T0374940

NAOROJI

NAOROJI

Pioneer of Indian Nationalism

DINYAR PATEL

Harvard University Press

Cambridge, Massachusetts, and London, England   2020

Library of Congress Cataloging-in-Publication Data

Names: Patel, Dinyar, author.
Title: Naoroji : Pioneer of Indian Nationalism / Dinyar Patel.
Description: Cambridge, Massachusetts : Harvard University Press, 2020. |
Includes bibliographical references and index.
Identifiers: LCCN 2019035455 | ISBN 9780674238206 (cloth)
Subjects: LCSH: Naoroji, Dadabhai, 1825–1917. | Nationalists—India—Biography. |
Legislators—Great Britain—Biography. | India—Politics and
government—1857–1919. | Great Britain—Colonies—Asia.
Classification: LCC DS475.2.N354 P373 2020 | DDC 320.540954/092 [B]—dc23
LC record available at https://lccn.loc.gov/2019035455

For Parinaz

CONTENTS

A NOTE ON TERMINOLOGY
AND STYLE

The spellings of nineteenth-century Indian names vary widely. In this book, I have tried to adopt the most commonly used spellings for particular individuals. Parsis and many other Indians did not adopt a standardized use of surnames until the late nineteenth century; therefore, some individuals, such as Navrozji Fardunji, are referred to by their given name (Navrozji, in this case) in subsequent references.

The name Dadabhai Naoroji presents a conundrum. Naoroji was his father's name, and the family's surname, which they occasionally used, was Dordi. In India, he was regularly referred to by his given name, often as "Mr. Dadabhai." In Great Britain, Naoroji was increasingly recognized as his surname, and he often went by "Mr. D. Naoroji." It is a good example of the hybrid world that Dadabhai Naoroji inhabited. In this book, I have treated Naoroji as his surname. His children and grandchildren eventually adopted Naoroji as their surname, dispensing with Dordi.

To avoid confusion, I have retained the colonial spellings for Indian cities; therefore, Mumbai remains Bombay, Kolkata remains Calcutta, Chennai remains Madras, and so on. I have employed the term "Anglo-Indian" to mean Britons resident in India. To describe individuals of mixed Indian and European heritage, I have used the term "Eurasian."

Naoroji's correspondents, who wrote their letters in a tearing hurry, frequently abbreviated common words. For clarity, I have lightly edited quotations and fully spelled out such abbreviations. For example, "yr" has been rendered as "your," and "shd" has been rendered as "should."

NAOROJI

Introduction

IT CAME DOWN TO THREE VOTES, a margin later widened to five. A handful of ballot sheets, however, proved enough to make history. Late on a July evening in 1892, telegraph wires emanating from London lit up with the name of Dadabhai Naoroji and some very improbable news: an Indian had been elected to the British Parliament. A Parsi from Bombay, a man who claimed to represent some 300 million downtrodden subjects in the faraway Indian subcontinent, now also represented Central Finsbury, a constituency at the very heart of the British Empire. Only a few years beforehand, the British prime minister, Lord Salisbury, had declared Dadabhai Naoroji to be a "black man" unworthy of an Englishman's vote. Now Salisbury watched uncomfortably as Naoroji prepared to bring a reform-minded Indian political agenda to the halls of power at Westminster. Shoals of congratulatory messages and telegrams poured in from places as far away as Bulgaria and Shanghai, the Cape Colony and Zanzibar. Nationalist newspapers in Dublin, which clamored for Irish political autonomy and occasionally made common cause with Indian leaders, hailed the news. So did *Native Opinion*, the first African-owned broadsheet in South Africa, which praised the admission of Salisbury's black man into the House of Commons.[1]

Among the Indian political elite, the atmosphere was euphoric. In Dadabhai Naoroji's native Bombay, a group of prominent citizens sent a

1

picture book of their city to the constituents of Central Finsbury. They included a portrait from a recent session of the Indian National Congress, the political party that Naoroji had helped establish in 1885 in order to advance India's interests. It was at the Congress's first-ever session, among delegates of a vast and diverse country, that the Parsi leader enunciated a farreaching objective: having "the actual government of India transferred from England to India." Bal Gangadhar Tilak and Lala Lajpat Rai, emerging radical voices within the Congress, believed Naoroji's election to be a fillip to the Indian nationalist movement. Two other men, soon to be household names in the subcontinent, agreed. From the gallery of the House of Commons, Muhammad Ali Jinnah, a candidate for the bar at Lincoln's Inn, watched Naoroji deliver his maiden parliamentary address and "thrilled" at his defense of free speech. "There he was, an Indian, who would exercise that right and demand justice for his countrymen," reminisced the founder of Pakistan. Meanwhile, in the South African town of Durban, a young lawyer drew encouragement from events in faraway Westminster. While bolstering Indians' claims for the electoral franchise in Natal, Mohandas K. Gandhi reminded the colony's legislators of "the fact of an English constituency returning an Indian to the British House of Commons."[2]

Naoroji's election was not exclusively a topic of interest for the elite. Far away from the hubs of Indian political life in Bombay, Calcutta, Madras, and elsewhere, the new Parsi parliamentarian became a household name. The residents of Chikmagalur, a small town in Mysore state hemmed in by coffee plantations, penned a testimonial to the electors of Central Finsbury, offering them "our sincere and heartfelt thanks for the honour done to India." A Congress volunteer in rural Satara district observed a mass meeting of villagers—"four thousand agriculturalists and the backward classes," in his words—gathering to discuss the election and a host of other political matters. Other members of the Indian diaspora, in a vein similar to Gandhi's, took heart at Naoroji's achievement. Indian residents of Georgetown, capital of the steamy South American colony of British Guiana, appended their signatures to a lengthy memorial to the new member of Parliament (MP). "We need hardly say," their statement began, "that altho' we are thousands of miles separated from you, it will be ever our foremost interest to read of your career, and earnestly trust that success will attend your undertakings both politically and otherwise."[3]

Finally, a broad spectrum of Britons expressed enthusiasm about Naoroji's win. Trade union leaders, ordinary workingmen, and campaigners for women's suffrage hoped that the Central Finsbury MP would champion their interests. Even the *Times* of London, a stodgy Conservative paper that usually frowned upon the Indian leader's activities, allowed that "the appearance of a native of India in the British Parliament is an interesting and almost romantic event, if romance can enter into politics." Among the congratulatory messages that continued to pour into his office, Naoroji received a curious note from a political organizer working with farm laborers in rural Northamptonshire. The organizer assured him that "you may be sure that by no class of our Countrymen is your return to Parliament a matter for greater congratulation than it is among our agricultural workers." While the farm laborers "could not pronounce your name," they believed Naoroji to be their representative as well.[4]

British agricultural laborers, Indian villagers, female suffragists, Irish nationalists, and Indian emigrants in South Africa and South America—all of these individuals saw Dadabhai Naoroji's parliamentary victory as their victory. What explained the Parsi leader's diverse appeal? How did he knit together the interests and aspirations of so many different constituencies?

We can find answers in his long and pathbreaking career. Naoroji was arguably the most significant Indian nationalist leader before Gandhi. Popularly known as the "Grand Old Man of India," he directed almost all aspects of the emerging nationalist movement and authored some of the most hard-hitting arguments against British imperial rule. By the 1880s and 1890s, Naoroji became the first modern Indian political figure to gain a truly national appeal, enjoying broad-based support across the subcontinent. But he was also much more than just an Indian leader. He was a pioneering anti-imperialist, someone who relentlessly hammered away at the ideologies of empire while forging links with progressive and emancipatory movements around the world. Naoroji's ultimate achievement was to make British India—and the scandalous poverty of its people—into the preeminent symbol of the wrongs inflicted by European imperialism. And he did so while convincing a broad spectrum of Britons that he was correct.

Dadabhai Naoroji, oil on canvas portrait by M. F. Pithawala.
Reproduced with permission from *Portrait of a Community,* Chemould
Publications and Arts, 2002.

Dadabhai Naoroji lived for nearly ninety-two years and spent five decades of his life fighting for Indian rights. When he was born in 1825, the
British East India Company had just recently extinguished Maratha authority, once an existential threat to English ambitions in the subcontinent. By the time of his death in 1917, India was only three decades away
from independence. Here was a man who, in his earliest years at a Bombay
schoolhouse, imbibed lessons on the recent feats of John Malcolm—a
Scotsman who helped vanquish Tipu Sultan of Mysore in 1799—and who,
in his last years, made a deep impression upon the founders of independent India and Pakistan. His life and career spanned the high noon of
British imperialism and the first stirrings of modern political life in India.

The Grand Old Man's election to Parliament in 1892 was only one high-light in a long and varied career. In Bombay of the 1840s and 1850s, he was a respected professor, journalist, and religious and social reformer. In the princely state of Baroda during the early 1870s, he was the diwan or prime minister. Between the 1860s and 1880s, as he constantly shuttled between India and Great Britain, Naoroji undertook groundbreaking research and analysis of Indian poverty, demonstrating that British colonial rule was facilitating a spate of famines that carried away millions of Indian lives. Throughout his life, he mentored generations of Indian students in the United Kingdom, encouraged reform-minded Indian princes, dabbled in Bombay civic politics, and consorted with leading European thinkers and scholars. Finally, in 1906, in the eighth decade of his life, the Grand Old Man demanded swaraj, or self-government for India, a declaration that reverberated around the globe. Gandhi summed up Naoroji's career by anointing him as the father of the nation and a mahatma—titles that in India today are reserved for Gandhi.[5]

These events help us flesh out a life marked by constant change. Dadabhai Naoroji's career evolved in three distinct stages. In the first stage, lasting from the mid-1860s through 1885, the Parsi leader advanced a highly controversial thesis: Britain was draining India of its wealth, bleeding the country white (Chapter 2). He developed his drain theory, as it became known, in an era when many Britons took it for granted that imperialism was a beneficent force and a stimulus for growth and prosperity in their colonies. Through a colossal assemblage of facts and figures, rigorous interrogation of official data, and the collection of testimonies from across the subcontinent, Naoroji demonstrated otherwise. Indians, he established, were desperately poor. Moreover, due to the drain of wealth, they were getting poorer by the year, pushed closer to the precipice of mass starvation. With the steady diminution of money and material, how could anyone express surprise at the worsening cycles of famines gripping India?

In Naoroji's estimation, the biggest drain on Indian resources was the Indian civil service. This was an elite cadre of colonial administrators, overwhelmingly British in its makeup and beholden to British imperial interests. As a corollary of sorts to his drain theory, Naoroji put forth a suggestion that laid bare political motivations for his research on poverty. If more Indians were employed in the civil service—and if more Indians were in control of their own government—the drain of wealth would be stanched. India would grow more prosperous. In order to test this proposition, Naoroji looked toward the princely states of India, semi-autonomous units that were dispersed across the subcontinent. He argued that these states, administered by Indians rather than Britons, were largely buffered from the drain of wealth and were therefore more prosperous and stable than Indian territories under direct British rule. The political and economic success of several princely states influenced Naoroji to speak enthusiastically about Indian self-government by the conclusion of the first stage of his career.

Aside from a brief foray into the administrative affairs of Baroda state, Naoroji increasingly trained his sights on the British Parliament. During the second stage of his career, from 1886 until 1895, he attempted to directly influence British policy toward India (Chapters 3, 5, and 6). "All the most fundamental questions on which hinge the entire form and character of the administration here are decided by Parliament," Naoroji told delegates of the Congress's second annual session, held in Calcutta. "No matter what it is, Legislative Councils, the Services,—nothing can be reformed until Parliament moves and enacts modifications of the existing Acts."[6] Aside from lobbying MPs and officials, Naoroji determined to influence Westminster from within: he would stand for Parliament, contesting a seat in the House of Commons and throwing in his lot with the Liberal Party of William Gladstone.

Indian representation in the Commons—even if it was through a local English constituency—was not a new idea. Naoroji received notable encouragement from several British statesmen and officials who were sympathetic toward Indian grievances. Nevertheless, standing for Parliament required Naoroji to broaden his horizons beyond exclusively Indian concerns. He had to engage with the dynamic and chaotic political processes of late Victorian Britain. Naoroji reached out to the leaders of various progressive movements—organized labor, socialism, feminism and female suffrage, and Irish home rule—in order to popularize Indian political demands and turn Indian affairs into a voter issue. Political exigencies made him momentarily prioritize issues such as Irish home rule over Indian self-government. These efforts paid off in 1892 when, after a long and hard-fought campaign, those five critical votes made Naoroji the MP for Central Finsbury.

In the Commons, Naoroji formulated a distinctly Indian legislative agenda. He pushed for simultaneously holding Indian civil service entrance examinations in the United Kingdom and India. This was, on the surface, a mundane bureaucratic tweak, but it had profound implications. The examinations had previously been held only in Britain, which practically barred most Indian candidates. If the examinations were held across the subcontinent, Naoroji reasoned, the doors would be thrown open to the thorough Indianization of the colonial bureaucracy. It would be a first step toward self-government. He cobbled together a broad alliance of fellow MPs to augment India's voice in Westminster. And he traveled throughout Britain and India to whip up support for reform. All of this came to naught. Barely two years into his parliamentary career, Naoroji realized that most of the Commons cared little for Indian concerns. Fellow Liberal Party MPs thwarted his agenda. He lost his seat in 1895.

Embittered and disillusioned, Dadabhai Naoroji embarked on the final phase of his political career, radicalizing considerably (Chapter 7). He threw caution to the wind, condemning British imperialism and predicting an imminent rebellion in disaffected India. He evolved into a truly global exponent of anti-imperialism, reaching out to like-minded thinkers and political actors across Europe and North America. Swaraj now became his primary concern—although, by initially allowing for "Self-Government under British Paramountcy," he struggled to define how much autonomy India could wrest from the most powerful empire in human history. Presiding over the Calcutta session of the Congress in December 1906, Naoroji invoked the drain of wealth—the horrors of famines, pestilences, and unfathomable impoverishment—to demand swaraj. This was not the first time that an Indian leader had made that demand. Indeed, by the early twentieth century, many other nationalists went further than the Grand Old Man, calling for the country's full separation from the British Empire, by violent means if necessary. However, Naoroji's declaration in Calcutta was significant for its own reasons. It constituted the most prominent and publicized demand for self-government to date, one that bound the entire Congress organization to this objective. At the twilight of his political career, Naoroji took a Congress agenda of piecemeal reforms and reconfigured it toward the achievement of one concrete, overarching goal.

The first phase of Naoroji's career was marked by theorization. In the second phase, he attempted to apply his theories on Indian poverty to the legislative domain. Agitation was the hallmark of the last phase—unflinching protest and a rousing call for self-government. Each phase of Naoroji's career was shot through with an abiding concern about Indian poverty. Unlike other Indian nationalists, such as Gandhi, the Grand Old Man did not develop philosophically nuanced strains of political thought. He had limited interest in considering the broader sweep of Indian tradition and history in order to understand the country's colonial predicament. His brand of nationalism was simple, direct, and marked by immediacy: India was desperately poor, it needed to control its own government, and any delay in reform condemned millions to death. True, this blinded Naoroji to certain concerns that dominated later phases of the nationalist movement, such as questions of caste, untouchability, and minority representation. But it gave Indian nationalism a moral, humanitarian appeal that, much like Gandhi's thought, upended many smug Western notions of civilizational superiority. "Is it necessary that, for your benefit, we must be destroyed?" Naoroji asked Britons.[7] Few had an effective answer.

Dadabhai Naoroji is a seminal figure in the history of modern India, Victorian Britain, and the British Empire. On a more global level, he ranks among the great non-European thinkers and reformers of his era. His life can be read side by side with that of the intellectuals who attempted to modernize Qing China, Meiji Japan, or Ottoman Turkey in the late nineteenth and early twentieth centuries. A number of parallels even emerge between the Grand Old Man and African American leaders such as W. E. B. Du Bois, who shared Naoroji's passion for hard-hitting scholarship, socialist politics, and forging ties with emancipatory movements around the world. In terms of anti-imperialist thought, Naoroji's work complemented that of Karl Marx and J. A. Hobson. He added a colonized subject's perspective on the links among capitalism, race, and empire. His drain theory, furthermore, was a powerful indictment of classical economic theory—and the use of such theory to explain away desperate poverty in the colonial world. "It is not the pitiless operations of economic laws, but it is the thoughtless and pitiless action of the British policy; it is the pitiless eating of India's substance in India, and the further pitiless drain to England; in short, it is the pitiless *perversion* of economic laws by the sad bleeding to which India is subjected, that is destroying India," he lectured the British secretary of state for India in 1880. "Why blame poor Nature when the fault lies at your own door?"[8]

And yet Naoroji remains strangely forgotten today. In India, many people recognize the Grand Old Man as an important early nationalist leader, but few can pin down precisely *why* he was important. For decades after Naoroji's 1892 victory, as the British Empire swelled in size and then spectacularly collapsed, the landmark election of an Indian to the British Parliament elicited surprisingly little commentary in the United Kingdom. It became a forgotten episode in spite of the growing multicultural makeup of both Naoroji's former constituency and the country at large. On the broader global stage, Naoroji is even more of an unknown entity.

Surprisingly little has been written about his life. Gopal Krishna Gokhale, a leading moderate nationalist, and someone whom an elderly Naoroji identified as a torchbearer for many of his ideas and politics, intended to write the Grand Old Man's biography. He was unable to begin this endeavor before his untimely death in 1915. In 1939, Rustom P. Masani, a Bombay civic leader, published a lengthy biographical tome. Although hagiographic, it remains the most detailed account of the Grand Old Man's life and career. Masani, who lived next door to the Naoroji family in the early twentieth century, had the luxury of interviewing his subject as well as Naoroji's relatives and associates. He relied upon countless letters, articles, and documents that have since withered away in the heat and humidity of Bombay.[9]

Within the world of academic scholarship, remarkably few historians have examined Naoroji's ideas and achievements. Most of them have focused on his published economic writings, particularly his drain theory. A handful of scholars have looked at the 1892 parliamentary campaign. Others have incorporated Naoroji in broader studies on British anti-colonialism, the British Indian community, the Parsis, the Indian liberal tradition, or the early nationalist movement. For the most part, however, professional historians have neglected to consider how these various components of his life fit together.[10]

There are a few explanations for this neglect. First, historians of South Asia, who are very prone to the vagaries of academic fashion, have been loath to accept biography as a legitimate form of scholarship. Although there are promising signs of change, scholars of South Asia have almost reflexively shunned political elites. Such elites do not mesh well with the Marxist and postcolonial traditions that still dominate the academy. Second, many historians have taken a dim view of early Indian nationalism. They have dismissed its leaders as being ineffective and overly Anglicized, and their movement as being hopelessly cut off from the rest of Indian society. Early nationalists have been unfairly portrayed as "collaborators" of empire or, less imaginatively, "proto-nationalists." Last, for any scholar, writing a biography of an Indian leader is an extremely difficult task. Due to shoddy record keeping, dismal archives, and stunning historical neglect in modern India, many important personal collections have been damaged, destroyed, or rendered inaccessible. Thankfully, Naoroji's personal papers do survive, but they are forbiddingly vast. They are also very difficult to utilize due to damage and incomplete organization. Consequently, only two or three historians, at most, have closely engaged with his correspondence. The overwhelming majority of scholarship on Naoroji is based exclusively on his published writings—which tell a very incomplete story of the man.[11]

The book in your hands attempts to correct these various deficiencies. A biography is the only way to restore the centrality of Dadabhai Naoroji and his ideas to the development of modern Indian politics. Through the lens of biography, furthermore, we are able to rediscover the intellectual richness and dynamism of the early Indian nationalist movement—a movement that harnessed technology, international alliances, and financial networks to coordinate political activity across two continents. I have engaged in more than two years of study of Naoroji's private correspondence, examining around fifteen thousand documents and discovering significant new material in English and Gujarati. In addition, I have conducted extensive research in other collections in India, Great Britain, Ireland, and the United States. From this research, Naoroji emerges as a far more radical and complex political figure than has otherwise been commonly believed. He was no "proto-nationalist" or "collaborator."

Furthermore, by writing a biography, I have also explored the worlds beyond Indian nationalism that Dadabhai Naoroji inhabited. Take mid-nineteenth-century Bombay, for example (the topic of Chapter 1). Although born into relative poverty, Naoroji benefited from the city's distinct educational tradition, one that crafted his reformist ethos and eventually gave his family the means for a better livelihood. In Bombay schoolhouses, he imbibed rationalist strains of thought, developed a pronounced fervor for empirical research, and honed his progressive impulses. He participated in a burst of institution building in the 1840s and 1850s, extending Bombay's educational tradition by inaugurating a pioneering network of schools for young Indian girls. Naoroji helped make Bombay a locus of Indian intellectual activity. But the city also shaped the Grand Old Man in multiple ways.

So did his community. As a Parsi, Naoroji was a member of one of India's most microscopic ethnoreligious communities, descendants of Zoroastrians who abandoned Iran for Gujarat a thousand years beforehand. Naoroji's own father was a humble Zoroastrian priest from rural Gujarat. By the early 1800s, however, Parsis exercised phenomenal commercial influence in the bazaars and countinghouses of Bombay—and had amassed extraordinary wealth and influence. As a young reformer, Naoroji relied on fellow Parsis for financial and organizational assistance. More importantly, his coreligionists helped him to build broader, cross-communal alliances for endeavors such as female education. Naoroji continued to rely heavily on Parsi networks of finance and influence for the rest of his career.

In 1855, a Parsi commercial venture gave the Grand Old Man, then thirty years young, his first opportunity to reside in Great Britain. By the time he left British shores for the last time, in 1907, he had passed nearly five decades of his life in the country, mostly in the imperial capital. Naoroji took on multiple roles in London, functioning as an Indian emissary, a scholar, a crusader against racism, and a community leader for an emerging British Indian diaspora (Chapter 4). I have used Naoroji as a prism for understanding the networks of people, organizations, and ideas that increasingly bound together Britons and Indians. These ranged from temperance to Freemasonry. The following pages are animated with some relatively well-known figures: Henry Hyndman, for example, who founded Britain's first socialist party, and Behramji Malabari, a prominent champion of Indian women's rights. But they also feature numerous ordinary men and women who played significant roles in sustaining Naoroji's activities.

I have relied on biographical methods in order to demonstrate the richness and complexity of numerous lived experiences, not just that of Dadabhai Naoroji. It is only through such methods that we can bring alive the debates, discussions, and activities of a generation of individuals—Indians and Britons, as well as a diverse cast of other men and women dispersed around the globe—who set in motion India's journey toward self-government and freedom.

CHAPTER 1

Young Dadabhai,
Young Bombay

ON THE TWENTY-SIXTH OF JUNE, 1855, Dadabhai Naoroji inadvertently caused a major traffic jam on the streets of Bombay. That evening, crowds turned out at Apollo Bunder, a promontory jutting out into the city's harbor, to watch Naoroji board the steamer *Madras* and thereby begin his first-ever voyage to Great Britain. It was a momentous event. Naoroji's departure made the headlines of local newspapers. Despite the threat of a monsoonal downpour, well-wishers turned out in force, turning the muddy lanes off Colaba Causeway into a sea of horse carriages and people. Leading Indian citizens of Bombay marked the occasion by presenting Naoroji with scrolls of honor and purses of money.

By the midpoint of the nineteenth century, the departure of an Indian for Europe was no longer a rare occurrence. Why, then, did part of Bombay come to a halt to send off a twenty-nine-year-old Parsi? There are a few possible explanations. On that June evening, Naoroji left Bombay in order to help start what was reputed to be the first Indian mercantile firm in Great Britain. Along with the Camas, a wealthy Parsi business family, he planned to set up shop in London and Liverpool and, from the heart of empire, stake out a portion of the Indian textile trade that had hitherto been controlled entirely by Englishmen. This was a daring and risky endeavor, but one that understandably excited many Indians. A few days after the *Madras* steamed out of the harbor, a Bombay learned society, the

Jamsetjee Jejeebhoy Philosophic Institute, held a special lecture entitled "The Probable Effects upon India of the New Mercantile Relations between India and England Formed by the Establishment of a Parsee Mercantile Firm in London."[1]

But many Bombay citizens were probably drawn to Apollo Bunder for a far more prosaic reason: to catch one last glimpse of a man who had risen from desperate poverty to become one of the city's most recognizable figures. In mid-nineteenth-century Bombay, Dadabhai Naoroji symbolized transformation—both individually and at the community level. Over the past several years, he had emerged as one of the greatest champions of social reform and educational activities in the city. Hailing from a poor Parsi family that escaped famine-stricken Gujarat, Naoroji seized upon various educational opportunities to rise to the uppermost strata of Bombay's civic life, consorting with Indian merchant princes and British officials while still in his mid-twenties. By the time he agreed to join the Cama family in their business venture abroad, he had already steered the affairs of one of Bombay's most popular and progressive newspapers, helped orchestrate major Parsi religious and social reform activities, and participated in the city's first major political organization, the Bombay Association. In 1854, he became the first-ever Indian appointed as a full professor at a government college. Naoroji clearly staked great importance on this last achievement. "Several honours came to me during my lifetime," he noted toward the twilight of his career, "but no other title created in me that sense of pride which I felt in being known as a Professor."[2]

His statement should elicit little surprise. Naoroji was in many ways the product of a distinct educational tradition in western India, one that shaped the contours of social and political development in the region— perhaps to a greater extent than in any other region of India. Amid the powerless and poverty that marked British colonial rule, education was one of the few arenas where Indians in and around Bombay could exert significant leadership and promote broad social improvement. As such, processes of social, religious, and—eventually—political reform in Bombay were firmly tied to the classroom. This left an indelible mark on Naoroji's career. During his youth, Bombay's mercantile elites helped provide free or subsidized education in new schools and, ultimately, an institution of higher learning, Elphinstone College. Naoroji, having achieved a distinguished record at these places of learning, then helped translate Bombay's educational tradition into a burst of reformist activity in the late 1840s and 1850s. Popularly known as "Young Bombay," this movement championed the further spread of education. Its greatest undertaking was the promotion of education for young Indian girls. Here Naoroji laid the foundations for a truly unique movement in colonial India: the creation of a network of girls' schools that was funded, administered, and staffed almost entirely by Indians themselves. Unlike in Madras, Bengal, and other parts of India, educated Indians—rather than foreign missionaries or British instructors—pioneered female education on a mass scale.[3]

Underlying Naoroji's activities was a clear understanding, gained through both lived experience and detached study, of the relationship between poverty and education. By educating girls, attacking social and religious customs deemed irrational or harmful, teaching in Elphinstone College, and disseminating educational material through mass-produced publications and newspapers, Naoroji endeavored to break down as many barriers as possible to social and economic advancement for impoverished Indians. This, he believed, was his solemn responsibility, since he had benefited from an early form of public education. "I realised that I had been educated at the expense of the poor, to whom I myself belong," he noted later in life. "The thought developed itself in my mind that as my education and all the benefits arising therefrom came from the people, I must return to them the best I had in me. I must devote myself to the service of the people."[4] Naoroji's long public career, therefore, began in the classrooms of colonial Bombay.

Humbled to Dust

For Dadabhai Naoroji, poverty was not simply a topic of academic interest. It was a lived reality. Like millions of others across the subcontinent, Naoroji, along with his parents and grandparents, was subject to the steady impoverishment of India, an invidious process set in motion by British colonial rule in the late eighteenth and early nineteenth centuries. This experience of poverty contrasted with his family's fortunes prior to the advent of the East India Company. Naoroji was a member of the Dordi family of Navsari, a Parsi stronghold located along the once prosperous coastal littoral of southern Gujarat, not far from Surat. Navsari was known as *dharamni tekri*, "the summit of the religion," since it had been a vital center of the Zoroastrian priesthood. And the Dordis had been an important part of Navsari's ecclesiastical tradition: through a long, un-broken line of priests, they could trace their descent down through the centuries to Zarthosht Mobed, supposedly the first member of the Parsi clergy to settle in the town. Like most Parsis, Naoroji's ancestors pros-pered under Mughal rule. In 1618, two priests from the family, bearing goblets of Navsari's famous attar (perfume), presented themselves as Zoroastrian emissaries before the emperor Jehangir at Ahmedabad, receiving in return both land and money. Some decades later, an-other family member, Framroze Sorabji, became a leading Parsi merchant in Surat, which flourished spectacularly as the Mughals' premier port. Framroze's nephew, Behramji Mehernosji, was reckoned to be Navsari's wealthiest man.[5]

During the late 1600s and early 1700s, however, southern Gujarat went into economic free fall due to Maratha raids, crumbling Mughal authority, and, finally, the growing commercial and political stranglehold of the East India Company. British trade and taxation policies inflicted a lethal blow to the indigenous cotton and silk textile industry, which had long been a foundation of Navsari's wealth. By the beginning of the nineteenth century, Naoroji's grandfather had been reduced to being a humble agri-culturalist on a Dordi family estate in nearby Dharampore, a minor princely state pressed against the Western Ghats. Dadabhai's father, Naoroji Palanji, worked as a practicing priest and also tilled the soil in Dharampore. But he eagerly sought escape from rural poverty. In pre-vious decades, this would have meant migration to Surat. Now, how-ever, the erstwhile Mughal entrepôt had been, in the words of one English observer, "humbled to dust"—its bazaars depopulated, its mansions abandoned, and its fabulous wealth only a distant memory.[6] Instead, Naoroji Palanji, like thousands of other destitute Gujaratis, trained his eyes on a new destination: Bombay.

We have no records to tell us precisely when Naoroji Palanji and his wife, Manekbai, quit Dharampore. It is quite likely, however, that famine, another consequence of the impoverishing effects of British rule, played a role in the timing of their departure. After a failed monsoon in 1824, much of Gujarat stared into the void of an acute food shortage. In previous times, administrators and rich merchants would have absorbed price shocks and opened reserve supplies of grain. Now, however, British officials affected an attitude of sheer indifference, while struggling grain merchants in Surat were forced to barricade their stores against starving peasants.[7] Famines snapped individuals' ties to the land and their families; the crisis of late 1824 likely did this for the Dordis as well. When Naoroji Palanji and Manekbai migrated from Dharampore, they helped push along a much broader process whereby Gujarat was absorbed into the hinterlands of Bombay city, while once dynamic commercial centers like Surat and Navsari became transformed into the mofussil, outposts of reduced significance and fortune.

Dadabhai Naoroji was born in Bombay on September 4, 1825, his parents' first and only child. At the time of his birth, Bombay's fortunes were riding high due to a brisk trade in opium destined for China and, increasingly, raw cotton to feed England's hungry textile mills. Recent migrants from Gujarat's famine tracts had swelled the island city's population to over 150,000.[8] Britons and rich Indians lived in large houses huddled behind the soot-blackened town walls in Fort, which occupied a narrow strip of land between the harbor and Back Bay. To the north and west of Fort stretched a vast open space, the Esplanade, littered with cotton bales and the white canvas tents of European visitors. Having largely outlived its original defensive purposes, the Esplanade now functioned as a cordon sanitaire, separating Fort from the teeming Native Town, where the bulk of Bombay's Indian population lived.

Naoroji's family occupied a humble dwelling in Khadak, a warren of streets located in the Native Town's northeastern fringes, close to today's Masjid Bunder railway station. Chances are that the Dordis lived in very squalid conditions. In 1826, an average dwelling in the locality housed 8.7 people, the second-highest occupancy rate in Bombay. Naoroji's neighborhood was one of many parts of the Native Town distinguished by open sewers "a foot or so wide" on both sides of the street; as a later municipal report noted, these sewers were "in actual contact with and soaking into the foundations of the whole street frontage of each house." In spite of the stink and disease, Naoroji had the fortune to live in one of the most religiously and culturally diverse parts of Bombay. In the early nineteenth century, this part of the Native Town was home to Parsis, Bohra and Khoja Muslims, Kacchis, and the city's original inhabitants, the Kolis. Directly south of Khadak was Israeli Mohalla, a bastion of the Jewish Bene Israel community. North of Khadak, meanwhile, were the spacious and desirable neighborhoods of Byculla and Mazagaon, populated by wealthy Britons, Parsis, Baghdadi Jews, and the descendants of Portuguese landowners. From a very early age, therefore, Naoroji was exposed to Bombay's startling heterogeneity, described in wonder by a contemporary Indian chronicler as "fifty-six languages and eighteen castes with different head-dresses." It was a starkly different environment from the relatively homogenous Parsi *wads* of Navsari or the farmlands of Dharampore that his parents and grandparents inhabited.[9]

Old Navsari traditions nevertheless weighed heavily on young Dadabhai. Indeed, these traditions had already determined his future vocation. As a firstborn son, he was expected to maintain family tradition by joining the Zoroastrian clergy. This meant that Naoroji could look forward to a frugal, difficult life: after rigorous training, perhaps in a Zoroastrian *madressa* (seminary) in Navsari, he would have to spend his days performing rituals, reciting ancient Zoroastrian prayers by rote, and tending to the holy fire. But then, at the age of four, he lost his father. Naoroji Palanji's sudden death cast a long shadow over Dadabhai. "One of the first fancies which took possession of my mind as a little child was that, as my father was dead, the moon, like other friends, was in sympathy with me," he remembered decades later. "And whether I went to the front or back of the house, the moon always seemed to go with me." His father's death, however, most likely relieved Naoroji of a career in the Zoroastrian priesthood. While he did complete the *navar* ceremony, the first step toward entering the clergy, he never became a practicing priest. Instead, Manekbai, his widowed mother, put Naoroji on a different course and enrolled him in an indigenous school run by a Gujarati *mehta* or instructor. He entered this school at a moment of great change in the educational landscape of Bombay, a moment that also had profound ramifications for the social and political dynamics of western India.[10]

As Dadabhai Naoroji began receiving instruction sometime in the early 1830s, new educational institutions—schools with British or British-trained instructors, Western pedagogy, and occasionally instruction in the English language—attracted ever increasing numbers of Indian students in Bombay city and across the presidency. Many later commentators interpreted the appearance of these schools as a dramatic break with the past, when knowledge and learning began rooting out pervading ignorance. "As far as education was concerned there was darkness or at the best visible darkness," Dinsha Wacha, one of Naoroji's closest nationalist allies, remarked about the early 1800s.[11]

This was, to say the least, quite an exaggeration. If Western education proved popular among Naoroji's generation in Bombay, then its success can be partly attributed to the rich networks of indigenous education that prevailed beforehand in Gujarati- and Marathi-speaking districts. Bombay's educational tradition had deep roots. Reports and surveys carried out by the Bombay government in the 1810s and 1820s offer some tantalizing clues about the scope and extent of these indigenous schools. Far from documenting a dim, benighted world of pervading ignorance, such reports point to diverse systems of schooling that reached a relatively wide spectrum of western Indians. After the British defeated the Maratha peshwa in 1818, Mountstuart Elphinstone, the new governor, recognized the importance of these educational networks—and state patronization of education—in the Company's newly annexed domains. Noting the "present abundance of people of education," Elphinstone worried that "unless some exertion is made by the Government, the country will certainly be in a worse state under our rule than it was under the Peishwa's [*sic*]" because of the large number of teachers now without a royal patron. From this position of relative vulnerability, the governor sketched out a policy for supporting vernacular-medium schools throughout the presidency, publishing schoolbooks in vernacular languages, and also pursuing a limited program in English-language education for Indian schoolchildren. Thus, compared to the situation in contemporary Bengal—where the Orientalist-Anglicist controversy pitted British supporters of "traditional" Indian education against advocates of western pedagogy—Elphinstone's educational policies were shaped much more by immediate political realities than by ideological considerations.[12]

Hardly any information survives about the indigenous school that Naoroji attended. It was, quite likely, similar to the many other such institutions that dotted Bombay and its hinterlands: *pathshalas* and madrassas that were relatively informal in nature, meeting at the houses of instructors or public venues such as temples or mosques. Minimal fees helped keep enrollment figures relatively high. With some assistance from her brother, Naoroji's widowed mother was able to easily bear the nominal charges of her son's schoolmaster. In Bombay, Gujarati indigenous schools were known for producing students remarkably adept in mathematics. Naoroji did not prove an exception. His mehta was in the habit of exhibiting Naoroji's mathematical prowess on the streets of Bombay "amid the loud *wawas* (cries of bravo) of the admiring audience."[13]

But sometime in the 1830s, at the urging of the very same mehta, Naoroji's mother withdrew her son from the indigenous school and placed him in a new institution, a school run by the Bombay Native Education Society. The society, which had been established in 1822 with Mountstuart Elphinstone as its president, administered a growing number of government-supported schools around the Bombay Presidency. A relatively equal number of Britons and Indians sat on its board of directors, including some of Bombay's most influential *shetias* or Indian merchant elites. By the time Dadabhai's name was entered on the Native Education Society's rosters, its schools were attracting some of the best pupils from indigenous institutions, in part because of their near monopoly in instruction of the English language. Additionally, the society had moved toward free education, at the same time instituting supplementary scholarships for select pupils. For Naoroji's mother, this was the critical factor. "Had there been levied the fees of the present day, my mother would not have been able to pay them," Naoroji noted in an autobiographical article that he wrote in 1904. Unlike most Parsi children, who were enrolled in the society's Gujarati-medium school, Naoroji attended its central English school, which had much stricter rules of admission. Candidates had to pass an examination on the grammar of their native language as well as arithmetic and algebra. Young Dadabhai evidently cleared these hurdles with little trouble.[14]

Thus Naoroji became part of a generation of Bombay schoolchildren that received a distinctly hybrid education, partly in the indigenous school of the mehta and partly in a new classroom presided over by English schoolmasters. Inside the central English school, Naoroji and his classmates confronted an environment and curriculum that were strikingly new and unusual. Instead of informal instruction in a house or public space, students gathered in a dedicated schoolhouse situated along the Esplanade, where stern portraits of Mountstuart Elphinstone and his successor as governor, John Malcolm, stared down at them. Lessons were oriented around heavy standardized textbooks on grammar, algebra, and geography. Students encountered a few completely foreign subjects, such as Western classics and English history, often approached through dramatic performances. In 1838, Naoroji played the part of the Roman senator Sempronius, opposite another Indian student donning the robes of Cato, in a school production. Another time, Naoroji's teacher induced him to perform as King Canute, placing him upon a table where he was to deliver a rousing oration to his schoolmates, acting the parts of Anglo-Saxon ministers, gathered below. Once the performance was over, the teacher raised Naoroji's hand, revealing the torn, ragged sleeve of an evidently poor child. "This is our Canute the Great," he told an amused English visitor.[15]

Off the stage, Naoroji's hybrid education developed in other ways. From the bookshelves of his school's library, he devoured works of English literature. Among his favorite books was *The Improvement of the Mind,* a treatise on logic penned in 1727 by Isaac Watts, an English non-conformist. He was deeply moved by the biographies and writings of two British individuals who had undertaken rigorous empirical research in pursuit of social and political reform: Thomas Clarkson, an abolitionist who detailed the horrors of the slave trade, and John Howard, who advocated the improvement of prison conditions. Meanwhile, among his family and community members, Naoroji leafed through stories from the *Shahnameh,* the great Persian epic. He soon acquired a reputation for reciting Gujarati translations to Parsi crowds. "To read with pleasure and enthusiasm the heroic deeds of long past Persian ancestors," he remembered, "to be influenced by the reading, and to see the audience entering with patriotism and excitement into the spirit of the deeds was a sight and experience that could not be forgotten."[16]

But mathematics remained Naoroji's true forte. Like his erstwhile mehta, Naoroji's British teachers occasionally put his skills on public display. At one such public mathematics examination, held in the central English school's library in the mid-1830s, the British travel writer Marianna Postans was in the audience. She recorded her impressions of young Dadabhai in her subsequent book on western India, thus penning the earliest published account of the Grand Old Man. "A little lad of seven years of age, with an overhanging forehead, and small sparkling eyes, peculiarly attracted our attention," she noted.

> The moment a question was proposed to the class, he quickly took a step before the rest, contracted his brows in deep and anxious thought, and with parted lips and finger eagerly uplifted towards the master, silently, but rapidly worked his problem in a manner peculiar to himself, and blurted out the solution with a startling haste, half painful, half ludicrous. The little fellow seemed wholly animated with the desire of excelling.[17]

Naoroji did indeed excel at the central English school. His success stemmed, in part, from many commonalities that linked together the Native Education Society school with the old institutions run by mehtas. For example, a large group of Indian monitors and tutors at the central English school helped mediate and explain lessons, oftentimes also translating concepts into vernacular languages. And the indigenous school's flexibility and informality were complemented in the Western school by a surprising absence of discipline. "So lax was discipline that often we would coolly march out of school and spend the whole day in games," Naoroji remembered, adding that, while skipping class and heading out to Bombay's wide grassy Esplanade, he developed particular skill in *gilli danda,* commonly referred to as Indian cricket.[18]

Just before adolescence, Dadabhai was temporarily pulled away from the classroom and gilli danda pitch. Instead, his mother placed him under a *mandap* (canopy), where Naoroji found himself seated next to a seven-year-old girl, Gulbai, the daughter of a family acquaintance. Zoroastrian priests instructed the children to clasp hands and, after the ritual tying of a white thread, pronounced them husband and wife. Naoroji, age eleven, was now a married man.

Promise of India

Having returned from his wedding—child marriages were commonly practiced in the Parsi community through the late nineteenth century—Naoroji continued to demonstrate exceptional academic promise. His teachers at the central English school eventually recommended him for a course of further education. In Bombay of the late 1830s, this meant attending Elphinstone College. Established in 1835, the college represented the educational hopes of both the government and a broad spectrum of the indigenous elite. It originated in 1827 when, upon Mountstuart Elphinstone's departure for England, Bombay's shetias pledged an endowment for one or two professorships, giving the outgoing governor the privilege of filling the chairs with scholars of his choice. Princes in outlying parts of the presidency added a considerable sum to this endowment, Rs. 215,000, signaling their desire to promote knowledge of "the languages, literature, sciences, and moral philosophy of Europe." In 1839, the Bombay Native Education Society included Naoroji's name in a list of fifty students for possible transfer to the college. Naoroji's fellow candidates included many future notables of Bombay: Atmaram Pandurang, who became the founder of the Prarthana Samaj, the reformist Hindu association; Keru Laxman Chhatre, later an astronomer and professor at the Deccan College in Poona; and Ardeshir Framji Moos, who would join Naoroji in numerous reform activities within the Parsi community. On May 1, 1840, Naoroji, then nearly fifteen years old, was formally enrolled as an Elphinstonian and awarded a special scholarship in the name of a recent governor of Bombay, the Earl of Clare. It totaled the princely sum of 16 rupees.[19]

Naoroji entered Elphinstone College when the institution was in great flux. It had a ready group of professors and assistant professors, the strong support of Bombay's indigenous elite, and a talented yet admittedly small cadre of pupils. British officials in London and Bombay, however, dith-ered in their commitment toward the college and in 1839 nearly shut down the institution on the pretext of low enrollment figures. Elphinstone Col-lege almost fell victim to a central contradiction in British rule: in spite of lofty rhetoric about the need to "improve" and "civilize" Indians, colo-nial policymakers were driven by a desire to spend as little money as pos-sible on educating their subjects. That the college survived at all was largely a testament to Indians, such as the shetia members of the Bombay Native Education Society, who raised vociferous protests. As a student, Naoroji was exposed to a constant tussle between a miserly government and Indian stakeholders demanding more resources and better funding. He did not have to look far beyond the classroom walls to observe the many yawning gaps between imperial rhetoric and reality.[20]

Despite the looming threat of its dissolution, Elphinstone College man-aged to play a truly seminal role in the history of midcentury Bombay. It birthed a generation of Indian students committed to rationalist precepts, scientific inquiry, social reform, and the material improvement of their country. This was largely on account of the college's gifted faculty. Naoro-ji's professors bore little resemblance to the evangelical, arch-imperialist dons who presided over missionary institutions in Calcutta and else-where. As the historian Naheed Ahmad notes, "In their ideas the Elphin-stone College professors were far from being aligned to the Raj." They were a relatively freethinking lot. Missionaries, in fact, regularly assailed the college as an insidiously anti-Christian establishment. In 1850, George Bowen, an American attracted to western India in the hope of winning over hapless native souls, charged that the principal of Elphinstone Col-lege was "an infidel and freely ridicules the Christian religion before the pupils."[21]

Who were these professors? Between the 1830s and at least the 1870s, the college faculty was dominated by a notably large number of Scotsmen and Irishmen, many of whom exhibited a decisively progressive and lib-eral political bent. Intellectually, several of these instructors were distant heirs to the rational schools of thought from the Scottish Enlightenment. For example, John Harkness, the college's principal during Naoroji's school years—as well as the target of George Bowen's vitriol—studied moral philosophy at the University of Edinburgh, where he came under the influence of James Pillans, a prominent classicist and educational reformist who was a student of the philosopher Dugald Stewart. As Dinsha Wacha recalled, Harkness was greatly attracted to the philosophical thought of William Hamilton, another Edinburgh don who was in turn influenced by Immanuel Kant.[22]

Not saddled by particular prejudices, many of these instructors established close and lasting relationships with their pupils, something that heightened their intellectual influence on Bombay society. John Bell, a Scotsman who taught Naoroji "natural philosophy" (a precursor to modern physics) and chemistry, was effusive in his praise for his students. "It would be difficult for any teacher to be otherwise than kind to the youth of an Indian Seminary," he noted before a large audience of Britons, Indian alumni, and students in May 1846, "where insolence and disobedience are unknown; where the scholar is as eager and anxious to learn, as the instructor is to teach; and where, consequently, the business of instruction is not so much an irksome task, as a delightful social enjoyment." Joseph Patton, an Irishman and graduate of Trinity College who taught mathematics, was wildly popular with Naoroji's generation of Elphinstonians—and deeply mourned after his premature death in 1852. "It is to Patton we owe all the new life the Parsees got in the early 50s," Khurshedji Rustomji (K. R.) Cama, another Elphinstone student several years younger than Naoroji, noted retrospectively.[23]

But Europeans were not the only ones who taught at Elphinstone College—its faculty included a number of Indians as well. Naoroji was deeply influenced by two remarkable assistant professors, Bal Gangadhar Shastri Jambhekar and Navrozji Fardunji. Indeed, it was Jambhekar who had the foresight to formally select Naoroji for admission into the college, overruling a teacher (most likely British) at the central English school who ranked him near the bottom of his class on account of his young age and impoverished background. Like Dadabhai, Navrozji and Jambhekar were products of a hybrid education. Jambhekar, whose family hailed from the southern Konkan coast, was most likely educated in Sanskrit by his father, a well-known *shastri,* before he was brought to Bombay in 1826 and enrolled in the central English school.

Navrozji, the son of a Parsi landholder, attended a vernacular school in Bharuch, moved on to Surat to receive further instruction from a British missionary, and finally enrolled in the central English school in Bombay in 1830.[24]

Inducted as assistant professors at Elphinstone College mere years after finishing their schooling, both men established a polymathic tradition of academic study at the institution. Surviving educational records tell us little about Navrozji's time in Elphinstone; nevertheless, in his other activities he displayed an obvious facility for languages. In 1837, the British diplomat Alexander Burnes recruited Navrozji as his translator for his mission to Kabul. Navrozji had the good fortune to leave Afghanistan before a mob massacred Burnes and the rest of his colleagues in 1841. Back in Bombay, he embarked on less life-threatening endeavors, such as helping to compile the first-ever Gujarati-English dictionary. And around this time he first became acquainted with his fellow Parsi, Naoroji, forging a lifelong friendship and partnership in pursuit of social and political reform.[25]

Jambhekar, meanwhile, juggled responsibilities in multiple subjects. "Small in person, diffident and unpretending in manner, Bal-Shastree is yet no ordinary man," Marianna Postans remarked after observing him at work in the classroom. Aside from instructing Naoroji and his classmates in advanced mathematics and optics, Jambhekar assisted John Harkness in lecturing on the merits of Shakespeare's *Julius Caesar* and *The Merchant of Venice* as well as Alexander Pope's *Essay on Man*. When Elphinstone's mathematics professor, Arthur Orlebar, went on furlough to England due to ill health, Jambhekar took over his responsibilities and specially tutored two of his star pupils, Naoroji and Atmaram Pandurang, in integral calculus and analytical geometry, catching Orlebar by surprise upon his return to Bombay. "On no occasion before I left India have so many been able to pass examinations in the higher mathematics," a rejuvenated Orlebar praised his temporary replacement. Jambhekar dabbled in astronomy, journalism, Marathi etymology and grammar, and paleography—he frequently contributed papers to the Bombay branch of the Royal Asiatic Society although, as an Indian, he was barred from entering its premises—before succumbing to typhus at the tragically young age of thirty-three.[26]

Under the mentorship of Jambhekar, Navrozji, and progressively in-
clined Scotsmen and Irishmen such as Harkness and Patton, Dadabhai
Naoroji thrived academically. Like his two Indian professors, he distinguished himself as a polymath. Elphinstone's faculty in 1843 recognized
him as one of the top students in chemistry, natural philosophy, and
history; the "most promising pupil" in the study of optics; and—
importantly—deserving of a prize for his performance in political
economy. In a letter of recommendation dating from 1846, a tattered
scrap of which survives among Naoroji's personal papers, John Harkness alluded to his pupil's broad talents. "In point of scholarship, and
attainments in the different branches of literature & sciences," Elphinstone College's principal stated, "he has all along maintained the highest
character with his different teachers; & has repeatedly carried off the
first prizes at the successive Annual Examinations." Orlebar, Naoroji's
mathematics professor, was more succinct in his praise. He pronounced
Naoroji as the "Promise of India."[27]

Dadabhai Naoroji finished his studies at Elphinstone College in 1845.
Having advanced in education as far as was possible in Bombay, he now
faced a unique challenge: what to do next? "Promise of India" or not, this
was no simple dilemma. In spite of their degrees and distinctions, many
Elphinstonians faced great difficulty in finding meaningful vocations.
The most dynamic city in western India had little to offer them aside from
the business houses of the shetias or middling governmental clerkships.
Yet as Naoroji completed his last months of college, Erskine Perry, chief
justice of the Bombay supreme court—and someone who had taken deep
interest in Dadabhai's scholarly progress—floated an ambitious plan. He
proposed sending Naoroji to England to qualify for the bar, even offering
to pay for half of his expenses if Parsi community leaders chipped in the
remaining amount. These community elders, however, angrily shot down
the scheme. Still reeling from an infamous incident in 1839 when the Scottish missionary John Wilson converted two Parsi boys to Christianity,
they suspected—unreasonably—that Perry's real intent was to coax yet
another Zoroastrian to apostatize from the faith. Thus Naoroji lost a
chance to become the first-ever Indian to qualify for the English bar.[28]

AGE 20.
From a Photo. by Rustumjee Jamsetjee, Poona.

Naoroji at the age of twenty, around the time he finished
his studies at Elphinstone College. *Strand Magazine,*
July 1892.

Courtesy of the Irvin Department of Rare Books and Special
Collections, University of South Carolina, Columbia.

With plans for a legal career derailed, Naoroji considered other employment options, including an offer to join the Bombay secretariat as a government servant. But he ultimately chose to return to his alma mater. In
November 1845, he joined Elphinstone College as an assistant master, responsible for elaborating upon the lectures delivered by his British

superiors and occasionally translating them into vernaculars. It was a relatively lowly position, with a starting salary that did little to ameliorate the Dordi family's poverty, but Naoroji used the experience to further distinguish himself as a polymath. One of his old classmates, Dadoba Pandurang, invited Naoroji to demonstrate various chemistry experiments before his class at Bombay's normal school, which had been founded by Bal Gangadhar Shastri Jambhekar to train new generations of Indian teachers. At public gatherings in the college, Naoroji lectured on diverse topics such as the workings of the steam engine, the philosophy of mathematics, astronomical principles, and "the duties of a teacher." As he plunged deeper into his academic responsibilities, he was steadily rewarded with pay increases. These finally banished the specter of impoverishment from the Dordi family home. By 1849, Naoroji had become the highest ranked non-professorial instructor in the college, commanding a salary of Rs. 100 a month. In 1851, he rose to the rank of assistant professor, filling the post that had lain vacant since Jambhekar's death. Identifying Jambhekar's old pupil as "one of the most experienced as well as able men ever educated within the walls of the Institution," the Elphinstone faculty stated in their annual report, "We have a strong hope that he will fill in a worthy manner the place of his esteemed predecessor."[29]

Surviving reports of the Bombay Board of Education (the successor body to the Bombay Native Education Society) provide a glimpse of Naoroji's teaching career at Elphinstone, where he lectured on mathematics, astronomy, and natural philosophy. In examination papers, he asked his pupils to prove the value of pi, perform integral calculus, define particular theorems, and solve complex trigonometric problems: "What is the declination of the Sun, when he is on the horizons of Bombay and Madras at the same instant; their respective latitudes being 18° 56′ N., and 13° 5′ N.; and their longitudes 72° 57′ E., and 80° 21′ E.?" Fulfilling the hopes of other faculty members at Elphinstone, Naoroji, like Jambhekar, displayed an infectious enthusiasm for teaching and a strong dedication to engagement with his students. He spoke eloquently in favor of the many benefits derived from studying mathematics, arguing that a student of this discipline "is inured to strict inquiries, is enabled to guard himself against credulous simplicity, and the meanness of yielding a slavish submission to the absolute dictates of authority or of any species of mental tyranny."[30] Mathematics, in other words, provided excellent training in rational thought, and it was through the study of the subject that Naoroji passed along the rationalist ideas of his teachers to a new generation of students.

Naoroji was not satisfied with confining his instruction within the four walls of the classroom. He took his students on an "outdoor lesson"—under the night sky—in order to reinforce particular astronomical principles. While lecturing on mechanics, Naoroji relied on texts from Trinity College in Dublin but, after noticing that his students "did not acquire a sufficiently clear comprehension" of the workings of the steam engine and locomotive, complemented these lessons with several field trips. He convinced two leading members of the famous Wadia family of shipbuilders, Ardaseer Cursetjee Wadia and Hirjibhai Merwanji Wadia, to allow his pupils to see their dockyard facilities at Mazagaon and the inside of a steamer anchored there. Later, Naoroji brought his students to the Bori Bunder station in order to inspect that great modern wonder, the steam locomotive, which plied the brand-new Great Indian Peninsula Railway, India's first railroad.[31]

Through his dedication and creative teaching methods, Naoroji succeeded, like Jambhekar, in molding a new generation of Indian educators, men who would shape the contours of education across western India for the remainder of the nineteenth century. Among his pupils were Ramakrishna Gopal Bhandarkar, the prominent Indologist and social reformer who taught at both Elphinstone and Deccan Colleges; Mahipatram Rupram Nilkanth, future principal of the Gujarat Training College in Ahmedabad, which supplied instructors for the proliferating number of primary schools across Gujarat; and Javerilal Umiashankar Yajnik, an active member of various scholarly associations in the presidency and, later in life, a member of the Bombay Municipal Corporation and Bombay legislative council. Finally, Naoroji began putting his own stamp on educational policy in western India when, in 1851, he was appointed as a member of the Bombay Board of Education. Here, although still in his late twenties, he worked alongside some of the most eminent Indian and European civic leaders in the city.

Naoroji's meteoric rise at Elphinstone was facilitated by two important factors. First, both students and instructors, whether Indians or Britons, enjoyed remarkably cooperative relations at the college. Second, due to the influence that Indians exercised as instructors and financial benefactors, the educational infrastructure in Bombay was to a great degree geared toward the promotion of Indian talent. In their original endowment of the Elphinstone professorships in 1827, shetia and princely benefactors had specifically stipulated that the posts were to be held by Britons "until the happy period arrives when natives shall be fully competent to hold them." These were not empty words. The donors, many of whom were members of the Bombay Native Education Society and the Bombay Board of Education, had enough influence and clout to enforce this stipulation and determine when such a "fully competent" candidate materialized. This occurred in 1854. That year, Elphinstone's faculty formally appointed Naoroji as a full professor of mathematics and natural philosophy, making him the first-ever Indian professor at a government college in the subcontinent. They were careful to describe his appointment as "a measure so entirely in accordance with both the letter and spirit of the resolution" of the 1827 endowment.[32]

Particular British officials also assisted in the promotion of Indian talent, broadening this cooperative environment into elements of the educational bureaucracy. Naoroji remained very close to Bombay's chief justice, Erskine Perry, who also served as the president of the Bombay Board of Education. Perry appears to have coaxed Naoroji to pursue the full professorship at Elphinstone, dispelling the young scholar's doubts that he had "done nothing hitherto to show the world that I have any good claim to apply for such a place." In the 1850s and 1860s, George Birdwood, a professor at Grant Medical College and later the registrar of Bombay University, was widely respected for his willingness to cross racial barriers and forge lasting friendships with both his students and Bombay's leading shetias. Birdwood's own friendship with Naoroji ultimately spanned nearly six decades. This environment of close cooperation did not last, of course: by the mid-1860s, when Indian influence in the educational bureaucracy began to wane, following the deaths of some leading shetias and a deep commercial crisis precipitated by the end of the American Civil War, Bombay bureaucrats became much more interested in employing fellow Britons in the college rather than seeking out Indian talent.[33] But while it did last, the unique environment at Elphinstone

College propelled the Young Bombay generation to the fore, ushering in a moment of social, religious, and nascent political reform. The progressive, liberal agenda of Young Bombay was firmly tied to the classroom. Naoroji and his colleagues made education a central feature of their reform projects.

The Benefit of Fresh Air

What, precisely, was "Young Bombay"? The term was sparingly used at the midpoint of the nineteenth century and—when it was used at all—was often deployed in a negative way. In September 1851, for example, the *Times of India* contemptuously sneered, "We were not till now aware that Chuckerbuttyism had taken root amongst us,—that there was a Young Bombay as well as a Young Bengal, desirous of reforming the abuses amongst themselves with a view to their release from the foreign thralldom under which they and their fathers have been restrained from the national pastime of robbing and cutting each other's throats when it so pleased them!"[34] "Chuckerbuttyism"—a snide reference to Bengali reformist ambitions—and the *Times*'s general tone of derision aside, the comparison with Young Bengal was telling. It linked a rising generation in Bombay with students of Hindu College in Calcutta who, under the brilliant Eurasian instructor Henry Louis Vivian Derozio, began in the 1820s to vociferously attack orthodox social and religious conventions.

Young Bombay was led by a new demographic in the city: a generation of Elphinstone graduates that possessed a clear "corporate sense of identity" born out of "an acceptance of the intrinsic value of a liberal Western education and of the knowledge which it imparted." As in Bengal, these men were positioned in opposition to a bulwark of orthodoxy. Many scholars, however, have pinned the weight of this social and religious orthodoxy upon the shetias, thereby framing an intrinsic conflict between the old shetia elite and the new intelligentsia. This is not entirely correct. Naoroji and his Western-educated peers—men such as Navrozji Fardunji, Bhau Daji, Ardeshir Framji Moos, and Karsondas Mulji—certainly consolidated a distinct sense of identity through their schooling and their commitment to social and religious reform. But they also forged strong alliances with the shetia elite, many of whom actually supported and bankrolled their reformist programs. Naoroji was responsible for creating and maintaining some of the alliances that were most critical to the movement's success.[35]

Therefore, instead of classifying Young Bombay as yet another case of competing elites—or even clear generational conflict (as in Young Bengal)—it is more useful to see the movement as the product of cooperation between Naoroji's fellow Elphinstone graduates and certain liberal-minded shetias. On account of the decades of Indian leadership in educational activities—in the Bombay Native Education Society, the Bombay Board of Education, and elsewhere—Young Bombay was in many ways the natural outcome of the strong educational tradition in western India, a tradition that produced receptivity to reform. If the late 1840s and early 1850s can be defined as a liberal moment, then it was liberal precisely because it was tied to the educational project championed by Indian elites. Many of the movement's key reformist planks were centered around the further extension of education and learning to underprivileged constituencies, most notably women.

Dadabhai Naoroji stands out during this period for his involvement in creating a new institutional fabric for Bombay. Between 1848 and 1855, he took a leadership role in a variety of new associations. He was the founder and first editor of the Parsi Lekhak Mandli, a society for Parsi writers, and was instrumental in raising funds for the Framji Cowasji Institute, which gave Bombay citizens a new forum for lectures and public gatherings. Upon its establishment, Naoroji exhorted educated Indians to use the institute's pulpit for teaching their countrymen to "emulate Newton or Watt"—to cultivate a spirit of inquisitiveness and industriousness. Not surprisingly, given his earlier record in student performances at the central English school, Naoroji also became a founding member of the Parsi Natak Mandli (Dramatic Society). Through its performance of a Gujarati rendition of *Rustom and Sohrab* in October 1853, this association raised the curtains for that great cultural institution of the late nineteenth and early twentieth centuries, Parsi theater. Additionally, Naoroji took a leading role in Parsi efforts to ameliorate the conditions of the remaining Zoroastrians of Iran, who suffered from terrible oppression and poverty.[36]

Naoroji's first foray into institution building was also one of his most significant. In the summer of 1848, he took great pains to revive

Elphinstone College's Native Literary Society—over which Bal Gangadhar Shastri Jambhekar had presided—by roping students and professors into a new and more ambitious organization, the Students' Literary and Scientific Society. While Professors Joseph Patton and Richard Tuohill Reid served as mentors, students took turns delivering fortnightly lectures on a range of topics. Some of these lectures skirted controversial political and social issues: "European Colonization in the East and West," "On Opium and the Opium Trade," "Condition of the Bombay Poor," and "Condition of the Lower Classes of Hindus Compared with Those of England." Naoroji also chalked out a detailed agenda for the society that went well beyond these fortnightly lectures. One of the specific objectives of the society was the dissemination of knowledge and learning, and to this end the society welcomed corresponding members in distant locations such as Surat and Dharwar. In July 1849, Patton challenged student members to create a body of "National Literature," enjoining young Elphinstonians to "write for the people" and produce works "which would influence the native mind."[37]

Naoroji was already busy laying the groundwork for this effort. Three months after the inauguration of the society, he helped create the Dnyan Prasarak Mandli (Society for the Diffusion of Knowledge), a branch of the society that held public lectures and produced popular journals in Gujarati and Marathi. Naoroji and his co-organizers specifically intended for these journals "to promote the diffusion of knowledge among the uneducated masses" and therefore kept prices very low to ensure wide distribution.[38] As the first president of the Mandli and editor of its Gujarati journal, Naoroji deepened working relationships with fellow Elphinstonians.

But he also relied extensively on the support of an energetic shetia, Kharshedji Nasarvanji Cama. Naoroji and Cama's collaboration serves as perhaps the best example of how shetias and young Elphinstonians cooperated to achieve particular reforms. A member of one of Bombay's wealthiest and most prominent Parsi mercantile families, Cama lacked a formal education and spoke halting English. Many of his closest relations were strictly orthodox and looked at the young Elphinstonians with suspicion. In spite—or because—of these handicaps, he threw himself into the task of widening the distribution of the Mandli's publications. "It was his worship, his love of human intellect," Naoroji recalled years later, that was the reason behind Cama's zeal for reformist activities. Cama (with Naoroji's additional contribution) paid out of his own pocket the monthly salaries of the Mandli's writers. Beginning in the early 1850s, he sponsored monetary prizes for Gujarati-language essays on topics such as "the importance of smallpox vaccinations" and "the wrong superstitions of astrologers."[39]

Kharshedji Nasarvanji Cama was involved in two other endeavors that Naoroji helped begin in 1851, the Rahnumae Mazdayasnan Sabha (Society of the Guides of the Mazdayasnan Path) and the Gujarati newspaper *Rast Goftar* (*Truth Teller*). Both the Sabha and *Rast Goftar* waded into the deeply treacherous waters surrounding Parsi religious and social reform, something that put Naoroji and his colleagues into direct confrontation with the orthodox Parsi priesthood and laity. The Sabha, with Naoroji serving as secretary and Navrozji Fardunji as president, gave itself the task of reforming and rationalizing Zoroastrianism by removing supposedly foreign and inauthentic customs and practices. In this regard, Navrozji was a logical choice to head the organization: in the wake of earlier Christian missionary attacks on Zoroastrian religious texts and doctrine, he had taken a leading role in defending the faith and disputing missionaries' allegations. Navrozji drew on a wide variety of sources—ranging from Voltaire and Thomas Paine to contemporary European orientalist scholarship—to rebut missionary polemics and characterize Zoroastrianism as a religion marked by reason and rationality.[40] Dadabhai threw his support behind the rationalist perspectives of his old teacher, thereby launching his own career as a Parsi religious reformer.

But the activities of the Sabha were momentarily forgotten when, barely two months after its inaugural meeting, Bombay was convulsed by riots between the Parsi and Muslim communities after a Parsi journalist published an insensitive account of the life of Muhammad and, in a masterstroke of bad judgment, included it alongside a depiction of the Prophet. In the wake of the riots, where many Parsis felt that both the government and the community's Parsee Punchayet had offered them inadequate protection, Naoroji published his first edition of *Rast Goftar,* which was bankrolled by Kharshedji Nasarvanji Cama. While its initial numbers dealt exclusively with the fallout from the riots, *Rast* moved on to take up a diverse array of reformist positions such as the discontinuance of child marriages, the inappropriateness of nautches, and the rights of women in adopting certain items of European clothing (the paper was a particularly staunch defender of Parsi women who, somewhat bizarrely, desired to wear stockings in the heat and humidity of Bombay).[41] Together, Naoroji's paper and the Sabha evolved into strong mouthpieces for certain reforms that went well beyond the limits of the tiny Parsi community, influencing western Indian society at large.

In the larger narrative of reform and education in Bombay, *Rast Goftar* and the Rahnumae Mazdayasnan Sabha were significant for three major reasons. First, the activities of Dadabhai Naoroji and Navrozji Fardunji—identifying and weeding out supposedly foreign aspects of practiced Zoroastrianism—bore the clear imprint of ideas and philosophies learned within the walls of Elphinstone College. Aside from portraying Zoroastrianism as a rational faith, they helped usher in a very Protestant search for doctrinal authenticity. The one unfortunate consequence of this development was that both men succumbed to orientalist stereotypes of Hindu and Islamic decadence and corruption, something that had visibly crept into Elphinstone's curriculum. Thus, Navrozji specifically and deliberately tarred certain Parsi practices he found undesirable—particular marriage and funerary customs, various forms of black magic, and superstitions—as borrowings from the two major religions of India, further underscoring their inauthenticity and harmfulness.[42] For better and for worse, therefore, Young Bombay's reforming impulse was guided by lessons learned in the classroom.

Second, both *Rast* and the Sabha envisioned themselves as pedagogical instruments for combatting ignorance. They had a clear educational agenda and purpose, as is evidenced from the language they deployed. At the Sabha, Dadabhai Naoroji charged certain orthodox Parsis with being "ignorant or following traditions without understanding." Navrozji Fardunji, meanwhile, pronounced that "their thoughts should be reformed, and arrangements should be made to fill them with precious and useful knowledge." *Rast Goftar* adopted an almost populist tone in its first edition, mourning a general atmosphere of ignorance and resolving to "spread the practice and habit of reading a paper among the poor people." To this end, both the Sabha and *Rast* followed the lead of the Dnyan Prasarak Mandli by aiming for mass distribution. While Navrozji resolved to publish inexpensive educational pamphlets for the Sabha, Kharshedji Nasarvanji Cama shouldered the costs for free distribution of a thousand copies of the first numbers of *Rast,* an unprecedented circulation in those days. These tactics garnered remarkable success. With time, *Rast* established itself as a redoubtable organ reckoned to have the largest newspaper circulation in all of India.[43]

Cama's largesse brings us to the last, and perhaps most important, point of significance for *Rast Goftar* and the Rahnumae Mazdayasnan Sabha. They drew together a wide spectrum of reform-minded elites who would sustain much of Bombay's civic life over the next fifty years—and many of whom would prove themselves vital interlocutors in Naoroji's future political career. Dadabhai Naoroji helped solicit financial support from prominent Parsi mercantile families such as the Banajis, Petits, and Readymoneys. He relied extensively on the support of Parsi Elphinstonians. This included men such as Sorabji Shapurji Bengali, who became one of the most ardent voices of social reform in Bombay, and K. R. Cama, the pioneering Parsi scholar of Zoroastrianism who later in his career helped popularize in India new philological methods of religious study brought from Europe. But Naoroji did not just rely on members of his own community. Karsondas Mulji, the prominent Gujarati social reformer and journalist, eventually became one of the eight members of the "syndicate" that ran *Rast,* enabling it to break out of an exclusively Parsi mold, while Maharashtrians and Gujaratis such as Dadoba Pandurang, Vishwanath Narayan Mandlik, and Javerilal Umiashankar Yajnik contributed columns in English. Last, Naoroji counted on assistance from some of Elphinstone's European faculty members. Joseph Patton, keen on seeing his former student's *Rast Goftar* succeed, apparently "used his personal influence with the leading natives to make them subscribers." Naoroji, bereaved at the loss of this pillar of support in 1852, eulogized Patton in *Rast* as his "father and protector."[44]

This coalition of individuals—students and shetias, Parsis and non-Parsis, Indians and select Europeans—would sustain what was the greatest single example of Young Bombay's cooperative spirit: the endeavor to promote female education. Before the American Missionary Society and

Scottish Missionary Society opened the first girls' schools in Bombay in the late 1820s and early 1830s, government reports could point to only a few scattered instances in the presidency of elite Muslim and Parsi families educating their daughters at home.[45] It is remarkable how quickly opinion shifted in favor of girls' schools thereafter.

In mid-nineteenth-century India, the question of female education was, with a few notable exceptions, entirely decided by men. Little material survives to tell us what, precisely, motivated the men of Young Bombay to start extending the fruits of learning to women. They were no doubt aware of some remarkable instances of female assertiveness against oppressive gender norms. In May 1848, for example, a Bombay Parsi woman created a sensation as far away as Bengal when she flung aside the purdah at her house in Fort, marched out of the city, and set up a tent among the forests of then-remote Malabar Hill, anxious for "the benefit of fresh air." The incident created some momentary hand-wringing among Bombay's patricians about the welfare of their womenfolk.[46]

However, for the vast majority of Bombay's champions of female education, the welfare of women was not the chief priority. Many Elphinstonians were instead fired by the ideal of national regeneration. In this vein, an Elphinstone student senior to Naoroji, Govind Vitthal Kunte, better known as Bhau Mahajan, criticized the government for inaction in the columns of his Marathi weekly, *Prabhakar*. "To this date, the Government has not started any schools for girls," he wrote in 1843. "This must be done without any delay, for so long as our women remain in ignorance there is no hope for the progress of this country." Other young reformers worried about how ignorant mothers would raise their sons. "It is needless to dilate on the advantage of female education," opined Kaikhoshru Hormasji, a student at Elphinstone in 1850. "It will suffice us if we were to mention that philosophers like Bacon, and linguists like Jones, who afterwards became so famous for their learning, were indebted in their early lives to their learned and intelligent mothers, under whose care their youthful minds were formed." Last, as Rustom P. Masani, Naoroji's first biographer, suggested, the new crop of young educated men rued the domestic unhappiness caused by uneducated wives: "No wonder several of them were driven to seek pleasure outside the home."[47]

Naoroji probably agreed with all of these observations. Indeed, his own marriage appeared to be unhappy partly due to the fact that his wife, Gulbai, was illiterate and possessed little interest in being educated. Although none of Naoroji's writings from the 1850s on female education seem to have survived, we can glean some of his motivations from a statement that he composed for a government educational commission in 1882. Like Kaikhoshru Hormasji, Naoroji believed that "good and educated mothers only will raise good and educated sons." But he also possessed notably progressive views on female education, arguing that it was a fundamental pillar for establishing gender equality. Indians, he argued, would one day "understand that woman had as much right to exercise and enjoy all the rights, privileges, and duties of this world as man, each working toward the common good in her or his representative sphere." In making such an assertion—relatively unprecedented in late nineteenth-century India—Naoroji most likely had in mind the towering example set by his own mother. After all, Manekbai Dordi, although illiterate, had made the critical decision to enroll young Dadabhai in a school run by the Bombay Native Education Society—a decision that ultimately rescued the family from the clutches of worsening poverty. She was also a staunch proponent of female education. Naoroji, therefore, had something in common with many of the leading social reformers of his day, men such as Behramji Malabari in Bombay and Ishwarchandra Vidyasagar in Bengal: the influence and example of that most resilient of characters in the Indian family, the strong-willed and independent-minded matriarch. "She helped me with all her heart in my work for female education and other social reforms against prejudices of the day," Naoroji recalled many decades later. "She made me what I am."[48]

Since British administrators in Bombay refused to extend government support for girls' schools, members of the Students' Literary and Scientific Society decided to intervene. In October 1849, Dadabhai Naoroji joined twelve other Maharashtrian and Parsi Elphinstonians in opening up six schools—three for Parsi girls and three for Hindu Maharashtrian girls—run under the umbrella of the society. Naoroji and one of his college students were initially in charge of a girls' school located outside of Fort's walls. From 1849 until the early 1850s, this band of thirteen ran the schools on a purely voluntary basis. They went door-to-door pleading

with parents to send their daughters to the new schools, oftentimes receiving threats of violence from fathers outraged by the very idea of educating their female offspring. Early in the morning, before Elphinstone's
doors opened, Naoroji and his colleagues taught the handful of girls who
assembled in makeshift classrooms.[49]

In spite of grave financial challenges, the whims of students' fathers,
and wildly fluctuating attendance, the society's schools began yielding
impressive results. In 1849, Naoroji and his colleagues counted fewer than
fifty pupils; by early 1853, more than five hundred girls crowded onto
school benches. There was, furthermore, a significant trickle-down effect. Students returned home to impart school lessons to their female relatives, oftentimes also teaching mothers, aunts, and elder sisters how to
read. At least one Parsi girl and one Maharashtrian girl were judged qualified enough to begin teaching classes. And in a schoolhouse in Fort,
teachers nurtured one girl with pronounced learning disabilities into a
star pupil, one who knew "a great deal more than the first girl of the first
division."[50]

A number of shetias soon stepped in to lend support. One of the first
donors was Jagannath Shankarsheth, a respected merchant and a
founding member of the Bombay Native Education Society. Jagannath,
who had educated his own daughters at home, bequeathed to the society
a building on his estate to be used as a girls' schoolhouse. Two Parsi
magnates—Framji Cowasji Banaji, at the end of his distinguished life as
a merchant and agricultural pioneer, and Cowasji Jehangir Readymoney,
a relatively new force in Bombay civic affairs—offered Naoroji additional
funding and moral support. Jamsetjee Jejeebhoy, the influential Parsi bar-
onet, summoned Dadabhai and a vocal critic of female education to his
office. Weighing both perspectives ("But what do females want education
for? It will only spoil them," charged the critic. "You see, you should not
supply more oil to a lamp than it can bear, for, otherwise the light is sure
to extinguish itself"), Jamsetjee sided with Naoroji and eventually bankrolled four additional girls' schools. But it was Naoroji's connections with
the Camas that proved most critical. "This is a happy day for me," Naoroji
recalled Kharshedji Nasarvanji saying when he first broached the subject
of formal education for young girls. The Camas threw their support
behind female education and presented the Students' Literary and Scien-

tific Society with the whopping sum of Rs. 4,800, enabling the society to cover rent for its Hindu and Parsi schools and also pay its teachers. The family was, therefore, instrumental in making sure that the society's girls' schools were put on solid and permanent footing.[51]

While Naoroji's fellow Parsis initially led the way with female education, they were soon joined by members of other communities from across the presidency. Gujarati Hindu traders endowed a girls' school outside Fort in 1851; three years later, Mangaldas Nathubhai, a progressive-minded Bania merchant and banker, inaugurated another institution. Support for female education spread quickly through Bombay's hinterlands. In Ahmedabad, the city's powerful Jain *nagarsheth* or head merchant expressed his "heartfelt gratification" at the success of girls' schools in Bombay and transmitted funds to the society's coffers, while another wealthy benefactor, Maganbhai Karamchand, donated Rs. 20,000 to open two girls' schools in the erstwhile capital of Gujarat. Further south, in relatively remote Ahmednagar, Dadoba Pandurang, Naoroji's old classmate, noted in the mid-1850s the existence of two private girls' schools and reported on some Muslim girls attending a Muslim religious school.[52]

All of these developments had profound implications for Naoroji. His role in laying the groundwork for female education and his strong ties to prominent shetia philanthropists such as the Camas augmented his position of leadership in Bombay society. His leadership also earned him support from powerful British officials. Erskine Perry, in his last full year as secretary of the Bombay Board of Education, harangued the chief engineer of the Bombay public works to give Naoroji assistance in building a girls' schoolhouse outside of Fort's ramparts. When the chief engineer proved noncommittal, Perry contacted the governor, Lord Falkland, for help and convinced him to make an official visit to the girls' school that Naoroji managed. Naoroji evidently reached out to Indian princely states as well for financial contributions: he received a small sum from the diwan of Indore "for prizes to some good girls in the Fort [Parsi] school."[53] Contacts with princely states, British officials, and a broad spectrum of shetias and educated youth all hint at how Naoroji, still in his late twenties, vigorously pursued an agenda of social reform by creating an expansive and diversified network of support.

These networks sustained Young Bombay's final turn toward political reform in 1852, when Elphinstonians joined hands with shetias to form the Bombay Association. The association was part of a new burst of civic life across the subcontinent, as wealthy Indians in presidency towns, members of the tiny minority that had prospered from British rule, sought to influence their colonial rulers. While Jagannath Shankarsheth presided over the organization—drawing in fellow commercial elites such as Jamsetjee Jejeebhoy, the Konkani Muslim merchant Muhammad Ali Roghay, and the Baghdadi Jewish magnate David Sassoon—the younger generation, including Dadabhai Naoroji, Navrozji Fardunji, and the Maharashtrian polymath Bhau Daji, set an agenda for policy inquiry and petitioning the government over various grievances. Like the Students' Literary and Scientific Society, Rahnumae Mazdayasna Sabha, and *Rast Goftar*, the Bombay Association placed great faith in the transformational and regenerative qualities of education. Its inaugural meeting was, appropriately, held at Elphinstone College. In his first address as president, Jagannath specifically pointed to the institution and the city's Grant Medical College as proof of the beneficial aspects of British rule, asking rhetorically how the association could ever be in opposition to a government that endowed these places of learning.[54]

But Indians could advise on improving governance, and to this effect, members of the association—led by Navrozji Fardunji, Bhau Daji, and possibly Naoroji—began drafting a petition to the British Parliament in relation to the renewal of the East India Company's charter in 1854. In comparison to the petitions sent by its sister organizations, the Native Association of Madras and the British Indian Association of Calcutta, the Bombay Association's memorial was remarkably brief. But while all three organizations complained about official miserliness toward schools, the Bombay Association made education a central plank of its petition to Parliament, proposing the establishment of universities in India and boldly arguing that "all the reforms and all the improvements sought for; or in the power of your honourable House to make, are but secondary in importance compared with the necessity of introducing a complete system of education for the masses of the people."[55]

This was a significant call to action, and it indicated how the petitioners sought to ingrain Bombay's educational tradition within government policy. We have no direct evidence that Naoroji helped draft the Bombay Association petition. However, its strong language and its central demand for both broadening and deepening the extent of education within Indian society certainly suggest that he played an important role. These were, after all, ideas that Naoroji would actively champion for the rest of his life.

Dadabhai, What a Fall!

Dadabhai Naoroji's early career, when he concentrated his energies on being an educator and a reformer, ended on June 26, 1855, as the steamer *Madras* slipped beyond view from Bombay's shores and charted its course in the direction of Europe. On board the ship, Naoroji was joined by three other Parsis: Rustomji Behramji Parakh, a bright young candidate for the East India Company's medical service; K. R. Cama, Dadabhai's friend and reformist colleague; and Mancherji Hormusji Cama, destined to lead the Cama family's business operations in Great Britain. Together, these four men were heralded as representatives of a new educated, professional class of Indians—Young Bombay out to make its mark on the world.

In spite of the well-wishers who had crowded onto Apollo Bunder to send off the erstwhile professor, not everyone was happy with Naoroji's decision to turn to commerce. "Dadabhai, what a fall!" Elphinstone College's principal apparently exclaimed when he learned the news. Naoroji hoped to keep his sojourn in England brief. After agreeing to join the Cama business venture in England, he filed a request with Bombay educational authorities for a simple two-year leave of absence from his professorial duties at Elphinstone. The Bombay Board of Education was so anxious to retain Naoroji's services that it even consulted the governor on the matter.[56]

But Naoroji never returned to teach at the college. Regardless, the year 1855 did not mark the end of his involvement with educational matters in Bombay. As he embarked on a business career and made his earliest forays into politics in London, he remained engaged with friends advancing the cause of education back home. Naoroji solicited financial support from wealthy Britons for new girls' schools in Bombay, floated plans for a fellowship at the recently established Bombay University, and outlined another scheme for a loan company, "intended for the benefit of all of India," which would finance Indian students traveling to Great Britain and other European countries. In London, he befriended Mary Carpenter, the founder of the "ragged school" movement for British street children. As Carpenter's educational interests turned to India—and, in particular, female education—he assisted with her fact-finding visits to the country, which Naoroji and his Bombay colleagues deftly used to pressure colonial authorities for more financial support for girls' schools. In 1871, Naoroji helped inaugurate the London branch of Carpenter's National Indian Association in Aid of Social Progress in India, which became one of the most important organizations dedicated to the welfare of Indian students enrolled in British schools and universities.[57]

In short, Dadabhai Naoroji continued to shape—and be shaped by—Bombay's distinct educational tradition, exerting significant leadership and initiative in spite of his distance from India's western shores. Increasingly, however, Naoroji channeled his energies into protest. By the 1860s, he began attacking the colonial government's miserliness and indifference toward Indian education. This was a significant development: examining educational policy, he fashioned some of his earliest and most hard-hitting critiques of colonial rule. He also drafted some of his most progressive and farsighted proposals. In 1868, Naoroji submitted a petition to the India Office on female education, complaining to the secretary of state for India about official indifference to girls' schools in Bombay. Demonstrating the skills in empirical research that he had honed at Elphinstone College, he marshaled facts and figures to his advantage. He showed that while the governments of Bengal, Punjab, and the North-West Provinces each annually expended around Rs. 30,000 on girls' schools, Bombay officials had forked over precisely Rs. 341 in the past year. This stood in marked contrast to the endowments funded by Indians of Bombay, which he estimated were in excess of Rs. 340,000. By 1871, growing progressively more impatient with non-responsive Bombay officials, Naoroji decided to set his sights significantly higher. In evidence submitted before the British Parliament, he called for a "comprehensive plan of national education, both high and popular," in India.[58]

By proposing "national education," Naoroji enunciated what was one of the earliest demands for mass public education in India. The idea, evidently, had been brewing in his mind for some time. Naoroji's experience at the Bombay Board of Education's central English school, where his mother did not have to pay a single rupee in fees, had made him "an ardent advocate of free education." He thereafter championed "the principle that every child should have the opportunity of receiving all the education it is capable of assimilating, whether it is born poor or with a silver spoon in its mouth." This was a revealing statement: Naoroji's advocacy of public education in India was, like his earlier activities in Bombay, premised on the relationship he observed between poverty and education. In 1882, he composed a memorandum for the Commission on Indian Education that examined how the twin evils of the country's "extreme poverty" and the government's unwillingness to properly fund schools fed off each other. Once more assembling a damning set of statistics, Naoroji calculated that only one in 114 children in India attended a primary school, a figure that meant "nearly 25,000,000 children needing primary education only grow up in ignorance." Noting that, per head, the United States, United Kingdom, and even other parts of the British Empire lavished large sums on public education, he condemned the British colonial government in India for only being able to muster "the wretched 8 3/4 pies per head of population, or *hardly a penny,* from all sources—voluntary, and taxation and rates or cesses." These statistics told "a sad, sad tale . . . about India—wretched as she is materially, still more wretched is she educationally."[59]

By the 1880s, however, Dadabhai Naoroji knew that education alone could not reverse India's economic fortunes. It could not attack the disease at the heart of India's colonial predicament, one that every year reduced the country to even more extreme levels of poverty and subjected millions to even more catastrophic famines. That disease was the drain of wealth. It is to poverty and the drain—and the first phase of Naoroji's political career—that we will now turn.

CHAPTER 2

Of Poverty and Princes

AS THE *MADRAS* steamed westward from Bombay harbor in late June 1855, Dadabhai Naoroji encountered a world diverging to extremes of wealth and poverty, power and powerlessness. He dispatched impressions of his journey to Britain in a series of Gujarati-language articles published in *Rast Goftar*. The Indian Ocean, once teeming with trade between the ports of Africa, Arabia, and the subcontinent, was now eerily silent and empty. In Aden, the first port of call, Naoroji commented on the piteous condition of Somali laborers, while noting disapprovingly that the town lacked even one proper school. Egypt, which the Parsi travelers passed through under a blazing July sun, presented a study in contrasts. Naoroji admired the wide roads and European-style buildings of Alexandria, and he praised the reform-minded pasha for having begun construction of a railway line and telegraph network. But everywhere, and at all times of day and night, he heard the cry of "baksheesh" from poor Egyptians holding out their hands for alms.[1]

Beyond Egypt, in contrast, lay a "new world." He marveled at the volume of ship traffic in the Mediterranean, a marked contrast to the empty sea-lanes between India and Arabia. After making landfall at Marseilles, Naoroji boarded a series of trains heading north and was simply stunned by the prosperity of the French countryside. He marveled at the networks of canals, abundant fields, and bustling market towns. In Paris, he took in the scientific and technological wonders of the Exposition Universelle. The City of Light, with its modern infrastructure, handsome buildings, and evident wealth, made even the grandest streets of Bombay pale in comparison. All of this left a profound impression on the young man who, not long before, had distinguished himself as a star pupil of political economy. "I make a fervent wish," Naoroji told readers of *Rast Goftar,* "that God instills in the subjects and leaders of my dear country the enthusiasm to try to make it as prosperous as France."[2]

On his first-ever voyage beyond Indian shores, therefore, Dadabhai Naoroji was clearly thinking about the economic condition of his homeland and how it compared with other parts of the world. He had more opportunity to do so when, in late August 1855, he and his Parsi business partners reached Britain and established their mercantile firm, Cama & Co., in London and Liverpool. Here, in these two great Victorian metropolises, the former Elphinstone professor no doubt had ample occasions to study how Indian resources enriched Great Britain. Shuttling back and forth between London and Bombay in the late 1850s and early 1860s, while he rode the highs and lows of the cotton trade, Naoroji must have even more keenly felt the stark difference between mother country and colony. For England was the undisputed locus of power and prosperity: home to the newly established India Office, which took over the reins of power from the East India Company without interrupting the flow of wealth from the subcontinent. India, in contrast, lay shattered after the Mutiny of 1857 and enervated from a spate of deadly famines. It seemed to be the very byword for poverty and powerlessness.

Naoroji soon abandoned such anecdotal comparison in pursuit of detailed economic study of India. Between the late 1860s and early 1880s, he produced a prodigious amount of literature—containing extensive calculations, international comparisons, compilations of historical evidence, and refutation of government pronouncements and statistics—highlighting the stark impoverishment of Britain's Indian subjects. Significantly, he established a direct causal link between poverty and British rule. "So far as my inquiries go at present, the conclusion I draw is, that wherever the East India Company acquired territory, impoverishment followed their steps," he argued. The instrument of this impoverishment, Naoroji famously contended, was the "drain of wealth"—whereby as much as one-fourth of the annual tax revenue raised in India went into British coffers rather than being reinvested in the country. While its mechanisms were complex, Naoroji clearly understood that the drain was, fundamentally, a question of colonial policy. "I wonder when this Hydra headed policy will ever be broken," he confided to a friend and political ally in Bombay, Behramji Malabari. "These Englishmen cannot understand that the wealth *they* carry away from this Country is the *whole* & *sole* cause of our misery. . . . *They* take away our bread and then turn round asking us why we are not eating it."[3]

The link between policy and poverty is important. Naoroji was hardly the first person to notice the drain of wealth from colonial India: numerous Britons and Indians, from as early as the 1770s, wrote about the phenomenon. Indeed, Naoroji had been exposed to Indian accounts of a drain while a student at Elphinstone College. Among his elder classmates was a group of Maharashtrian students who, in the early 1840s, wrote and debated about the causes of Indian poverty. They formed a "secret society," and Naoroji, who attended the society's meetings, recalled that it was "as rebellious as it could possibly be."[4]

In contrast with these British and Indian antecedents—as well as later studies of Indian poverty pursued by thinkers such as Mahadev Govind Ranade and Romesh Chunder Dutt—Naoroji's innovation was to make economic scholarship and theory serve an explicitly political objective, the achievement of swaraj or self-government. He progressively drew upon Indian poverty and the drain theory to justify political reform in the direction of swaraj. The key link between these ideas was the Indian civil service. By the 1870s, Naoroji argued that the "excessive employment" of Britons in the civil service—specifically, the cost of their salaries, pensions, and other benefits, which weighed heavier on the Indian taxpayer with each passing year—was the main cause of the drain of wealth. Consequently, he crafted a political corollary to the drain theory. If the employment of Britons was depleting the country's wealth and worsening Indian poverty, then the solution to the drain would be to employ Indians instead, whose earnings would circulate back into the Indian economy rather than being funneled to British coffers. This was a powerful argument in favor of political reform.[5]

Naoroji's writings on poverty and the drain were therefore polemical in nature: while firmly rooted in data and detailed empirical observations, they were not meant to be neutral, objective analyses of the Indian economy. Other historians have puzzled over Naoroji's economic work, wondering why, out of all the possible causes for the drain of wealth, he obsessed over just one source, a European-dominated civil service. The political corollary helps explain this nationalist preoccupation with civil service reform, something that has otherwise been unfairly chalked up to the self-interest of Indian elites for employment and greater social standing.[6]

The political corollary also explains other arenas of early nationalist activity that have been mostly overlooked. One such arena was nationalist engagement with Indian princely states, semi-autonomous domains ruled by indigenous royalty. Starting in the late 1860s, Naoroji forged close relationships with the darbars (courts) of several princely states, especially those in Gujarat. Since such states enjoyed a degree of autonomy from colonial rule and had bureaucracies that were staffed by Indians rather than Englishmen, Naoroji theorized that they were buffered from the drain of wealth and, consequently, were more economically robust than British India. They could, therefore, serve as laboratories for experiments in Indian political and economic reform—experiments that were impossible to undertake in British India as long as the civil service remained a nearly exclusive British club. In 1873, Naoroji accepted the position of diwan or prime minister for Baroda state and sought to catalyze key administrative reforms and modernizations. Significantly, he recruited several products of Young Bombay in order to help with implementation. Whereas, in his writings on poverty and the drain, Naoroji was limited to the world of theory, Baroda gave him the opportunity to put his ideas into practice.

In the midst of these endeavors, Naoroji had to deal with the vagaries of family life and endure wild fluctuations in his business fortunes. When he first sailed away from Bombay in 1855, he left his young wife, Gulbai, in the care of Manekbai, his mother. It was unthinkable in those days for a Parsi, no matter how reform-minded, to take a female relation beyond Indian shores. Manekbai, evidently, began to regret her choice of a daughter-in-law. By the late 1850s, she actively encouraged her son to take up a second wife; bigamy, after all, was commonly practiced by Parsi elites in the mid-nineteenth century. Naoroji would have none of it. From London and Liverpool and on return visits home, he rebuffed his mother's entreaties, even taking part in efforts to outlaw bigamy through a new Parsi marriage act put before the Bombay government. Manekbai eventually dropped the subject.[7]

But soon after, the somewhat restored domestic tranquility of the Dordi family home in Bombay was rocked by an incredible rumor spread by one of Naoroji's original business partners at Cama & Co., Mancherji Hormusji Cama. Cama was staunchly orthodox and had, in the early 1850s, even set up a rival organization to counter Naoroji's reformist work at the Rahnumae Mazdayasnan Sabha. The two men somehow let pursuit of profit smooth over these earlier animosities—until 1858, when Naoroji left Cama & Co. and established his own mercantile firm in London, Dadabhai Naoroji & Co. Perhaps smarting from accumulated ill will, Cama around 1863 propounded a bizarre story that Naoroji was keen on converting to Christianity and marrying an Englishwoman. Naoroji was so distraught by this rumor that he immediately sailed back to Bombay in order to quash it. He returned to England more than a year later, bringing along with him his mother, wife, and two young children—his son Ardeshir, born in 1859, and a newborn daughter named Shirin—thereby breaking the taboo on Parsi womenfolk traveling abroad (and no doubt causing further insult to Cama's orthodox sentiments). Almost immediately after settling in London, the reunited family suffered a terrible financial catastrophe as Dadabhai Naoroji & Co. plunged into bankruptcy. Naoroji spent much of the next fifteen years feverishly trying to repay accumulated business debts.[8]

Thus began the first phase of Naoroji's career and political philosophy— against an occasionally tense family backdrop, as well as a momentary worry that poverty would return to stalk his household. Naoroji soldiered on in spite of these difficulties. This phase of his career unfolded partly in Britain, partly in British India, and partly in the princely states. It involved pauperized Indian peasants, British civil servants that Naoroji characterized as "European leeches," and reform-minded maharajas.[9]

And it dramatically pushed forth the agenda of an emerging band of Indian nationalists.

The Poverty of India

Between 1867 and 1880, Dadabhai Naoroji expounded upon the drain of wealth from India through a series of detailed papers and published statistics. He presented most of these papers in London, before British audiences. This was no mere coincidence: Naoroji felt duty-bound to change the tone of Indian policy debate in the capital of the empire. To this extent, in late 1866 he established the East India Association, a forum for discussion of Indian affairs that, in London as well as in a branch society in Bombay, drew a large cross section of bureaucrats, politicians, students, and intellectuals.

It is difficult to say why, precisely, Naoroji chose the late 1860s to launch into sustained discussion of Indian poverty and the drain. No letters or papers survive to explain his rationale. Quite likely, however, Naoroji was moved to action by twin crises unfolding in the subcontinent at the time. The American Civil War prompted the first crisis. Opening volleys from Fort Sumter's cannons brought to a halt the South's cotton trade with Britain, causing a spike in the price of Indian cotton. This benefited a handful of Indian cotton merchants, including Naoroji, while wiping out the last remaining weavers in the Indian countryside, who were no longer able to purchase raw materials. Once peace returned to the United States, the price of Indian cotton cratered. Indian merchants faced economic ruin—this was the reason Dadabhai Naoroji & Co. was forced to declare bankruptcy and temporarily shutter its London office. For India, the American Civil War was a one-two punch that sent financial shudders through both city and countryside, demonstrating the precariousness of the colonial economy.[10]

The second crisis was far graver. In 1865, following a capricious monsoon, famine began stalking India's eastern shores. Panic spread through the region of Orissa after the colonial governor coolly refused to intervene and provide emergency supplies of grain. By 1867, as much as one-third of Orissa's population was dead. The Orissa famine was, for Naoroji, a stark example of India's perilous economic and political position. It prompted him to investigate how mass famine had been a hallmark of British rule in India—and how the specter of starvation and disease had significantly worsened in the past decade. "What an appalling, what a sad picture we have before us!" he concluded upon tabulating recent death figures. "Have all the wars of the past 100 years destroyed as many lives and property as the famines of the past eight years?" From the East India Association's lectern, Naoroji began speaking with urgency about Indian poverty, mass famine, and the drain of wealth as interconnected phenomena. He first sought to establish the gravity of Indian poverty in order to highlight the country's inability to bear further outflows of its meager resources and finances. Naoroji's immediate task, therefore, was political in nature: urging swift policy changes that would acknowledge and rectify the drain.[11]

When Naoroji began speaking about poverty and the drain, however, he confronted a Himalayan obstacle. It was extraordinarily difficult to convince British audiences, both policymakers and the general public, that India was a fundamentally impoverished country. During the second half of the nineteenth century, this notion went against conventional wisdom in the United Kingdom—in spite of grim headlines emanating from the latest famine-stricken districts. How was poverty possible in a land that had produced the British nabobs of the previous century, one that continued to buoy the fortunes of the City of London, the empire's financial heart, and fill British docks and warehouses with luxury goods of every sort? Could India really be a poor country when, year after year, an increasing number of Indian professionals, princes, and wealthy merchants streamed into London, consorting with the commercial and political elite of Britain and the empire? And wasn't Naoroji—educated, Anglicized, and relatively wealthy by the mid-1860s—himself an example of imperial beneficence? As naive as these observations might seem today, they were important components of British imperial imagination. They were premised on the common belief that India, precisely because of its abundant wealth, was the linchpin of the empire's prosperity and political, economic, and military strength. Famine was a bizarre aberration, the result of Indian laziness or fecundity rather than systemic poverty.[12]

The British Indian government did not make Naoroji's task any easier. Each year, mandarins in the India Office in Whitehall assembled the *Moral and Material Progress Report*, deploying official statistics to claim significant social and economic progress in the subcontinent. Many of these statistics, however, were simply wrong. In 1871, Naoroji addressed London's Society of Arts, mentioning a recent India Office report given to Parliament. As proof of the "General Prosperity" of India, the report cited a "great excess of exports above imports," a stunning 188 percent increase in exports during the 1840s and 1850s, and a 227 percent increase in imports in the same period. These were, an incredulous Naoroji stated, "fallacious statements." And they were also symptomatic of a much larger problem. "I am constrained to say, after my residence in this country for fifteen years, that the knowledge of the public here about India is not only imperfect, but in some matters mischievously incorrect," he declared. Due in part to such reports and statistics, there was "the almost universal belief that India is rich and prosperous, when it is not so."[13]

Naoroji's attempts to hammer away at this universal belief were hampered by many factors other than ignorance, bad information, and rosy official pronouncements. There were, for example, particular derisory attitudes among Britons toward Indians. One irate Anglo-Indian, writing to the *London Review* in response to some of Naoroji's opinions about Indian poverty, complained that Naoroji was simply repeating "the common native argument that the English have drained India of its treasure and reduced it to misery." But what truly outraged the writer was that an Indian had the audacity to make these claims before an audience of eminent Britons—current and former officials and "many practical men"—and then publish his paper for distribution, something that suggested "a most mischievous character."[14]

Such were the attitudes that greeted Naoroji's first forays into discussion of Indian economic matters. On May 2, 1867, he inaugurated the East India Association in London by delivering a paper titled "England's Duties to India." The title sounded innocuous enough. But before an audience that included eminent members of the India Office, men who helped compose the annual *Moral and Material Progress Report*, Naoroji detailed the horrific dimensions of the Orissa famine. The famine forced Naoroji to weigh the advantages and disadvantages of British colonial rule. "Security of life and property we have better in these times [under the British], no doubt," he stated, "but the destruction of a million and a half lives in one famine is a strange illustration of the worth of the life and property thus secured." While he lavished praise upon the British for granting India several supposed boons—"law and order," "the enlightenment of the country" through Western education, and a "new political life"—Naoroji grappled with a fundamental tension between, on one hand, piecemeal social and political advancement and, on the other, unfathomable impoverishment.[15]

Aside from broaching the topic of mass famine, Dadabhai Naoroji's "England's Duties to India" was significant in one other sense: it established his quantitative, statistical approach for proving the existence of Indian poverty. While his focus in this paper was India's heavy financial tribute to its colonial master, Naoroji soon turned his attention toward the economic condition of the Indian people themselves. In July 1870, he delivered another paper, "The Wants and Means of India," at London's Society of Arts. With a touch of irony, Charles Trevelyan—a hated figure in Ireland due to his mortality-inducing policies during the potato famine of the late 1840s—presided over the meeting. Naoroji posed a basic question to Trevelyan and other attendees: "Is India at present in a condition to produce enough to supply all its wants?"[16]

In order to answer this question, Naoroji developed several innovative methods for quantifying and describing India's stark poverty. First, and most significant, he made the first-ever estimates of the country's gross income per capita (technically, gross production per capita). His calculations were simple and difficult to disprove. "The whole produce of India is from its land," Naoroji observed. Working backward, he took land revenue figures for the year 1870–1871 and, by noting that the government collected around one-eighth of total produce in the form of land revenue, calculated that the gross product of the country per annum was in the neighborhood of £168 million. Adding gross revenue from opium, salt, and forest products, and factoring in coal production as well as revenue from appropriated land, Naoroji set a very conservative final estimate of £200 million. By simply dividing this amount by the total population of

India, he arrived at a figure that caused scandal in London: a paltry 27 shillings per Indian subject. In comparison, average income in the United Kingdom was nearly twenty-five times higher, around £33 per head. Naoroji offered a more conservative estimate of 40 shillings per head in India in order to account for any industry and manufacturing, which he held to be negligible. Either figure, he cautioned, was undoubtedly too high, due to the concentration of wealth in a microscopic upper and middle class. "Can it be then a matter of any surprise," he asked his audience, "that the very first touch of famines should so easily carry away hundreds of thousands as they have done during the past twelve years?"[17]

Naoroji's second method involved perfecting the art of statistical comparison. Figures on Indian poverty might startle and shock members of the British public, but well-formulated comparisons could also make them viscerally uncomfortable. In "The Wants and Means of India," Naoroji pioneered economic comparisons between India and other countries, especially the United States and the United Kingdom. But it would take a few more years for him to make some of his most striking statistical comparisons. In another paper, "Poverty of India"—delivered in 1873 to a parliamentary committee but not published until 1876—he compared the plight of the average Indian peasant unfavorably with that of an Indian prisoner or coolie emigrant. Once more, Naoroji's method of calculation was simple, turning the limited official statistical data on the country to his advantage. Consulting government reports, he located figures for basic provisions—food, clothing, and bedding—provided to inmates at Indian penitentiary facilities and recommended for coolies making their outward sea voyage from Calcutta. These provisions, Naoroji emphasized, were for "simple animal subsistence," allowing for "not the slightest luxury . . . or any little enjoyment of life." Yet, he declared, they were beyond the reach of the vast majority of Indians. Naoroji illustrated, province by province, how the amount expended on maintaining an inmate could, in some cases, be twice as high as the average income of a peasant. "Even for such food and clothing as a criminal obtains," Naoroji concluded, "there is hardly enough of production even in a good season, leaving alone all little luxuries, all social and religious wants, and expenses of occasions of joy and sorrow, and any provision for a bad season." This was a prophetic observation. Just a few years later, during the so-called Great Famine of Madras in 1876–1878, an American missionary recorded how starving weavers begged to be arrested so that they would at least receive some food while in jail.[18]

Statistics, however, could only go so far in convincing interested parties in Britain and India. Therefore, Naoroji increasingly relied on a third and final strategy. While speaking on Indian poverty, he began employing the testimony of British Indian officials to prove his own points.[19] This required assiduous research. Naoroji pored through books and documents in Bombay and London libraries. Two high-ranking officials, Erskine Perry and Mountstuart Elphinstone Grant-Duff, gave him free access to the India Office library in the 1860s and 1870s—something that the latter official eventually came to regret. Here, within the grand confines of the newly completed India Office building in Whitehall, where long marble corridors and Italianate arcades attested to the strength and wealth of the Raj, Naoroji must have combed through legions of reports, memoirs, parliamentary records, and other sources in search of official documentation of India's desperate poverty.

In "Poverty of India," Naoroji assembled from these sources a set of particularly damning testimonies. Some material had long been used by imperial skeptics and critics of Indian policy. But Naoroji dug deeper into the archives, uncovering, with great irony, descriptions of stark poverty in some editions of the *Moral and Material Progress Report*. Further investigation yielded offhand remarks by some of the highest-ranking officials—viceroys John Lawrence and Lord Mayo as well as Mountstuart Elphinstone Grant-Duff himself—acknowledging the destitute state of their Indian subjects. It was understandably difficult for the Indian government and India Office to contradict such statements.[20]

In spite of these occasional admissions by the ruling sahibs, Naoroji still had to contend with those "fallacious statements" in government reports and statistical abstracts that suggested India's prosperity. He now concentrated his energies on undercutting such statements by calling official statistics into question. In "Poverty of India," he detailed the extreme difficulty of formulating a cohesive economic picture of the subcontinent: most Indian provinces could not supply complete sets of statistics on agricultural prices and productivity. The few available statistics, furthermore, suffered from a fatal flaw. As he explained, provincial governments calculated average commodity prices by adding up prices in each district and then simply dividing by the number of districts. Similar methods, employing straightforward division, were used to formulate other vital statistics, such as average produce per acre. Thus, government statisticians entirely ignored important ground realities: that some districts were bigger than others, that quantities of produce might differ by locality, and that area under cultivation and land productivity were not uniform. "The result, therefore, is wrong, and all arguments and conclusions based upon such averages are worthless," Naoroji declared, adding, "These averages are not only worthless, but mischievous."[21]

Having dismissed government statistics, Naoroji came full circle in his attempts from 1871 to calculate India's gross income per capita. While government estimates for average prices and production were "fallacious," he realized that the raw data used to make these estimates could instead be utilized to bolster his claims about Indian poverty. This was a tactic that Naoroji would consistently employ for the rest of his political career: the use of official data to debunk official pronouncements. And with each subsequent estimate of total production, Naoroji took care to incorporate more and more raw data, producing increasingly sophisticated calculations that stood in vivid contrast to vague government declarations of general prosperity. Thus in "Poverty of India" he relied on facts and figures collected by officials in the intervening years— commodity prices, patterns of land cultivation, crop patterns and crop yield, and acreage under irrigation—to make detailed estimates of total production by province. Naoroji processed a simply staggering array of figures and indicators. He backed up his calculations with detailed tables enumerating produce down to bushels. In the case of Madras, he even factored in differing crop acreage based on thirty identified grades of soil. Ultimately, Naoroji declared that India's total production could be no more than £340 million—which left 40 shillings as income per head "for an average *good season*," though, given the recent cycles of drought, famine, and pestilence, the figure was much more likely to be 30 shillings per head. This, of course, was not far off from his earlier estimate of 27 shillings.[22]

In 1880, Naoroji concluded more than a decade of focused economic study by producing one final estimate of gross production, addressed to the secretary of state for India and later published as a thick pamphlet, "Condition of India." This study, based on his most detailed and extensive calculations to date, merits a closer look. It indicates how Naoroji's economic analysis developed in three distinct stages: approximations based on scanty data such as land revenue, as was undertaken in "The Wants and Means of India"; estimates based on rigorous analysis of official raw data, seen in "Poverty of India"; and, finally, Naoroji's supplementation of this raw data with his own collected statistics and observations, enabling even more nuanced estimates and pointed refutation of government figures. In "Condition of India," Naoroji limited his calculation of gross production to just one province, Punjab. He had, so far as we know, never set foot in the land of five rivers. Nevertheless, by focusing on Punjab, Naoroji could test his thesis about Indian poverty in one of the country's most productive and prosperous agricultural regions—one that had also, due to its relatively recent annexation by the British, suffered less from the drain of wealth.

"Condition of India" analyzed production in Punjab through twenty-one key agricultural commodities, fifteen types of manufactured goods, and other activities such as mining and livestock—even taking into account marginal occupations such as fishing. Evidently, Naoroji had by 1880 developed a deep familiarity with—and almost encyclopedic knowledge of—agricultural products and yield patterns in the subcontinent. Interrogating figures on Punjab's cotton production per acre, for example, he pointed out that officials had not differentiated between unclean seed cotton and the final product, thereby inflating total production. Turning to sugar, Naoroji identified flaws in average price figures listed in a government publication. "The average price, as obtained on the basis of the prices given in the Report, is, for '1st sort' or what is called Misri," he explained. "But there are different qualities of sugar, viz., Gol, Red Sugar, ordinary 2nd sort sugar, and best or 1st sort sugar." Impressive figures for sugar yield per acre in relatively arid Delhi district, furthermore, were evidently a "mistake"; how could they be higher than in comparatively more fertile Ludhiana? Aside from this intense scrutiny of existing government data, Naoroji appears to have relied on sources on the ground, who supplied additional data and observations. He alluded to at least one anonymous "Punjab farmer" who provided missing data on certain commodities and assessed figures collected by the Indian finance department. Wading through these numbers and making necessary corrections, Naoroji determined that Punjab's total annual production was £35.33 million, working out to £2 per head. This was precisely 40 shillings, Naoroji's more conservative estimate from 1871 for all of India. Thus even in "one of the best Provinces of India," Naoroji declared, poverty was stalking the land.[23]

By 1881, therefore, Dadabhai Naoroji proved that India was an exceedingly poor country. But did he succeed in getting Britons to abandon or at least modify their fantasies of Indian wealth and prosperity? Although it is impossible to assess broader attitudinal changes, it is clear that by publishing and disseminating his studies, he put Anglo-Indians on the defensive. Some of them, such as James Mackenzie Maclean, editor of the *Bombay Gazette*, challenged Naoroji's figures and the methodologies behind them. Maclean charged, for example, that Naoroji's dismal numbers in "Poverty of India" had failed to account for Bombay's booming cotton goods manufacturing sector. This was easy enough to disprove: Naoroji simply reached into his large storehouse of collected data and, using Maclean's own numbers on Bombay cotton mills, recently published in the editor's *Guide to Bombay*, proved manufactured cotton goods output to be inconsequential. In subsequent years, prominent British Indian officials—men such as Frederick Charles Danvers, a public works official at the India Office, and James Caird, a well-known agricultural expert who served on the Indian famine commission of 1878–1879—penned detailed and sophisticated responses to Naoroji's estimates, suggesting that he did not take into account various other sectors of vital economic importance to the country. These rebuttals, at least, acknowledged the existence of *some* level of poverty in India by arguing in favor of modest additions to gross production.[24]

Not all critiques, however, addressed the specifics of Naoroji's papers. Several respondents were simply unable to muster statistics and economic observations to their side of the debate. Instead, grasping at straws, they resorted to mockery, weak arguments based on race, and that most favorite Anglo-Indian tactic, charges of political disloyalty. Maclean, evidently frustrated at being outwitted, thundered in the *Bombay Gazette* that Naoroji—along with Navrozji Fardunji, who joined his former pupil in investigating Indian poverty—were promulgating "the extraordinary doctrine that the British Government of this country was an unmitigated curse." Meanwhile, in London, Hyde Clark, a railway executive and promoter of Indian railway interests, took offense at Naoroji's references to the British as foreign rulers. "It is strange, too, that these reproaches come from the Parsees," Clark stated, "who are equally foreigners in their relations to the other races, and who owe their present freedom to us." William Sowerby, a Bombay-based civil engineer and cotton merchant, complained—with irony that was probably lost on him—that statistics were "the greatest delusion of the age." He sarcastically laid out a future scenario where Naoroji would preside over the liquidation of the Raj, order all Europeans to depart India on troop ships, tear up the railways and return them to Britain, and finally invite the Americans to India to demonstrate "how to establish a republic." Sowerby concluded his fulminations with a crude appeal to Naoroji's racial instincts, arguing that if the British were to leave India's shores, "before one revolution of the moon every Parsee in Bombay would be either murdered, beggared, or wandering about the country as a homeless fugitive."[25]

Such accusations and hollow arguments only went so far. In time, Naoroji found confirmation of changing attitudes toward Indian poverty among Britons. And it came from a relatively unexpected source: Evelyn Baring, the future Lord Cromer, haughty standard-bearer of empire in Egypt. As finance member in Lord Ripon's viceregal cabinet, Baring in 1882 made the colonial government's first official estimate of India's gross production. We have no concrete evidence to prove that the finance member's undertaking was in direct response to Naoroji's outpouring of economic analysis, but this was likely the case. Baring concluded that average income per head could be no more than Rs. 27, about 54 shillings, which was not significantly higher than Naoroji's various figures. "Though I am not prepared to pledge myself to the absolute accuracy of a calculation of this sort," he noted, "it is sufficiently accurate to justify the conclusion that the tax-paying community is *exceedingly poor.*" Naoroji, understandably elated to see official acknowledgment of widespread indigence, dashed off a note to Baring and requested to see his calculations. Baring, not surprisingly, declined the request, and the government of India never published the full estimate.[26] The ruling sahibs of Calcutta, it seems, were eager to forget about the finance member's statistical exercise and pretend that it had never happened in the first place. Thus, even when British officials acknowledged the destitute state of their Indian subjects, they did so in a very grudging manner. But this acknowledgment proved to be a key victory for Naoroji: it further propelled discussion of the political corollary that he had crafted for the drain theory.

Sapping Vital Blood

In Dadabhai Naoroji's formulation, the Indian civil service—and, specifically, the lack of a significant number of Indians in this administrative corps—was the primary reason for Indian impoverishment. He posited a direct link between the preponderance of Britons ruling the country and the scale of the drain of wealth; this, in a nutshell, was the political corollary to the drain theory. For Naoroji, therefore, civil service reform was a subject of vital economic importance, a matter of life or death to millions of famine-weary Indian peasants.

Naoroji did not enunciate the political corollary until the 1870s. However, we can trace its roots back to his maiden political speech, delivered at the inauguration of the Bombay Association in August 1852. In this speech, Naoroji, then in his late twenties, suggested a link between faulty governance and poverty. The impoverishment of the Kunbis or peasants, he noted, might be the product of "bad administration." Government administrators, "being drawn from England, do not, except after a long residence and experience, become fully acquainted with our wants and customs." Consequently, these British officers were "often led, by their imperfect acquaintance with the country, to adopt measures calculated to do more harm than good." The solution, therefore, was to recruit knowledgeable Indians for government service. In 1859, four years after relocating to Great Britain, Naoroji took up the case of the very first Indian candidate for the civil service, Rustomji Hirjibhai Wadia, who was unceremoniously barred from taking the service's entrance examination by the India Office's last-minute reduction of the age limit.[27]

Although in Wadia's case his pleas to authorities fell on deaf ears, Naoroji persisted in speaking and writing about the need for more Indian administrative officers. Like many other political reformers in Calcutta, Bombay, Madras, and elsewhere, he concentrated his energies on protesting against the formidable difficulties faced by Indian candidates: a low age limit; the fact that exams were only held in England, necessitating a long and costly voyage from the subcontinent; and the content of the exams, which privileged knowledge of European classics and literature over subjects such as Arabic and Sanskrit, where Indian candidates would have a significant advantage. Indian agitation led to some official concessions. In 1865, the India Office reversed its decision to further deemphasize Arabic and Sanskrit in exams after Naoroji submitted a petition on the topic, questioning the government's commitment to fairness for aspiring Indian officers. Naoroji increasingly framed the civil service issue as one of Indian rights, dropping his earlier arguments about the problematic consequences of an Indian administration dominated by Britons unfamiliar with Indian culture and opinion.[28]

Naoroji's 1867 address before the East India Association, "England's Duties to India," represented another important transformation in his views about how the civil service caused poverty. It was at this moment that Naoroji suggested, for the first time, that India's impoverishment was the result of a pronounced economic drain. While he did not use the term "drain" specifically—he spoke of financial tribute and "home charges"—Naoroji asserted that British rule had resulted, to date, in the transfer of a whopping £1.6 billion from the subcontinent to imperial coffers. Relying on parliamentary returns, he calculated that Great Britain continued to siphon, conservatively, £33 million each year from its Indian possessions, or roughly one-fourth of tax revenues collected in India.[29]

The drain and its devastating impact upon India constituted the first half of his paper. In the second half, Naoroji dwelled on the political injustice that Indians faced under British rule, with the civil service as the main grievance. "Either the educated natives should have proper fields for their talents and education opened to them in various departments of the administration of the country," he warned, "or the rulers must make up their minds, and candidly avow it, to rule the country with a rod of iron." The best way to secure Indian officers was with simultaneous examinations; in other words, ensuring that the exams of "a portion, however small at first," of candidates take place in India as well as Britain. Thus Naoroji continued to think of civil service reform mostly in terms of the rights of Indians. But he made one critical observation: that a European-dominated civil service was a major source of the drain, since these Britons regularly sent portions of their salaries home and also drew pensions after they retired to the British Isles. Examining government revenues, Naoroji tallied the salaries of British bureaucrats, administrators, and soldiers, concluding that India annually lost about £4.36 million through remitted salaries. This was, of course, far short of his calculations for the total annual drain, and Naoroji therefore had to account for additional sources. He suggested a profoundly unfavorable trade imbalance. In a later paper, delivered after the Abyssinian War, where Great Britain borrowed Indian troops and then served Indian taxpayers with a bill for expenses, Naoroji placed blame upon the great costs of maintaining a large military. By 1871, he was focusing on land tenure, arguing that unduly high rates of assessment were imperiling both zamindars (landlords) and ryots (peasants).[30]

During the late 1860s and early 1870s, Naoroji's proposed solutions to the drain were relatively limited in scope. Somewhat incredibly, he believed that part of the drain was justified. In exchange for the supposed political, moral, and social benefits of British rule, it was "inevitable" that India had to sacrifice some of its wealth. "If India is to be regenerated by England, India must make up its mind to pay the price," Naoroji reasoned. The critical problem was that the drain, while impoverishing ordinary Indians, also sapped India of capital that could otherwise support indigenous commerce and industry and, consequently, lighten the effects of this financial tribute. If India were economically more robust, it would be easier for the country to bear the burden of what he termed the "legitimate portion of the drain."[31]

In order to further clarify this relationship between the drain, capital, and Indian poverty, Naoroji turned to John Stuart Mill's *Principles of Political Economy*. "Land and labour are both useless unless we have sufficient capital," he stated. "Mr. Mill distinctly proves that industry is limited by capital, that law and government cannot create industry without creating capital. Capital, then, is the great and imperative want of India,

as much for the existence of the foreign rule as of the people themselves."
Since the drain robbed India of its own capital, Naoroji suggested that Great
Britain finance, through long-term loans, major public works projects in
the country to stimulate growth. "If sufficient foreign capital is brought
into the country," he declared, "all the present difficulties and discontent
will vanish in time." Naoroji put particular faith in the transformative effects of railways, irrigation projects, and similar "*large* public works."[32]

While speaking on the drain and championing a solution through
public works, Dadabhai Naoroji did not lose sight of civil service reform.
In addition to vigorously challenging British allegations that Indians were
not mentally fit, capable, or trustworthy enough to hold high administrative positions, he sketched out plans for steady Indianization of the services. These plans became more ambitious with time. In 1868, he held
out hope that the British majority in the services could be reduced to two-
thirds or three-fourths, while allowing that "certain places of high executive power should remain in their hands only." Naoroji categorically
dismissed any moves toward self-government and the eventual transfer
of all administrative posts to Indians. "In my belief," he asserted, "a greater
calamity could not befall India than for England to go away and leave her
to herself."[33]

But his evolving demands for Indianization of the civil service betrayed
a different sentiment. In 1871, while addressing a select parliamentary
committee in London, he discarded his earlier stance that "high executive power" should be the sole province of the British. Instead, Naoroji
now called for the appointment of Indians to legislative councils, the India
Office, and "all grades" of the government. It was a simple question of government efficiency: how, Naoroji asked, was it possible for British officials, who rotated in and out of the country, to properly administer an
entire subcontinent? This system, furthermore, denied Indians any opportunities to gain experience in governance and administration. Here
we see the germ of what Naoroji later termed the "moral drain": the loss
of administrative experience whenever a British official retired and left
India, further condemning India to misgovernance. Indianizing the civil
services could, therefore, remedy a drain that had both moral and financial components. Importantly, for Naoroji, civil service reform was no
longer just a question of Indian rights.[34]

During these early speaking engagements, the former professor also began to reflect—on a somewhat abstract level—on India's particular predicament of being colonized by a European power. Like his nationalist contemporary and fellow Elphinstonian, Mahadev Govind Ranade, Naoroji stressed the inability of classical economic theories to explain the financial predicament of colonial India. Whenever Britons acknowledged severe poverty in India, he noted, they "talk of the pitiless operations of economic laws, but somehow they forgot that there is no such thing in India as the natural operation of economic laws" due to the drain of wealth. But British rule, in Naoroji's analysis, did much more than just turn accepted economic wisdom on its head: it created a distinct historical disjuncture. The administration of both Company and crown had a strange, decisively foreign quality that deviated from patterns of previous imperial conquest and rule in the subcontinent, a trait that was undermining India's national cohesiveness. Naoroji was not immune to orientalist notions of Indian history: he agreed that previous empires, such as the Mughals, had subjected India to "the usual Oriental despotism," resulting in "utter stagnation and gradual retrogression." Nevertheless, he observed that "when all other foreign invaders retained possession of the country, and became its rulers, they at least became *of* the country." They did not remain foreign and aloof, and, consequently, their administration was not economically extractive. "If they plundered the rich and screwed the ryot, the wealth was still *in* the country," Naoroji noted. "If individuals were plundered or oppressed, the country remained as rich as ever. But entirely different has been the case with the foreign rule of the British." By electing to remain a distinctly foreign power, the British were sapping the country's "vital blood"—not simply its material wealth—and endangering its very "vitality and vigour."[35] This was a serious indictment of British colonialism that could not be expressed in purely economic or political terms.

"Poverty of India," as we have seen, constituted an important turning point in Dadabhai Naoroji's efforts to highlight the impoverishment of the subcontinent. Delivering this paper in 1873 before the Select Parliamentary Committee on East India Finance, Naoroji painted a grim picture of India's economic condition by arguing that the average Indian fared far worse than a prisoner or emigrant coolie. In terms of the evolution of Naoroji's thoughts about the drain, "Poverty of India" was also a landmark document. It is quite likely that Naoroji was radicalized by a tour in south Gujarat, Kathiawar, and Kutch that he undertook during the 1871 monsoon "with a view to acquaint himself personally with the condition of the agricultural classes of those provinces." There is some evidence that, along with Navrozji Fardunji, he undertook a follow-up survey in Gujarat in early 1873. Regardless, once he returned to London, Naoroji came before the Select Committee with far sharper views on poverty and the drain, shorn of many of his earlier beliefs regarding possible solutions. The committee chairman, Acton Smee Ayrton—and, most likely, Mountstuart Elphinstone Grant-Duff, undersecretary of state for India—balked at the contents of his submitted statement and refused to publish it in the committee's final report. It was not until 1876 that Naoroji delivered this statement, in two parts, before the Bombay Branch of the East India Association and published it as a pamphlet.[36]

While he had been sharply condemnatory of British Indian administration in the past, it was only in "Poverty of India" that Naoroji began directly referring to colonial policy as "evil." Turning to the drain, he identified as causes exclusively "two elements": salaries and pensions paid to British officials and remittances made by Anglo-Indian civilians. He made no mention of other factors such as military expenses. Gone, furthermore, was any discussion of the supposedly "legitimate" portion of the drain that India was obligated to pay. Naoroji had also now abandoned his faith in public works projects, especially railroads: the necessary British capital injected into India, Naoroji realized, would most likely land up in the pockets of Britons and British interests. This foreign capital, paradoxically, would further feed the drain of wealth. Providing an innovative spin on Mill's *Principles of Political Economy*, Naoroji concluded that the drain produced an ever-worsening spiral of impoverishment. "The candle burns at both ends," he noted, "capital going on diminishing on the one hand, and labour thereby becoming less capable on the other, to reproduce as much as before." Thus, the burden of the drain became heavier and more lethal with each passing year.[37]

In order to highlight the unique nature of India's predicament, Naoroji began drawing international comparisons. He was particularly intrigued by the experience of the United States. By the mid-1870s, Naoroji began poring through US government reports and statistical data, and he also initiated correspondence with officers and directors in the US Army Corps of Engineers and the Departments of Agriculture, Treasury, and the Interior. Naoroji turned to the flurry of railway construction in America to illustrate how India would not benefit from a similar construction program. In the creation and operation of the American railway network, he observed, "every man is an American; every farthing taken out of the produce of the country for its conveyance remains in the country." Americans reaped the wealth derived from increased production, while the interest on loans cycled back into the national economy. This was not the case in India. British railway loans, he noted, largely went to the Britons building and operating the Indian network. Interest on these loans, similarly, went "out of the country" and back into British coffers. To drive home this point about an externally produced drain, Naoroji scoured works of history, particularly the writings of the American scholar John William Draper, to sketch out another international comparison—with pre-Reformation England. As a tributary to the Pope, he argued, England withered from an "Italian drain," weighed down by an alien clergy and heavy remittances to Rome. The system also exacted a heavy toll in terms of England's political and intellectual advancement. "India cannot but share the same fate under similar causes," warned Naoroji.[38]

As he suggested in his comparison with England and the Catholic church, Naoroji held that the drain could not simply be measured in terms of sterling. The drain of wealth, rather, was a "triple evil." British policy caused the "loss of wealth, wisdom, and work to India," constituting a peculiarly noxious combination of financial and "moral" outflow. Here Naoroji fully elucidated the concept of a "moral drain," explaining how the preponderance of British civil servants both robbed Indians of employment and crippled Indians' abilities to develop administrative and political experience. "All experience and knowledge of statesmanship, of administration or legislation, of high scientific or learned professions, are drained away to England, when the persons possessing them give up their service and retire to England," he declared. This situation further highlighted the strange, unnatural nature of European colonial rule: skilled Indians were denied an outlet for their talents in their own country. "All the talent and nobility of intellect and soul, which nature gives to every country, is to India a lost treasure."[39]

Naoroji now presented a trump card of sorts. In the years and decades after 1857, Anglo-Indians and British officials remained terrified about the possibility of another mutiny. Naoroji clearly understood these anxieties, harnessing them as early as 1867 in order to warn about Indian disillusion with colonial policy: "No prophet is required to foretell the ultimate result of a struggle between a discontented two hundred millions, and a hundred thousand foreign bayonets." He now channeled colonial anxieties in a different direction. Educated Indians, he argued, remained a bastion of loyalty to the crown—but their faith was being steadily eroded by exclusion from the civil service and observation of the drain of wealth. "It will be a *very, very* short step from loyalty to disloyalty," he cautioned. For added effect, Naoroji brought up the Russian bogey, skillfully playing on another source of colonial paranoia. In case the Cossacks began streaming over the Khyber Pass, he asked, how could British suzerainty be ensured when the masses were impoverished and the educated were disillusioned?[40]

Hence, by pursuing its current policies, the British Raj was sowing the seeds of its own destruction. How, then, was it possible to remedy the multiple evils resulting from the drain? Naoroji responded to this question by setting out the first plank of his political corollary. He had already singled out "the excessive employment of Europeans" as the cause of so much economic and political turmoil. The solution, therefore, was to thoroughly and comprehensively Indianize the civil service. It was too late for piecemeal reform. With a preponderance of Indians in the bureaucracy, "the economical result to India will be pure gain." Thus, in one stroke, Naoroji used the drain to formulate a powerful argument in favor of civil service reform. Indianization was not simply a matter of Indian rights; it was the answer to the country's dire financial and economic straits. Within a few years, Naoroji began referring to the issue as a "question of life and death to India." Maintaining the status quo meant risking certain economic disaster and, eventually, rebellion. On the other hand, by putting Indians in charge of their own government, authorities in

London and Calcutta would be "increasing [India's] capital and prosperity," ensuring that India "may be strengthened and confirmed in its loyalty and gratitude to the British nation."[41] How could policymakers not fail to make the correct choice?

There was a second and obvious plank to the political corollary of the drain theory: that the drain decreased in proportion to the reduction of British officers ruling India. Through the remainder of the 1870s and the 1880s, Naoroji continued to clamor for simultaneous examinations in Britain and India, something that would quickly increase the proportion of Indians in the government. However, at the same time, he began taking this second plank to its logical conclusion. There was a fine line between championing a government where Indians were proportionately in the majority and a one where, with the exception of a handful of spots at the very top reserved for Britons, Indians occupied *all* posts. Naoroji crossed this line in 1884, less than ten years after presenting "Poverty of India" to Bombay audiences. That year, as Lord Ripon wound down his relatively liberal viceroyalty, Naoroji penned a memo on the Indian civil service that was submitted "for the consideration of the late and present Viceroys, and some other high Officials."[42]

In this document, Naoroji drew upon Ripon's most forward-looking proposal—"local self-government" at the provincial level—in order to sketch out a far more ambitious scheme. He envisioned a day when simultaneous examinations would give way to examinations held exclusively in India, with only select positions such as the viceroy and governorships "mainly reserved" for Britons. In order to clarify the power dynamics of such a political structure, Naoroji made quite a bold declaration: "*Never* can a foreign rule be anything but a curse to any country, except so far as it approaches a native rule." A few months later, at a speech in Bombay to mark Ripon's retirement, Naoroji invoked, for the first time in public, the goal of self-government for India. Linking together the ideas of the drain and political autonomy, he stressed that the "greatest questions" facing the country were "our material and moral loss, and our political education for self-government." He nevertheless looked forward to a day when India would be "a self-governing and prosperous nation"—albeit one that was still "loyal to the British throne."[43]

Naoroji chose his words carefully, couching them in declarations of loyalty and gratitude, but there was no mistake about the significance of his message. Thus, in the middle of the 1880s, at the high noon of British imperialism, we can witness the birth of the idea of swaraj within mainstream Indian nationalist politics.

A Splendid Prospect for the Future

At precisely the same time that Dadabhai Naoroji deployed the drain theory to argue for political reform in the direction of self-government, he was immersed in the affairs of several Indian princely states. This was not a coincidence. Naoroji's involvement with these states—ranging from lobbying efforts in London to serving as diwan in Baroda in 1873–1874—was, in many ways, the practical application of the political corollary to the drain theory. Princely states were an arena where Naoroji attempted to put into practice many of the ideas he expounded within lecture halls in London and Bombay between the 1860s and 1880s. This is an aspect of Indian political reform and early nationalism that has been almost completely unnoticed.

In both works of history and popular imagination, India's various maharajas and nizams (as well as the occasional rani or begum) have often been characterized as mere stooges of the British, and their states depicted as petty fiefdoms distinguished by autocratic governance and social and political retrogression of the worst sort. But princely India was never a uniform entity. Rather, it was a patchwork of more than six hundred states with varying degrees of political autonomy and administrative sophistication. Political reformers in Bombay quickly recognized this diversity: after all, roughly half of all Indian princely states, around 361 in number, were located in their immediate vicinity, constituting one-third of the territory of the Bombay Presidency exclusive of Sindh. And within this assemblage, Naoroji and his colleagues sought out what were known as "progressive" states, larger realms with rulers keen on administrative modernization. Here, by the early 1870s, Naoroji hoped to test both the drain theory and his ideas for political reform.[44]

Unlike the drain theory, where we can at least rely on a steady stream of published talks and papers from the late 1860s onward, it is extremely difficult to reconstruct the evolution of Naoroji's thought with regard to princely states. With the exception of one East India Association paper, some India Office records, and fragments of his Gujarati and English correspondence, hardly any relevant material survives prior to Naoroji's arrival in Baroda in late 1873. But some of Naoroji's earliest associations offer clues about influences on his thought in the 1850s and 1860s. A few of his elder classmates in Elphinstone College—the same group of students who formed a "secret society" to discuss the steady impoverishment of India under British rule—spoke vigorously in defense of princely states' autonomy. For example, Bhaskar Pandurang, the brother of Naoroji's classmate Atmaram Pandurang, loudly condemned the annexation of Satara, a Maratha principality south of Poona, in 1848. Additionally, as the editor of *Rast Goftar*, Naoroji was most likely aware of the Bombay press's strident support of Indian rulers. The *Bombay Samachar*, a Parsi-owned broadsheet, excoriated the governor-general, Lord Dalhousie, for aggressively annexing states in the final years of Company rule, labeling him as "that notorious pindaree and plunderer of the Rajas."[45]

The British policy of annexation simultaneously caused deep discomfort among a small group of Britons and Anglo-Indians—known as the Friends of India—that Naoroji joined by the early 1860s. One of these Britons was John Dickinson, a furious critic of British Indian policy who in 1853 founded the India Reform Society in London. Dickinson and his society took a particularly favorable view of Indian rulers. A society pamphlet from 1853, titled "The State and Government under Its Native Rulers," contrasted the prosperity and stability of India under Akbar, Shivaji, and Hyder Ali with the economic ruin and political chaos that the British brought upon Bengal after Plassey. It thundered against contemporary British policy toward Satara and Awadh, eventually annexed in 1856. Many decades later, Naoroji wrote an introduction and concluding note to the pamphlet, republished by the British socialist Henry Hyndman. "What a splendid prospect is in store for the future," he observed, if British policy allowed full freedom to princes to develop their "own Native Services."[46]

While we have limited information on Naoroji's precise relations with Dickinson, there is little doubt that this friend of India was an important mentor. But we know much more about another associate, Evans Bell, a major in the Madras Staff Corps stationed in Nagpur through the 1850s. Bell was a particularly zealous defender of princely states and their rulers: after Nagpur was annexed in 1853, he fought tirelessly for proper reparations for the deposed Bhosle family, a task that led to his being charged with insubordination shortly after the Mutiny. Back in London, and probably already acquainted with Naoroji, Bell turned to writing, producing a prodigious amount of literature decrying the policy of annexation. The further extinction of states, he reasoned, increased Indian discontent, diminished chances of fostering enlightened Indian polities, and harmed imperial security. Annexation, he concluded, was "exceptionally unjust, injurious, imprudent, and unprofitable." Consequently, he wielded his pen against attempts in the 1860s to dispossess the Wodeyar house of Mysore state (already under direct British rule for some thirty years), as well as similar moves against the nizam of Murshidabad and the raja of Dhar. Along with Dickinson, Bell became one of the earliest members of Naoroji's East India Association, ensuring that the affairs of princely states remained a prominent topic of discussion in London's political circles.[47]

Through the influence of John Dickinson and Evans Bell, Naoroji in the late 1860s focused his energies on imminent threats to various princely domains. In 1867, he joined the chorus of protest against British policy toward Mysore. While acknowledging a degree of misgovernance by the Wodeyars before direct British rule, Naoroji pinned greater blame on British Indian administrators. "The picture of an Englishman holding off the savage ruler from his victim is no doubt a very pretty and gratifying one," he told an audience of the East India Association, "but unfortunately there is a little want of truth in it, and a little daub in it." At the same time, he charged, direct British rule and the threat of dispossession constituted gross violations of treaty terms between Calcutta and Mysore. Were the viceroy and secretary of state in danger of "sink[ing] down to the level of the despotic Hindu rulers" they so roundly disparaged? Naoroji also cited Mysore as a dangerous example of British imperial overreach, comparing dispossession and possible annexation with London's simultaneous enlargement of the empire outside of the subcontinent:

> To destroy the native rule in Mysore it is pressed that as Englishmen have settled there, it ought to be taken into English possession.

This I suppose is an invention of the nineteenth century. What a fine prospect this opens up of conquering the whole world without much trouble. Some Englishmen have only to go and settle in a country, and then the English government has simply to say, "You see English people cannot be managed by you, therefore you should give up the country to us"; and there is a conquest! But, unfortunately for the inventor, those stupid fellows the French and other continentals, the Americans and such others, won't see it.[48]

Mysore was not the only state that concerned Naoroji. In the northern reaches of the Bombay Presidency was Kutch, where Kazi Shahabudin, one of Naoroji's early political associates, was serving as diwan to the ruling *maharao*, Pragmalji II. Working with Kazi, Naoroji helped defuse a tense standoff between Calcutta and Bhuj: when, in 1868, the Indian government proposed investing local *bhayads* or zamindars with greater administrative authority vis-à-vis the maharao, Pragmalji threatened to resign and hand over authority of Kutch to the British. Naoroji counseled British Indian authorities to rethink their proposal, arguing that diminishing the maharao's powers would set a terrible precedent for relations with other princely states. "The policy of weakening the power of any Native Ruler, except for the introduction of constitutional checks is a retrograde movement," he cautioned. Instead, Naoroji urged British officials to preserve the authority and ruling power of princes, allowing for the centralization of resources and the development of an "efficient administration" in the domains over which they presided.[49]

Thus, Naoroji followed the lead of Dickinson and Bell by directly entering the fray between troubled princes and the British Indian state. Between 1868 and 1873, however, he began to build on his mentors' ideas about the political and economic significance of princely India, factoring these states into discussion of the civil service and Indian poverty. The darbars and bureaucracies of princely states, Naoroji realized, were excellent proving grounds for the administrative capabilities of Indians. There was, by and large, no British-dominated civil service with which to contend, no white sahibs to stymie Indian talent. In an 1868 memo titled "Admission of Educated Natives into the Indian Civil Service," Naoroji reminded Stafford Northcote, the secretary of state, that several highly regarded Indian ministers had emerged from princely darbars: Salar Jung in Hyderabad, Dinkar Rao in Gwalior, and T. Madhava Rao in Travancore. As he laid out his drain theory before British and Indian audiences, Naoroji suggested that the princely states, as semi-autonomous units, possessed a degree of immunity to this hemorrhaging of finances and resources. Aside from a relatively small tribute—which, Naoroji calculated, was a comparatively trifling sum of £720,000 per year for all states combined—they did not have to bear the burden of paying salaries to British officers. Nor did they have to contend with a moral drain. Furthermore, Indian merchants, rather than British ones, largely controlled the economies of these domains, ensuring that profits from trade did not get siphoned off to London.[50]

Consequently, Naoroji revived an old debate that had been contested by reformers and civil servants alike: whether princely India was more prosperous than British India. He came out strongly in favor of the former. Naoroji's views on the subject most likely crystallized in the early 1870s in tandem with the political corollary. He observed that native states, especially the cotton-producing ones in Gujarat and opium-producing entities in Rajputana, constituted some of the most important economic engines of the subcontinent. As a result, merchants and capital from princely states played a significant role in the commercial activities of British India, and especially in Bombay. Convinced of the wealth of princely states, Naoroji sought to leverage these financial resources for Indian political reform. During his extended tours through the Indian countryside between 1871 and 1873, which had such a transformative role on his views on Indian poverty, Naoroji succeeded in securing vast subscriptions in princely domains for the East India Association. Pragmalji of Kutch, no doubt grateful to Naoroji for his role in resolving the bhayad controversy, transferred Rs. 50,000 into the association's coffers, while smaller yet still substantial donations came from Maharaja Holkar of Indore, the maharaja of Patiala, the nawab of Junagadh, the jam sahib of Jamnagar (Nawanagar), and the rulers of several smaller states in Kathiawar. As noted by a young Mahadev Govind Ranade, then managing the affairs of the East India Association's branch in Bombay, three Gujarati princes distinguished themselves as the organization's most munificent patrons. Wealthy subjects in these states furnished additional subscriptions.[51]

And then there was Baroda. Sometime in 1872, Naoroji approached Malharrao, the newly installed ruling *gaikwad* of the state, for financial assistance for the East India Association. The gaikwad expressed little interest in donating, but some months later he hurriedly summoned Naoroji, then in Indore, to his darbar and brought up an entirely different topic of concern. Malharrao was currently embroiled in a tense standoff with Bombay authorities over seating arrangements. The gaikwads had long enjoyed the privilege of seating visiting British dignitaries, such as the governor of Bombay, to their left in darbars and other ceremonies. William Vesey-Fitzgerald, the current governor, now insisted on sitting to the gaikwad's right, infuriating Malharrao and triggering a flurry of heated correspondence between London, Bombay, and Baroda. The gaikwad turned to Naoroji for assistance in resolving this diplomatic row. Drawing upon his experience of defending the authority of the maharao of Kutch, Naoroji dispatched a carefully worded *yad* (memorial) to the India Office, urging the secretary of state not to rob Baroda of prestige, which would cause the state "to be degraded in the eyes of all India at your Lordship's hands." Naoroji's interference appeared to soften the resolve of Bombay authorities, and a grateful Malharrao summarily pledged a reward of Rs. 50,000 in the form of a trust for the children of his Parsi advisor.[52]

This gift set in train two distinct series of events. In London, Naoroji became firmly—and suspiciously—identified with the interests of princely states. British officials accused him of being a paid agent of the gaikwad and other rulers, while in the House of Commons Naoroji was buttonholed by a member who warned, "If you are going to give any evidence about Native Princes, I should look out for you." Naoroji was finally compelled to make a public statement in August 1873 before the East India Association, justifying his acceptance of the monetary reward and denying that he was a secret operative for any darbar.[53] Meanwhile, in Baroda, as officials in the *khazana* (treasury) drew up the trust deed, Malharrao dangled another offer in front of Naoroji. He invited him to be diwan of the state.

Malharrao had, apparently, long been interested in employing Naoroji to modernize the state's bureaucracy and establish better relations with the government of India. And in spite of warnings from two Anglo-Indian officials on friendly terms with Naoroji, Bartle Frere and Erskine Perry, about significant political problems within the gaikwad's realm, the Parsi leader leapt at the opportunity to try his hand at actual administration. By early November 1873, he had departed London and was in Italy, moving south toward Brindisi in order to catch a Bombay-bound steamer. Both before and after arriving in Baroda, Naoroji worked fast to assemble a cabinet of skilled ministers and bureaucrats. Here he relied heavily upon his links to Young Bombay and the subsequent generations of educated Indians produced by Elphinstone College and other western Indian institutions of learning. In order to prove the administrative capabilities of Indians, Naoroji looked to some of the brightest minds in the Bombay Presidency. Ministerial candidates included Nana Moroji, Naoroji's classmate at Elphinstone who had subsequently distinguished himself as a Marathi educator and a presidency magistrate; Vishwanath Narayan Mandlik, another Elphinstone contemporary who dabbled in journalism (he edited *Native Opinion*) and government service before becoming a highly successful lawyer at the Bombay High Court; and Mahadev Govind Ranade, then just beginning his judicial career.[54]

None of these three individuals, unfortunately, was willing or able to leave his career for the uncertainty of the Baroda darbar. But Naoroji's eventual cabinet included other equally prominent names. Kazi Shahabudin, having resigned as the diwan of Kutch, took control of the gaikwad's revenue department. Bal Mangesh Wagle, one of Naoroji's students at Elphinstone—and, along with Ranade, among the first graduates of Bombay University—left his position as an advocate before the Bombay High Court to become chief justice. As chief magistrate, Naoroji chose a fellow Parsi, Hormusjee Ardeseer Wadya, a Kathiawar barrister who probably first met the new Baroda diwan while studying at University College in London. Naoroji clarified to his ministers that they were not simply working for Malharrao, but rather had as their goal the welfare and advancement of princely India. "We have not come to serve the man; we have come to serve the cause," he advised Wadya.[55]

From the limited surviving evidence about the actual diwanship, it appears that Naoroji and his colleagues concentrated their efforts on reducing the financial burdens and obligations placed upon some of

Baroda's poorest subjects. Economic considerations, as well as the promotion of administrative efficiency, motivated their policies. First, they overhauled the judicial system, making it more transparent, accountable, and accessible. "The chief foundation of the State," Naoroji declared in a note to Malharrao, "must be laid upon justice and fairness." Wagle, the chief justice, began eradicating practices such as *nazarana*—the pledging of gifts to the gaikwad—which had degenerated into a method of buying justice in courts. He also forbade judges from privately interviewing witnesses and instead ordered all cases to be conducted in public. Wadya, meanwhile, prosecuted local officials accused of corruption and the general mistreatment of peasants. This move, Naoroji alleged, "was simply astonishing to the people, to see Vahivatdars and Fozdars and other officials (supposed to possess influence at high quarters) accused of corruption or oppression, tried in open Court or thoroughly cross-examined as witnesses, and made to feel the weight of law and justice when found guilty." Furthermore, Naoroji, Wagle, and Wadya began preparing new criminal, civil, and penal codes modeled on English ones.

The ministry's second target of reform was the revenue system. Kazi Shahabudin conducted a detailed survey of revenue collection and subsequently ordered the remission of one-fourth of land assessments, specially requiring all local revenue officers "to notify and explain to the cultivators the object of this Proclamation." In his survey, Kazi had admitted that land assessments were in many cases too high—rates had not been reduced since the time of the American Civil War, when the demand for Baroda cotton burgeoned—and proposed a reduced settlement until the time when "the available statistics might be expected to be efficiently reliable to form the basis of a more scientific measure."[56]

Taking account of all of these achievements, Naoroji, after he resigned as diwan, defended his ministry in a statement he dispatched to the British Parliament. By sweeping aside the founts of corruption and laying the foundations of a modern, accountable administration, he and his colleagues had displayed to the people of Baroda "the difference between pure and impure justice in general administration, and between honesty of purpose and shams and intrigues." "The mark we have left and the confidence we have inspired among all classes of the people, (except the harpies, the intriguers and their dupes)," he concluded, "will take a long time to be forgotten."[57]

Of course, the mere fact that the ex-diwan felt a need to defend his ministry before MPs—let alone make reference to "the harpies, the intriguers and their dupes"—indicates that something also went terribly wrong in Baroda. Dadabhai Naoroji, unfortunately, could not have picked a worse time to come to the state. In 1873, Baroda was being torn asunder by two of the worst systemic features of Indian princely states: the concentration of power within the ruling family and the presence of a British resident who could freely interfere in the affairs of the darbar. When Naoroji arrived in Baroda, he was immediately drawn into a bitter war between ruler and resident—which was part of a larger, messy struggle between the Bombay government and the government of India. Malharrao's rule had been, admittedly, disastrous: during his three short years on the *gadi* (throne), the gaikwad had alienated the peasantry through high taxation and tolerance of corruption, lost the trust of many sirdars and other elites, and surrounded himself with a coterie of venal yet sycophantic ministers and advisors—many of whom were close relations. The gaikwad, furthermore, did not seem to be a very pleasant man. He was remembered, some five decades after his death, as "undersized, of uninviting presence and coarse complexion, with eyes looking in different ways and lips kept asunder by projecting black teeth." Even a modern historian of princely India admits that Malharrao's "propensities to violence and sadism were well-known." Not surprisingly, the British resident at Baroda, Robert Phayre, successfully convened a special government commission to examine misrule and corruption in the state.[58]

But Phayre was no model official, either. A self-righteous, fault-finding figure with a touch of messianic Christianity, Phayre had a tendency to exceed his brief. He had also established a track record, of sorts, of grievously offending Indian princes. For example, in August 1870, the panicked commissioner of Sindh informed the governor of Bombay that Phayre, then a political superintendent in the frontier region, had hurled unsubstantiated accusations against the khan of Kalat, subsequently opening lines of communication with rebel sirdars in exile in Afghanistan.

Bombay officials removed Phayre from his post and later, in a decision that betrayed either severe incompetence or a sharp sense of irony, assigned him to the Baroda residency. Here Phayre trained his sights on Naoroji, whom he accused of being "a traitor" to the British Empire. Before even boarding his Bombay-bound steamer at Brindisi, the future diwan received a telegram that the resident had prohibited his entry into Baroda. Phayre had taken a dim view of Naoroji's advocacy of princely states. "It is impossible not to be deeply impressed with a sense of the mischief which political adventurers like this Dadabhoy Nowrojee are doing amongst the native princes & chiefs of India," he wrote to the Bombay government in April 1873. While he eventually allowed Naoroji to enter the city, Phayre remained deeply suspicious of him and his new ministers: in a report from May 1874, he labeled them as "artful intriguers from England" bent on placing the gaikwad "in direct antagonism to the British Government." Naoroji and Kazi Shahabudin were particularly suspect since both were "prominent members of the East India Association in London." Consequently, Phayre took the incredible step of not recognizing Naoroji's appointment, crippling the diwan's abilities to govern and communicate with administrators in Bombay and Calcutta. The resident apparently warned Malharrao that Naoroji's diwanship meant "war not peace, and that it would bring about His Highness' ruin in three months."[59]

Malharrao did not make his diwan's tasks any easier: he never fully put his authority behind Naoroji's program of reform. Family members, friends, and other *darbaris* exercised enough influence over Malharrao to stonewall major administrative changes. Even the Bombay government realized this: early in 1874, one of its sharper officials correctly predicted that "the Gaekwar and his agents would be enabled to shelter themselves behind Mr. Dadabhai's reputation, and he would be powerless for any reform of abuses." Malharrao was unwilling to purge the darbar of previous officials and ministers, creating the absurd situation of Baroda possessing, in Phayre's words, a "duplicate Cabinet," with each of Naoroji's selected ministers having a counterpart from the old regime. Naoroji was not spared: the gaikwad created a new position, that of the *pratinidhi*, in order to retain his old diwan, Shivajirao Khanvelkar, who was also his brother-in-law.[60]

The resident, for his part, exploited the situation to the hilt. In reports dispatched to Bombay, he condemned Naoroji for being unable to rid the court of corrupt older officials. He then embraced the same officials as allies against the diwan. Between a weak gaikwad, a spiteful resident, and resentful darbaris—Phayre claimed that "the whole of the old Karbharees rose up in arms at the idea of a Foreigner becoming Dewan in a Mahratta State, that foreigner too being a Parsee commercial Agent unaccustomed to executive administration of any kind"—Naoroji had little room for maneuver. His only bargaining chip was the threat of resignation, something that would put Malharrao further at the mercy of the resident. Time after time, Naoroji and his ministers tendered their resignations in order to maintain or achieve particular reforms: for example, in July 1874, when Malharrao tried to undo judicial reforms, and in early August, when the ruler vacillated on abolishing nazarana and dismissing the duplicate cabinet. In each case, the gaikwad was the first to blink.[61]

But in late December 1874, when Naoroji ordered Malharrao to replenish the exhausted public exchequer through the privy purse, the ruler had had enough—the tide of reform was now sweeping away some of the gaikwad's most cherished royal prerogatives—and he let his diwan follow through on his threat to resign. Naoroji and his colleagues departed Baroda via train on January 11, 1875, leaving half-completed their attempts to radically reform the state. It was, in hindsight, an eminently fortuitous decision. Affairs in Baroda were rapidly taking on a markedly bizarre—and murky—quality. Two months earlier, on November 9, 1874, Phayre had taken two or three sips of his daily morning glass of pomelo juice, sensed a "most unpleasant metallic taste in the mouth," and quickly spat out the contents before being overtaken by dizziness and "confusion of thought." The resident hurriedly telegraphed Bombay: "Bold attempt to poison me." Chemical tests performed at the Grant Medical College in Bombay revealed the juice to contain traces of arsenic and powdered glass or quartz. After Phayre began sending out a stream of correspondence loudly accusing Malharrao of being behind the plot, Calcutta officials intervened and, perhaps with Phayre's conduct in faraway Kalat in mind, finally decided to remove the resident from his post. Naoroji enjoyed excellent relations with the new resident, Lewis Pelly, and both men cooperated closely in investigating the poison attempt. In the final days of

Naoroji's diwanship, they started to stumble upon evidence that Phayre's accusations against Malharrao might not have been so baseless after all. On January 14, a proclamation was published at Fort William in Calcutta stating that the government of India had temporarily taken control of affairs at Baroda. British troops swooped down into the city and arrested Malharrao. The deposed gaikwad was eventually convicted of attempting to poison Phayre and sent into exile in Madras. A parliamentary inquiry in Westminster finally closed this sordid chapter in the history of Baroda.[62]

Thus Naoroji—a staunch advocate of princely interests, a vocal opponent of British intervention in princely states, and a strong proponent of experimenting with political reform in these domains—discovered that some "progressive" states were not so enlightened after all. He experienced firsthand the sheer difficulty of achieving significant reform against the will of ruler and resident, and witnessed the extraordinary deposition of a ruling gaikwad by the British. There was little scope for testing the drain theory, or applying its political corollary, when Baroda was riven by internal dissent and ruled over by a man suspected of attempted murder.

While understandably embittered by the experience, Naoroji, quite remarkably, did not allow his Baroda diwanship to diminish his enthusiasm for princely states or his resolve to advocate their interests. He engaged in voluminous correspondence with various rulers, diwans, and darbaris in the years after 1875. Within Gujarat, Naoroji was in regular contact with the courts of Bhavnagar, Jamnagar, Gondal, and Kutch. Under Malharrao's successor, Sayajirao, the ex-diwan enjoyed excellent relations with Baroda. Scattered letters in Naoroji's personal papers from Hyderabad, Indore, Mysore, and Travancore hint at broader correspondence now lost. A number of minor states sought assistance from Naoroji. Suchet Singh, a contender for the throne of Chamba, a Himalayan fastness between Jammu and Lahaul, exchanged letters in Hindi with Naoroji, who advised him on financial affairs. Tulaji Raje Bhosle, heir to the throne of Akalkot—the state where, decades beforehand, young Dadabhai's professor at Elphinstone College, Bal Gangadhar Shastri Jambhekar, had served as a royal tutor—turned to Naoroji for help in a conflict with the India Office. Naoroji mediated a dispute between Dharampore, where his father and grandfather had lived as agriculturalists, and the Rajput state of Alirajpur (after Naoroji's

1892 election, the ruler of Dharampore even asked the new MP to bring the matter before Parliament). By the early 1880s, Naoroji and an English friend, W. Martin Wood, established a formal agency in London for lobbying the India Office on the affairs of princely states. Over time, a reciprocal relationship developed between rulers and early nationalists like Naoroji: the politicians lobbied on behalf of princely interests, while the princes helped fund the politicians and their activities.[63]

Beyond issues of finance, Naoroji continued to incorporate these states in his political thought with regard to poverty, the drain, and swaraj. During his first parliamentary campaign in 1886, for example, he compared William Gladstone's proposal for Irish home rule with the "native states which possessed Home Rule" in India, arguing that there was room for political autonomy within the empire. And in the 1880s he returned to the question of whether princely India was more prosperous than areas of the subcontinent under direct British administration. Once more amassing statistics and other forms of data, Naoroji demonstrated that several states were, in comparison to British India, able to raise far greater revenues at much lower rates of taxation. This was, as he stated in an article published in the *Contemporary Review* in 1887, a sure sign of "improved government, and of the increasing prosperity of the people." "I have no doubt that Native States will go on rapidly increasing in prosperity as their system of government goes on improving," he declared. "I know from my own personal knowledge as Prime Minister of Baroda for one year that that State has a very promising future indeed." Without a significant drain of wealth, states such as Baroda, Bhavnagar, and Gondal were building their own railways—largely with their own capital and labor, unlike neighboring territories under Calcutta's thumb—while Gwalior was lending large sums of money to the Indian government. "Will this ever be in British India under the present policy?" Naoroji asked rhetorically. "No." Princely states, therefore, continued to figure prominently in Naoroji's campaign for Indian political reform—and these states exercised the imaginations of other early nationalists, too. As Hormusjee Ardeseer Wadya declared to the ex-diwan of Baroda, "There is no cause better calculated to secure India's national regeneration in her present circumstances than the ensured wellbeing and independent progress of our Native States."[64]

An Inspirer of Pessimistic Articles

Exactly two decades elapsed between when Dadabhai Naoroji introduced the drain theory in "England's Duties to India" and when he wrote about the comparative wealth of princely states in the *Contemporary Review*. These twenty years represented a period of staggering intellectual activity for Naoroji, something that had a deep and lasting impact on early Indian nationalism. By calculating the extent of India's impoverishment, Naoroji significantly undermined a key ideological justification of imperialism: that British rule brought stability, development, and prosperity to India. Furthermore, by attacking government statistics and exposing faulty methods of calculation, he put Anglo-Indians on the defensive, forcing many of them to acknowledge India's devastated economic landscape. Naoroji's formulation of the drain theory gave teeth to the argument that British policy in India was "evil" in nature. This was a landmark moment in the development of anti-imperialist thought. Colonized subjects, after all, had rarely dared to publicly condemn their rulers in such a direct manner, and Robert Phayre's behavior in Baroda stands as a testament to how Naoroji's outspokenness rankled particular officials. The political corollary to the drain theory, meanwhile, provided a solution to India's woes, establishing a firm relationship between the progressive Indianization of the civil service and the country's prosperity.

Naoroji has hitherto been seen as a founding father and leading figure of an explicitly economic form of nationalism. This seems to be a somewhat naive assumption. During the early nationalist era, there was no clear dichotomy between economic nationalism and its political variant; rather, political and economic arguments were deeply embedded in one another. Naoroji and his peers did not address Indian poverty and the Indian civil service as separate issues. They saw both as integral components of a single, unified demand for fundamental political reform, which Naoroji eventually conceptualized as self-government. Thus, we can perceive a logical progression of thought: from Naoroji's early activism for admitting Indians into the civil service to his enunciation of the drain theory and through his diwanship in Baroda.

Naoroji's influence, however, extended far beyond emergent Indian nationalist circles and the halls of power in Calcutta and Westminster. He quickly developed friendships with activists and thinkers from diverse political backgrounds. One such figure in Great Britain was Henry Hyndman. Brash and confrontational, with a flowing red beard that accentuated his stocky build, Hyndman leapt across the political spectrum before undertaking study of British colonialism in India. Researching the Raj's history of economic exploitation helped transform Hyndman into the so-called father of British socialism. In the late summer of 1878, Hyndman came across "Poverty of India," in pamphlet form, at King's parliamentary bookseller in Westminster. He drew heavily upon Naoroji's work, especially the drain theory, in a subsequent article titled "The Bankruptcy of India," published in *Nineteenth Century*. By the end of August the two men were in correspondence, with Naoroji sharing his figures and economic calculations. Through the 1880s, Hyndman's views and concerns largely paralleled those of Naoroji: he chalked up the drain of wealth to the preponderance of Britons in the civil service and believed that princely states were wealthier than British India. The Anglo-Indian press was quick to pick up on their collaboration. The *Pioneer* of Allahabad, for example, identified Naoroji as "the inspirer of the pessimistic articles" penned by the socialist firebrand.[65]

But their collaboration might have had one other tantalizing consequence: influencing the thought of another stocky, bearded socialist thinker in London, Karl Marx. In February 1881, Hyndman, who had recently pored through *Das Kapital*, informed Marx, "I want you very much to meet Mr Dadabhai Naoroji to whom I am much indebted for facts and ideas about India." Only a few days later, in a letter to the Russian economist Nicolai F. Danielson, Marx spoke of a drain of wealth from India in language remarkably similar to Naoroji's. He railed against how the British pried fortunes from India through "rent, dividends for railways useless to the Hindus; pensions for military and civil servicemen, for Afghanistan and other wars." "What they take from them without any equivalent and quite apart from what they appropriate to themselves annually *within* India," Marx claimed of the British, "amounts to *more than the total sum of income of the 60 millions of agricultural and industrial labourers of India!* This is a bleeding process with a vengeance!" Does such language suggest that Marx and Naoroji could have met each other? There is a slight possibility. Even if such a meeting did not transpire, it is very likely that

Hyndman transmitted to the sage of Hampstead, then in the twilight of his life, the gist of Naoroji's political and economic thought.[66]

As Karl Marx briefly dabbled in the idea of a drain of wealth, the first phase of Naoroji's career drew to a close. Nearly two decades of furious research, writing, and political work had taken an immense physical toll on the man. In late 1883, while in India, Naoroji's health collapsed, requiring him to pass several months in convalescence at the Gujarati seaside town of Tithal. He began suffering from persistent respiratory problems and sleeplessness.[67]

Naoroji's workaholic regimen was not the sole cause of his ill health. Family affairs contributed to his worries and stresses. Ardeshir, his son, spent several formative years of his youth with him in England and, consequently, experienced a rough transition back to life in India. When he returned to Bombay as a teenager to attend Grant Medical College, he was unable to communicate in Gujarati, an unthinkable circumstance for a Parsi in those days. Culturally alienated, he developed a disturbing fascination with firearms. It did not help matters that Ardeshir was not the most careful marksman: he grazed himself from several misfires, and while cleaning his rifles he occasionally sent a stray bullet whizzing through the corridors of the family home in Khetwadi. Naoroji's dismay was palpable from faraway London. He fretted over Ardeshir's lax study habits, haranguing him in homeward letters to put away the guns, stop skipping classes, and instead devote his full energies to medical science. "I see that your uppermost thoughts, and such as you think worthwhile communicating to me at the distance of so many thousand miles are those of the same childishness & laziness with which you have distressed me enough for two years," he lectured his son in March 1879.[68]

During his long sojourns in London and Baroda, Naoroji kept the rest of his family—his wife, elderly mother, daughter Shirin, and another daughter born in 1868, Maki—in Bombay in the care of Mancherji Merwanji Dadina, one of his former pupils at Elphinstone College. Dadina managed the family's occasionally straitened financial circumstances (eased by the Rs. 50,000 trust fund that Malharrao had endowed in 1873 for Naoroji's children) and informed Naoroji of various household dramas ("Gulbai wants to control the son and the son insists on controlling the mother!" he wrote shortly after Ardeshir's return from England). In 1875, not long after his resignation as diwan of Baroda, Naoroji suffered a grievous blow when his beloved mother, Manekbai, passed away. But there were happier moments, as well. Ardeshir wedded Dadina's daughter, Virbai, in 1880. In time, two further marriages would unite the families: between Shirin and Dadina's elder son, Fram, and between Maki and Dadina's younger son, Homi.[69]

Ardeshir successfully completed his studies at Grant Medical College, thereafter earning a plum position in charge of a civil hospital in Mandvi, in the princely state of Kutch. With an expanding family of his own—Ardeshir and Virbai's first child was born a year after their marriage, and seven more children would follow in quick succession—he beseeched his father to return to India for good. Naoroji, it seems, was already contemplating such a possibility. "Much agitation and a greater interest has now arisen here in Indian matters," he wrote to Ardeshir from London in 1879, "and it seems as if the labour of my life is now bearing fruit." Consequently, he pondered winding up his firm in the City and retiring to Bombay in order to continue writing and speaking about Indian poverty.[70]

But there were serious temptations to stay. Naoroji recognized that any hope for translating his ideas into political reform lay solely in Westminster, and that his ability to influence matters of Indian policy would be seriously undercut if he left the imperial capital forever. "We must remember that *all* the great principles of Indian administration must be ultimately decided in England," he had noted as early as 1872. "The fountain-head of power is in England, and there only have all Indian interests their ultimate fate."[71] Although he gave in to family demands and sailed back to Bombay in 1881, friends including Henry Hyndman prevailed upon Naoroji to keep his stay in India short so that he could return to engage directly with the British public and Parliament. Soon enough he was once more at Apollo Bunder, gazing out at Bombay's wide harbor and ready to board a Europe-bound steamer. Thus began the second phase of his political career, where Naoroji sought to take discussion of Indian poverty and political reform to the floor of the House of Commons—as an MP.

CHAPTER 3

Turning toward Westminster

WHY WOULD AN INDIAN want to stand for the British Parliament, and how could he expect any chance of election? These were questions that vexed many of Dadabhai Naoroji's friends and well-wishers as he made plans to sail from Bombay to London in early 1886. A few historians have subsequently attempted to provide answers. They have suggested Naoroji's campaigns resulted from his "robust faith in British justice," a search for Indian "respect and respectability" from their colonial masters, or a quest for some sort of "imperial citizenship" in a more liberal empire.[1]

None of these explanations quite suffices. Dadabhai Naoroji was not so naive as to trust the supposed magnanimity of the British public. India's dire poverty, rather than respectability, was his primary concern. And although he occasionally pronounced his countrymen to be British subjects, such declarations in no way precluded his vision of India as a nation. In order to truly understand why Naoroji embarked on the second phase of his political career, we must consider the establishment of a new political party, the Indian National Congress. Buoyed by the relative liberality of Lord Ripon's rule as viceroy, and encouraged by his support for "local self-government" at the provincial level, political leaders across the subcontinent scrambled to coordinate their various agendas. Bombay emerged as the locus of activity. Here an energetic Scotsman, Allan Octavian Hume, a former civil servant with a keen sense of Britain's injustice toward its Indian subjects, took the lead. Spending the winter of 1884–1885 in Bombay, Hume met with Naoroji and other western Indian leaders such as Navrozji Fardunji, Kashinath Trimbak Telang, Behramji Malabari, Mahadev Govind Ranade, Pherozeshah Mehta, and Dinsha Wacha. He organized a series of secret meetings—many held at the Breach Candy bungalow of William Wordsworth, grandson of the poet and a professor at Elphinstone College—where these leaders hammered out the foundations of "a National Indian Association" to articulate political demands. With a formal organization, Naoroji would have a solid platform for amplifying his calls for the Indianization of the bureaucracy and fleshing out his ideas about the eventuality of self-government.[2]

But there was a significant obstacle. In spite of Ripon having briefly raised some hopes, Indian nationalists remained deeply skeptical about their ability to wrest any concessions from the government of India. The preserve of some of the most reactionary and racist Anglo-Indians, the colonial bureaucracy saw no need to reform its authoritarian ways. It brooked no opposition, and leaders from across the subcontinent understood this all too well. From Madras, M. Viraraghavachariar, cofounder of the *Hindu*, declared, "I do not think that our Viceroys and Governors can do anything for India so long as they are surrounded by that wretched civil service whose sole aim is self aggrandizement." From Bombay, Dinsha Wacha sensed the grave threat to India posed by Anglo-Indian officialdom: "They are forging stronger iron chains for us so that we may not be able to unfetter ourselves for the next century to come." Naoroji agreed with these sentiments. "The authorities in India can never be expected to desire to move in that direction [toward reform]," he stated. "On the contrary they would do all to thwart."[3]

The prospects for achieving reform within India, therefore, appeared grim. For this reason, the founding generation of the Congress looked for alternative paths. The best path seemed to lie through Westminster. Parliament, after all, possessed authority over the government of India, and it had the right to modify Indian policy. Within the House of Commons, there were several MPs, including John Bright, the radical Liberal statesman, who had long track records of speaking in favor of Indian reform. Furthermore, going to Parliament was not a new idea. Under

Company rule, Indians had taken their disputes to both houses, occasionally winning their cases while rattling the nerves of directors sitting in East India House. Many Indians, including the great Bengali liberal Rammohun Roy, had pressed the case for Indian parliamentary representation. Naoroji already possessed a long resume of petitions addressed to Parliament and testimony given before its committees. Importantly, since the late 1860s, he had also worked behind the scenes to advocate Indian interests in the Commons, operating through sitting British MPs who agreed to take on the additional mantle of "member for India." Thus, for the Congress, Parliament was a weapon of the weak, but it was nevertheless a weapon that had yielded some modest results in the past. Here lay the most promising hope for pursuing the new body's agenda. It was for this reason that in the months prior to the formal establishment of the Congress in December 1885, Hume based himself in London, holding a marathon series of meetings with MPs, Liberal Party officials, and members of the press in order to drum up support for the association.[4]

Naoroji's decision to stand for Parliament, therefore, was absolutely in keeping with the early policy of the Congress. Moreover, his first-ever campaign, waged in the central London constituency of Holborn during June and July 1886, was very much a Congress endeavor. The organization played an indispensable role in giving Naoroji a fighting chance to win election. Members of the Congress coordinated support from India and provided Naoroji with vital contacts in Great Britain. In fact, being Indian actually *helped* Naoroji during his early electoral work: he capitalized on the many personal and professional connections with India that these contacts possessed, winning influential allies and making inroads into the Liberal Party establishment. With these new allies, the prospective candidate began constructing broad-ranging networks across the British political sphere, securing support from various constituencies. Both during and after his Holborn campaign, Naoroji made special efforts to reach out to progressive movements. He struggled to interest socialists, workingmen, and even women suffragists in the need for political reform in India, hoping to win allies while also broadcasting his political agenda among a public unfamiliar with affairs in its largest colony. Support from these constituencies, in turn, helped bolster the standing and public recognition of the Congress.

But the constituency that Naoroji courted with the greatest zeal was the Irish. During the 1880s, Irish home rule—specifically, the creation of a separate parliament in Dublin—dominated British headlines, especially after the prime minister, William Gladstone, indicated in 1885 his intention to bring a home rule bill before Parliament. In seeking alliances with the Irish, Naoroji was once more treading upon familiar ground. Irish and Indian political activists had deep links. "Probably no other country in the world has exercised greater influence on the course of Indian nationalism, both as an example and as a warning, than Ireland," notes the historian S. R. Mehrotra. Naoroji's activities in the 1880s indicate the sheer breadth of Indian nationalist interest in England's oldest colony. Irish leaders had, similarly, been intrigued by the commonalities experienced by Indians under British rule: famine, worsening poverty, and authoritarian governance. These were commonalities that Naoroji now foregrounded on the campaign trail in order to declare himself an ardent Irish home ruler. Thus, in the second phase of Naoroji's political career, we witness a curious development in his thought and strategy. He temporarily abandoned conceptualization of Indian self-government in order to champion home rule for Ireland. It was a tactical move that, in the long run, increased Naoroji's chances of returning to Indian matters as a sitting MP.[5]

The Idea of Indian MPs

In 1885, Lalmohan Ghosh, a Calcutta barrister and one of the city's rising political stars, made history by becoming the first-ever Indian to stand for Parliament, campaigning as a Liberal from a southeastern London constituency.[6] Ghosh's attempt, while unsuccessful, dramatically brought to light how Indians were beginning to seek political representation in the heart of empire. However, Indian interest in the British Parliament—and the interest of some Britons in seeing a few Indian representatives sitting in the House of Commons—long preceded the Bengali barrister's maiden campaign. The idea of parliamentary representation for the subcontinent was, fundamentally, part of a lengthy tradition of Indian engagement with Westminster in order to modify and influence policy.

Under the autocratic sway of the East India Company, Indians were quick to appreciate the value of petitions, memorials, and occasional visits to Parliament in order to make up for the deficit of political power at home. One such Indian was Rammohun Roy, often touted as the "father of modern India" for his pioneering religious, social, and political reform activities. In 1828, Rammohun dispatched petitions to both houses of Parliament protesting the Company's intention to restrict membership in grand juries only to Christians, a matter that he vigilantly pursued in Westminster after sailing to Great Britain in 1830. Recognizing the broad public significance of his agitation against the jury act, Prasanna Kumar Tagore, a prominent Calcutta lawyer, hailed Rammohun as India's unofficial MP.[7]

Such pronouncements hinted at an important development in modern Indian political thought: the belief that Indians' rights as British subjects extended to representation at the highest levels. Shut out of government affairs in their own country, Indians could maneuver around the Company administration and aspire to something as lofty as a parliamentary seat, from where they could exercise influence over policy in a much more direct and effective manner. As the historian Lynn Zastoupil notes, elites in both Calcutta and London fostered hopes that Rammohun—whose period of residence in Great Britain coincided with the failure of a parliamentary franchise reform act in 1831 and the passing of the Reform Act of 1832—would contest a seat in the Commons. Amid the clamor and debate over widening the franchise, Joseph Hume, a radical MP (and father of Allan Octavian Hume), and Robert Montgomery Martin, editor of the *Bengal Herald* of Calcutta, argued in favor of imperial representation in Parliament, including representation for India. Hume's colleague in the reformist Parliamentary Candidate Society, the utilitarian philosopher Jeremy Bentham, proposed Rammohun as an MP for India who would sit alongside "a half caste, and a negro" in order to lend some voice to British imperial subjects and "subdue the prejudices of colour." The idea of an Indian MP, therefore, fit in with movements in Britain for parliamentary reform, popular representation, and early experiments with conceptualizing an imperial federation, although India always sat at the very margins in such schemes. Rammohun, for his part, was apparently ready to take a seat in the Commons so as to "pave the way for his countrymen."[8]

Rammohun's death in 1833 robbed India of any chances of claiming a pre-Victorian parliamentary candidate, although his close friend Dwarkanath Tagore kept the subject alive by debating the merits of Indian MPs with William Gladstone in the 1840s. It is quite likely that Rammohun played an indirect role in influencing Bombay's growing interest in Parliament: long after his death, the city's newspapers continued to discuss his ideas and political activities. In 1848, Gopal Hari Deshmukh or Lokahitawadi—one of Naoroji's contemporaries and a fellow social reformer—wrote in favor of Indian MPs in a Marathi newspaper. These ideas filtered down into Young Bombay. In early 1852, the Young Bombay clique of the Bombay Association—which might have included Naoroji—made a list of sweeping demands for political reform, which included "admission of representatives into the British Parliament" alongside the Indianization of the civil service, reform of the revenue system, creation of municipal corporations, and mass education. Thus, parliamentary representation began to be popularly discussed in the subcontinent, a component of a broad reformist agenda forged by a new generation of educated Indians.[9]

While Indian interest in parliamentary affairs naturally increased after the assumption of crown rule in 1858, public discussion of Indian parliamentary representation tapered off, perhaps on account of overabundant caution following the Mutiny. It was Naoroji who eventually revived the conversation. In his "England's Duties to India," read before the East India Association in May 1867, Naoroji neatly tied together the idea of Indian parliamentary representation and the inability of Indians to take part in or influence their own government. He then linked these issues to broader questions brought up earlier by the likes of Martin, Hume, and Bentham: the supposed rights of British subjects, expansion of the franchise, and representation of other imperial domains in Parliament. Naoroji framed these questions from the standpoint of the Indian taxpayer, underscoring the fundamental injustice of the current system:

> There is again the almost total exclusion of the natives from a share and voice in the administration of their own country. Under former rulers there was every career open for the talented. For the voice of a few small boroughs Parliament has been wrangling for years,

while the Indian budget of over 40 millions is voted before scarcely a dozen honourable members, and without a single voice to represent the millions who pay taxes. Why should not 200 millions of your fellow-subjects who contribute so largely to your wealth and prosperity, and who form an integral part of the British empire, have a few representatives in the Imperial Parliament to give their voice on imperial questions?[10]

Although Naoroji's proposal mustered little response from his British audience, it continued to be pressed forward by an increasing number of Indians involved in political activities in Britain. Naoroji's East India Association in London served as an important forum for debate on parliamentary representation, which took place in the context of broader discussion on whether Indians could enjoy the same political rights and freedoms as their colonial rulers. For example, two months after Naoroji read "England's Duties to India," W. C. Bonnerjee—the man who in 1885 would become the first president of the Indian National Congress—took to the association's lectern in London and delivered a remarkable speech calling for the immediate institution of representative institutions for his countrymen. Invoking the Italian patriot Giuseppe Mazzini and refuting the claims of Thomas Macaulay and John Stuart Mill that Indians were unfit for liberal government, Bonnerjee declared the "common people of India" to be as intelligent as the average Briton. He held up panchayats— institutions of "self-government *par excellence*"—as an example of how Indians had long enjoyed a modicum of democracy at the village level. While several British members expressed incredulousness about the young Bengali barrister's ideas and attempted to cut off further discussion, Bonnerjee's speech evoked a chorus of support from Naoroji, Navrozji Fardunji, and two other promising young lawyers from Bombay in the audience, Pherozeshah Mehta and Badruddin Tyabji. Significantly, a former Irish MP, Thomas Chisholm Anstey, a champion of Irish Catholic interests and a supporter of the Irish leader Daniel O'Connell, also rose in the chamber to voice his support for Bonnerjee's proposal. "There is no nation unfit for free institutions," Anstey declared, recalling that he had, decades beforehand, "stood almost alone in the House of Commons" in advocating representative government in British India.[11]

Having made the case for representative institutions in the colony, members of the East India Association returned to Naoroji's proposal for seating Indian MPs in Westminster. In early 1874, a five-member committee—including Navrozji Fardunji, John Dickinson, and Edward B. Eastwick, a Conservative MP and former member of the Bombay civil service—began hammering out a petition to the Commons on the subject. The petition revealed the extent to which the idea of Indian parliamentary representation was evolving. Navrozji and his colleagues enumerated advocates of Indian representation such as Joseph Hume and Edward Creasy, a historian and former chief justice of Ceylon, and even claimed Adam Smith as a supporter of sending Indians to Parliament. Eight seats in the Commons, they felt, would be sufficient: two members each for Calcutta, Madras, and Bombay, and one each for the North-West Provinces and Punjab.[12]

In this sense, Indian subjects would enjoy rights of representation similar to those of other colonized people in the French, Spanish, and Portuguese empires. Committee members noted that the French National Assembly included fifteen colonial representatives, including one from France's Indian possessions, while colonial representatives also sat in the *cortes* in Madrid and Lisbon. The glaring absence of similar representation for an empire as large as British India was, in contrast, "calculated to increase the dissatisfaction which is undoubtedly felt by our own fellow-subjects there." Recent inventions, furthermore, had removed obstacles that stood in the way of calling Indian MPs to sit in the Commons. Steamships and the Suez Canal reduced travel time between India and Britain to three weeks, while the telegraph facilitated rapid correspondence between London and India's major urban centers. With speedier transportation and communication, "a representative of India would be practically in a better position, so far as regards contiguity to those who elected him, than were the representatives of the more distant parts of Scotland and of Ireland at the beginning of the present century."[13]

The East India Association's petition excited interest in the subcontinent. Contacts in Bombay and Calcutta eagerly telegraphed their support to Dickinson, while the Poona Sarvajanik Sabha, the premier political organization in the Deccan, dispatched a further petition to Westminster, signed by more than twenty-one thousand individuals and demanding eighteen Indian seats. Unfortunately, the association's petition never made it to Parliament. In spite of Navrozji's strong advocacy, other members of the association found the proposal too "revolutionary" and, simultaneously, "impracticable" and "utterly hopeless." It was ultimately withdrawn. In debates over creating an imperial federation or a truly imperial Parliament, demands for representation for white settler colonies such as Canada, Australia, and New Zealand took significant precedent over any similar proposals regarding India.[14]

The idea of an Indian MP failed to go away, however. Beginning in the late 1860s, Naoroji, Bonnerjee, and certain British allies increasingly sought out the next best thing: relying on a sitting MP to advocate Indian political demands. The strategy had a clear precedent. In the 1830s, the assembly of Lower Canada hired John Arthur Roebuck, MP for Bath, as its agent; New South Wales later appointed Francis Scott, MP for Roxburghshire, to bring its business before Parliament. While John Bright had long advocated Indian concerns in the Commons, the mantle of "member for India" eventually fell upon Henry Fawcett, the blind MP for Brighton, a professor of political economy at Cambridge and a radical Liberal. Not surprisingly, given their shared academic interest in economics, Fawcett pursued in the Commons many of the same issues that Naoroji was addressing in public meetings in Britain and India. Fawcett expounded upon the dire poverty of India, called for the Indianization of the civil service, protested against India being burdened with the expenses of imperial military adventures in Abyssinia and Afghanistan, and questioned the India Office's free reliance on the Indian exchequer for numerous dubious purposes.[15]

Naoroji worked closely with Fawcett on two critical matters. First, in 1868, Fawcett introduced a resolution into the Commons on simultaneous civil service examinations, which he subsequently continued to bring up every year. Second, he called for the formation of a select committee of Parliament to inquire into Indian financial issues, which sat in the early 1870s but was finally dissolved before it could issue a report (Naoroji's "Poverty of India" was originally a submission to this committee). For his steadfast advocacy of Indian interests, Fawcett enjoyed great popularity in India. When the "member for India" lost his actual seat in Brighton in 1874, public associations in India raised £400 for Fawcett to use in contesting another constituency. Several years after Fawcett's death in 1884, Bonnerjee, working with Eardley Norton, an Anglo-Indian lawyer from Madras and a member of the Congress, recruited Charles Bradlaugh as the new "member for India." Bradlaugh was a leading radical figure who, as a declared atheist, courted a constant stream of controversy in Victorian society. Indian political leaders, therefore, continued to find friends among some of the most advanced radicals in Parliament.[16]

One sympathetic advocate in the Commons was, of course, hardly enough. Beginning with the general election of 1880, Indian political leaders borrowed an Irish nationalist tactic and attempted to influence the way that British electors voted. They significantly stepped up their efforts for the next general election, held in 1885. Here Lalmohan Ghosh was at the fore, having secured the Liberal candidacy in Deptford, a working-class and Irish constituency created by the Third Reform Act of 1884. In India, meanwhile, political associations busied themselves with two tasks: raising campaign funds for Ghosh and the sympathetic Anglo-Indian journalist William Digby—who, through his pamphleteering, sought to make India a major electoral issue—and lobbying voters. Three Indians—Narayan Chandavarkar, from the Bombay Presidency Association (a successor organization to the now-moribund Bombay Association); S. R. Mudaliar, of the Madras Mahajana Sabha; and Manmohan Ghosh, representing the Indian Union of Calcutta—embarked on a speaking tour across Britain.

The "most controversial step" taken during the election was the Poona Sarvajanik Sabha and Bombay Presidency Association's decision to publicly support or oppose particular candidates for Parliament. Naoroji, not surprisingly, was closely involved in this task. In late September 1885, he maneuvered the Bombay Presidency Association to endorse eight Liberal candidates beyond Ghosh and Digby—including Lord Hartington, John Bright, John Slagg, and Wilfrid Scawen Blunt—and oppose Richard Temple, Lewis Pelly (the former resident at Baroda), and three other Conservatives. In an impassioned speech on the importance of the elections, he singled out the importance of Parliament in achieving Indian reform. "Almost entirely we have to depend upon the people and Parliament of England to make those great reforms which alone can remove the serious evils from which we are suffering," he declared. "It is in Parliament that our chief battles have to be fought. The election of its members, especially those who profess to speak on Indian matters, requires our earnest attention." As the deliberations of the inaugural Congress session in 1885 would demonstrate, Naoroji was becoming one of the strongest advocates of an Indian nationalist strategy premised on achieving political reform almost exclusively through Westminster and Whitehall.[17]

Naoroji spoke with feeling on the topic because, by the fall of 1885, he was eagerly awaiting his own opportunity to contest a seat. Only a few years after advocating Indian MPs in his "England's Duties to India," Naoroji began to seriously consider his prospects for election to the Commons. In an October 1884 letter to W. Martin Wood, an ally in princely state matters, Naoroji revealed that he "had laid a sort of foundation" for a parliamentary run as early as 1872, just before getting caught up in affairs in Baroda. Responding to Wood's encouragement to once more look toward Westminster, he confessed that he did not at the moment have sufficient funds for a campaign and that the deliverance of such funds depended on the largesse of a Kathiawadi prince. Naoroji informed Wood that he had "done some work for a Prince," and although this business had been successfully concluded, "saving both 'Izat' [honor] and money to the Prince," he had not received the promised payment from the darbar.[18]

In a subsequent confidential letter sent to a contact in Rajkot, Naoroji revealed that the prince in question was the nawab of Junagadh. "The Junagar Durbar not having fulfilled their promises with me I am unable to carry out my wishes to try to get into Parliament," he complained.

> As far as I am personally concerned I am willing to give my labour
> and the rest of my active life to the accomplishment of some of . . .
> the most pressing reforms needed by us. And this can be done only
> in England and best in Parliament. I have not the necessary means.
> I can only offer my personal work and those who have means must
> supply them.

Naoroji indicated that another friend was corresponding on his behalf with two other potential princely donors, the rulers of Kutch and Bhavnagar. While his correspondence does not reveal how he eventually procured funds—some letters suggest that the darbars of Junagadh and

Bhavnagar may have eventually come through on their respective obli-
gation and promise—by early April 1885 Naoroji was speaking confidently about wrapping up affairs in Bombay and returning to Britain.
We do not know how he convinced his long-suffering wife and children
to agree to another prolonged absence from home. But friends in London
provided Naoroji with encouragement. "I should like to see you in this
country trying to get into Parliament," wrote Nasarvanji J. Moolla, a fellow
Parsi, from his office on Old Broad Street in the City. "They ought to send
you here from Bombay instead of that lazy fellow [Lalmohan] Ghose."[19]

Naoroji eventually decided against sailing to Britain ahead of the general elections held in November and December of 1885. He was undoubtedly compelled to stay in Bombay because of the imminent first meeting
of the Congress—and he probably also wanted to assess how Lalmohan
Ghosh fared with British voters. He did not have to wait long for the next
electoral tussle. With the Liberal prime minister, William Gladstone, intent on introducing his controversial Irish home rule bill before Parliament, Naoroji gambled on the likelihood of a fresh poll. He sailed from
Bombay in late March 1886, arriving in London on April 12 amid frigid
weather and the "great excitement" caused by the home rule bill, and immediately began reconnecting with old Liberal contacts while dispatching
letters of introduction to prospective new allies.[20] For the next two
months, Naoroji kept a frenetic schedule of meetings, interviews, and
dinner appointments with party leaders, journalists, and key public figures. Persistent networking helped Naoroji land a nomination from Holborn once new elections were announced in early summer.

A Forlorn Hope

On the morning of June 25, 1886, hardly ten days before electors in his
constituency went to the polls, Dadabhai Naoroji wrote a lengthy letter
to William Wedderburn, a progressive-minded civil servant in Bombay
and an enthusiastic member of the nascent Congress. Naoroji pronounced
his campaign in Holborn to be "a forlorn hope"—an arduous trial necessary in order to advance his cause. He was not being unduly pessimistic.
Holborn, the congested warren of streets sandwiched between the Strand
and Bloomsbury in central London, was difficult territory for a Liberal

candidate. Its electors—a mix of non-resident shopkeepers, lawyers from Lincoln's Inn and Chancery Lane, wealthy homeowners clustered around Russell Square, and less fortunate individuals huddled in the tenements of St. Giles—were overwhelmingly Conservative. Moreover, as Naoroji readily admitted, the incumbent Conservative MP, Francis Duncan, was a "popular man," having won by a comfortable margin in the previous general election. Naoroji, in contrast, was an unfamiliar character in Holborn. "The great difficulty I have to contend with," he informed Wedderburn, was that electors replied to his overtures with a standard line: "We don't know you, we cannot experiment at present."[21]

Holborn was indeed a "forlorn hope," but it was a calculated risk on Naoroji's part. During the 1886 general election, his primary objective was not to win, but rather to make his name known among Liberal power brokers and electors—and thereby position himself for the next poll. Naoroji was also motivated by the opportunity to advertise Indian political demands while on the hustings. "Success or failure, the Indian cause will be advanced a stage this election," he reassured Wedderburn.[22] But India was important for another reason. In order to forge relations with Liberal Party officials and leaders, Naoroji relied heavily upon their Indian connections. After all, many senior party members—men like Lord Ripon and the Duke of Argyll, the former secretary of state—had also been senior Indian administrators, while other prominent MPs, such as John Bright, had long records of speaking on Indian affairs. In this sense, being an Indian was actually politically advantageous for the prospective candidate: Naoroji could rely upon several mutual friends and acquaintances for appointments and letters of introduction. And these friends and acquaintances—many from Bombay or with important ties to the city—formed the first of several overlapping networks of support that allowed Naoroji to gradually penetrate to the very core of the Liberal establishment. Between early April and late June 1886, when Gladstone finally dissolved his government and called for general elections, Naoroji leveraged these networks in order to assemble a broad base of support across the British political spectrum. Aside from Liberal stalwarts, this support base included a smattering of Conservative contacts and a large contingent of Irish leaders. Holborn might have been a "forlorn hope," but it succeeded in facilitating Naoroji's emergence as a recognized figure in late Victorian politics.

Naoroji's first network of support included the Congress leadership, based mostly in Bombay. The so-called inner circle of the Congress—men who had taken the lead in establishing the organization, with Allan Octavian Hume at its head—specifically assisted with Naoroji's foray into Liberal politics. The social reformer Behramji Malabari, for example, was a close confidant of Lord Ripon and probably helped Naoroji reconnect with the ex-viceroy in London. William Wedderburn, then employed at the Bombay secretariat, facilitated contact with individuals at the India Office, where Lord Kimberley, a chief ally of Gladstone, was secretary of state.

But it was Hume who provided the most important contacts. While promoting the Congress in the United Kingdom during the summer and autumn of 1885, he had become acquainted with some of the most powerful and influential figures in the Liberal establishment. He now passed along to Naoroji a thick file of letters of introduction before the latter departed Bombay in March 1886. Addressees included parliamentarians and party seniors such as John Bright; Joseph Chamberlain; John Morley; Lord Dalhousie, a navy admiral and supporter of Irish home rule; Robert T. Reid, a Scottish MP and critic of Indian policy; and a young Alfred Milner, the future imperial proconsul in South Africa. There were important media figures, as well: C. P. Scott, editor of the *Manchester Guardian*; Henry Yates Thompson, owner of the *Pall Mall Gazette*; and Henry Dunckley, editor of the *Manchester Examiner and Times*. Hume introduced Naoroji to Florence Nightingale—the "lady with the lamp" had an interest in Indian affairs dating from the 1860s. Finally, he penned letters to prominent anti-imperialists, such as Richard Congreve, a disciple of Auguste Comte and a long-standing champion of the political liberation of India and Ireland. Another contact was Wilfrid Scawen Blunt, who had taken up the cause of Egyptian nationalists on the eve of the Anglo-Egyptian War of 1882 and, the following year, attended a conference in Calcutta organized by the Bengali leader Surendranath Banerjea.[23]

With Hume's letters in hand, Naoroji immediately set to work making appointments. Five days after arriving in London, he called upon John Bright. The aged radical agreed that "it would be good if Indians got into

"OUR OWN CONGRESS COOLIES."

[In proposing a vote of thanks from the I. N. Congress to the British Committee, Mr. Dinshaw Eduljee Wacha made a telling speech. He said :—" Among the hardest workers there could be no three names more well known to you than those of Sir William Wedderburn, Dadabhai Naoroji and A. O. Hume. These have been working incessantly. For months past our ears have been deafened with cries of certain exalted personages, who say that they work for fourteen hours a day like a man in the coal-pit. They are, no doubt, exalted-coolies but they earn from ten to twenty thousand rupees. But there are some of our own Congress coolies who work far more than they."]

[*Hindi Punch, Dec., 1904.*]

Cartoon from the *Hindi Punch* of Naoroji (left), Allan Octavian Hume (center), and William Wedderburn (right) as "Congress coolies." Naoroji, Hume, and Wedderburn were recognized as the guiding forces of the Congress during its first two decades.

Cartoons from the Hindi Punch (for 1905), ed. Barjorjee Nowrosjee (Bombay: Bombay Samachar Press, 1905), p. 11. Reproduction © The British Library Board, IOR, SV 576.

Parliament" but cautioned that "the difficulties were great" for a non-Briton. When Naoroji pressed him for active support of his parliamentary ambitions, Bright hesitated, "but it appeared from the general tone of his conversation that if a good movement were made, he might help." Other individuals were more forthcoming. Reid, for example, mused enthusiastically about the effect that an Indian MP would have upon Parliament. Naoroji expressed his fears that he would have little traction with other members of the Commons, but Reid immediately dismissed his concerns: "Oh! there is no fear about it. The House is sure to listen to you as an Indian." Here Reid indicated his commitment to Naoroji's prospective campaign: he offered to "write to Birmingham." This meant approaching the National Liberal Federation, one of the party's two great nodes of power, commanded by its formidable secretary,

Francis Schnadhorst. Milner was equally supportive and enthusiastic. Over a three-hour-long breakfast, he explained to Naoroji that he wished, at all costs, to prevent India from becoming another Ireland—a hotbed of radicalism and sedition. "As regards India he said he should never like to see matters driven so far as they had been with Ireland," Naoroji noted in his diary. "India's desires should be met in good time and with good grace." Milner pledged to "do all he could to help" Naoroji. He approved of Reid's outreach to the National Liberal Federation, hoping that Naoroji could land a large speaking event in Birmingham.[24]

Thus, largely through Hume's contacts, Naoroji steadily made inroads into the Liberal establishment. But he kept his political options open. George Birdwood—another old friend from Bombay, now an India Office official with pronounced Tory leanings—expressed his determination to get Naoroji into Parliament "by one door or another," and offered to set up meetings with leading Conservative politicians. Through one of Hume's contacts, Naoroji learned that Benjamin Disraeli, the deceased Tory statesman, had supported the idea of electing an Indian candidate from an English constituency. There is some evidence that Naoroji briefly mulled over the prospect of standing as a Tory—he discussed the matter with Blunt, who counseled that Naoroji had "no chance" with the party. Meanwhile, on the far left of the political spectrum, Naoroji reconnected with Henry Hyndman, who now commanded Britain's first socialist political party, the Social Democratic Federation. Naoroji, however, treaded carefully with his socialist friend, recently charged with sedition after a workers' rally had descended into a full-scale riot in Trafalgar Square. He was conscious of "the disfavour in which his name was among the people and the Press."[25]

But one party continued to attract Naoroji: the Irish nationalists. The general election of 1886, as Naoroji well understood, was largely a referendum on Gladstone's proposal for Irish home rule. And Ireland had dominated his discussions with Liberal leaders. Bright had confided to Naoroji that he could see "no satisfactory settlement of the Irish question." Milner, who had despaired about India becoming another Ireland, argued with Naoroji about the viability of a separate Irish legislature. Naoroji had no such qualms, identifying himself as a firm supporter of Gladstone's home rule bill. After all, in his analysis, Ireland, like India, was beset by poverty and famine caused by illiberal governance. In language strikingly similar to his earlier examinations of India's economic woes, Naoroji declared the current administration of Ireland to be "a *certain* evil" and maintained that with home rule "Ireland would rise in prosperity."[26]

Naoroji was, therefore, deeply invested in Irish political concerns. Luckily, many Irish parliamentarians also expressed great interest in the political affairs of the subcontinent, allowing Naoroji to once more use Indian connections to his advantage. During his earlier periods of residence in London, he had become acquainted with two of the most towering leaders in the Irish camp, Charles Stuart Parnell, head of the Irish Parliamentary Party (commonly known as the Home Rule Party), and Michael Davitt, founder of the Irish National Land League. In 1883, Davitt had even suggested to Parnell that Naoroji stand for Parliament from an Irish constituency. Naoroji now actively worked to renew his friendship with the two men. He also reached out—through one of Hume's contacts—to T. P. O'Connor, a Parnellite MP from Liverpool, who subsequently offered to give Naoroji "the Irish vote in some constituency where we are powerful." Furthermore, Naoroji sought out speaking engagements on Ireland, desiring to publicly associate his name with the home rule cause. William Digby tried to land Naoroji a seat at a Liberal Party conference supporting Gladstone's policy; meanwhile, Henry Hyde Champion, secretary of Hyndman's Social Democratic Federation, offered to include Naoroji in a home rule demonstration being staged by Irish MPs.[27]

With expanding networks of support among both Irish home rulers and prominent Liberal MPs, Naoroji now focused his attention on the key power brokers in the Liberal Party and allied clubs and associations. In late May, Francis Schnadhorst agreed to meet with him. This gave Naoroji a significant boost: the National Liberal Federation secretary pledged to work with Digby in order to search for a suitable constituency. Naoroji also turned to the Federation's sister organization in London, the Liberal Central Association. Indian connections once more proved useful: the Association's secretary, Francis Wyllie, was an ex-civil servant from Bombay. Florence Nightingale, meanwhile, helped Naoroji get in touch with Arnold Morley, the party's chief whip, and Ripon strengthened Naoroji's hand by sending Morley a letter of endorsement. Morley

summoned Naoroji to the association's chambers and evaluated his fitness for standing in an election. Did he have the necessary funds? "I said I
was fully prepared," replied Naoroji. How would he, an Indian, appeal
to British electors? "I had explained to him that though India was my
chief subject I was not quite a stranger to English politics," he responded,
"as I had spent the best part of my manhood in this country."[28]

Naoroji now turned to Manchester, an important Liberal stronghold
with a large Irish population. Here, in the great industrial center whose
fortunes were so dependent on the flow of raw materials from the subcontinent, he received a warm welcome. Arthur Symonds, secretary of
the National Reform Union, an assemblage of Liberal-leaning merchants
and manufacturers, promised to assist Schnadhorst in finding Naoroji a
constituency. The heads of two influential city organizations, the Reform
Club and the Athenaeum, invited Naoroji to deliver talks on India before
their members. Finally, Naoroji left a favorable impression with Hume's
media contacts, C. P. Scott and Henry Dunckley, thereby ensuring that
the *Guardian* and *Examiner and Times* were on his side.[29]

Thus, by the beginning of June 1886, Naoroji had assembled a vast and
diverse group of supporters and well-wishers. Irish home rulers, sitting
Liberal MPs, critics of imperialism, socialists, and Manchester civic leaders
had all—through a common interest in Indian affairs—been enticed by
the prospect of an Indian sitting in Parliament. Naoroji and his friends
now set to work finding a constituency that was similarly amenable to
the idea. Contacts suggested a broad range of locales. Hodgson Pratt, a
peace activist and former member of the Bengal civil service, believed that
he should try in Scotland. "The Scotch were far more liberal than the liberals of England," he advised. Meanwhile, Frederick W. Chesson, secretary of the Aborigines Protection Society, an early humanitarian organization, recommended an Irish seat. Others proposed Manchester;
Oldham, a hub of cotton textile manufacturing; or even somewhere in
scenic Cornwall. By the middle of June, various local Liberal associations
were actively courting Naoroji. St. Albans offered him its ticket, but
Naoroji, aware that the constituency had polled heavily Conservative in
the previous election, rejected its overtures, choosing instead to investigate leads in North Paddington and South Kensington.[30]

While Naoroji continued to search for constituencies, events moved quickly in Westminster. On June 8, the House of Commons defeated Gladstone's home rule bill on its second reading, leaving the prime minister with little option but to dissolve Parliament and call new elections. Naoroji, relatively sanguine about the bill's chances of success, was clearly caught off guard. "The dissolution came upon me too soon," he admitted to Wedderburn on June 17. "The plan now is to select the least expensive Constituency I can get and try a chance, and considering over the whole matter, my present intention is to do so." As Naoroji mulled over his prospects in South Kensington, Henry Hyde Champion, Hyndman's lieutenant, suddenly alerted him about a vacancy in Holborn. Although the Liberal candidate there had been soundly defeated in the previous election, when Parnell had called upon his supporters to abandon Gladstone's party, Champion believed that the current Liberal-Irish alliance gave Naoroji a fighting chance. *"The Irish vote I imagine would secure you the seat,"* he declared. On June 18, Naoroji, citing this sizable Irish electorate as his deciding factor, formally approached the Holborn Liberal Association, which unanimously endorsed his candidature.[31] He was now officially standing for Parliament.

There was, however, little time to celebrate this achievement. Since Gladstone was on the verge of officially dissolving Parliament, it was a matter of weeks, if not days, before polling places were expected to open. Immediately after nominating its candidate on the evening of June 18, the Holborn Liberal Association drafted, printed, and distributed flyers introducing Liberal electors to Dadabhai Naoroji, describing him as "an eminent native of India." Naoroji hurriedly published a circular letter the following day. "To many of you I am a man of strange name and race," he acknowledged. But, Naoroji continued, "with English life and English politics I am familiar; I have voted at British Elections; I have worked for Liberal Candidates."[32]

This was the essence of Naoroji's strategy on the campaign trail: he played up his long residence in the United Kingdom, as well as his previous associations with British politics. He proclaimed himself to be a fervent admirer of certain British values, something that no doubt helped compensate for his foreignness. During the Holborn contest, we find some of Naoroji's most florid pro-British statements, which sometimes jarred uncomfortably with his earlier opinions expressed in his writings on Indian poverty and the drain of wealth. "I have lived in this country actually for twenty years," he declared before a packed audience at Holborn Town Hall. "And I say that if there is one thing more certain than another that I have learned, it is that the English nation is incompatible with tyranny."[33]

Additionally, Naoroji drove home his support for Irish home rule. Most of his campaign speeches, in fact, addressed Ireland rather than any Indian concerns. He heaped praise on its people: "If ever I have found a warm-hearted people in the world, I have found the Irish." He railed against the rampant prejudice to which the Irish were subjected. "If they are bad now, it is your own doing," Naoroji scolded Englishmen. "You first debase them, and then give them a bad name, and then want to hang them." And he recruited Irish MPs, including Michael Davitt, to speak at his rallies. But he was also careful to link Ireland to English and Indian affairs. For example, Naoroji cast home rule as a patriotic cause. It was something that would endow British history with "a brighter chapter than any it at present contained," since it vindicated the Englishman's characteristic commitment to justice. He also dismissed fears that home rule would put Ireland on the path toward complete secession: the Irish would not want to relinquish "a share in the most glorious Empire that ever existed on the face of the earth." Turning to subcontinental matters, Naoroji struggled to link Irish home rule with political reform in India. India, like Ireland, he reminded voters, lacked representative government. The plight of both countries demonstrated that "no one race of people can ever legislate satisfactorily for another race." As polling day approached, Naoroji increasingly conflated Irish and Indian affairs. He appealed for electors' votes "on behalf of the five millions in Ireland and 250,000,000 of India."[34]

Naoroji's efforts to get into Parliament had begun with the Congress's inner circle, and it was the inner circle that now helped him conclude the Holborn campaign. Here Behramji Malabari took the lead. Utilizing the National Telegraphic Union, a Congress organ designed to counteract the influence of Anglo-Indians upon the British media, Malabari started to organize a uniquely transnational movement in the 1886 general election. Toward the end of June, he fired off telegrams to Congress leaders and newspaper editors across the subcontinent, from Madras to Lahore, imploring them to organize local demonstrations in favor of Naoroji and, to a noticeably lesser extent, Lalmohan Ghosh (who had been nominated once more as the Liberal candidate in Deptford). "Pray delay not public meetings, Bombay holds last," read one such message that radiated across the telegraph lines spanning India.[35]

By the final days of the month, replies began trickling back into Bombay. From Calcutta, the Indian Union and the Indian Association transmitted resolutions of support for Naoroji and Ghosh, expressing gratitude to Holborn and Deptford for considering their candidacies. From Agra and Karachi, correspondents reported "enthusiastic" public meetings. Locals in Dhulia (Dhule) and Ratnagiri organized more public demonstrations of support, while further south, the inland town of Dharwar hosted a "monster and influential meeting of more than 2,000 people." Malabari transmitted these reports to Naoroji, who incorporated them into his final campaign speeches. Through the Telegraphic Union, he also sent the reports to major British dailies and press associations, adding that the demonstrations represented all parts of India and all communities. Consequently, Naoroji's name—and the ringing endorsements he received from across India—appeared in numerous British papers in early July, ranging from the *Pall Mall Gazette* and *Daily News* of London to local broadsheets in Yorkshire and Devon.[36]

Just before the polling day for Holborn, July 5, there were some encouraging signs. The *Daily News* reported that Naoroji was receiving "an increasing amount of support for his candidature." Henry Hyndman agreed with the assessment. "It is a pity you have not more time as you certainly gain ground as you go along," he wrote to Naoroji after attending an evening rally. In the last few days of campaigning, Naoroji stepped up his efforts. He knocked on electors' doors in the daylight hours and held multiple open-air meetings each evening, shuttling between different corners of Holborn and other areas of London until well after 10:00 P.M.[37]

But it was still not enough. According to the official tally, ready by the early morning hours of July 6, the Tory incumbent, Francis Duncan, polled 3,651 votes, while Naoroji mustered 1,950 (the small voter tallies were the result of franchise restrictions and markedly low voter turnout). In light of electoral trends across the country, the defeat was hardly surprising. Once the staggered general election came to an end in late July, the Gladstonian Liberals had been utterly routed, defeated by an alliance of Conservatives and breakaway Liberal Unionists that had stood firmly against Irish home rule. "The present defeat is entirely general of the Gladstonian party," Naoroji wrote to Malabari on July 23.[38]

Holborn was, indeed, a "forlorn hope," but Naoroji emerged from the general elections as a much stronger contender for a future race. He had polled a decent number in spite of being a foreign figure and a complete outsider in the constituency. While on the campaign trail, he had leveraged connections with Liberal and Irish leaders, and had consequently built up a popular following in central London. "The Irish and the working men I think did fairly well for me," he remarked about the Holborn electorate. And Naoroji had generated a great deal of publicity, both through his outspokenness on Irish affairs and through the demonstrations of support in India that had been orchestrated by the Congress. Hyndman had observed as much when he penned a short note to Naoroji just before voting commenced. "You have made a gallant fight; you have got your name well before the political world; you will, I am sure, poll well, even if you do not win," he wrote. "Win or lose, you have made an excellent propaganda for India in the heart of London, besides being certain of a seat next time."[39]

My Work Is Here

With the general elections behind him, Dadabhai Naoroji weighed two possible courses of action. He could return to India—at least for the short term—and take a wider role in the work of the Congress. Gulbai, Ardeshir, Shirin, Maki, and other family members anxiously held out hope for this possibility ("You feel lonely and I do the same here," Naoroji wrote in one homeward letter, making a rare, understated acknowledgment of the emotional cost of prolonged separation). Conversely, he could stay on in the United Kingdom in order to not waste a minute preparing for the next opportunity to enter the Commons. The choice seemed obvious to

Naoroji. "Every day advices and conviction force themselves upon me that my work is here, and more so because there is nobody else here, European or Indian, to do this work," he wrote to William Wedderburn from London. "The labours of the last National Congress of Bombay, or of any other similar Congress, cannot bear any fruit unless there is somebody here to work for and support them. For all the objects resolved upon in that Congress can be attained only here."[40]

Some members of the Congress's inner circle in India, however, had a different perspective. In the months after the Holborn defeat, they increasingly began to resent Naoroji's insistence on staying in Britain. "From this distance it is difficult to judge, but for the most part we regret your determination to remain in England," Wedderburn replied from Poona. "There is so much work to be done here & no one so well fitted to do it as yourself." Malabari claimed that Naoroji's absence was taking a visible toll on the Congress. "You are the only cohesive plaster for the body politic with its numerous disintegrating diseases," he argued. "*All* have confidence in you—which few have in few others. Splendid opportunities are going by for lack of organized action." While Malabari agreed that the Congress must train its focus on Parliament, he reminded his friend that necessary logistical, financial, and organizational work could only be carried out in India. Naoroji, in sum, had to be in two places at once. "The trouble is we are unable to help you in the good cause without your being here helping us to help the country."[41]

Other Congress members offered far blunter criticism. In September 1886, Malabari warned Naoroji that two of the inner circle's best legal minds, K. T. Telang and Pherozeshah Mehta, were deeply unhappy about his continued absence from Bombay. They expressed their unhappiness in sharper terms some months later, when Malabari called on them at their respective houses. "Telang has no belief in your mission to England," he informed Naoroji. "You are wanted here, he says. With this as his *conviction*, it was useless proceeding with arguments." Mehta—interrupted during his bath—"showed himself more firm even than Telang in his *conviction*."[42]

However, by the middle of 1887, Naoroji was receiving help, of sorts, from unexpected quarters in winning over his critics. Ripon's successor as viceroy, Lord Dufferin, who had originally welcomed the foundation of the Congress, began turning against the organization. In Bombay, rumors circulated about the government's intentions to discourage higher education for Indians and rein in the powers of the city's municipal corporation, an emerging forum for Indian political assertiveness. Meanwhile, in Madras, the governor, Mountstuart Elphinstone Grant-Duff, was busy distinguishing himself as one of the most unpopular Anglo-Indian officials in living memory. Prospects for reform in India looked even grimmer. These developments convinced members of the inner circle to renew their faith in Naoroji's parliamentary ambitions. "I am therefore even more convinced than before that the hope of India lies on your side," Dinsha Wacha wrote to Naoroji. There was no point in trying to reason with reactionary officials such as Dufferin, whom Wacha described as being "as vindictive as a woman." Allan Octavian Hume, in equally colorful language, offered the view that "his lordship is an ass, & a weak & touchy ass to boot."[43]

With opposition from inner circle members receding, Naoroji stepped up his activities in London. He already possessed enough name recognition and connections to secure a Liberal nomination in some constituency or another. But in order to get nominated for a truly competitive seat—one where he had a fighting chance—Naoroji needed to do more. From the late 1880s onward, Naoroji began forging ties with a variety of progressive constituencies in Great Britain. He sought support from anti-imperialists and colonial critics as well as from camps more removed from colonial affairs, ranging from religious non-conformists and positivists to anti-vivisectionists and temperance advocates. Aside from Irish nationalists, his emerging coalition relied on two important constituencies. One consisted of the working class and its socialist and trade unionist advocates. The other—somewhat unexpectedly, since they were denied the vote—consisted of female suffragists and women's rights activists. Naoroji labored to connect these various causes to the struggle for Indian political reform, stressing commonalities across disparate movements. Consequently, he developed a distinct politics of empathy, one that put him at the center of networks with various progressive causes.

Irish home rule continued to dominate the headlines in spite of Gladstone's defeat. Increasingly, Naoroji tried to raise the prominence of Indian political demands through direct association with the Irish cause.

"The Irish question naturally brings into the front the Indian question," he wrote to Wedderburn in late August 1886, "and we must be ready and on spot to take every favourable opportunity to push on the Indian question as far as we can." Consequently, Naoroji joined Irish organizations, such as the United Kingdom Home Rule League, and, as he informed Wacha, began an extensive course of study of Irish history.[44]

He also took an increasingly prominent role in Irish rallies and demonstrations. In June 1888, for example, Naoroji presided at a large meeting in Clerkenwell protesting the imprisonment of John Dillon, the nationalist leader who was behind a prolonged campaign of land agitation in Ireland. Around two months later, Naoroji presided at another Irish meeting, where he confessed to the audience that he could not understand how the British, "the most strenuous advocates of self government," had for more than seven hundred years "made every possible effort to exterminate the Irish people instead of making them feel as brethren." When Charles Conybeare, a radical Liberal MP, was arrested for giving bread to dispossessed tenants in Donegal—a crime under the draconian Irish Coercion Act—Naoroji, not surprisingly, figured among his core group of supporters. In short, Naoroji labored to demonstrate his thorough commitment to Ireland and Irish causes, a commitment that extended well beyond the 1886 home rule bill.[45]

These activities succeeded in catching the attention of the Irish nationalist leadership. In May 1888, Michael Davitt—who in 1883 had privately floated the idea of Naoroji standing for an Irish seat—revived the possibility of an Indian MP for Ireland. Significantly, he did so in a very public manner, while stressing Irish-Indian solidarity. Writing to the *Freeman's Journal*, Ireland's leading newspaper and a nationalist organ, Davitt proposed that Naoroji stand from an open seat in Sligo, on the island's northwestern coast. "What I write to you, sir, to propose is, that Ireland shall give in Westminster what England denies in India to these myriads of our fellow-sufferers—a direct vote and voice," Davitt addressed the paper's editor. The Irish, he held, must make common cause with the Indian struggle for political rights:

A proposal of this kind may, at first sight, appear to ask too much from an Irish Nationalist constituency; but I venture the opinion that the more it is pondered over the more strongly will it recommend itself to every Irishman who is anxious to win for his country a reputation for active sympathy with every people "rightly struggling to be free," while every Nationalist who hates and despises the butchering and plundering rule of England should be glad of any and every opportunity to help the friends of liberty or to strengthen the hands of the enemies of oppression.

Naoroji, Davitt reminded readers, was "honestly devoted to the cause of Home Rule," and would thereby become a vocal pro-Irish nationalist voice in the Commons. The prospective Indian candidate, furthermore, had pledged himself to support and vote with Parnell.[46]

Naoroji appears to have been an enthusiastic collaborator in Davitt's scheme. Shortly after the *Freeman's Journal* ran the letter, he wrote a short note to Parnell, offering to meet and enclosing biographical material. Parnell seems to have been receptive to the idea of Naoroji standing from Sligo. But there were mixed reactions from other quarters. George Birdwood was horrified, arguing that Naoroji's alignment with Parnell would taint the Congress with Irish radicalism. "Let it never come to accepting the patronage of Parnellites—never—never—never," he cautioned his old friend. "Give up your Parliamentary career rather." Some Congress leaders, as Malabari informed Naoroji from Bombay, evidently agreed with Birdwood's assessment. "It will doubtless help you with the Irish, but will make you unpopular with the English official class, here and in England, who will say the Indians wish to take up the Irish role," Malabari worried. "You give our enemies a handle." Wacha, meanwhile, despaired that "Dadabhai and Davitt will become synonymous, one for fomenting Indian and the other for the Irish rebellion." To the relief of Birdwood, Malabari, Wacha, and others in the Congress, no formal offer materialized from Sligo. By mid-July, Naoroji confided to Malabari that there was "*very little, if any, chance*" of him getting an Irish seat. This turn of events, however, had no appreciable effect on Naoroji's interest in Ireland—he continued to weave home rule into his speeches and writings. And in late August 1889, Naoroji may even have joined a special Home Rule League delegation to Dublin. Thus, while Davitt's proposal fizzled, Naoroji still benefited handsomely from the press coverage and a direct association with the top brass of the home rule party.[47]

Similar to the Irish, the working class was emerging as an important voting demographic in urban British constituencies. While suffrage in Britain had long remained a highly limited privilege, subject to certain property qualifications, the Third Reform Act of 1884 had given the vote to many laborers, and had amplified their voice through the redistribution of constituencies. Significantly, their enfranchisement and empowerment occurred as labor unions and socialist organizations gained ground. Partly due to his long association with Henry Hyndman, Naoroji was familiar with both socialists and the labor movement. Holborn had given Naoroji further exposure: Henry Hyde Champion helped him reach out to working-class voters, and in the local Liberal association Naoroji befriended Sidney Webb, the leading light of the Fabian Society.[48]

Naoroji now worked to actively identify himself as a champion of labor and a supporter of certain socialist causes. At public demonstrations, his name increasingly appeared on the speakers' roster alongside some of the most prominent socialist and labor voices of the day. Among those sharing the platform with Naoroji at a November 1888 rally at Clerkenwell Green—a favored venue for radical protests—were William Morris, the famous designer and founder of the Socialist League; Eleanor Marx Aveling, a labor and women's rights activist, as well as the daughter of Karl Marx; and Robert Bontine Cunninghame Graham, the first openly socialist MP and a founder of the Scottish Labour Party (and eventually the Scottish National Party). The following month, Hyndman's Social Democratic Federation booked Naoroji as a speaker at a midnight rally for unemployed Londoners. Naoroji was once more in esteemed company: fellow speakers included John Burns, the militant labor leader, and a young Annie Besant, a recent convert to socialist thought who would later become an outspoken leader in the Indian nationalist movement. Naoroji, therefore, had adeptly maneuvered himself into the front ranks of British socialism.[49]

Before these audiences, Naoroji declared his support for a handful of policy proposals designed to ameliorate the conditions of the British working class. He championed free education, fairer workers' contracts, the eight-hour workday, and a "free breakfast table"—the abolition of duties on essential foodstuffs. He condemned how "the rich became richer, and the poor poorer," and asserted the need for "a better distribution of wealth." In October 1888, Naoroji turned to Sidney Webb for coaching on rent and land policy, subsequently delivering two speeches that broached the hot-button topics of land redistribution and land nationalization. While cautioning against direct confiscation of land, he condemned the avarice of the landed aristocracy, citing John Stuart Mill to argue that laborers were the rightful owners of the soil upon which they worked. "There should be some compulsion," Naoroji believed, "by which the land should provide food in sufficient abundance for the people to live upon it."[50]

In a related vein, Naoroji endorsed the Lockean concept of property in labor; that is, the ownership rights of producers of material goods. Elaborating on this idea in an 1890 pamphlet, "The Rights of Labour," he advocated the creation of special industrial courts to ensure that laborers received a fair share of profits from their employers. He rejected certain principles of classical economics: the laborer's fair share, Naoroji maintained, could not be adduced from the price of a good, but was rather the product of "the practical facts of the social resistances and frictions of people's necessities and circumstances." Industrial courts, Naoroji believed, should be given extensive powers to determine such needs and circumstances, as well as to investigate costs of production. Trade unions, he continued, could closely assist in the work of these courts.[51]

In his speeches and writings directed to the British working class, Naoroji made no explicit references to Indian labor. But he did not hesitate to bring Indian political grievances to the attention of laborers and labor leaders. For example, Naoroji actively courted John Burns's support of Indian political reform, sending him copies of Congress publications. "The information contained therein has whetted my appetite for more," Burns enthusiastically replied after reading the report of the Congress's 1887 Madras session. In time, Naoroji found many more sympathizers for Indian reform among labor leaders, including James Keir Hardie, a key founder of the Labour Party.[52]

Naoroji also made frequent reference to Indian grievances in his talks to working-class audiences. While addressing skyrocketing unemployment rates in central London, he assured listeners that "however deep the poverty was here they could form no conception of what it was in India." Here he employed an innovative method to drive home his point. Britain, he contended, also suffered from a drain of wealth, a drain that was caused by the persistence of poverty in spite of the nation's overall prosperity. Poverty exacted social and financial tolls in various ways. British authorities, for instance, spent vast sums every year prosecuting petty criminals, many of whom were poor laborers. Poor rates—taxes levied in order provide some meager support to the burgeoning underclass—drained wealth away from property owners. Added to these expenses were general losses of production and consumption. Finally, the liquor trade—which profited overwhelmingly from the poor's misfortunes—dissolved more than £13 million annually that could otherwise be deployed for more productive uses. Naoroji let his audience reflect on how the drain of wealth in India—so much larger and so much more invidious—caused an unending spiral of social problems and deeper impoverishment for an already destitute people.[53] Through such stark comparisons, he pulled at the heartstrings of British electors, especially those newly enfranchised working-class voters who were familiar with the curse of poverty. Perhaps they, like the Irish, could sympathize with Indians and extend a hand of support.

Naoroji's emerging progressive coalition, therefore, embraced two large and influential blocs in the political landscape of Victorian Britain: the working class and the Irish. The third constituency in this coalition was a small but dedicated band of women's rights activists and female suffragists. The Parsi politician was a committed supporter of women's voting rights. In an interview with the *Daily Graphic*, he identified women's suffrage as "the most important" issue that had been left out of the Liberal Party's platform. Naoroji's associations with women's rights activists dated from much earlier than his alliances with the Irish or laborers: they were a natural outgrowth of his leadership in female education and social reform during the Young Bombay period, in the late 1840s and early 1850s. Since the worlds of Indian social reform and British feminism overlapped, Naoroji was most likely familiar with many suffragists well before his return to London in 1886. This overlap, furthermore, enabled the prospective Liberal candidate to forge especially strong links between the causes of British women and the campaign for Indian political rights.[54]

One particular social reform endeavor facilitated some of the first ties. Shortly after the Holborn defeat, Naoroji joined hands with women's rights activists in order to protest the draconian Contagious Diseases (C.D.) Acts in India. First implemented in 1868, the C.D. Acts were meant to counter spiraling rates of syphilis and other venereal diseases among soldiers of the British Indian army by giving sweeping powers to the government to register and compulsorily examine prostitutes as well as so-called kept women. Given the difficulty of defining who, precisely, fit into these categories, many Indian social reformers roundly condemned the acts, arguing that they transgressed upon the privacy and liberties of Indian women. Meanwhile, in London, Naoroji found a ready ally in Josephine Butler. Butler, one of the most prominent British social reformers of the Victorian era, had earlier worked with Florence Nightingale to overturn the United Kingdom's own C.D. Acts and was now secretary of the International Federation for the Abolition of State Regulation of Vice, which crusaded against similar legislation across western Europe.[55]

Naoroji and Butler's alliance was mutually beneficial. For Butler, Naoroji provided a vital link to the Indian political elite. In December 1887, for example, the International Federation formally requested that Naoroji coordinate an organized movement for repeal of the C.D. Acts among the "leading natives of India." "We believe that no one could be more powerful than you in assisting to produce such an expression of opinion," Butler and her associates declared. Naoroji did not disappoint. As the secretary of state for India began to consider the possible repeal of the acts, Naoroji reached out to Malabari, Wacha, and Hume, stressing the need for concerted action among Indian political associations. After all, "what can all our struggles to improve the position of woman be worth if she is publicly and legally declared to be only worth satisfying the vice of man," he asked Malabari. Significantly, Naoroji remained committed to the cause of the International Federation well after the C.D. Acts were suspended in July 1888. The following year, in the middle of September, he traveled to Geneva in order to serve as a delegate to its congress.[56]

Naoroji's association with Josephine Butler appears to have facilitated further involvement with women's rights activities in Britain. By the 1890s, for example, he was serving as a vice president of two major feminist associations, the Women's Progressive Society, a socialist organization that targeted parliamentary candidates opposed to women's suffrage, and the International Women's Union, which had members in the United States and Europe as well as in India, Persia, Brazil, and Japan. Naoroji also had a long-standing association with the Women's Franchise League, which was led by some of the most prominent suffragists of the late Victorian era, including Elizabeth Clarke Wolstenholme Elmy, Emmeline Pankhurst, and Ursula Bright. He was a member of the league's council and was regularly sought by Elmy and Bright to speak in public. In 1890, for example, he delivered a lecture on the condition of Indian women at a major conference organized by the league, the International Conference on the Position of Women in All Countries, held at Westminster Town Hall. A draft program for this conference lists Naoroji, remarkably, alongside Rukhmabai, the Indian child bride who had kicked up a legal storm in Bombay after refusing to cohabit with her husband, and Elizabeth Cady Stanton, the American suffragist, as distinguished attendees.[57]

By the early 1890s, therefore, Naoroji was part of a broad network of feminist leaders and organizations—one that embraced women's activists and prominent sympathizers from across the world. But what advantages, precisely, did the prospective candidate derive from his association with people who still did not possess the vote? First, just as Butler relied on Naoroji for access to Indian leaders during the anti–C.D. Acts agitation, Naoroji benefited from feminists' access to prominent radical Liberals and major public opinion makers. Ursula Bright, for instance, was the wife of a sitting MP, Joseph Bright, and the sister-in-law of John Bright. Mynie and Tina Bell—the widow and daughter, respectively, of Naoroji's old ally in the cause of princely state autonomy, Evans Bell, and ardent suffragists in their own right—inducted Naoroji into their wide circle of activist and freethinker friends, which included George Jacob Holyoake, leader of the secularist movement, who later gave public support to Naoroji during his Central Finsbury campaign. And in early 1888, as Naoroji stepped up his efforts to find a suitable constituency, Butler helped reintroduce Naoroji to T. P. O'Connor, the Irish MP and journalist. Naoroji profited from this important connection between a feminist and an Irish leader. O'Connor, Butler recounted, subsequently declared to her that "we must get Mr. Naoroji into Parliament." Disenfranchised women, therefore, were vital facilitators in Naoroji's efforts to cobble together support from a variety of constituencies that did possess the vote.[58]

Second, Naoroji found feminists to be especially receptive to the cause of Indian political reform. The lack of the vote, the absence of absolute legal rights, and the utter nonexistence of any form of representation no doubt played a major role in fostering empathy and a sense of common cause between the two movements. Surviving correspondence indicates that Naoroji very deliberately tried to provoke interest in India among his feminist contacts. In December 1886, for example, he began sending his papers and essays to Josephine Butler. Butler was greatly moved by the issues of Indian poverty and misgovernance, comparing the situation to that in Ireland. She quickly promised to write letters to the *Liverpool Daily Post, Newcastle Leader,* and other Liberal papers, advocating immediate reforms for India. Significantly, Butler also began querying Naoroji on touchy historical subjects—such as the "morality" of the British conquest of India and the chief reasons for the Mutiny of 1857—indicating that Naoroji helped nudge along her growing skepticism about imperialism. A little over a year later, Butler was still writing to Naoroji about her journalistic activities—this time her attempts to counsel the influential editor of the *Pall Mall Gazette,* William T. Stead, to be more sympathetic toward Indian political matters.[59]

Historians have argued that when it came to Indian social reform, British feminists' activities were shot through with colonial and social Darwinist prejudices. They were, in their own ways, the handmaidens of empire.[60] But Naoroji's correspondence helps us see matters slightly differently. While certain prejudices were no doubt evident, it is quite clear that many women's rights activists were also motivated by a deep sense of injustice, whether that injustice was found at home or in Britain's imperial domains, and were not solely bound by imperial considerations. Butler, for example, adopted and espoused Naoroji's equation between the rights of British women and the rights of Indians, suggesting an almost universal struggle for justice. She saw Naoroji's political career as a reflection of this struggle:

> It has long been very much on my heart that you should gain a seat in Parliament, and I should like to add my little word of testimony

to others which you have received in regard to the confidence we have in you. It is not so much as a mere Liberal that I hope for your election, but because you are one of the most uncompromising friends of womanhood. You have already upheld the necessity of equal law for men and women, and your moving appeals on several occasions at our meetings have sunk deeply into our hearts. We have at this moment more than ever painfully the interests of your country women and our fellow-subjects in India on our hearts and I hope that our efforts may result before long in a greater measure of legal justice for the women of India. Your clear insight into all that is false and unequal in our British laws regarding women has not been, to my mind, surpassed in any instance, even of our own countrymen experienced in these matters.[61]

By pursuing a politics of empathy, premised on a shared sense of injustice, Naoroji won allies among diverse constituencies and placed India within the ranks of the leading progressive causes in late Victorian Britain. Consequently, in the years after Holborn, he helped promote a surge of interest in Indian political affairs among Britons. Finally, and importantly, as Butler's comments indicate, he also won some valuable, well-connected friends who were eager to see Naoroji elected to Parliament during the next general election.

Black Man

During the 1880s, with the expansion of the franchise and the birth of mass politics, Great Britain passed through an especially fruitful moment of reformist activity, one in which various progressive causes overlapped and converged. Within this convergence lay great opportunities for an Indian leader to build political alliances. Dadabhai Naoroji's allies, after all, included the old guard of anti-slavery activists, men like Frederick W. Chesson, who now turned their attention to Indian reform; longtime India reformers, such as Evans Bell, who were involved in the secularist movement; secularists, most notably George Jacob Holyoake, who moved in suffragist circles; and suffragists, especially Josephine Butler, who possessed Irish home ruler contacts. Henry Hyndman appeared to know everyone. The 1880s were, furthermore, a moment of many firsts in Westminster—a direct consequence of the parliamentary reforms of 1884. T. P. O'Connor's election in 1885 made him the first-ever Irish Catholic MP returned by an English constituency. The first openly socialist MP, Robert Bontine Cunninghame Graham, took his seat in the Commons in 1888. Charles Bradlaugh, an avowed atheist, became the first individual to sit in Parliament without taking a religious oath. An Indian candidate was still a far more unexpected figure than an Irish Catholic, socialist, or atheist, but electors appeared open to new possibilities. Congress leaders in the subcontinent, who closely monitored political developments among their colonial masters, were savvy enough to recognize these shifting dynamics. And they were shrewd enough to see the potential for advancing a reformist Indian agenda through these expanding networks among progressive causes.

Thus by the late 1880s, Naoroji, and his views on Indian politics, had become quite well known within British activist circles and among the political elite. But something much more significant was happening: Naoroji was developing popular recognition among the British public. His name—albeit frequently and creatively misspelled—appeared with more regularity in the columns of British newspapers; his pamphlets and writings circulated widely and gained greater readership; his speaking invitations increasingly emanated from locations far removed from the imperial capital. Even the *Times* grudgingly admitted that Naoroji was now a "well-known" personality. But it was none other than Lord Salisbury, the Conservative prime minister, who truly illustrated the extent to which the Indian leader had shot to national prominence. At noon on November 29, 1888, Salisbury began addressing a large audience that had assembled in Edinburgh's Corn Exchange. In the course of a long and rambling speech, the prime minister, accomplished in the art of making verbal gaffes, alluded to the 1886 contest in Holborn:

> Colonel Duncan was opposed to a black man (laughter), and, however great the progress of mankind has been and however far we have advanced in overcoming prejudices, I doubt if we have yet got to that point where a British constituency will elect a black man to represent them. (Laughter.) Of course, you will understand that I am speaking roughly and using language in its ordinary colloquial

"COLOURABLE SHAKSPEARIAN IMITATION."

Othello, M.P. for Central Finsbury (saluting Sarum, Doge of Vestminster). "Haply that I am
Black——" [Doge shudders, but feels unable to withdraw.]

A *Punch* cartoon from July 1892 of a "black man" in the House of Commons. Naoroji,
recently elected as an MP, is satirized as Othello, while Lord Salisbury, now out of power,
is the "Doge of Vestminster." Nearly four years after the "black man incident," London
papers and magazines continued to make productive use of Salisbury's verbal gaffe.
Punch, July 23, 1892, p. 33. Reproduced from Widener Library, Harvard University.

sense, because I imagine the colour is not exactly black; but at all
events he was a man of another race who was very unlikely to represent an English community.[62]

Thus transpired the "black man incident," which kicked off a furious
storm of protest in Britain and India. Through this jibe, Salisbury did not
simply acknowledge public recognition of Naoroji, but inadvertently did
the Parsi politician a tremendous favor by greatly enhancing it. In the days
and weeks that followed, the prime minister and the so-called black man
were splashed across the pages of newspapers and journals from Dublin
to Calcutta. The *Pall Mall Gazette* expressed shock and dismay, recom-
mending that Salisbury lather his tongue with Pears soap; the *Weekly*

Dispatch joined several other broadsheets in finding Naoroji utterly unworthy of the insult; the *Daily News* fretted over how this would deepen Indian grievances about British rule; and *Punch* had a grand time satirizing the fallout. Far too many column-inches of print were spent debating whether the Parsi candidate was, in fact, lighter in complexion than the swarthy prime minister. Regardless, the black man incident achieved something for which Naoroji had long struggled: truly wide-ranging, favorable, and sympathetic press coverage. From faraway Bombay, Behramji Malabari marveled at how "our adversaries are often our best friends."[63]

Critically, many newspapers wondered how the black man incident would impact Naoroji's chances at the next general election. And it was the *Freeman's Journal,* the home ruler periodical in which Michael Davitt had suggested Naoroji's nomination for an Irish seat, which made the boldest prediction. "One result of Lord Salisbury's insulting taunt is that Mr. Naoroji is almost certain to be returned to Parliament at the next general election," the paper declared. "This, indeed, is the only real reparation that can be made to the Indian people."[64] Amid similarly encouraging pronouncements from friends and allies, Naoroji now set course for a new campaign in a new constituency, Central Finsbury.

CHAPTER 4

An Indian Emissary in
the Heart of Empire

EARLY IN THE MORNING of January 2, 1891, Dadabhai Naoroji might have been rudely woken up by a telegram from the London police. Sometime the previous evening, a C. K. Desai—one of hundreds of Indians resident in Great Britain as students, professionals, or menial laborers—was arrested for public drunkenness and thrown in a cell at the Vine Street police station. It was here, around 1:00 A.M., that Desai dictated a brief telegram to a police inspector indicating that he wanted Naoroji to post his bail.[1]

We do not know if Naoroji complied with his poor, hung-over compatriot's request, nor do we know if C. K. Desai even knew Naoroji personally. But the telegram from the London police, now brittle with age, is much more than a bizarre historical find. It is part of a large trove of material in Naoroji's private correspondence that allows for a detailed, vivid reconstruction of British Indian life in the late Victorian era. Out of the thirty thousand or so documents that survive in this collection, the overwhelming majority of items date from Naoroji's last period of residence in London, from 1886 until 1907. This includes around two thousand letters to or from recognized Indian political figures—Behramji Malabari, Dinsha Wacha, William Wedderburn, and others. A few hundred additional items consist of correspondence with prominent social and political figures in Britain. But the rest of the correspondence involves

individuals who, like C. K. Desai, are for the most part completely forgotten today: fellow British Indians as well as minor Liberal Party functionaries, leaders and secretaries of social and fraternal organizations,
doctors, booksellers, journalists, and ordinary Britons.

These letters indicate precisely how Naoroji's career unfolded in the
heart of the British Empire—and the methods he employed to advocate
India's interests. They demonstrate how Naoroji took on myriad social
and cultural responsibilities in addition to his political tasks. Well before
the black man incident with Lord Salisbury propelled the prospective MP
to the front pages of British dailies, he was publicly recognized as a
spokesman and authority on subjects related to India and Indians. As
early as the 1860s, Naoroji began playing the role of an Indian emissary:
a resource for Britons on political and cultural issues, a leader in organizations advocating Indian interests, and an outspoken critic of contemporary racial attitudes toward his co-nationals. This was a role that
he fine-tuned after returning from Bombay to London in 1886.

Due to the sheer volume of correspondence dating from his parliamentary campaigns and early Congress work in Britain, we can also observe
how Naoroji became an active participant in the vibrant British public
sphere. He joined numerous social, fraternal, and political associations
that, while having no direct link to Indian political affairs, nevertheless
helped him enhance his political and social standing. By wading through
Naoroji's miscellanea—thousands of ordinary receipts, subscription notices, and circulars—we can reconstruct the specific networks within
which he operated. Moreover, such miscellanea tell us about Naoroji's
daily itineraries and the routine operations of his candidacies and early
Congress activities—the everyday life of political leaders and political
movements. Advocating Indian interests in the imperial capital was an
arduous endeavor. It required marathon schedules of letter writing, endless cycles of meetings and appointments, close coordination with colleagues scattered around India, deft networking within local branches of
the Liberal Party and numerous other associations, and constant travel.
This was a schedule that Naoroji maintained into his early eighties, although it took a noticeable toll on his health. Analysis of this everyday
life reveals how early Indian nationalism was not simply a matter of

abstract high politics: it was a movement sustained by a furious stream of on-the-ground activity.

Finally, within Naoroji's correspondence, we are introduced to hundreds of C. K. Desai's fellow British Indians. During his nearly five decades of residence in Great Britain, Naoroji created networks and organizations that gave this emerging community—composed of Indians from different regional, religious, and linguistic backgrounds—a sense of cohesion. Letters from countless British Indians indicate how Naoroji was acknowledged as a community leader. Students and professionals turned to him for mentorship, advice, and financial assistance. He was also the first point of contact for many visitors from the subcontinent as well as other diasporic settlements. Naoroji's office and drawing room hosted a dazzling array of guests: Anagarika Dharmapala, the Buddhist revivalist from Ceylon; Prafulla Chandra Roy, the eminent chemistry professor and entrepreneur from Calcutta; Sister Nivedita, Swami Vivekananda's Irish-born disciple; and, finally, Mohandas K. Gandhi, who benefited from Naoroji's political connections while lobbying colonial officials in London in 1906. Letters from these individuals show, once more, how Naoroji was much more than a political figure. While in Britain, he performed many roles for many different people, well beyond that of a potential stand-in for the bail bondsman.

The Time for This Excuse Is Gone

What roles did Parsis and other Western-educated Indian elites play in colonial society? Several historians have lumped them together under the rather unflattering banner of "mediators" and "interpreters" for British rulers—or, more darkly, "compradors" and "collaborators."[2] Yet these characterizations can be a little misleading. Admittedly, there were a number of wealthy, Anglicized Parsis—their chests brimming with imperial medallions, their names suffixed with CIE or KCIE—who at least proclaimed themselves to be fulfilling roles as mediators and interpreters, and who by the early twentieth century were making ridiculous suggestions that they shared more affinities with Englishmen than with their fellow Indian neighbors, friends, and business partners.

But there was a marked difference between rhetoric and reality. The labels of "interpreter" and "mediator" presume a certain neutrality and detachedness on the part of elites, traits that they might very well express in published English works for a British readership. However, upon further examination of private correspondence, it is clear that many such elites were firmly embedded within the broader currents of Indian society, quite regularly affirming their Indian identity and a sense of patriotism. This is the case for a supposedly confirmed cultural mediator such as the Parsi social reformer Behramji Malabari, and it is certainly so for Dadabhai Naoroji.[3] Naoroji and the many other Indian elites who closely interacted with Britons, both in India and in England, played far more nuanced and complex roles. We might better think of them as emissaries. Aside from advocacy of Indian political interests, they promoted knowledge of Indian society and culture, facilitated Indians' contact with British elites, and supported certain economic endeavors. They were sought after by Britons interested in the politics, business environment, history, cultures, and religions of the subcontinent. During the late Victorian and early Edwardian eras, Naoroji was, unquestionably, India's chief emissary in the United Kingdom.

Naoroji first took on this role through his work as an educator. While employed at the Cama family firm in London and Liverpool during the late 1850s, the former Elphinstone professor—like his business partner and Young Bombay colleague K. R. Cama—distinguished himself for his ability to be easily distracted from commercial matters. In 1859, Cama traded the countinghouse for the classroom, plunging into the world of ancient Iranian studies and working under some of its leading scholars at European universities. Naoroji, although he did not fully cease mercantile activities, also made forays into the Western academy, once more taking up the duties of a professor. In March 1856, he was appointed as professor of Gujarati at University College in London. In this capacity, Naoroji soon became the Gujarati examiner for Indian civil service candidates, where he sat alongside the orientalist Friedrich Max Müller, who tested candidates' Sanskrit abilities, and the legal scholar Henry Maine, who administered papers on law.[4] Naoroji was, consequently, quickly drawn into circles that included some of the most prominent thinkers and scholars of the Victorian era. He joined leading institutions such as the

Royal Asiatic Society, the Liverpool Athenaeum, and the London Ethnological Society. Within these societies, he emerged as an academic and eventually popular authority on all matters subcontinental.

In 1861, Naoroji was invited by two Liverpool societies to address British audiences. His talks were, appropriately, on his own community, the Parsis, and its recent experiments with social and religious reform. On March 13, 1861, he presented "The Manners and Customs of the Parsees" before the Liverpool Philomathic Society, and then, on March 18, read his paper "The Parsee Religion" to the Liverpool Literary and Philosophical Society. Naoroji provided his audiences with a unique, firsthand account of some of the activities of Young Bombay while also producing his own translations and interpretations of Zoroastrian religious texts. As these were some of the few English-language sources on Zoroastrianism composed by an actual follower of the faith, the papers gained wide popularity in the United Kingdom after they were published as pamphlets. Naoroji's talks were quoted extensively and cited as recommended reading on Zoroastrianism in various books, magazines, and encyclopedias— oftentimes alongside the works of the most prominent Zoroastrian scholars of the time. They also provoked a warm response from Max Müller. Thus, Naoroji continued to be drawn into networks of intellectuals in Great Britain.[5]

These talks could have helped Naoroji launch a promising career in religious studies, perhaps even as a counterpart to his old friend K. R. Cama. But the Liverpool- and London-based cotton trader was far more focused on immediate political concerns. From the mid-1860s onward, he helped create institutional space in the imperial capital for discussion of Indian affairs. Naoroji was an active member of the National Indian Association and the Northbrook Indian Association, two societies that allowed Indians and Britons to socialize, converse, and debate issues on a relatively level playing field. However, his most significant contributions to London's institutional life began in 1866, when he founded the East India Association. This association constituted "the most ambitious attempt ever made to set up a comprehensive organization in London of all those who took any interest in India."[6] Aside from its political mission—lobbying MPs on Indian policy—the East India Association was designed to promote general knowledge of the country and its inhabitants, serving almost like a cultural bureau. Naoroji stocked its Westminster premises with an extensive library and promoted the association as a clearinghouse for information on India, a resource for the public as well as Parliament.

The body's membership reflected its diverse functions. The East India Association brought together British Indian officials and Indian political leaders—for example, Lord Salisbury, then secretary of state for India, and Navrozji Fardunji, who regularly launched salvos against the India Office. It was a testing ground of early nationalist cooperation, providing a platform for a younger generation of leaders that included Pherozeshah Mehta, Mahadev Govind Ranade, and Romesh Chunder Dutt. But Naoroji also recruited a galaxy of other individuals. There were industrialists like Jamsetji Tata of Bombay and Ranchhodlal Chhotalal of Ahmedabad; scholars such as the Calcutta native Rajendralal Mitra, a noted historian and Indologist, and Ramakrishna Gopal Bhandarkar, Naoroji's former pupil at Elphinstone; journalists including Robert Knight of the *Times of India* and Kristodas Pal of the *Hindoo Patriot;* and educators and social reformers like Sayyid Ahmad Khan and Ishwarchandra Vidyasagar. Several members of the Tagore family were in its ranks—Debendranath, Prasanna Kumar, Jatendra Mohan, and others—as were numerous Indian merchants in Hong Kong. Indian princes rounded out the membership rosters.[7]

For its era, the East India Association was unique in the sense that it did not exclusively draw members from a narrowly defined region—say, Bombay and its hinterlands or Bengal. Politically, it flopped. A conservative Anglo-Indian clique took a jaundiced view of the organization, complaining that it was "too Radical" and therefore needed to be "stamped out rather than patronized." By the early 1870s, this clique wrested control away from Naoroji and his allies, ending any ambitions that it would serve as a progressive political lobby. But through this body Naoroji significantly advanced Indian interests in other ways, putting its leaders, businessmen, cultural figures, and educators in the same social circles as the British elite.[8]

Naoroji did not entirely give up on the idea of a central, London-based institution for Indian political, economic, cultural, and social affairs. After becoming a member in 1886, he made the National Liberal Club, affiliated with the Liberal Party, a locus of India-related activity, ushering a steady stream of subcontinental visitors through its grand entrance hall. Slightly farther down Victoria Embankment, Naoroji helped open the Congress's London office, the British Committee of the Indian National Congress, which became another locus of activity from the late 1880s onward. By this time, however, Naoroji had fully taken on the mantle of Indian emissary and carried out much of this work by himself. Countless Britons wrote to Naoroji seeking information and assistance on matters concerning India. Political issues dominated, not surprisingly: numerous churches, social clubs, guild and fraternal organizations, and political associations invited Naoroji to address their members on the need for Indian political reform. Other bodies, such as the Warwick and Leamington Women's Liberal Association, simply enquired about recommended reading on current Indian affairs.[9]

Yet Indian politics was not the only topic of concern. In November 1892, the secretary of the Society for the Suppression of the Opium Trade asked Naoroji to join their deputation to Lord Kimberley, the secretary of state for India. The society desired "to make China, not India, the prominent subject on this occasion," but felt that Naoroji's participation would give "some indication of the real feeling of educated India on the question" (Naoroji had been a lifelong critic of the opium trade). The following month, James Hole, a member of the Association of Chambers of Commerce of the United Kingdom, asked Naoroji to review his draft book chapter on Indian railways. Hole's fellow businessmen and industrialists flooded the mailbox of India's emissary. A textile manufacturer in Stockport, near Manchester, floated a proposal to harvest rhea (ramie) fiber—"of which there is an unlimited quantity in the Native States"—and start a new textile industry in India, one that could possibly generate stiff competition for English cotton goods. Two young friends from Brixton, meanwhile, sought an appointment with Naoroji to discuss their plans to emigrate to India and enter the building trade. Other correspondents sought diverse forms of assistance. A London publisher, binding several books for India, asked Naoroji to identify the language in which they were written ("sent transliterations of 2 booklets," Naoroji noted in the letter margin). And in the fall of 1889, Naoroji helped a West Kensington Park resident, a Mrs. Pogosky, fulfill her wish of acquiring a vessel of *ganga jal* or holy water from the Ganges.[10]

In addition to letters from the general public, Naoroji was constantly barraged by interview requests from the British media. During his sea voyages to and from India, some enterprising journalists even went to the extent of telegraphing the next port of call of Naoroji's steamer in order to scoop a story on Indian political developments. But, like Pogosky, these writers and newspapermen also reached out to Naoroji on matters of social and cultural interest. On October 22, 1894, Naoroji sat down with W. J. Frost, a reporter from *Chums*, a "high class boys paper," to discuss "What Indian Boys Play At." Frost and Naoroji explored the similarities between Indian and British childhood games: *chandani andhari*, for example, was very similar to tug-of-war, while they discovered that Bombay lads played marbles with different methodologies than their London counterparts. Naoroji grew particularly animated while discussing *chopat*, a board game that was "so exciting that it was played by men as well as boys," and he reminisced about childhood gilli danda matches. But, he concluded, games had changed considerably since his childhood, and "at the present time Indian boys go in largely for English games (cricket especially)."[11]

Four years later, in 1898, the *Vegetarian*—edited by Mohandas K. Gandhi's close friend Josiah Oldfield—interviewed Naoroji about Indian eating habits. The interview was conducted by a man named Raymond Blathwayt, who, incidentally, had earlier relied on Naoroji for procuring certain Indian contacts. It began in a somewhat unusual manner:

> "You are a Vegetarian, I presume, are you not?" I said.
>
> "No," replied Mr. Naoroji, "I am not."
>
> "That's rather awkward!" I said, "because I am not one either."

After this rather unpromising start, Naoroji, claiming that he was too old to give up his meat-eating ways, nevertheless offered a spirited defense of India's vegetarian traditions. "The wonderful thought and philosophy and the highest intellect of India are, I think, due to Vegetarianism," he maintained. When Blathwayt suggested that a lack of meat weakened "both the physical and moral fibre" of Indians, Naoroji shot back at once, debunking this classic imperialist argument. Laborers who carried massive cotton bales in Bombay, after all, "are entirely Vegetarians," while among Brahmins and Buddhists, vegetarianism had cultivated a high moral regard for life. The problem lay instead with the overindulgent Englishman. "The English who go to India eat far too much meat; there is no doubt that they would be stronger and healthier if they took less, and also drunk less, or not at all." In Britain, meanwhile, excessive meat-eating had made people "much more ferocious than is either right or desirable." "And are we here in this world only to fight and grab?" he questioned Blathwayt. "Is that your highest ideal of patriotism?" Naoroji, ever the politically minded individual, could not resist an opportunity to rebuke Britain on its imperialist ways, even within a conversation on dietary habits.[12]

Blathwayt concluded his interview with a discussion of a portrait he saw in Naoroji's possession. It showed the former MP next to Lord Salisbury, with a line of text underneath asking, "Which is the Black Man?"[13] Reference to the notorious black man incident of 1888, as well as Blathwayt's stereotypical assessment of Indian vegetarianism, brings us to one of Naoroji's greatest responsibilities as an Indian emissary: responding to and combating the prejudiced, racist attitudes that many Britons exhibited toward their Indian subjects. While taking on some of the Victorian era's greatest exponents of bigotry, the Indian leader drew heavily upon his own academic training and the scholarly networks he had forged since Young Bombay.

His first foray into Victorian racial politics had taken place as early as 1866, when he delivered a paper titled "The European and Asiatic Races" before the London Ethnological Society. Naoroji's paper constituted a lengthy rebuttal to the rants of the society's octogenarian president, John Crawfurd, a politically influential, self-styled orientalist who, in papers with titles such as "Colour as the Test of the Races of Man," exhibited some of the worst racial prejudices of his time. In spite of his extreme positions, Crawfurd was a formidable opponent: his close friends included men of power and influence such as Mountstuart Elphinstone, Henry Thomas Colebrooke, Wilhelm von Humboldt, and Alexander von Humboldt.[14]

It appears that a lecture Crawfurd delivered on February 13, 1866, "On the Physical and Mental Characteristics of the European and Asiatic Races of Man," particularly riled Naoroji and provoked him to respond. The president of the Ethnological Society declared "Asiatics," broadly defined, to be markedly inferior to Europeans in terms of judgment, taste, imagination, creativity, enterprise, and perseverance. Aside from deploying hackneyed theories of oriental despotism and superior European physical prowess—"The most natural attitude of the European is to stand erect, that of the Asian to sit"—Crawfurd declared that Asian societies lacked some of the basic elements of civilization, such as great literary traditions. He singled out the *Shahnameh,* one of Naoroji's favorite literary sources during his childhood, and claimed that it was simply "a series of wild romances of imaginary heroes, and is of such slender merit that no orientalist has ever ventured on presenting it in a European translation." In a series of sweeping generalizations, Crawfurd also declared that Asians lacked any moral sense, enjoyed no good government, and were habitual polygamists, meting out especially cruel treatment to women.[15]

It took Naoroji a few weeks to produce a suitable rejoinder. Sometime after eight o'clock in the evening of March 27, 1866, he took to the lectern at the Ethnological Society, hammering away at Crawfurd's racial arguments well into the late night hours. By propounding on the innate inferiority of Asians, Crawfurd had made a grave mistake, "one of those which foreign travellers and writers are very apt to fall into from superficial observation and imperfect information." Naoroji ranged about him diverse sources on the histories of Arabia, Persia, India, and China. He spoke of the literature of Kalidasa and Confucius, cited authorities ranging from Strabo to Abu'l Fazl, and assembled parliamentary testimony on current educational advances in India. Jesus, he reminded Crawfurd, was technically an Asian. Delving into contemporary scholarship, he quoted freely from William Jones's work on ancient Indian grammatical analysis, John Malcolm's descriptions of the literary output of ancient Persia, and Andrew Crichton's arguments on the West's indebtedness to Arab science. This careful and detailed research, standing in vivid contrast to Crawfurd's motley collection of stereotypes and crank racial theories, made the former Elphinstone don's rejoinder all the more powerful.[16]

Naoroji, furthermore, skillfully employed one particular intellectual tradition, that of ancient Iran and Zoroastrianism, in order to disprove claims that Crawfurd indiscriminately applied to an entire continent. Here Naoroji had a critical advantage: he possessed immense knowledge of his own religious tradition and, significantly, had built up a wide network of scholarly contacts. He liberally cited from his personal correspondence with these scholars in the course of his paper. In order to address claims about the supposed lack of literary output from Asian civilizations, Naoroji focused on Crawfurd's assault on the *Shahnameh*. He turned to Edward B. Eastwick—an influential voice on Persian affairs, translator of Saʿdi's *Golestan*, and personal friend—who opined that Firdausi's epic poem was on par with Homer's *Iliad*. Refuting Crawfurd's assertion that the *Shahnameh* had merited no proper European translation, Naoroji produced personal correspondence with Julius von Mohl, K. R. Cama's old tutor at the Collège de France and currently the secretary of the Société Asiatique in Paris. Mohl, Naoroji read from a letter, was in the process of producing his fifth volume of a French translation of the *Shahnameh*. The Paris-based scholar also offered a sharp rebuke to Crawfurd's Eurocentric attitudes. "Oriental literature can only take its place in the universal literature of mankind," Naoroji quoted from Mohl's letter, "when intelligent historians show its value for history in its largest sense . . . and show, too, how large has been the past of the East, and how great in some respects its influence."[17]

Naoroji must have been particularly perturbed by Crawfurd's generalized comments on women. Addressing his declarations on the polygamous tendencies of Asians, Naoroji—after asking his opponent to consider the case of Mormonism in the West—pulled out letters from Friedrich Spiegel, the respected professor of oriental languages at Erlangen and another former teacher of K. R. Cama. Spiegel, Naoroji noted, could not find any evidence of polygamy in the Zoroastrian religious texts and agreed with his correspondent that Parsis had always been largely monogamous. Last, in order to draw from another Asian intellectual tradition and thereby argue in favor of the universal value of truthfulness, Naoroji instanced correspondence with his colleague at University College, Theodor Goldstücker, professor of Sanskrit, who pointed to how truth was celebrated, and untruthfulness condemned, in the Rigveda and Yajurveda.[18]

Having offered a defense of Asian civilizations, Naoroji moved in for the attack. He asked his audience to consider how an Asian resident in London for a period of time might perceive European culture and civilization. Cleverly using the observations of an anonymous Parsi friend, Naoroji took the opportunity to elaborate on the many social problems evident in Victorian Britain, problems that rendered hypocritical any claims of Western moral and civilizational superiority. He spoke of the extreme poverty in the cities, the abundance of illicit activities in London, corruption in politics, the duplicitous dealings of merchants, soaring crime rates, and rampant marital infidelity. Moreover, he pointed out, these were the same people who had conquered a nation on the premise of trade, who drew exorbitant revenues from it every year, taxed its people to death, and still managed to claim that they had great moral purpose in ruling India. This Parsi friend, Naoroji claimed, had ultimately concluded that "the only God the English worshipped was gold; they would do anything to get it. . . . If it were discovered that gold existed in human blood, they would manage, with good reasons to boot, to extract it from thence."[19] Given his emerging views about Indian poverty and the drain of wealth, it is possible that Naoroji himself was the anonymous Parsi observer of British life and society. Regardless, he was able to conclude that if Crawfurd could declare Europeans to be superior to Asians, then an Asian could declare London to be the most immoral and hypocritical place on earth.

By the end of the evening's deliberations, Naoroji had decisively turned the tables against John Crawfurd, mobilizing a barrage of evidence to challenge him on his own ground of scholarly authority, within the very society where he was president. The transactions of the Ethnological Society, unfortunately, do not provide us with any idea of Crawfurd's reactions to Naoroji's paper, although one contemporary journal remarked on "the interchange of vigorous and forcible repartees, of a sort not usually encountered in scientific transactions."[20] Naoroji's rejoinder seems to have taken the steam out of the octogenarian president, who delivered a scant few more papers—none of them featuring the vitriol and stark prejudice that marked his earlier rants—before passing away in May 1868.

Crawfurd's death, of course, did not bring to an end racial debates or the Indian emissary's participation in them. As Indian nationalist demands became bolder, prejudicial attitudes in Britain only seemed to worsen. Hardly a month after Crawfurd breathed his last, Naoroji took up Anglo-Indian and British criticism of a petition he had dispatched to the India Office, one that called for the Indianization of the civil service. Perturbed by his critics' allegations that Indians lacked the integrity necessary for positions of power, he urged an audience at the East India Association to "observe a little more around themselves, observe the amount of fraud and 'doing' in this metropolis." How could Britons talk about the integrity of others when there were "convictions for false weights, the puffs of advertisements, the corruption among the 'independent and intelligent electors,'" and many other such sordid examples under their very noses? Some years later, exhausted by the persistence of prejudiced attitudes regarding civil service reform, Naoroji declared before the Hunter Commission on Indian Education that "the time for this excuse of native unfitness and want of command of influence and respect is gone." These were obviously not the words of an impartial mediator or cultural interpreter.[21]

Naoroji continued to combat bigots and bigotry after returning to London in 1886. Barely two months before Lord Salisbury uttered the words "black man" before his Edinburgh audience, Naoroji felt compelled to deliver a talk on Zoroastrianism—a modified version of his 1861 papers—on account of "prejudice raised against me on the score of religion," most likely in relation to his recent nomination as the Liberal candidate for Central Finsbury.[22] The black man incident, therefore, did not occur in isolation. It was part of a long chain of events that put India's emissary at the center of vicious racial politics in Britain.

Artificial Teeth

After arriving in London in mid-April 1886, Dadabhai Naoroji appears to have kept all incoming correspondence, regardless of importance. Consequently, within Naoroji's surviving personal papers, letters of great political importance jostle alongside ordinary commercial receipts, subscription forms, medical prescriptions, random press clippings, and the

nineteenth-century equivalent of junk mail. There is a veritable moun-
tain of miscellanea. We learn from an eyeglass prescription from 1894
that, politics aside, Naoroji really was farsighted. A note from William
Hutchinson & Co., a Charing Cross–based banking firm, informs us that
in October 1901 Naoroji's account was overdrawn by £7.17s.10d.—an embarrassing personal drain of wealth that occurred just a month or so
after his landmark volume *Poverty and Un-British Rule in India* was published. A different sort of drain had plagued Naoroji a few months
earlier: F. W. Ellis, a plumbing contractor from Upper Norwood, gravely
informed him that his toilet was plugged. And shortly after returning
from the 1906 Calcutta Congress, where he had endorsed the swadeshi
movement emanating from Bengal, an octogenarian Naoroji entered into
correspondence with Messrs. Jacobs & Clark of Camden Town for the
purchase of a decisively *videshi* (foreign) item, "English and American Artificial Teeth." Reams of newspaper and journal clippings, meanwhile,
reveal a man with a broad range of interests. Amid pieces on British South
African policy, American Progressive politics, and alien labor laws in
British Columbia, we stumble upon a yellowing article praising the qualities of that versatile South American pack animal, the llama.[23]

It is easy to dismiss such documents as trivial and unimportant, having
little value other than providing occasionally humorous anecdotes. Put
together, however, these random items help us reconstruct, to a startlingly
detailed degree, the activities and routines of Naoroji and his political allies in London. They help us understand the everyday life of political
leaders and political movements. Fulfilling the duties of an Indian emissary, standing for Parliament, and nurturing the Congress were, after all,
not easy tasks. They required Naoroji and his colleagues to maintain
grueling schedules, balancing hours of letter writing with private
meetings, participation in London's public sphere, speech and article
drafting, speaking engagements, fundraising activity, and financial accounts work. There were cultural challenges as well. Working in London
necessitated adjustment to a society, physical climate, and urban environment that were vastly different from the familiarities of Bombay. Naoroji
had to contend with nuisances such as pollution-laden fog, bone-chilling
winters, vast commutes, bad food, a dramatically higher cost of living, and
the occasional overzealous Christian evangelist. And, prior to shutting

down Dadabhai Naoroji & Co. in 1881, he had to do all of this while running his own business. Through examination of miscellanea, we gain an unrivaled perspective on how Naoroji's routine, everyday activities undergirded the broader nationalist movement.

How, for example, did an Indian dress in Victorian Britain? Some, like the arch-Anglophile W. C. Bonnerjee, unhesitatingly donned the Englishman's garb. "We have not an Indian dress in the house," noted his son, K. S. Bonnerjee. Uncomfortable with the wholesale adoption of Western attire, Naoroji crafted a hybrid outfit. He wore a broadcloth coat and black trousers, tying around his neck a silk handkerchief that was held in place by a gold ring. Some of Naoroji's Parsi protégés, such as Pherozeshah Mehta and Hormusjee Wadya, adopted the same costume during their stints in London. Naoroji was far more reluctant to compromise on headgear. He continued wearing the traditional Parsi *pagdi* on the streets of the City and Westminster. Once he decided to stand for Parliament, however, Naoroji knew that he could no longer dress as a half-Indian, half-Briton. William Digby, he noted in his diary, "strongly recommended to change the head dress to an English Hat." On the hustings, the Parsi candidate was often hatless, dressed in a somber double-breasted suit and tie. Yet there remained a streak of sartorial creativity. On his return to Bombay after winning election to Parliament, Naoroji stunned the colonial governor, Lord Harris, by wearing pink silk trousers to an appointment at Government House ("I wish his constituents had seen him," Harris dryly noted).[24]

Food—at least, tasty food—was another challenge. Naoroji, his appetite perhaps dulled by the painfully bland fare on offer in London, regularly skipped breakfast and downed three or four raw eggs for lunch, which he ate while standing. He was no doubt relieved when Bhikhaiji Cama, the fiery revolutionary nationalist, visited London in January 1906 and invited him for a Sunday "Parsee lunch." Aside from spicy food, Naoroji and his fellow expatriate Indians pined for mangoes. The king of fruits makes frequent appearance in his correspondence. During his frantic last few weeks of campaigning in Central Finsbury in June 1892, Naoroji took time out of his schedule to profusely thank Mancherji Bhownaggree, a Parsi political ally who later gravitated toward the Tories, for the "little basket of mangoes" sent across from Bombay. The industrialist Jamsetji Tata sent Naoroji at least one consignment. Another homesick Indian correspondent, residing in Glasgow, wondered aloud to Naoroji whether their co-nationals could open a special shipping line to transport mangoes and other dearly missed subcontinental produce to Europe.[25]

For an Indian elite in London, Naoroji maintained a comparatively simple lifestyle, something that most likely complemented his workaholic ways. Bonnerjee settled his family into a sprawling house in Croydon, which he named "Kidderpore," while Bhownaggree lodged in the tony new garden suburb of Bedford Park in Chiswick. Naoroji, meanwhile, chose to reside where he worked: in July 1886, he rented a room at the National Liberal Club in Westminster, where he conducted most of his meetings and interviews, where he had easy access to Parliament and the India Office, and where he became a fixture in the letter-writing room. It was an arrangement that allowed him to take on even more tasks and responsibilities. He was evidently a man in a hurry. One visiting reporter at the National Liberal Club expressed amazement at the rapidity with which Naoroji spoke, especially while delivering an analysis of Indian exports. At the end of the MP's monologue, the reporter wryly commented, "Here Mr. Naoroji paused to perform an operation known as breathing, which, I am informed by medical friends, is a process that human beings cannot safely neglect for any length of time."[26]

We know much more about Naoroji's life at 72 Anerley Park, or Washington House, an abode near the Crystal Palace where he lived between 1898 and 1904. Here, as an Indian visitor reported, there were "loaded bookshelves" and "piles of books arranged against the walls of almost every room." Although a septuagenarian at the time, Naoroji continued to maintain a punishing schedule. He began wading through correspondence at ten in the morning—Naoroji admitted that "I am not what is called an early riser"—arrived at another office in Lambeth by two o'clock, and returned home by midnight, oftentimes putting in an extra one or two hours' work before sleeping. It was probably in this Lambeth office that, in 1906, he met with Mohandas K. Gandhi, who described it as a garret approximately eight feet by six feet in size, "with hardly room in it for another chair." As for holidays and breaks from work, Naoroji claimed not to know them. When, in 1903, a journalist expressed skepticism and pressed him on the matter, Naoroji admitted that he had taken a month's leave at the seaside resort of Bournemouth—about fourteen years earlier, and because of his doctor's strict orders that he leave London and conduct no work. He appears, nevertheless, to have violated these orders. A note from his campaign secretary indicates that while in Bournemouth, Naoroji delivered at least one public address on Indian affairs.[27]

In order to maintain his frenetic schedule, Naoroji relied heavily on the assistance of a number of agents and secretaries. One of these individuals, J. C. Murkerji, was Indian; all others were Britons. His longest-serving secretary, R. M. H. Griffith, steered Naoroji's affairs during his tortuously long campaign in Central Finsbury and his short term in Parliament. A Finsbury native of Welsh extraction, Griffith apprenticed as a cabinetmaker before dabbling in accountancy, journalism, and, ultimately, the affairs of the local Liberal Party branch. His correspondence with Naoroji serves as an encyclopedic resource for the constituency, shedding light on long-forgotten local power brokers and the feuds that animated its politics. It also provides a vividly detailed picture of how an ordinary Briton, someone with no outside connection to India, worked with Naoroji for the same political cause. Griffith was, evidently, fiercely devoted to the Central Finsbury candidate. "You may rely upon my loyalty to the end," he concluded one letter, during a period when local Liberal Party power brokers hostile to Naoroji were attempting to push him out of the race.[28]

Griffith was also, like his employer, a consummate workaholic. His letters, written in a tearing hurry, read like colossal run-on sentences; he evidently had no time for punctuation. In his daily dispatches to Naoroji, often sent by the midnight post, Griffith's taxing schedule unfurls: meetings at various local political associations, which occasionally descended into near-brawls and shouting matches; appointments with important constituents, Liberal Party leaders, and members of the Metropolitan Liberal and Radical Federation; and constant negotiations with printers, publishers, and operators of public halls. Interspersed in this correspondence are Griffith's urgent telegrams to Naoroji hinting at numerous crises encountered and defused (May 13, 1890: "Not tonight can you call this afternoon"; September 25, 1890: "Crowded court reporters present makes suppression undesirable"; April 13, 1891: "Special messenger coming on to you now").[29]

Griffith, more than any other individual, helped transform the Indian emissary, a foreign figure with a name unpronounceable for many Finsbury locals, into a worthy parliamentary representative for a working-class central London neighborhood. It was Griffith, for example, who suggested that the candidate go by "D. Naoroji," which would be "shorter and easier." He made countless other decisions on relatively trivial matters that, taken together, ingratiated Naoroji with his would-be constituents. Wading through the reams of letters from local residents and associations, Griffith decided which meetings Naoroji should attend, which social causes Naoroji should support, and even what type of attire he should wear to particular functions. Once Naoroji was elected to Parliament, the secretary's work took a markedly different direction. He shielded the busy MP from numerous frivolous requests, such as that of a "little old lady" who in July 1893 wanted to press her claim that the British government owed her £300 million. Conscious that "people have a particular notion of what a Parsi is and sometimes misunderstandings arise," Griffith took care to edit Naoroji's speeches, adding references to certain universalist religious principles. In the everyday life of Naoroji's parliamentary campaigns and career, Griffith was a simply indispensable figure—someone who, although virtually unknown outside of Finsbury in his day, and now entirely forgotten, played a vital role in the propagation of India's political demands. It was therefore entirely appropriate that, in his presidential address to the Lahore Congress of 1893, Naoroji paid tribute to his tireless secretary, singling him out as "one of my best friends and supporters."[30]

As a parliamentary candidate, MP, and Congress leader—someone with one ear to the ground in England and the other directed toward India—Naoroji found the rhythms of his workday dictated by the dispatch and delivery of three particular items: letters, telegrams, and newspapers. Correspondence with Griffith and other London contacts was swift and easy—mail was delivered several times a day—but letters to and from India were another matter altogether. The early Congress was, in terms of its organizational and geographic breadth, a pathbreaking movement: its leaders sought to coordinate activity between London and the far-flung cities of the subcontinent. But this was no easy task. "The Mail"—it was deliberately referred to as a proper noun—came on weekly steamers that plied between London and Bombay, Madras, or Calcutta.

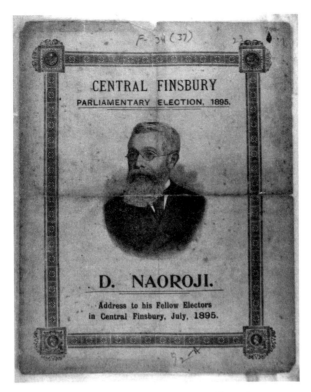

Cover page for Naoroji's "Address to his Fellow Electors in Central Finsbury" for the 1895 general elections. His campaign secretary, R. M. H. Griffith, suggested that "D. Naoroji" would be easier for Britons to pronounce.
Dadabhai Naoroji Papers, National Archives of India.

A frantic burst of letter-writing activity occurred before mail was collected and dispatched either eastward or westward. Nationalist political activity, therefore, happened in spurts: if Naoroji asked Behramji Malabari to collect Congress donations and subscriptions in western India, he would have to wait a minimum of two weeks for any response. Rather simple activities took months to coordinate. For example, it took around five months to prepare and print the official report of the first Madras Congress, held in December 1887, since its authors and contributors were dispersed between Madras, Bombay, and London.[31]

To overcome such delays, as well as the frequent miscarriage of letters and packages, Naoroji and his Congress colleagues increasingly relied on the telegraph. This was not a faultless technology, either: Malabari occasionally complained about unanswered telegrams, while operators sometimes garbled the content of their messages. Newspapers, at least, seemed to arrive relatively regularly at Naoroji's offices. He received a steady stream of the principal papers and journals published in London and Bombay, as well as others such as the *Amrita Bazar Patrika* (published out of Calcutta) and the *Hindu* (printed in Madras). Correspondence, receipts, and subscriptions provide an idea of other periodicals on his reading list: occasional editions of the *New York Sun* and *New York Post*, the *Women's Suffrage Record*, and the *Journal of the Indian Mathematical Society*.[32]

Naoroji's receipts and subscriptions also reveal that between the late 1880s and early 1900s he was deeply involved in a variety of societies and organizations across the United Kingdom. At first glance, it is difficult to fathom his motivations for maintaining certain affiliations. Why would an Indian emissary join the Church of England Burial, Funeral, and Mourning Reform Association—dedicated to objectives like the institution of cheaper, decomposable coffins, limited floral decoration, and curtailed funereal feasting—or serve as a vice president of London's Goldsmiths and Jewellers' Annuity and Asylum Institution? What, precisely, was the Independent Order of Rechabites and why was Naoroji an honorary member?

For answers, we must take into account Britain's vibrant public sphere during the late Victorian era. Through participation in this public sphere, Naoroji fraternized with the British elite, forged myriad connections with other movements, and burnished his own political and social standing in and beyond his constituency (Central Finsbury, for example, had a high concentration of goldsmiths and jewelers). Freemasonry was an extremely important institution for Naoroji and other early nationalists, both in India and in Britain. Naoroji had been a founder, secretary, and the first Indian master of the Marquis of Dalhousie lodge in London, as well as a member of at least two Crusaders lodges in the capital city. R. M. H. Griffith, who ran a "Masonic and General Business Newspaper" in Finsbury, inducted the Indian parliamentary candidate into the Masonic life of the constituency. But Naoroji was involved in many other fraternal organizations. He seemed particularly active in those dedicated to temperance, such as the Independent Order of Good Templars, where he was a lodge president in 1900 (the Rechabites, mentioned previously, were also against drink). Other affiliations confirm Naoroji's progressive political leanings. He was a fellow committee member with Keir Hardie in the Democratic Club, joined Sidney Webb's Fabian Society, and was a vice president of the Free Land League, committed to the abolition of primogeniture and customary tenure. More surprisingly, we find the septuagenarian MP serving as the president of the Central Finsbury Football Club and vice president of the North London Institute Cricket Club. "One would really imagine you to be a God of Cricket," R. M. H. Griffith declared to his boss in 1895. For Naoroji, the public sphere evidently included the sports field.[33]

Receipts and subscriptions tell us about one other important way that he took part in the public sphere: through liberal philanthropy. From 1886 through his retirement in 1907, the Indian emissary clearly had access to large reserves of funds that he used, in part, to donate to various British institutions, associations, and charities. Some of this money was most likely from India, from a number of rich benefactors who had pledged support for political activity in Britain. Some also came from shrewd investments. Naoroji held shares in a number of British publications, presses, and commercial firms. John Chapman, proprietor and editor of the *Westminster Review*—the forum for Herbert Spencer, John Stuart Mill, and Eleanor Marx Aveling—recruited Naoroji as a company director and relied upon him to enlist further Indian shareholders. Naoroji might also have invested in First Garden City, Limited, the company that built Letchworth (the world's first planned garden city and a prototype of the modern suburb), and an enterprise constructing Buenos Aires's tram system.[34]

Naoroji developed a distinct philanthropic strategy, donating to institutions within his chosen electoral constituencies and those that complemented his political and social interests. As the Liberal candidate and MP for Central Finsbury, he signed relatively large checks for local hospitals, labor union chapters, dispensaries, almshouses, and schools. Outside of the constituency, Naoroji's donations tended to go to unions, educational endeavors, women's associations, and temperance activities. Philanthropy is, of course, a two-way process. Naoroji donated to causes with which he sympathized, but the leaders of such causes identified him as a sympathizer and actively sought his support. From analysis of donation sources, we can, furthermore, observe a distinct pattern of political radicalization. In the early 1890s, Naoroji donated to numerous Liberal Party affiliates and organizations, many in the vicinity of Finsbury. By the end of the decade, he was donating to, and receiving requests for donations from, outfits that were much further to the left: Henry Hyndman's Social Democratic Federation, the London Socialist Sunday School Union, and a First of May Celebration Committee ("Representing Trade Unions, Socialist Bodies, and other Working Class Societies").[35]

While wading through miscellanea, we can discern one final, especially critical factor in the everyday lives of Naoroji, his Congress peers, and other associates: health. Naoroji and his correspondents regularly signed off their letters by wishing good health to one another. This was no mere formality. Due to overwork, constant travel, and the particular urban environments in which they lived, early Indian nationalists were extremely vulnerable to sickness. Naoroji was affected by London's pollution as well as cold spells, regularly complaining of colds and throat infections. In letters dispatched to William Wedderburn in the late 1880s, he occasionally gave equal weight to his search for a parliamentary constituency and his latest consultations with a throat specialist in New Cross, J. W. Bond. While residing at the National Liberal Club, Naoroji was literally in the thick of the city's noxious fog, and also next to the fetid Thames. Consequently, he seized upon a handful of opportunities to escape the heart of the metropolis. One refuge was the home of a Parsi friend, Nosarvanji J. Moolla, who resided in Lee, a suburb due south of Greenwich. Here Naoroji enjoyed a few days in "pure air—out of the smoke of London," while still being able to commute to appointments in Westminster. Health, it appears, was the prime reason that Naoroji vacated his room at the National Liberal Club and eventually relocated to suburban Anerley Park. But sickness still haunted him: during the "khaki election" of 1900, he was too ill to contest a parliamentary seat.[36]

Halfway across the world in India, Naoroji's correspondents fared little better. Allan Octavian Hume complained of constant indisposition. Malabari was afflicted by a bizarre recurrent fever "which comes on 2nd or 3rd year regularly." He experienced stress-related illnesses that on one night, with the unfortunate assistance of some "bad fish," produced cholera-like symptoms. "Have had some 30 motions and am very weak," he told Naoroji, sparing no details. And Gopal Krishna Gokhale, who suffered a concussion of the heart while on a train en route to London in early 1897, sent terrifying reports of the plague upon returning to Poona, excusing himself from political work in order to look after two recently widowed aunts and a cousin "in a precarious condition."[37]

Naoroji's personal papers indicate how, amid the gloom of Victorian London and receipt of these depressing missives from India, he attempted to maintain a healthy lifestyle. From the presence of a few vegetarian recipes, for example, we can surmise that he altered his diet, perhaps even diversifying beyond raw eggs for lunch. From letters written to physicians and health experts, we learn about Naoroji's daily exercise regimen: light weightlifting in the morning and evening, several half-hour walks, and some aerobics. A note from 1906 even raises the possibility that Naoroji practiced hatha yoga. These materials give us little indication of the efficacy of Naoroji's lifestyle choices. But—when considered alongside the receipts, subscriptions, and ordinary correspondence that make up the bulk of his personal papers—they help humanize Naoroji as well as other early Indian nationalists, who have otherwise been unfairly portrayed as staid, remote, and even downright dull figures.[38]

Chief of All Indians in England

During his many decades of residence in Great Britain, Dadabhai Naoroji was acknowledged as the leader of the country's growing Indian community. Both Britons and Indians recognized him as their first point of contact in the event of any problems or other urgent matters. Consequently, Naoroji's London letterbox was regularly filled with notes, requests, entreaties, and friendly letters from Indians scattered across the British Isles, in addition to countless other dispatches announcing the imminent arrival of students, professionals, dignitaries, and tourists from the subcontinent. Indians in Britain beseeched Naoroji for a variety of forms of assistance. Many requested academic guidance or professional advice. Others pleaded for emergency loans. Numerous Indians hoped to take advantage of Naoroji's political connections by asking for tickets to the House of Commons gallery or admission to the National Liberal Club. They asked repeatedly for letters of recommendation. In between such routine requests came many others: advice on where to bank, assistance in managing the affairs of Indians who died in Britain, help in getting out of a lunatic asylum, and even how to get an audience with the queen.

Within Naoroji's correspondence, there are thousands of such letters, emanating from hundreds of British Indian correspondents. These letters provide matchless insight into the lives of British Indians as well as how the British Indian community—and, in particular, the Parsi community in Great Britain—developed in the late Victorian era. Not all British Indians communicated with Naoroji: poor lascars (sailors), who inhabited the dock areas in London, Glasgow, Cardiff, and elsewhere, rarely reached out to him. Rather, the Indians who inhabited Naoroji's world in Britain were mostly elites who conversed in English, attended Oxbridge, studied for the bar, or worked in the City. Then there were the Indian princes, who began vacationing in England in the late nineteenth century or, in the case of the thakur of Gondal, Bhagvatsinhji, stayed on in order to earn multiple academic degrees. While not representative of the entire British Indian community, such individuals nevertheless provide us with clues about how Indians lived, worked, socialized, quarreled, made money, and went bankrupt in a foreign land. They tell us about the societies that Indians founded, the restaurants they frequented, and the businesses they ran. They speak of the hopes, fears, successes, and failures of an early generation of British Asians, one that inhabited a society awash with both vast opportunities and grave difficulties.

Where, and how, did Indians live in Britain during the Victorian era? A number of patterns and trends emerge. Those Indians who sailed to Britain in the 1850s and 1860s tended to engage in lucrative fields like the cotton trade and, therefore, congregated in great commercial centers such as London and Liverpool. Cama & Co., which Naoroji and his colleagues founded in 1855, had its offices in precisely those two cities. Not uncommonly, these Parsi businessmen lodged together, no doubt for reasons of convenience and cultural familiarity. In many ways, their lifestyles here mirrored processes of reform and change that the Parsi community was undergoing in India during Young Bombay. Naoroji and the Camas were divided along lines of religious and social practice. While Naoroji and K. R. Cama, as Young Bombay leaders, were reformists who urged the relaxation of purity laws that inhibited certain social contact with non-

Parsis, Mancherji Hormusji Cama, who was older and who later spread the rumor that Naoroji intended to convert to Christianity and marry an Englishwoman, was strictly orthodox. Consequently, Mancherji stipulated that they must have Parsi cooks and servants, since orthodox practice required all food to be prepared by a coreligionist.[39]

Despite reformist-orthodox fissures, all of the partners of Cama & Co. bowed to social pressure by refusing to take along their wives and dependents to Great Britain. Such prohibitions waned with time: in 1865, Naoroji brought his wife, mother, son Ardeshir, and daughter Shirin to live with him in Hornsey Rise in north London. Furthermore, he employed English servants at home. One of these servants, incredibly, named her own children after Naoroji's son and daughter, meaning that there was an English boy named Ardeshir and an English girl named Shirin in late Victorian London. Naoroji christened the Hornsey Rise abode "Parsee Lodge." It was an appropriate name: continuing the tradition of communal lodging, Naoroji hosted several Parsis who came through the imperial capital. There were a few other important centers of Parsi life in Victorian London, such as Mancherji Cama's home, which hosted some of the earliest meetings of the British Parsis' communal organization, the Zoroastrian Fund, and the commercial offices of Cama, Moolla & Co. on Old Broad Street in the City, which provided accommodations for the fund by the 1880s and 1890s. Near Earl's Court station stood Batliboi House, which was a popular lodging place for Parsis. Batliboi House was Naoroji's last known London residence: he stayed here before his final trip back to Bombay in October 1907. In 1911, British government agents monitored the house since one of its lodgers, Perin Naoroji, Naoroji's granddaughter, was known to be an active sympathizer of the militant nationalist Vinayak Damodar Savarkar, who had recently been arrested at Victoria Station.[40]

As the Indian community grew in size, it changed in nature from isolated residential clusters defined by caste and community to a diverse network of students and professionals scattered across London and the rest of the country. In 1885 and 1887, the Indian Magazine, published by the London-based National Indian Association, counted around 160 Indians resident in Britain, no doubt a significant underestimate. There was extremely high turnover in the community, the magazine noted, with an increasing number of students studying law at the expense of those preparing for careers in medicine, science, and engineering. This is borne out in Naoroji's correspondence, where many Indians listed their mailing address as Lincoln's Inn or the common room at Gray's Inn. A large number of these students found lodging in Bayswater, which began to be dubbed "Asia Minor." Professionals, on the other hand, could afford to leave the congested, smoky confines of central London. In June 1890, for example, Behramji Malabari, on a visit to the imperial capital, scribbled a hasty note to Naoroji mentioning that he was giving up accommodations in Bayswater in favor of suburban St. Catherine's Park. "London [is] intolerable," Malabari groused.[41]

Outside of London—and aside from the expected concentrations of Indians at Oxford and Cambridge—Naoroji had Indian correspondents in a variety of locales. Between 1901 and 1904, he was in touch with a Parsi doctor, K. D. Cooper, training as a medical officer in Lincoln and Bradford. More Indian medical students were to be found in Edinburgh, while a few other co-nationals were scattered elsewhere around Scotland. One of Naoroji's most colorful correspondents was Aziz Ahmad, a Lucknowi Muslim who, while an indentured laborer in Trinidad, converted to Christianity; then shuttled between British Guiana and Venezuela; enrolled for at least one term at the Yale Theological Seminary; and later moved to Glasgow. In Glasgow, Ahmad earned some money through speaking engagements, such as one where he promised to "appear in his native Muslim Dress, and give specimens of some Eastern Languages, with a quotation from the Quran, and the call of the Muazzin." He also printed two newspapers with sharply divergent aims—*Missions*, dedicated to converting other Indian Muslims to Christianity, and *Asia*, which supported the Congress. Writing to Naoroji in 1891, Ahmad mentioned that there was an Indian on the opposite coast in Perth who sold "*chutnee*." And in 1898, Naoroji received an appeal from an Englishwoman, a Miss Horscroft, asking him to contribute to a fund for P. R. Valladares, a Bombay native of Goan or East Indian extraction who "during his residence in Brighton for the past ten years, has made himself very popular," but had recently lost his sight. "It is hoped that the testimonial will serve, not only as a personal tribute, but also as a proof of the good feeling which English people entertain towards India, & the Indians," Horscroft added.[42]

Aside from medicine, law, engineering, and training for the Indian civil service, a number of Indians took up an additional vocation: standing for Parliament. Naoroji, as his correspondence attests, was hardly the only Indian hoping to take a seat in the House of Commons. Perhaps the best-known of these candidates was Lalmohan Ghosh, who stood as the Liberal candidate for Deptford in 1885 and 1886 and, although unsuccessful, mustered impressive support. Naoroji's contacts, however, seemed to relish meditating on the reasons behind Ghosh's ultimate failure. Frederick W. Chesson, a prominent abolitionist and one of Ghosh's mentors, apparently felt that he had a "want of social energy." Meanwhile, in his diary entry for April 19, 1886, Naoroji transcribed damning criticism offered by William Digby: that Ghosh was "very lazy" and that "the only thing he seemed to care for was smoking and drinking." Importantly, Naoroji noted that Ghosh harbored ambitions to make a third run after his 1886 defeat, mentioning in a letter to William Wedderburn that Ghosh was returning to Calcutta to work off campaign debts and wait for a suitable opportunity to return to Britain.[43]

While Ghosh's third campaign did not come to pass, several other prominent Bengalis tested the waters. W. C. Bonnerjee ran as a radical Liberal from Barrow-in-Furness in Cumbria in 1895. Before the next general elections, in 1900, Liberal Party officials approached Romesh Chunder Dutt about contesting a seat from Yarmouth. Dutt enthusiastically agreed to the proposal, and Naoroji even offered to extend Dutt an emergency loan for campaign expenses, but party officials evidently never followed up. Naoroji might have encouraged Dutt in 1903 to consider another campaign. Another candidate, about whom we know next to nothing, was Nandalal Ghosh. Ghosh offered himself to the electors of Tiverton in Devon in 1885. In January 1888, he was accepted as the Liberal candidate for North Lambeth—the constituency from which Naoroji would launch his final campaign in 1906—but he seems to have dropped out before the 1892 elections. An undated letter offers us clues on why this happened: Ghosh informed Naoroji that his "health has utterly broken down" and that his doctors had urged him to leave England "without another week's delay." Before departing to catch a steamer from Liverpool, however, Ghosh wished to talk to Naoroji "about Lambeth." Last, Aziz Ahmad, Naoroji's Christian convert friend in Glasgow, twice mentioned a Bábú

Kristna Lál Dátta who, "when he was in his teens," offered to stand as a candidate from Bridgeton constituency in Glasgow, and merited a degree of support.[44]

As is evident from both the places they worked and the constituencies from which a few chose to stand for Parliament, the geographical spread of the British Indian community was wide. However, this community was bound together by several associations and organizations that provided for rich social and intellectual life. Naoroji was the longtime president of the London Indian Society, which organized get-togethers, debates, and conferences for the city's Indian community. At Cambridge, there was the Indian Majlis, which invited Naoroji to its annual dinners, while further north was the Edinburgh Indian Association, which, in its "syllabus of meetings" for 1901 and 1902, featured a number of debates on contemporary Indian affairs. Finally, in the late 1880s, some sports-minded individuals formed the National Indian Cricket Club, which played against other local London teams on Saturday afternoons. The club's captain was Pandit Uma Sankar Misra, a Congress skeptic who had quarreled with Naoroji in the columns of the Times. Cricket appears to have soothed relations between the two men.[45]

The Parsi community had a particularly dense network of associations. The Zoroastrian Association or Zoroastrian Fund, established in London in 1861, was the first Asian religious organization in Britain. In spite of their personal animosities and divergent views on religious reform, Naoroji and Mancherji Hormusji Cama cooperated in steering the association through its first few years. Following a pattern typical in newly established Parsi settlements in the nineteenth and twentieth centuries, the fund was primarily concerned with providing a separate, sanctified space for the burial of the dead, and in 1862 it purchased land at Brookwood Cemetery in Woking from the London Necropolis Company. Under Naoroji's long presidency, which lasted from 1864 until 1907, the fund remained limited in its scope and activities: correspondence indicates that it continued to focus on funerary arrangements for Zoroastrian coreligionists. Occasionally, the fund organized a social event such as a navroze (Persian new year) or pateti (Parsi new year) dinner. A dinner for navroze in 1906, for example, was held at the fashionable Café Royal on Regent Street, with each plate costing 7 shillings "exclusive of wine."[46]

But it was clear that the growing community found these few dinners inadequate. In 1906, one member, Shapoorji A. Kapadia, formed a separate organization, the Parsi Club, for social get-togethers. Kapadia, it appears, founded the club with Naoroji's approval, for Naoroji agreed to preside at its inaugural dinner on May 1, 1906, held at the Florence Restaurant on Rupert Street. A flyer for this dinner survives, informing us that guests dined on "Mulligatawny," "Kari de Mouton à la Bombay," and "Glace à la Parsi." The Parsi Club was not the only community group to be founded that year. Around the same time as the inaugural dinner, Naoroji received a letter from Rustom H. Appoo in Scotland, informing him of the establishment of the Edinburgh Parsi Union. The union was meant to serve a different social purpose—providing a common meeting space for Parsi medical students in the city—and Appoo consequently asked Naoroji to become a patron and lend financial assistance so that the union could purchase quarters. Thus, by the end of 1906, the British Parsi community, which probably numbered no more than a hundred, boasted three separate organizations. Parsis across the country, furthermore, were united by their own newspaper, the *Parsi Chronicle,* edited by Nasarvanji Maneckji Cooper of Ilford. Cooper ran the paper from at least 1909 until 1911, when, tragically, he drowned himself in the Thames off Victoria Embankment.[47]

Cooper's suicide brings up an important point. In spite of the relative wealth of British Indians—and in spite of their educational achievements, degrees, professional qualifications, and links with the Westernized elite back in India—life in Britain could often be difficult and miserable. Community organizations and social clubs could not entirely mitigate these hardships. Newspaper accounts suggest that Cooper might have been distraught over a dispute he had with Mancherji Bhownaggree. But he could easily have been impacted by the racism, profound cultural differences, financial difficulties, sense of isolation, and homesickness that daily assaulted many of his fellow Indians. All of these problems are alluded to in Naoroji's correspondence with Indian students and professionals across Britain. In spite of the fact that Indians found Britons in the United Kingdom much warmer and more welcoming than their

Anglo-Indian counterparts in the subcontinent, racism remained a problem. K. D. Cooper, the Parsi doctor, complained to Naoroji in 1901 that "the prejudice the Indians have to overcome in this country are great and therefore I consider myself lucky to get into a hospital as an A.M.O. [assistant medical officer?] in such a strict & cathedral city as Lincoln. Matters are not so bad in London as out here." Shankar Abaji Bhisey, a brilliant inventor from Bombay, had the misfortune of having one of his inventions evaluated by technical experts in London the day after Madan Lal Dhingra, an Indian revolutionary, assassinated Curzon Wyllie, a former British Indian official, at the Imperial Institute. Owing to the fact that "the racial feeling was very tense in the city," Bhisey told Naoroji that he did not receive an objective review.[48]

Cast away from family, friends, and all the familiarities of home, many Indians sank into deep depression. "I am a stranger and quite friendless," S. Chelliah, an arts graduate from Calcutta now studying medicine in London, confided to Naoroji. Arthur Howell, perhaps a Eurasian, solicited help in finding a job: no one would hire him in spite of his distinction of serving under the famed journalist Robert Knight as a sub-editor for the Calcutta *Statesman*. "I am starving & overwhelmed by the awful loneliness of this great city," he wrote. An Indian residing at East India Dock Road, most likely a lascar, complained of being "a perfect stranger in England[,] penniless & friendless & not having come here of my free-will." Such sentiments were echoed by other correspondents from Aberdeen down through London. Another agonizing facet of life abroad was the remoteness and slow speed of communication from home. Naoroji learned of the deaths of friends and loved ones via telegrams or letters. Similarly, in 1901, the inventor Bhisey received a message by regular post informing him that his eighteen-month-old son in Bombay had passed away. Distance, coupled with the impossibility of frequent and instant communication, must have compounded their grief. Both Naoroji and Bhisey knew that a return home to be with family was itself a proposition fraught with financial and practical difficulties.[49]

Amid the isolation and uncertainty of British Indian existence, Naoroji played a vitally important role. He acted as a central hub of community life, mentoring and supervising students, dispensing professional and educational advice, counseling on cultural adjustment issues, extricating Indians from financial and legal difficulties, establishing and presiding over community-wide organizations, and facilitating a sense of national consciousness among Indians cast across the isles. He was, in the words of one medical student, the "Chief of all Indians in England."[50] In this sense, Naoroji's correspondence offers an unrivaled perspective on the most intimate of problems and concerns affecting the British Indian community—and, in a few instances, detailed information on how the Parsi leader helped his fellow Indians in overcoming their difficulties.

For a young Indian traveling to Britain for educational reasons, Naoroji was often his (and, increasingly, her) first point of contact. A desire to supervise and encourage students was, in fact, one of Naoroji's prime motivators for quitting his Elphinstone professorship and coming to London in the first place in 1855. In an interview that he granted in 1895 to a British magazine, he recalled that "I was induced to give up my mathematical chair in Bombay and enter into business here, partly in order that I might take charge of the young men who come to England to compete for these Services [Indian civil service examinations], and the very first year I had several under my care."[51] Naoroji's correspondence from the subsequent decades bristles with hundreds of letters of introduction from associates across the Indian subcontinent, who informed him of the imminent arrival in Britain of a relative, a family friend, a bright pupil, or a recent acquaintance. Indeed, prominent nationalists and political activists— such as Gopal Krishna Gokhale, Dinsha Wacha, Romesh Chunder Dutt, and Behramji Malabari—were especially keen to put promising students in touch with Naoroji, asking him to facilitate their smooth introduction to life in Britain and monitor their academic progress.

Others, who possessed no direct links with Naoroji, nevertheless wrote to him and asked for appointments or some form of help. Gandhi, for example, sailed to Britain in September 1888 with a letter of introduction to Naoroji from a Maharashtrian doctor who professed to not even know the intended recipient. "The fact is, you need no introduction to him," the doctor informed Gandhi. "Your being an Indian is sufficient introduction." Jivanlal Desai, who would later help Gandhi establish his first ashram in India, wrote to Naoroji in 1883—while he was still in high school in Ahmedabad—asking Naoroji for a loan so he could come to

London for the civil service examination; his parents were unwilling to foot the bill due to caste restrictions.[52]

Desai's request illustrates how Naoroji was widely recognized as a vital point of contact for ambitious Indians, no matter how young. "No student could come up to England for his studies without a desire to be introduced & recommended to you," remarked Hormusjee Wadya in 1896 while informing Naoroji of a young colleague in Kathiawar traveling to Britain for law studies. Wadya had himself benefited from Naoroji's mentorship while a student at University College in the late 1860s. Around the same time, Naoroji met and mentored two other promising students from India. The first was Romesh Chunder Dutt. Naoroji advised him to concentrate on studying for the civil service examinations first before taking up other activities—presumably, his desire to become involved in the East India Association. Dinsha Davar, later a justice on the Bombay High Court, was the second. "The first day I arrived in England I came to you for assistance & help," Davar recalled in a letter from 1897. As the cases of Wadya, Dutt, and Davar illustrate, Naoroji remained in close contact with many of his mentees, several of whom became important political allies.[53]

Aside from mentorship and guidance, Naoroji performed a variety of roles for Indian students as well as professionals. This included rather mundane tasks such as writing references, letters of recommendation, and certificates of good conduct. In 1898, for example, he provided a character reference to the owner of a house that Dutt rented in Forest Hill. Similarly, if Britons needed to contact anyone in the Indian community—or required references before they sealed business partnerships or rental agreements with any Indian resident—they dispatched letters to Naoroji's address. But one of Naoroji's most important tasks was dispensing financial assistance. London was an extremely expensive place for Indians, and many of them soon found themselves in deep financial trouble. In June 1902, for example, an S. Ghosh, introducing himself as a civil service candidate residing in Bayswater, informed Naoroji in a tone of quiet desperation that his wealthy relatives back in India had entirely failed to send him promised monetary aid. Ghosh pleaded for an appointment in order to discuss how to raise funds in Britain. His acute embarrassment concerning his situation was well apparent. "I cannot express, sir, what pains I feel in having to write such a letter as this," Ghosh confided.[54]

Naoroji's correspondence is littered with instances of the Parsi leader handing out loans and donations to other Indians in desperate straits: a £10 loan to N. B. Wagle, who had come to Britain in 1902 to study glass-making; a £50 loan to S. P. Kelkar, traveling to Rochdale to purchase "machinery that will help our hand-loom industry in India"; a £2 donation to Aziz Ahmad to help *Asia,* his struggling Glasgow-based newspaper. Even Gopal Krishna Gokhale, coming up short on cash during his 1897 visit to London, approached Naoroji for funds, and Naoroji seems to have given him a whopping £81 to cover expenses related to his testimony to a parliamentary committee. Naoroji's financial responsibilities extended to arranging for the return voyages of Indians stranded in Britain. As such, in 1894 he helped begin a public subscription to pay ship passage for a Manmohan Ghose and also contributed toward a return ticket for the widower of Anandibai Joshi, the first Indian woman to earn a Western medical degree. But even relatively wealthy and well-off professionals benefited from Naoroji's largesse. Out of the stacks of letters asking for a helping hand, one of the most interesting is from George Edalji, a Birmingham lawyer and the son of a Parsi convert to Christianity. At the close of December 1902, he dashed off a note stating that he was "in great distress through what is really no fault of my own" and beseeched Naoroji for *"any* aid, *no matter how slight."* Edalji was soon after accused of mutilating horses in what was called the "Great Wyrley outrages," precipitating a lengthy and racially charged court case, one where none other than the author Arthur Conan Doyle rallied to his defense. Naoroji offered Edalji 10 shillings.[55]

As the locus of the community, Naoroji regularly became a mediator in personal, financial, and family disputes that sometimes spanned the very ends of the British Empire. Mancherji Bhownaggree, who also assisted Indians in Britain, grumbled about the troubles created by "idiotic half witted Parsee boys" during their stints abroad; Naoroji, in contrast, treated his distressed coreligionists and co-nationals with a remarkable degree of sympathy and care. He appears to have offered advice to Bhagvatsinhji, who in the early 1890s was sued by an Englishwoman for "alleged seduction" and supposedly fathering her son, the rather royally named Albert Edward Bhagvat Sinhjee. But disputes became far more complex when they involved British Indians and their families back in the subcontinent. In 1901, for example, Naoroji rallied to the defense of Navrozji Fardunji's grandson, Phirozsha D. C. Furdoonjee, a student at University College, when his father threatened to cut off financial support. All seemed well by November 1901, when the father expressed satisfaction that Naoroji and George Birdwood had helped his son secure an apprenticeship in Liège, Belgium. Once this apprenticeship fell through, however, family pressure upon Phirozsha redoubled. Naoroji had to finally convince him to return home to Bombay.[56]

Phirozsha Furdoonjee's plight had, at least, been about money and academic performance. Most Indian parents were worried about the "vices" and "temptations" their children would encounter in the West, with conversion to Christianity, abandonment of Indian wives and families, or marriage to a Briton topping the list of undesirable outcomes. When parents' worst fears materialized, Naoroji was often quickly dragged into the mess. Thus, in April 1886 the despondent family of Shapurji D. Bhabha—who had converted to Christianity and moved to London—asked Naoroji to convince him to come home and return to the fold of Zoroastrianism. Naoroji did eventually meet with Bhabha and presented him with letters from his family, but he quickly recognized that the convert's Christian fervor was far too great to expect any religious reversion. Regardless, he told Bhabha that he could not help but sympathize with his father's "agony." Many years later, in 1898, Naoroji agreed to arbitrate a dispute involving a J. B. Dubash of Earl's Court, who had sailed from Bombay in 1881, leaving behind a young wife. Dubash's wife and family—after a period of seventeen years—now pressed Naoroji to counsel the absconding husband about his financial responsibilities to those remaining at home. While the final outcome of the dispute is not known, it is clear that Naoroji was pulled into murky family politics while arbitrating.[57]

Perhaps the most delicate situations involved interracial marriages. While Naoroji was socially liberal and seems not to have frowned upon marriages between Parsi men and British women, he nevertheless received a number of letters from parents in India anxious to avoid gaining English daughters-in-law. The situation became even more complex when Indian women started traveling to Britain in greater numbers. In June 1890, the Bombay-based family of Mary D. R. Colah, lodging at a place in New Cross called Bombay House, put out several feelers to Naoroji. Colah, as Naoroji was informed, had recently startled her family with the news that she was about to go to Australia in order to marry an Englishman. Colah's uncle begged Naoroji to intervene and convince her to not take a step that "will never do her any good and disgrace all her relatives." He was, however, fortunate in the sense that his niece at least kept in touch with her Bombay family. Naoroji received many other anguished letters from parents in India asking if he knew anything about why their children had stopped sending homeward letters altogether.[58]

By taking on the role of a mentor, guardian, and liaison between students and families, Dadabhai Naoroji often experienced some of the most unsavory and heart-wrenching aspects of life as an Indian in Britain. But his correspondence yields an important insight: that Naoroji—through his multifarious interventions in community affairs—took a keen and active interest in pushing British Indians to fulfill their professional and academic potentials. For both his co-nationals and coreligionists, he constructed and maintained community infrastructure while trying to minimize the overwhelming challenges that they faced in a foreign and unfamiliar environment. In this sense, Naoroji played a pivotal role in strengthening the community's foundations, allowing for further growth and consolidation during the twentieth century.

The True Causes of Our Poverty

One question remains. What compelled Dadabhai Naoroji—already an emissary, parliamentary candidate, and Congress leader—to take on the responsibilities of a British Indian community leader? Why did this already far too busy man get so deeply involved in the community's affairs?

Politics might provide us with an answer. It is quite apparent that Naoroji considered these community responsibilities to be a part of his broader political mission. He labored in the hope that British Indians, once they returned home, would become the successful civil servants, administrators, lawyers, engineers, doctors, and businessmen that India so desperately needed. A growing class of Indian professionals—trained in some of Britain's best universities and apprenticed in its best law firms or biggest businesses—could help challenge Anglo-Indian dominance in matters both political and commercial, thereby stanching the drain of wealth that Naoroji considered to be the source of all of India's woes.

To this end, Naoroji took special care to politically influence the British Indian community, imbuing its members with a nationalist consciousness. He inducted numerous young Indians into the National Liberal Club, where they could meet Indian political reformers such as William Wedderburn, William Digby, and Allan Octavian Hume. He invited Indians to political rallies and employed them as canvassers during his parliamentary elections. Naoroji gave explicit political direction to the London Indian Society, where, toward the end of the 1890s, he organized annual conferences that condemned aspects of British Indian policy and called for increased Indian political rights. These conferences provided early political platforms for men such as Bipin Chandra Pal, the face of radical politics in Bengal in the early 1900s. Eventually the conferences caught the attention of the India Office, which sent an undercover agent to monitor proceedings.[59]

But it was through his individual relationships with British Indians that Naoroji probably exercised the greatest influence. He sought to familiarize all Indian contacts—regardless of their vocation—with the salient political issues affecting their country. Thus, while the inventor Shankar Abaji Bhisey tinkered in London with electrical apparatuses for projecting store advertisements, he received Naoroji's pamphlets on the reasons behind India's dire impoverishment. "I really feel ashamed for not being sufficiently aware of the real state of my beloved country and the true causes of our poverty—which are so evidently and ably brought to bear on the subject by you that any *conscientious* man is bound to admit," Bhisey acknowledged after going through these pamphlets. In subsequent meetings with Naoroji, the Maharashtrian inventor seemed as keen to discuss political issues as his progress in inventing a more efficient typewriter.[60]

Naoroji's correspondence with a young Cambridge law student from Bombay, Joseph Baptista, also reveals the degree to which he encouraged the political awakening of a new generation of Indians. Having read Naoroji's copies of Congress reports and spoken at a London Indian Society conference in 1898, Baptista pledged himself to nationalist politics.

"I mean to devote my time fully to the work of our country after I have paid off the debt I have incurred," he wrote to Naoroji in 1899 before sailing home. Baptista did not disappoint. In 1901, he won a seat on the Bombay Municipal Corporation, which he held for several years. It was the start of a promising nationalist career: Baptista became a close associate of the radical leader Bal Gangadhar Tilak and a founder of the All-India Trade Union Congress. One of Baptista's campaign flyers, from 1900, survives in Naoroji's papers. Not surprisingly, the flyer prominently includes a brief letter of recommendation by Naoroji—one of hundreds of letters that Naoroji no doubt penned during his decades of residence in Great Britain. But this letter had significant consequences for Baptista: he acknowledged after his election victory that there was "no doubt that your name has won for me many supporters and helpers." Thus, in even that most mundane of tasks—writing recommendations—Naoroji wielded his pen in a manner consonant with his political ideologies and hopes. It is in this sense that Naoroji's community responsibilities in Britain were validated by an overarching political philosophy of Indian self-reliance and, eventually, Indian self-rule, a self-rule that became more tenable with each qualified and educated Indian sailing back home.[61]

CHAPTER 5

The Central Finsbury Campaign

"I PUT THE QUESTION PLAINLY," Dadabhai Naoroji addressed the Calcutta Congress of 1886, where he served as president. "Is this Congress a nursery for sedition and rebellion against the British Government (cries of no, no); or is it another stone in the foundation of the stability of that Government (cries of yes, yes)?"[1]

During the second phase of his career, Naoroji's political statements began taking on a markedly more loyalist and pro-British tone. Gone were references to British Indian policy being "evil." He largely abandoned his practice of quoting from the writings of certain Britons and Anglo-Indian officials who had, in their day, observed the plunder of Company rule and the deepening poverty of Indian subjects. The term "self-government," which Naoroji began to employ in his writings in 1884, disappeared from his letters and publications by the following year.[2] Instead, Naoroji spoke of the blessings of British rule, the justice and fair-mindedness of the British people, and the gratitude of Indians toward their colonial masters.

The Indian leader had not taken a sudden conservative turn. Naoroji maintained his political views but now took care about when, where, and how he explicitly stated them. During the first Congress session in December 1885, for example, he urged fellow delegates to "enunciate clearly and boldly our highest ultimate wishes" and "let our rulers know what our highest aspirations are"—but, ignoring his own advice for the moment, he did not use the term "self-government." Along with allies such as Allan Octavian Hume, Naoroji relegated discussion of major political objectives to private conversation. "Though we do not thus designate them as do the Irish," Hume wrote to Naoroji in a letter from 1887, "after all[,] all our efforts are directed towards Home Rule."[3]

What motivated this sudden cautiousness of speech among nationalist leaders? For Naoroji, at least, the answer is fairly clear: his continued ambition to win a seat in the House of Commons. After the Holborn campaign of 1886, Naoroji had consolidated a broad pro-Indian alliance among feminists, socialists, and leaders of the Irish cause. But in order to secure a winnable constituency, he had to appeal to a broader audience: various Liberal Party functionaries as well as the British electorate at large. For obvious reasons, Naoroji judged that stressing Indian loyalty, rather than outright condemnation of British policy, was more likely to gain him favor among this audience. Similarly, open discussion of Indian self-government was unlikely to improve his electoral prospects. Irish home rule, after all, remained an extremely divisive issue in England. As Naoroji looked forward to the next general election and cobbled together his campaign platform, he framed Indian political demands in the language of an empire loyalist and even a British patriot.

No amount of cautiousness and moderation, however, could offset what became the most contentious issue in Naoroji's campaign: race. In August 1888, he secured the Liberal nomination for the London constituency of Central Finsbury. Nevertheless, Naoroji gained a band of determined opponents within the Liberal Party who employed race and racist sentiment against the candidate. Naoroji's Indianness—already subjected to Lord Salisbury's choice opinions—became the defining issue in a bitter intraparty dispute that carried on until just before the general election of 1892. The irony of this situation was probably not lost on Naoroji: Central Finsbury enjoyed the reputation of being one of the most radical, progressive constituencies in the country, which was probably a major reason the Indian candidate considered standing here in the first place.

During this fraught campaign, Naoroji's political fate rested in the hands of four distinct groups. The first, as we have seen, included the leaders of various progressive movements who embraced the cause of

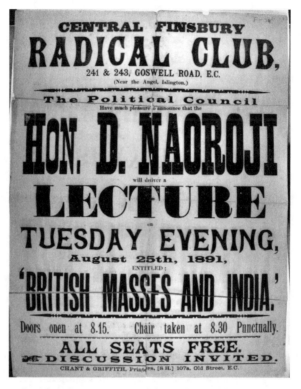

A flyer for a lecture Naoroji delivered in London in 1891 on
"British Masses and India."

Dadabhai Naoroji Papers, National Archives of India.

Indian political reform and integrated it within their agendas. Political allies in India constituted the second group. Congress members, especially
Behramji Malabari, drummed up popular and media support in the subcontinent for Naoroji's prospective campaign. They also solicited funds
for Naoroji's electoral coffers. Third were Liberal Party power brokers.
High-ranking leaders, such as Francis Schnadhorst of the National Liberal
Federation, figured within this category, but of equal importance were
officials in local constituency associations, who controlled the process of
nominating candidates. The last group was also the largest and most het-
erogeneous: ordinary British electors. In order to make Indian reform into
an electoral issue, Naoroji undertook a program of mass outreach to voters
across the country. He advertised Indian political grievances through
speaking tours, the publication and distribution of pamphlets and Con-

gress reports, and other journalistic endeavors. He strove, above all, to make Indian reform a popularly discussed issue among the electorate. And in spite of the racial barbs employed by his opponents, Naoroji's efforts met with a notable degree of success.

Our Fellow Subjects in India

Even before the black man incident catapulted Naoroji into the headlines, there were signs that his mass outreach to electors was bearing fruit. Naoroji placed great faith in the conscience of the average Briton, as well as his ability to convince these Britons of the immediate necessity of Indian political reforms. "We Indian people believe," he often stated before British audiences, "that, although John Bull is a little thick-headed, once we can penetrate through his head into his brain that a certain thing is right and proper to be done, you may be quite sure that it will be done." While such optimism might strike the modern reader as naive—especially when, as Naoroji himself pointed out, the very same Britons starved and impoverished their colonial subjects—the letters that streamed into Naoroji's mailbox indicate a degree of popular receptivity toward Indian demands. In the late 1880s, Naoroji established himself as a wholesale distributor of information on India, mailing out thousands of copies of pamphlets and reports in a veritable publications blitzkrieg. To cite only two examples, he appears to have distributed eight thousand copies of an article he penned in 1887, "Sir M. E. Grant Duff's Views about India," a scathing attack on the former governor of Madras, and at least ten thousand copies of the 1887 Madras Congress report. These materials were posted to universities, reading rooms, local Liberal associations, and workingmen's clubs across the British Isles.[4]

And they generated an active readership. Many of these British readers sent brief notes to Naoroji thanking him for bringing Indian affairs to their attention and occasionally remarking on how such literature had shaped or transformed their views. Having leafed through the report of the 1886 Calcutta Congress, Henry Lee, a resident of Sedgley Park in Manchester, concluded that "our Indian fellow subjects should be admitted to a much larger share in the government of their own country than they now enjoy." An affiliate of Rawdon College near Leeds declared that he felt "much sympathy" for the Congress. He vowed to "take an early opportunity of mentioning the movement for some share of self government by our fellow subjects in India" to the Liberal Council of Pudsey. Meanwhile, Archibald Duff, a professor at Airedale College in Bradford, took his copy of the Calcutta Congress report to the pulpit of his church, delivering a sermon on Indian political rights. "May the day of Home Rule in India soon come with stronger bonds than ever between all parts of the brotherhood gathered round the Queen, aye gathered round God's throne," the professor wrote to Naoroji.[5] As is indicated by Duff's language as well as by the common references to fellow subjecthood, Britons, rather than Indians, were often the ones who conceptualized a notion of imperial citizenship. They approved of the idea that colonial subjects deserved some rights, and they took it upon themselves to advocate this cause. Significantly, Naoroji's correspondents suggested that increased rights would strengthen the bonds of empire rather than disintegrate them.

Not surprisingly, many of the ordinary electors who corresponded with Naoroji were workingmen and Irishmen. Their letters imply that Naoroji did not simply limit his outreach efforts to the Irish and labor leadership in London. For example, one Irishman in Merseyside, F. L. Crelly, appears to have received and enthusiastically digested several of Naoroji's publications. "A greater interest will attach to the books you have sent me," Crelly declared, "owing to the great similarity between your demand & the demand of Ireland for Home Rule & which particularly recommends the cause of India to my sympathy as an Irishman." Another batch of reports and publications found its way to the Working Men's Club in Swansea, an important social institution for the laborers of this Welsh industrial center. There they caught the attention of a port employee, G. E. Wade. In late November 1887, Wade pressed Naoroji for more material on India, since he was anxious "to study at further leisure with my companions."[6]

Do such letters from Wade and his fellow workingmen point to a relative lack of prejudice in heavily working-class constituencies, something that was not the case among the more affluent sections of late Victorian British society? This might be partly true. The British working class had complex and often contradictory attitudes toward race and empire. A labor leader such as John Burns could whip up a crowd both with heavy doses of anti-Semitic sentiment and with declarations of solidarity with the Indian or Chinese people. Workers took pride in the empire while also realizing that it sustained a system of mass exploitation—one that kept them poor. But, as is evident from their correspondence, workers addressed Naoroji and his fellow Indians with the greatest respect. If correspondents broached the topic of race, it was usually from the standpoint of well-meaning curiosity about the diverse inhabitants of the subcontinent.[7]

Naoroji benefited from this ambiguity. Some workers were involved in industries dependent on Indian raw material and, therefore, were particularly keen to learn more about the colony's political grievances. James Blackwell, a resident of the gritty textile manufacturing center of Blackburn in Lancashire, wrote to Naoroji after reading copies of his speeches, pamphlets, and *India*, the magazine of the British Committee of the Indian National Congress. "I am quite took up [sic] with the way in which you have from time to time placed matters before the English public and I am quite satisfied that by continuously working on it will have its effect," he reassured Naoroji. Significantly, Blackshaw's interest in India translated into political activity. "I may tell you that I as a working man am doing all I can not only by putting in circulation what printed matter I can[,] by speaking at meetings myself[,] and also by advising them I come in contact with to do the same as me," he noted. Over the past two months, Blackshaw continued, he had spoken at several meetings, and he thought "that Lancashire people are beginning to see that it is to the advantage of the Empire at large" for Indians to receive a greater stake in governing their country. Individuals such as Blackshaw demonstrated that sympathetic workers could, on occasion, become important foot soldiers in the movement for Indian reform.[8]

Lord Salisbury's jibe against Naoroji had, perversely, only helped further ingratiate the "black man" with the common man. Naoroji and Indian politics became a regular topic of letters to the editors of major British dailies. For instance, J. Page Hopps, a minister in Leicester, wrote to the *Daily News* that Naoroji "ought to be offered a safe seat for Parliament." Only he, after all, could "confirm the loyalty of India, and . . . satisfy the millions who also are already beginning to whisper the pregnant phrase, 'Home Rule.'" Salisbury, by contrast, had stumbled upon "the way to lose India."

Aside from such printed letters in newspapers, Naoroji's inbox at the National Liberal Club overflowed with correspondence. By the end of December 1888, a month after the prime minister's verbal gaffe, Naoroji had received more than thirty-eight hundred letters, cablegrams, and telegrams of sympathy and support. Some were dispatched from India, Germany, Italy, the United States, Australia, Canada, New Zealand, and South Africa.[9] But the bulk was likely sent by British voters who were embarrassed and rattled by their prime minister's coarse language. Members of local clubs and political associations transmitted resolutions condemning Salisbury's comments and inviting Naoroji to address their audiences.

During the winter of 1888–1889, Naoroji took up many of these invitations, receiving warm receptions across the country. He addressed packed halls in Maidstone, Glasgow, North Ayrshire, and Cambridge. In Newcastle, where he delivered several talks, he was honored with a special breakfast at the city's Reform Club. There Robert Spence Watson, a prominent reformer and educationist, compared Naoroji to two previous honorees, an American abolitionist and a leader of the Hungarian revolution of 1848. Naoroji's audience in Loughborough, meanwhile, passed a resolution calling for "all reasonable demands of the Indian National Congress" to be met by Parliament and the government of India.[10]

With an outpouring of support for Naoroji and Indian political reform, Liberal Party power brokers entered the fray. William Gladstone wove the black man incident into a speech he delivered in Limehouse in the East End on December 15, 1888. He blasted Salisbury for giving "deep offence to many millions of our fellow-subjects in India" (but did a disservice to another subject race by claiming that Indians were certainly not Hottentots). His son, Herbert Gladstone, quipped before an audience, "I knew Mr. Naoroji very well, and I know Lord Salisbury by sight, and I am bound to say that of the two Lord Salisbury is the blackest." In their attempt to make the most political capital out of the incident, power brokers allowed Naoroji to appear before the public on the same platforms as its highest-ranking leaders. On February 19, 1889, Naoroji took a seat alongside Lord Rosebery, foreign secretary in Gladstone's last ministry, at a large rally held at precisely the same location where Salisbury had delivered his infamous remark, the Edinburgh Corn Exchange. Laden with symbolism, this event conveyed a strong message of Liberal Party solidarity with Naoroji. The National Liberal Club also organized a special dinner in Naoroji's honor, presided over by Lord Ripon and attended by several MPs, a Canadian delegate, and the consul general of the United States.[11]

All of this enhanced Naoroji's stature before the British electorate, consolidating their sense of goodwill toward him. Naoroji's correspondents were, of course, a self-selected group. Nevertheless, their support and sympathy illustrate how the Indian candidate's foreignness was not entirely a liability on the campaign trail. Foreignness could occasionally be a marker of distinction, something that aroused curiosity. There are some possible reasons for explaining Naoroji's popularity among ordinary Britons. A few historians have alluded to an "anti-racist" undercurrent in Victorian society, something that was propelled by politically radical leaders active in causes such as feminism, vegetarianism, and socialism. Public attitudes toward Naoroji indicate that this anti-racist undercurrent was much broader, embracing many non-elites. Such individuals, especially from the working class, held relatively tolerant views about race, sympathized with Naoroji's claims that Indians deserved the same political rights as Britons, and were deeply disturbed by the black man incident. It helped, furthermore, when racial differences were counterbalanced by familiar cultural and social traits. One Briton defended Naoroji against racist barbs by describing him as a "a highly cultured politician, an accomplished scholar, a refined thinker, and"—importantly—"essentially an English gentleman." Naoroji's Anglicized ways, his demonstrated erudition, and his fluency in British social and political matters made Salisbury's remark seem all the more reprehensible. And this disjuncture most likely prompted even more Britons to reconsider their attitudes toward Indians in general, something that further boosted Naoroji's appeal and improved public receptivity to his political demands.[12]

Both the Indian leader and Indian reform continued to be in the headlines through early 1889. Ahead of Naoroji's arrival in Newcastle in mid-February, Watson, who organized the breakfast at the city's Reform Club, spoke enthusiastically about how Salisbury's black man was generating wide media coverage and amassing speaking invitations. "I am really delighted to see how the Congress is taken up now by the English press," he noted. "I am half jealous of the places which are to have you before you come north."[13] From the Midlands to Scotland, and from the great industrial conurbations to rural agricultural settlements, Naoroji began to enjoy a broad degree of popularity and public recognition. In order to get into Parliament, of course, he needed to concentrate this popularity and goodwill within a specific constituency, winning over both electors and local power brokers.

Flung away in the Dunghill

This was where matters became more complex. In the search for a new constituency, Dadabhai Naoroji entertained offers from local Liberal officials in Deptford, where Lalmohan Ghosh had twice stood unsuccessfully, and Holborn, where at least one Liberal association, the Holborn Gladstonian Club, pledged its support. But he was increasingly drawn toward a constituency just to the north, Central Finsbury. Given Naoroji's progressive leanings, this constituency was an extremely attractive choice. Finsbury, alternatively known as Clerkenwell, was a solidly working-class district of some seventy thousand people that stretched northwest of the City, nearly touching King's Cross and giving way to Islington around Angel. In spite of having a sordid reputation for crime, poverty, and overcrowding—Charles Dickens's Oliver Twist roamed its narrow by-lanes—Finsbury was home to a large population of skilled artisans, especially watchmakers, jewelers, and goldsmiths. And it was a hotbed of radicalism. In the 1840s, Clerkenwell had been a major epicenter of Chartism, the working-class movement for parliamentary reform, and by the 1880s its residents were flocking to Henry Hyndman's Social Democratic Federation. In between, in 1867, the neighborhood played host to an audacious attempt to blast away the walls of the local prison in order to free a few Irish Fenian revolutionaries incarcerated there.[14]

While Central Finsbury electors were overwhelmingly radical Liberal and socialist in their political outlook, the constituency's local party branch, the Liberal and Radical Association, was hopelessly fractured. Due to incessant infighting between power brokers, the Liberal candidate during the 1886 general elections had lost to Frederick Thomas Penton, a

Conservative and, worse yet, a large landowner with significant property in the neighborhood (Finsbury's northern fringe continues to this day to be known as Pentonville). Amid the rancor and deadlock, the association withered from neglect and became even more dysfunctional. Its general committee—tasked with selecting candidates—was significantly hobbled by the fact that many of its three hundred listed members were dead.[15] Barring supernatural intervention, it was therefore quite difficult for the association to reach a quorum when it came to endorsing someone for election, even if a good number of its living members rallied to a particular individual.

Naoroji stumbled unawares into this morass. In February 1888, at the suggestion of some friends, he began investigating his chances in Central Finsbury, subsequently lecturing "at 4 or 5 places on India, in Clerkenwell and Islington," in March. He quickly earned the support of the Finsbury and Islington Radical Federation, most likely a splinter organization, which endorsed Naoroji as the "ablest and most experienced" among various contenders. By the end of July, Naoroji was shortlisted for consideration by the association's general committee. And on the evening of August 15, general committee members trooped into the association's hall on St. John Street in order to select a candidate. Members heard short speeches from Naoroji and three other individuals on the shortlist. The committee then held three separate votes, with Naoroji topping the list in all counts. By all appearances, therefore, Naoroji was now the official Liberal candidate for Central Finsbury. "I am selected to be the candidate for the next election," he confidently stated in a letter sent to family members in Bombay.[16]

It is difficult to piece together what happened next. According to many sources, after the last vote had been tabulated, pro-Naoroji committee members rejoiced at his selection and began filing out of the hall. One disgruntled member, however, charged the "Naorojians" with "creating so much disorder" throughout the entire meeting as to render the proper tabulation of votes impossible. He further alleged that after the final vote "the Naorojians broke up the meeting," thwarting any attempt at a recount. The chairman of the general committee (who acknowledged that he had backed a rival nominee) made similarly damning claims against the Indian candidate and his supporters. In his opinion, the three votes of that evening were null and void since, following the standard protocol of any good Victorian association, they needed to be ratified by a final motion and embodied in a resolution. But a motion had been impossible since Naoroji's supporters had already abandoned the meeting. In any case, the chairman continued, Naoroji's claims to winning were hollow since less than one-third of all three hundred general committee members were present that evening, and only half of those had raised their hands for Naoroji.[17]

Predictably, Naoroji's camp offered a different perspective. One supporter reminded the chairman that many of the absentee general committee members were, after all, dead. Another suggested that the anti-Naoroji power brokers in Finsbury were in the pocket of a major Finsbury landholder and were therefore actively working in favor of another candidate. Naoroji, meanwhile, maintained all along that the votes on the evening of August 15 had been legitimate. To prove this, he called a mass meeting and produced a letter from the secretary of the Central Finsbury Liberal and Radical Association offering his congratulations. Unfortunately for Naoroji, the secretary was in attendance and revealed that he had written the letter at the candidate's request. This caused an immediate uproar. According to one newspaper account, the revelation caused Naoroji's allies to be "drowned in the hoots" of the audience. "The meeting appeared to have resolved into a zoological collection, judging from the innumerable varieties of noises with which the speaker's remarks were accompanied." Amid more shouting and recrimination, the anti-Naoroji contingent of the general committee, along with the association's chairman, broke away and decided to hold a fresh vote for a candidate. Naoroji and his supporters on the committee branded this move as illegal and declined to attend the vote. As a result, a coterie of general committee members assembled on September 3 for an evidently stage-managed meeting, one where there was only a single candidate to consider: Richard Eve, the runner-up to Naoroji in the August 15 vote. Eve won handily.[18]

Thus by early September 1888, local power brokers in Central Finsbury were more divided and polarized than ever. There were now two Liberal candidates, both claiming to have official support. But matters were to take an even uglier turn. Naoroji soon found himself at the heart of a controversy involving two of the leading Liberal newspapers of London. One of these papers, the *Star*, began vigorously attacking Naoroji's candidacy, alleging that the support he had won among some Finsbury officials was the result of "skilful manoevring [sic]," possibly even "mechanical wire-pulling and sharp and skilful intrigue." The allegations must have deeply shocked the Indian candidate—not only because of their gravity and lack of substantiation, but also because of their provenance. The *Star*, after all, was a radical paper, in line with most of Naoroji's positions, and had been founded by T. P. O'Connor, a friendly acquaintance. Soon enough, the *Pall Mall Gazette* intervened, condemning the *Star*'s aspersions as "treason to the Liberal cause" and boldly hinting that the paper was subordinating "the interests of the party to those of an individual." By attacking Naoroji so vociferously, could the *Star* have been promoting the cause of a rival candidate? This is a very real possibility. It appears quite likely that a major shareholder of the *Star*—and the "individual" to which the *Pall Mall Gazette* alluded—was none other than Richard Eve.[19]

If the *Star* was indeed the mouthpiece of an Eve clique, then we have a probable answer as to why Naoroji evoked such strong opposition among certain Finsbury power brokers. Race was at the heart of the matter. The *Star* played up Naoroji's foreignness, claiming that it was a liability that would "make a present of the seat to the Tories." Eve's backers simply did not believe that electors in their constituency would vote for an Indian. "The experiment of running an Indian native for a London constituency has been already tried, and with disastrous results," the *Star* claimed, alluding to Naoroji's and Lalmohan Ghosh's previous runs.[20] It would be similarly disastrous, these power brokers reasoned, if a foreign candidate with a difficult name caused them to lose Central Finsbury once more.

Yet Eve's supporters and the *Star* were not motivated by electoral calculus alone. There was something more sinister at work. Whenever Naoroji responded to allegations published in the *Star*, the paper and Eve's supporters fell back on the standard line that he was, ultimately, an outsider, and therefore unable to appreciate proper political practices of conduct. An unfamiliar man was forcing himself on the constituency. One general council member commented that "Mr. Naoroji's long residence here has not taught him the rules." More disturbingly, it appears that his opponents, keen to further highlight his foreignness, descended to the level of calling him a "nigger, Indian, Hottentot, blackman, &c." These developments were transpiring two months *before* Lord Salisbury's remarks, within Liberal Party circles, and in one of the most progressive constituencies in the country. Thus, we can observe an important distinction in the political landscape of late Victorian Britain. While many ordinary Liberal voters did not allow Naoroji's foreign extraction to interfere with their support of him, Liberal power brokers were oftentimes beholden to some of the most prejudicial attitudes of the era and therefore made race a central issue of the campaign. In their ability to single out and malign Naoroji with racial epithets, party officials in Central Finsbury gave stiff competition to the Conservative prime minister.[21]

Naoroji chose to respond in a few ways. First, he reached out to some of his progressive allies, such as John Burns, who sent Naoroji a message of support and encouraged him to "not worry yourself unnecessarily" about the *Star's* attacks. Labor leaders were not the only ones to respond to Naoroji's call. In late September, around two thousand local workingmen gathered on Clerkenwell Green to protest against the Eve clique and pass a resolution recognizing Naoroji as the official Liberal candidate in their constituency. Second, with the help of another ally, William Digby, the Anglo-Indian journalist, Naoroji reached out to a senior Liberal Party power broker, Francis Schnadhorst. From his desk at the National Liberal Federation, Schnadhorst dashed off a note to Digby that expressed his disgust at the *Star's* campaign. "The object is of course to force Eve on the Constituency," he judged. "In my opinion although a Parsee is much handicapped in an English Constituency, Naoroji is not only the best man and politician of the two, but is more likely to win. Naoroji will become liked the better he is known. Eve just the opposite." Schnadhorst followed up this letter with a note to Naoroji, promising to do "any thing I can" to help him in Central Finsbury. "You have been fairly selected and it is our duty to support you," he declared.[22]

With support from Schnadhorst, Naoroji's position was strengthened. And in the aftermath of the black man incident, the groundswell of Liberal support for Naoroji appeared to take the wind out of Richard Eve and his supporters. After a relatively quiet period by the standards of Central Finsbury politics, Eve retired from the race in June 1890. It was a moment of understandable relief to Naoroji. While Eve did not explain why he was quitting, it is possible that he—and the local power brokers who supported him—came under outside pressure to terminate his candidacy. A local paper reported in early 1890 that "Socialists" had warned one of the Eve campaign's chief ringleaders, the colorfully named Mr. Wildbore, that "if Mr. Eve is chosen by the Council as the Candidate for Central Finsbury they will run a Labour Candidate." Could Naoroji and his supporters have relied upon an important progressive ally, Henry Hyndman and his Social Democratic Federation, to outflank their rivals? It is impossible to know for certain. Regardless, as Eve departed Clerkenwell, R. M. H. Griffith, the Parsi candidate's indefatigable secretary, wrote a letter to Schnadhorst seeking an assurance that Naoroji would "not be again impeded" by the actions of hostile local officials. Schnadhorst, as Naoroji later recalled, agreed that the National Liberal Federation would lend no support to any possible rival, promising that he "would endeavour to leave the road clear for me."[23]

Griffith's cautionary measure suggests that anti-Naoroji power brokers were not likely to give up so easily. They had, in any case, taken over the constituency's long-standing Liberal Party branch, the Central Finsbury Liberal and Radical Association—or at least its name, given that the body was for all practical purposes defunct—pushing Naoroji partisans to set up a rival Central Finsbury Liberal and Radical Council. Beginning in January 1891, the old Richard Eve clique began stirring to life once more, perhaps having used the previous few months to organize a more effective assault against Naoroji's campaign. In place of the *Star*, the clique's mouthpiece now appeared to be the *Finsbury and Holborn Guardian*, which adopted remarkably similar language in its descriptions of Naoroji. The Indian candidate, the paper declared, was "a carpet bagger of the first water." There were more claims of Naoroji's supposed campaign misconduct, conveniently without much elaboration. And, once more, Naoroji was portrayed as an outsider. If Indians stood for election, the *Guardian* asserted, "they must abide by the same rules as other Liberal Candidates." Then the punch line: "This is a case," the paper concluded, "of 'England for the English,' and we hope that he will see his way to stand out of the way and permit a fair fight." Here again was the familiar self-serving logic of the *Star*: Naoroji was conducting his campaign in an improper manner; he was doing so because he was a foreigner; and a foreigner would never be elected.[24]

Anti-Naoroji power brokers had swung back into action. Moreover, they had a new candidate: Frederick A. Ford, Central Finsbury's popular member of the London County Council, and a man as radical and progressive in his political outlook as Naoroji. Ford, incidentally, had polled third at the general committee's meeting of August 15, 1888, behind Naoroji and Eve. After his defeat, he had given assurances that he would stay out of the race. However, in January 1891, Ford suddenly and unexpectedly reversed his course. "Mr. Ford . . . a few weeks ago stated that he had no such intention [to run]," a panicked Naoroji wrote to Behramji Malabari. "He now comes out again by beginning with a personal attack upon me without any cause or provocation." Armed with strong connections within the Liberal Party establishment, Ford proved himself to be a far more serious threat than Richard Eve. He set about trying to, in Naoroji's words, "pack an association"—the Central Finsbury Liberal and Radical Association—"that would pass a resolution to resist my candidature." The association, furthermore, was laboring to get official recognition from the Liberal Party, something that would push Naoroji's rival council to the sidelines.[25]

There was, Naoroji informed Malabari, "a pretty good work looming for me." If Ford's supporters succeeded in getting recognition from the Liberal Party, they would press Naoroji to retire from the race, "which of course I will not do." He would rather stand as an independent candidate. But this was also a dangerous path to tread, as "diverse pains and penalties [were] threatened." Ford's backers warned Naoroji that if he stood as an independent, they would ensure that the Indian candidate was put on a Liberal Party "black list," something that would irreparably rupture his party connections and all but rule out any chance of standing for a seat as a Liberal in the future. "Here is a fine prospect!" he exclaimed to Malabari.[26]

Subsequent developments bore out Naoroji's worst fears. Through the spring of 1891, Ford and anti-Naoroji power brokers transformed their attacks into a vicious program of slander. They distributed circulars among Finsbury voters that accused Naoroji of peddling influence through "a lavish expenditure of money disbursed in the interest of the Native Indian Congress [sic]." In an interview with the *Finsbury and Holborn Guardian,* Ford similarly charged that his rival was "buying votes"— again, with no substantiation. Ford's backers also alluded to Naoroji's outsider status by insisting that "he can only succeed in making the Tories a present of the seat of a Radical borough." Other Finsbury officials eschewed indirect references to Naoroji's foreignness and went straight to the heart of the matter. At a meeting held inside a local schoolhouse, a Mr. Dighton, a man "strongly imbued with the idea of Nationality," delivered a speech where he "told the audience he did not want any foreign blackmen." Thus anti-Naoroji power brokers once more employed racism—both subtle and direct—as their weapon of choice. Significantly, many ordinary electors objected to these tactics, once more highlighting how power brokers and electors often had starkly different views on race. Dighton, for example, was shouted down by his audience and forced to "desist" from further speechmaking.[27]

Recoiling in horror from these attacks, Naoroji decided to reach out to Francis Schnadhorst, seeking delivery of the promises made after Richard Eve's retirement. Schnadhorst had, after all, been supportive of Naoroji since his campaign in Holborn. Now more than ever, the Indian candidate needed this support in order to rein in an increasingly vindictive opposition. Unfortunately for Naoroji, Ford and the anti-Naoroji lobby appear to have beaten him to the offices of the National Liberal Federation. Schnadhorst never responded to Naoroji. Week after week, as his rivals gained power and support, Naoroji struggled to connect with the federation secretary, recruiting William Digby to open up additional channels of communication. But Schnadhorst remained mysteriously silent, increasing Naoroji's suspicions that his opponents had won him over. Naoroji's letters to his friends and allies began to take on a markedly and uncharacteristically desperate tone by the summer of 1891. "Mr. Schnadhorst has been primed with a pack of falsehoods," he fumed to Digby. Matters worsened by early June, when the rival association decided to formalize Ford's campaign through a petition signed directly by electors. Naoroji immediately flung serious allegations of voter fraud at the rival camp. "I do not know how many signatures will be forged by the Canvassers, as they have done with the signatures for the Wards," he worried. In spite of worsening circumstances, Naoroji stubbornly refused to concede to his opposition. "I cannot after such a life as I have spent, and with the stakes I have upon me, allow myself to be flung away in the dunghill like a dead cat," he stated.[28] Determined to stay in the race, and unable to count on direct support from the National Liberal Federation, Naoroji surveyed his slender remaining options for salvaging a campaign under ferocious attack.

Indian Tea

Many of these options carried great risks or had extremely low chances of success. For example, Dadabhai Naoroji considered bypassing the National Liberal Federation altogether and appealing to a higher authority. In correspondence with William Digby, he raised the possibility of writing to "Mr G."—William Gladstone—and involving him in the dispute. But Gladstone's support was not guaranteed, and even if the former prime minister decided to wade into the fracas in Central Finsbury, his intervention would likely antagonize Francis Schnadhorst. It was best if Naoroji avoided gaining new enemies at this stage. He turned to progressive allies such as the Irish home rulers, seeking another constituency in case Central Finsbury became truly unwinnable. In early 1892, Naoroji approached Michael Davitt and asked him to find "a safe seat in Ireland for the next general election." Davitt, unfortunately, replied from Dublin that it would be "impossible" at the moment for "so complete an 'outsider' as yourself" to run on the home rule ticket. The Irish Parliamentary Party, after all, was in the midst of a bitter leadership dispute that had erupted in 1890 after Charles Stuart Parnell's relationship with a married woman was revealed. With extramarital affairs distracting from political affairs, Davitt reasoned, "the country could not be educated up to the diplomatic level of returning you for an Irish seat."[29]

As Naoroji's electoral prospects reached their nadir in the latter half of 1891, his Indian allies rallied to his side. Naoroji's India connections, which had played such an important role in his networking activities prior to the Holborn campaign of 1886, now proved invaluable in helping him struggle through an especially trying phase of the Central Finsbury contest. Opponents had long charged that the Congress was filling Naoroji's electoral coffers—Richard Eve snidely insinuated that "Indian tea" was buying off voters in Clerkenwell. While a large amount of Naoroji's funding did indeed emanate from the subcontinent (there is no evidence, however, of direct involvement of the Congress organization), Indians influenced the faraway electoral competition in a variety of other ways. In Calcutta, for example, Rustomji Dhunjibhai (R. D.) Mehta, a fellow Parsi and one of the city's most successful mill owners, served as a liaison between Naoroji and the Bengali political elite. With Mehta's help, Naoroji secured letters and resolutions of support from Calcutta's political associations, which were summarily forwarded to the British press and public. Dinsha Wacha volunteered to relocate to London in order to serve as Naoroji's private secretary, and by early 1892, William Wedderburn, having left both the civil service and Bombay, became an active participant in the campaign.[30]

But Naoroji's most significant Indian ally was Behramji Malabari, a man who became known in his day as "the right hand of Dadabhai Naoroji." Without Malabari, the Naoroji campaign likely would have collapsed for want of logistical, financial, and moral support during the winter of 1891–1892. It is a little surprising that the Parsi social reformer chose to take upon himself such weighty duties. By 1887, after all, he had left the Congress, publicly breaking with Naoroji over the organization's exclusion of social reform from its agenda. Their strong friendship most likely tempered these differences: Malabari helped look after Naoroji's family during the latter's absences in London, and in letters he fondly addressed the Indian candidate as "Dad." He threw himself into electioneering work with enthusiasm and dedication matched only by R. M. H. Griffith and the candidate himself. This is a facet of Malabari's career that has hitherto been completely unnoticed.[31]

From his spacious offices on Hornby Road in Bombay, more than four thousand miles away from the crowded tenements of Clerkenwell, Malabari took on diverse roles and functions. He served as the primary interlocutor between Naoroji and a host of political leaders, newspaper editors, and well-wishers scattered across the subcontinent. Thanks to his extensive contacts with British political figures and his deep knowledge of British politics—in spite of never having set foot on English soil before 1890—he regularly primed Naoroji with advice and intelligence. And on occasion he made his own unique contributions to the struggle for Indian parliamentary representation. At a particularly difficult moment in the Central Finsbury campaign, Malabari encouraged Naoroji to consider standing for Parliament from an entirely different locale: Bombay. Inspired by a letter recently submitted to his journal, the *Indian Spectator,* Malabari investigated King Charles II's charter of 1669 that granted the island of Bombay, then part of the royal dowry, to the East India Company. Noting that this charter recognized the island as part of the royal manor of East Greenwich, Malabari and a few friends argued that Bombay residents therefore had "all the rights and privileges of persons abiding and born in England." This included parliamentary representation.[32]

The argument that "the Island of Bombay is, by the Charter, virtually *in* England" might strike contemporary readers as bizarre—and certainly not something likely to rouse hopeful interest among Indian nationalists. But it fired Naoroji's imagination. Eager to test its possibilities, he asked Malabari to employ Bombay's sharpest legal minds—K. T. Telang, Pherozeshah Mehta, and Badruddin Tyabji—to verify the soundness of the proposition. "If it be a right that can be demanded by Bombay, to be represented in Parliament, it ought not to be lost," Naoroji argued, "but used as a splendid argument for representation for all India." Nothing further appears to have transpired from this correspondence—perhaps Bombay's famous legal trio weighed against utilizing King Charles's proclamation. However, in 1890, R. M. H Griffith employed similar logic while trying to prove Naoroji's British subjecthood in a local court. "Mr. Naoroji is a native of Bombay," Griffith stated, "and Bombay, although in India, is technically a part of the parish of East Greenwich."[33]

Although he was unable to establish that the residents of *urbs prima in Indis* had an inviolable stake in some Kentish constituency, Malabari was extremely successful in another endeavor: harnessing the Indian media for Naoroji's cause. As Frederick A. Ford's insurgent candidacy made inroads in Central Finsbury through the summer of 1891, Indian media support became a critical component of Naoroji's electoral strategy. He began actively styling himself as an Indian representative, someone who had the confidence of India's teeming millions. This was a strategy that had worked remarkably well in the past. At rallies and meetings, Central Finsbury electors had enthusiastically received Naoroji's predictions of "the blessings that the 250,000,000 of India would heap upon the constituency if it gave them a voice in Parliament." The London correspondent of the *Indian Spectator* reported that such exhortations "brought down the house." Even the *Star* admitted that Naoroji's claims to represent an entire subcontinent, and the ready evidence of support emanating from India, constituted his "trump card."[34]

Malabari was just the man to ensure the continuance of such support. As one of India's most celebrated journalists, he enjoyed strong relations with editors and proprietors of newspapers scattered across the country. And Naoroji had been quick to recognize this fact. Shortly after the black man incident, he asked Malabari, in not too subtle language, to actively encourage the production of sympathetic editorials in Indian dailies. "One thing will tell very powerfully here," he wrote from London, "viz. that the whole Native Press should express a desire that I should succeed in getting into Parliament." He made a similar plea in December 1891, as Ford continued to gain ground and Schnadhorst remained silent. Naoroji argued that "moral support" from Indian papers "would have a good effect here." Such press coverage, he continued, would resonate with local electors. "If the Congress, and the *whole* Indian Press, took up the matter warmly, that will help much here," Naoroji asserted. "A strong loud voice from India must be raised."[35]

Upon receipt of these messages, Malabari set to work. He dispatched two confidential circulars to editors and proprietors across India, informing them of the Indian candidate's dire straits in Central Finsbury. What Naoroji now desperately needed was "a strong and unanimous verdict in his favour." "Pray give it now and again in an emphatic authoritative manner," he urged. Malabari went so far as to suggest specific language. The Indian media, he believed, should warn the Liberal establishment that its mistreatment of Naoroji was jeopardizing educated Indians' allegiances to the party. "If we cannot afford to alienate the Liberal Party in this matter, can they afford to alienate us all in India?" Malabari asked rhetorically. "This is a line of argument likely to strike them."[36] Remarkably, Malabari felt that Indians, in spite of their complete and utter disenfranchisement, could exert influence over events in distant Westminster. He envisioned a sustained media offensive to rouse the attention of Schnadhorst, Gladstone, and other leaders.

By early February 1892, Malabari's circulars had provoked a good response. "The Native press is taking up your question well now," he
informed Naoroji. From across the subcontinent, editors mailed in clippings of articles they had run in their papers. Malabari, meanwhile,
scurried to find translators in Bombay in order to render vernacular
material into English, which could then be forwarded for use in London.
A Gujarati-language editorial in Bombay's *Kaiser-i-Hind* offers some clues
about how Indian papers acted upon Malabari's appeals. The paper criticized Liberal Party leaders for their current indifference to Naoroji's plight
after having profited from the black man incident and resultant public
outcry. It was now the duty of all Indians, the *Kaiser-i-Hind* continued, to
hold large demonstrations in support of Naoroji, appealing to Central
Finsbury voters that the candidate was the unanimously supported representative of the country. Aside from such pieces, Naoroji benefited from
a resolution passed at the 1891 Nagpur Congress that formally endorsed
his candidacy. And following the dispatch of the two circulars, the Poona
Sarvajanik Sabha informed Malabari that the organization wanted to directly "appeal to the electors" of Central Finsbury in some manner. Thus
by the early spring of 1892, Naoroji had at his disposal a battery of testimonials from India that he could employ in speeches, pamphlets, and
other publications. A letter from Griffith indicates one way that these testimonials were utilized: a Clerkenwell publisher, he informed Naoroji,
had just printed off two thousand copies of a leaflet entitled "Message
from India" that was to be distributed to electors.[37]

Naoroji's campaign, therefore, received a much-needed shot in the arm
from Malabari's journalist contacts. And, at roughly the same time, another set of Malabari's contacts raised Naoroji's hopes about rallying the
Liberal Party leadership to his side. In the course of his social reform activities, Malabari had forged strong relations with Liberal politicians who
had served in the government of India. Foremost among these was Lord
Ripon. While touring the United Kingdom during the final few months
of 1891, Malabari requested that Ripon lobby Liberal Party leaders on
Naoroji's behalf. "I should rejoice to see an Indian gentleman chosen by
an English Constituency," Ripon replied to Malabari, but cautioned that
"there are special difficulties in the way of the success of such a candidate."
Ripon believed that the best course of action was for Naoroji to retire

from Central Finsbury on Schnadhorst's explicit promise of assistance in finding him another constituency. By October 1891, according to Malabari, Ripon had begun setting this plan in motion, presumably negotiating with the National Liberal Federation chairman. A few months later, Naoroji received word that Ripon had embarked upon a much more ambitious course of action, and was now "endeavoring to get Mr Ford out, and to get the Party managers to declare for me." Regardless of precisely what happened behind closed doors at the National Liberal Federation's offices, Ripon's interventions at least gave Naoroji some encouragement and hope of success. As he explained to Malabari, his only other option vis-à-vis Schnadhorst was publishing their private correspondence, which would reveal the chairman's previous assurances of support. It would be a highly risky move, and there was no guarantee of it doing anything to change the dynamics of the split in Central Finsbury. Fortunately, Naoroji remarked, "this new, kind intervention of Lord Ripon" had "shut up my mouth."[38]

One other subject weighed heavily on Dadabhai Naoroji's mind: money. When Behramji Malabari first broached the topic of Naoroji's campaign with Lord Ripon, he revealed that the candidate had already expended nearly "a lakh of money" (Rs. 100,000) on electioneering. By early 1892, Naoroji had been canvassing Central Finsbury for three and a half years, and there were still no indications of a general election occurring anytime soon. Engaged in a protracted and extremely costly campaign, where could he expect to obtain the necessary funds? The answer once more lies with Malabari. Financial assistance was the last, and perhaps most critical, arena in which the Parsi social reformer aided the aspiring MP. Since at least September 1886, mere months after Holborn, Malabari had been actively soliciting donations in India and coordinating large transfers of cash to London. Finding adequate campaign funding had, from the start, been a persistent source of worry for Naoroji and his Indian allies. Friends such as Allan Octavian Hume had pointed out that Naoroji's coffers would largely have to be filled by supporters in India. But, at the same time, Hume despaired of any significant contributions from north India or Bengal, which had coughed up a relatively trifling sum in aid of

Lalmohan Ghosh. Furthermore, any donation from the subcontinent automatically lost one-fifth of its value on exchange. Faced with these challenges, Malabari opened a special account in Bombay, the Dadabhai Naoroji Public Work Fund, and began actively searching for committed donors, primarily in western India.[39]

He first sought out support among fellow Zoroastrians. However, this was an activity that came with a particular hazard—namely, having to deal with cantankerous old Parsi men. Dinshaw Petit, the Bombay mill baron, kicked up a fuss when he was approached for a donation. Malabari summarized his interaction with one of India's wealthiest sons, a man recently honored with his own hereditary baronetcy: "'Why should I pay?' asks this logical knight. Further, it appears he is anxious to have his contribution made public—which I have told him distinctly on no account to do." In the end, Petit handed over a mere Rs. 500. Padamji Pestonji, a wealthy coreligionist in Poona, appeared greatly disturbed by the idea of bankrolling any nationalist activity. "The fact is Poona Parsis as others in the mofussil not only do not appreciate the work but say it is a sin for Parsis to risk their all on Hindus & Mahomedans," an exasperated Malabari informed Naoroji. There are indications that Malabari also approached Jamsetji Tata, but we have no evidence that the industrialist ever wrote out a check in the name of the Public Work Fund. In the end, Malabari, bitter from his experiences with Parsis, looked outside of the community. He canvassed "upcountry Hindus and Mahamadans," while in Bombay he hoped to receive better responses from leading Muslims such as Fazulbhoy Visram and Rahimtullah Sayani. Malabari also made his own donations to Naoroji's electoral fund, transmitting at least Rs. 5,000 and perhaps as much as Rs. 20,000.[40]

Such funds, collected from industrialists, merchants, and professionals across India, helped somewhat defray mounting campaign expenses in Central Finsbury. But Malabari's greatest coup, something that single-handedly kept Naoroji in the race, was his success in winning financial support from the princely states of Gujarat. It is apparent that a group of princes—including many who had known and worked with Naoroji for decades, and some of whom had earlier donated to the East India Association—provided Naoroji with the overwhelming bulk of his financial reserves. We have limited evidence about their donations: Naoroji,

Malabari, and the princes very deliberately kept the transactions as secret as possible. A few passages and cryptic references in Naoroji and Malabari's correspondence, however, provide us some clues. In seeking the support of princes, Malabari once more turned to his coreligionists: many Parsis were employed as ministers and advisors to Gujarati rulers. As early as 1885—a year before Naoroji sailed from Bombay—Malabari had begun relying on this network of Parsi officials to lay the groundwork for princely support, approaching the darbars of Kutch, Junagadh, and Jamnagar.[41]

These early discussions paid off. By 1890, Naoroji appears to have been in possession of a substantial sum from "H. H. Rao," most likely Khengarji III, maharao of Kutch. Later, in 1892, Malabari played a role in securing several installments of cash—the first being for £1,000—from Sayajirao III of Baroda. Rustom P. Masani, Naoroji's first biographer, informs us that on the heels of Sayajirao's donation, the darbars of Bhavnagar and "other Indian States" provided "substantial help." "There is no need to go into details," Masani remarks mysteriously, perhaps confirming that this help was substantial indeed. However, it was another prince who provided Naoroji with the most liberal assistance: Bhagvatsinhji, the thakur of Gondal. The progressive ruler enjoyed excellent relations with both Malabari and Naoroji. It helped, furthermore, that while Naoroji waged his campaign in Central Finsbury, Bhagvatsinhji was conveniently in residence in Great Britain, earning a medical degree from Edinburgh. We know that the thakur presented a "big instalment," later revealed to be a lakh of rupees, to Naoroji in 1888. More arrived throughout 1891. In a letter from January of that year, Malabari let Naoroji know that "K."—most probably Kavasji Desai, the Parsi employed as Bhagvatsinhji's private secretary—would shortly send him a check for "25"—Rs. 25,000. Upon receipt, Naoroji was instructed to thank "the T."—the thakur—and then, following Desai's instructions, "ask for 50 more." By the end of the year, as Frederick A. Ford pressed his claims against Naoroji, Bhagvatsinhji appears to have made yet another large donation totaling at least Rs. 50,000.[42]

Thus, princely states, which figured so prominently in Naoroji's political and economic thought, helped plug up a very different drain of wealth, thereby influencing electoral dynamics in Central Finsbury. It is appropriate that some of the most enlightened Indian princes, men who had embarked on significant reforms in their states, provided the greatest help. They were no doubt motivated by a shared enthusiasm for political reform across India, as well as a deep interest in seeing an Indian in Parliament. But what other reasons help explain the particular liberality of a Sayajirao or a Bhagvatsinhji?

Bhagvatsinhji, at least, clearly understood that he enjoyed a reciprocal relationship with nationalist leaders, who lobbied on behalf of his interests before authorities in Bombay, Calcutta, and London. By no coincidence, the thakur cut checks to Naoroji just as the Central Finsbury candidate was trying to convince India Office officials to raise the number of honorary salutes offered for Gondal state. Additionally, both Naoroji and Malabari closely advised the thakur as he became embroiled in his paternity suit in Scotland in 1892.[43] This reciprocal relationship, therefore, worked exceedingly well for all parties.

Regardless of particular motivations, Indian allies proved themselves to be absolutely indispensable during all phases of the Central Finsbury campaign, furnishing Naoroji with much-needed logistical assistance, press coverage, and, of course, the vast sums of money needed to sustain his candidacy. By March 1892, rumors were growing of an imminent dissolution of Lord Salisbury's Conservative government, which would trigger the much-delayed general election. Naoroji responded accordingly, stepping up his correspondence with Malabari and making inquiries with Lord Ripon about the progress of negotiations with Francis Schnadhorst. And, not surprisingly, he penned a brief note to Bhagvatsinhji, requesting another sizable donation. "The coming Election and the opposition I have to fight against, entail upon me very heavy expenses," Naoroji explained. "Your help is my only support."[44]

The Hardest Struggle in the Metropolis

In the span of around fifteen weeks, between late March and early July 1892, Dadabhai Naoroji's parliamentary campaign went through its final, climactic stage. During this stage, the four groups that had influenced the course of events in Central Finsbury since 1888—progressive British allies, ordinary electors, Liberal Party power brokers, and Indian allies—pushed and pulled in various contradictory ways, creating a decidedly schizophrenic electoral denouement for Naoroji. The *Standard* of London predicted the Central Finsbury competition to be "the hardest struggle in the Metropolis."[45] And throughout this struggle, events transpired that caused the Indian candidate's electoral prospects to constantly rise and fall by increasingly dizzying proportions.

Power brokers cast the first shot. Toward the end of March, Lord Ripon finally announced to Naoroji the results of his discussions at the National Liberal Federation. In a lengthy letter, the ex-viceroy counseled Naoroji to accept arbitration in his dispute with Frederick A. Ford. Ripon offered to search out "an able and impartial person, of good position in the Party and entirely without bias," in order to judge who should become the universally recognized Liberal candidate from Central Finsbury. Naoroji was clearly stunned by the contents of Ripon's letter. For nearly six months, he had nursed hopes that Ripon was working toward a decisive show of support from the party leadership. Instead, Ripon had suggested a course of action that Naoroji's opponents most preferred and had long advocated. Arbitration, as was explained by J. E. Searle, one of the candidate's election agents, was simply a byword for forced retirement, compliments of senior power brokers:

> You have all to lose and nothing to gain. The answer to any arbitration would be "We are very sorry Mr. Naoroji. But we think you had better retire although we think you have acted very well. The Party is split and therefore there is a risk of the loss of a seat. You must be the one sacrificed." I know their ways quite well.[46]

Naoroji penned a brief and somewhat terse reply to Ripon, flatly ruling out the proposed arbitration. "I shall now go on as I think best for my honor and conscience," he concluded. This meant publishing his private correspondence with Francis Schnadhorst, which would reveal the latter's clear statements of support for the Naoroji campaign made in 1888 and again in 1890. In early April, Central Finsbury electors received this correspondence in the form of a pamphlet, "Mr. D. Naoroji and Mr. Schnadhorst." The pamphlet elicited a strongly worded letter from Arnold Morley, the Liberal Party whip, who threatened to bring the full force of the National Liberal Federation against Naoroji if he did not accept immediate arbitration. It appears that Naoroji dismissed the threat: R. M. H. Griffith responded by sending Morley copies of Naoroji's electoral handbills and pamphlets, assuring the party whip that on account of the candidate's "continued and increasing popularity, we are very hopeful indeed of winning the Central Finsbury seat for him and our common cause."[47]

Aside from antagonizing Morley, the pamphlet caused "much hurt" to Schnadhorst. Several Liberal newspapers also criticized Naoroji for his actions. By mid-April, it appeared as though Naoroji had made a fatal misstep, giving Ford and anti-Naoroji power brokers the upper hand. Yet the precise opposite seems to be the case. It is unclear what, exactly, transpired within the Liberal Party offices in late April and May of 1892. It is very likely that, aside from antagonizing a few key figures, Naoroji's pamphlets made the National Liberal Federation and the Ford campaign realize that the Indian candidate quite simply would not go down without a fight. "They think they can keep down the mild Hindoo," he had confided to a British friend at the very beginning of his campaign troubles. "I will show them." Those words proved to be prophetic.[48]

Given the very real possibility of a Conservative victory in Central Finsbury if two Liberal candidates remained in the race, an even messier fight was precisely what the federation was trying to avoid. Therefore, on the morning of June 11, Richard Causton, the Liberal MP for Southwark, paid a surprise visit to Naoroji at the National Liberal Club. Acting as an emissary of the federation, Causton asked for "some overture for peace." As the Ford campaign prepared for what would be, in hindsight, their last major meeting—deliberately designed to conflict with another local event featuring Naoroji—Causton all but acknowledged the legitimacy of Naoroji's nomination, giving assurances that the federation would work for him and expend "every effort" to repair divisions in the constituency so as to overcome the Conservative challenge. "He said he wanted to see me in the House and would do what he can," Naoroji informed William Digby.[49]

And thus sometime during the second week of June, Frederick A. Ford quietly and without explanation dropped out of the race. Anti-Naoroji power brokers, who had for so long argued that Naoroji was unelectable, were brought to heel by senior officials at the National Liberal Federation—who finally recognized the insurgent campaign as the true impediment. "Mr. F. A. Ford has formally announced his own retirement from the unequal contest," announced one local paper with evident relief, "and consequently Mr. Naoroji's candidature is no longer hampered by any rival in this direction." The Naoroji campaign now worked rapidly—in the span of mere weeks—to overcome four years of bitterness and factionalism. "I am breaking down ALL the barriers—and making firewood of them to keep enthusiasm warm and comfortable—things could not well be proceeding better," Griffith enthusiastically reported to his boss by mid-month. "Am glad to say that the tension is practically all over now so rest easy and prepare for the campaign in *quiet* earnest, it is all right now."[50]

We have evidence that at least one anti-Naoroji official eventually made amends with the Indian candidate. Henry Mundy, presumably an Irishman, wrote a brief note to Naoroji after Ford's retirement. "I may disagree with the manner you have thought right to pursue," Mundy stated, but "it becomes my duty and [that of] all other men calling themselves Radicals, not only to support but to work hard for the next few days to return you to the House of Commons by a large majority, which will gladden the hearts of all true Irish People, and crown with success the work of one of the greatest statesm[e]n [who] ever lived—W. E. Gladstone."[51] Party sentiment, and the desire for a decisive victory against the Conservatives, ultimately helped some of Naoroji's enemies overcome any lingering prejudice, mending a few of the divisions among Central Finsbury Liberals.

In order to rally electors, Naoroji now turned to progressive and Indian allies. Women were at the forefront. He asked Emmeline Pankhurst and Florence Nightingale to speak and write on his behalf. Naoroji also won the endorsement of at least one feminist publication, the *Woman's Herald*. "Whenever women want his help it is freely given, and we would appeal to women in return to secure his election," the journal advised. Many women, evidently, responded to the *Herald*'s call. Several wealthy ladies seem to have loaned their carriages for election day so that Naoroji's volunteers could drive Liberal voters to the polls. In the meanwhile, women volunteers canvassed Clerkenwell on behalf of the Indian candidate. An "army of ladies," Griffith remarked, filed into the campaign offices in order to manage various tasks and affairs. Farther afield in Bombay, Behramji Malabari worked with Indian allies to orchestrate another strong show of support from Indian political associations and the media. From his Hornby Road office, he dispatched urgent telegrams across the subcontinent to Poona, Allahabad, Nagpur, Calcutta, Lahore, Madras, and other cities, carrying instructions for immediate action. "Pray wire immediately, thro[ugh] Dadabhai or Digby message of cordial thanks to the electors urging them also to carry Dadabhai through for India's sake," he commanded. "I pay cost of wire if required." Princes helped as well: Sayajirao purchased the services of twenty carriages, which on election day plied the streets of Clerkenwell alongside the coaches loaned by Naoroji's female supporters (Lord Salisbury, meanwhile, provided carriages for the opposition).[52]

Finally, it was the turn of the electors of Central Finsbury to bring a long and tumultuous campaign to its conclusion. With polling day in Clerkenwell set for July 6, voters—inundated with leaflets and pamphlets, sifting through messages from India, and attending to house calls from women activists—weighed their choices carefully. Both candidates emphasized policy issues, although the Tories might have also tried to whip up racial sentiment against Naoroji. Frederick Thomas Penton, the Conservative incumbent, stressed the dangers of Irish home rule, cast doubt upon the eight-hour workday, and reminded his voters of the Conservative ministry's attempt to protect the British watchmaking industry—a critical component of the Clerkenwell economy—from foreign competition. Naoroji's agenda began with "Home Rule for Ireland" and ended with "Reforms for India." In between were declarations of support for "Free Education," public control of utilities and "ALL other Municipal necessities" in London, electoral reform consistent with the principle of "One Man One Vote only," "Legal Eight Hours" for workers, and "Abolition of the Hereditary System of Legislature."[53]

From the few extant letters penned by voters around the time of the election, it appears that Clerkenwell Liberals cast their ballots for Naoroji on account of his agenda and broader party considerations. There were hardly any references to Naoroji's ethnicity. Edward Breen, of 39 Gloucester Street, announced that he was cutting short a visit to Dover in order to vote for the Indian candidate. "I feel keenly anxious that Clerkenwell shall not again be misrepresented by a Tory," Breen mentioned, offering to volunteer for the campaign on polling day. Another local, George Bateman of 45 Millman Street, cited "the admirable manner in which you have supported the demands of labour—English Irish and Indian," and also placed his services at Naoroji's disposal.[54] In spite of the disarray of the long and drawn-out intraparty dispute, and in spite of the official candidate's foreign extraction, Clerkenwell Liberals rallied to Naoroji as a natural exponent of the district's progressive, radical political traditions.

The election was almost a dead heat. In the late evening hours of July 6, tabulators announced the final results: 2,959 votes for Naoroji and 2,956 for Penton. Naoroji had unseated the Conservative incumbent by three votes, a margin later widened to five votes in a recount. But he had won nonetheless. As night descended over central London, a crude contraption of electric lights mounted on the tower of the National Liberal Club along Victoria Embankment flashed one more win for Gladstone's party. Halfway across the world, Behramji Malabari heard of the victory while at the offices of the *Bombay Samachar*, having just called on Naoroji's wife and children at their Khetwadi residence. Seated at home, Malabari began writing a long letter to Naoroji. "The real work begins *now*," he reminded the new member for Central Finsbury.[55]

CHAPTER 6

Member for India

AMID THE SHOALS OF CONGRATULATORY MESSAGES and telegrams that streamed in from across the world, the newly elected Indian member of Parliament received two novel monikers. The first was "Dadabhai Narrow-majority," an obvious reference to his razor-thin margin of victory in Central Finsbury—and a name that rolled off the Englishman's tongue with relatively greater ease. The second was more enduring. Naoroji was hailed by Indians and Britons alike as the "Grand Old Man of India," a counterpart to the United Kingdom's Grand Old Man, William Gladstone, now once more prime minister. Like the seniormost Liberal statesman, Naoroji was recognized as the undisputed leader of an entire political program and movement. "Four and forty years have elapsed!" noted one Indian journalist about the Central Finsbury MP. "And the 'Grand Old Man' is still at his post of duty, hearty and hale, grown grey in his country's service but not weary."[1]

Naoroji had long played the role of an Indian emissary. While in the House of Commons, however, he declared himself to be an Indian representative, someone who enjoyed support from across the subcontinent. Testimonials to the "Grand Old Man of India" helped strengthen Naoroji's position. Much of the Indian media also looked up to the new MP as a leader of national standing. The *Kaiser-i-Hind* affirmed that, in the Commons, Naoroji would be "the representative of the whole country and not

THE MODERN COLOSSUS.

Naoroji depicted as a colossus straddling England and India, indicating his dual roles as a British MP and an Indian representative.

Review of Reviews (New York), October 1892, p. 279. Reproduced from Thomas Cooper Library, University of South Carolina.

of any particular class or community." Letters from ordinary Britons, as well as editorials carried in Liberal British broadsheets, likewise identified Naoroji with the political destiny of all of India. "Strange that nearly 300,000,000 of people should not have had a representative in the House of Commons up to now!" remarked Thomas Davies, a workingman from the mill town of Warrington.[2]

But not all Britons shared Davies's sentiments about the election's implications for India. Nor could many see their way to offer grudging acceptance of Naoroji's victory. Several Tory papers expressed noticeable unease about the presence of an Indian in the Palace of Westminster. "Is he the first link forged in a chain of Home Rule for India?" asked the *Bristol Times*. More worryingly, could Britons "wake up one fine morning to find that English members are in a minority in the Imperial Parliament"? Alarmed at Naoroji's election, many Conservatives sought to undermine claims that he could be an Indian representative. And they attempted to do so through the language of race. The *Spectator* held that "a Parsee is no more a representative of Indians, than a Nestorian Christian would be of Ottomans." *St. Stephen's Review,* meanwhile, offered the most damning verdict: "Central Finsbury should be ashamed of itself at having publicly confessed that there was not in the whole of the division an Englishman, a Scotchman, a Welshman or an Irishman as worthy of their votes as this Fire-Worshipper from Bombay."[3]

These differing responses to Naoroji's election set the tone for the rest of the MP's short term in Parliament, from the summer of 1892 until the next general elections held in mid-1895. His ability to represent Indians became a subject of occasionally fierce contestation. Furthermore, as the comments of the *Spectator* and *St. Stephen's Review* reveal, Naoroji's opponents seized on his Parsi identity in order to undermine his claims to be member for India: how could a Parsi, a member of a minuscule ethnoreligious minority, possibly represent a territory that was mostly Hindu and Muslim? Naoroji's foreignness, therefore, continued to be a lightning rod for his opponents (indeed, some of these opponents associated the Parsi MP with a much broader foreign threat: Naoroji's defeated Conservative rival, Frederick Thomas Penton, unsuccessfully attempted to reverse the election result by claiming that several Liberal voters in Central Finsbury were, in fact, unnaturalized immigrants from Italy, Germany, France, and elsewhere).[4] However, the MP's return to the subcontinent during the winter of 1893–1894, when he served as the president of the Lahore session of the Congress, largely dissipated any doubts about Naoroji being a popularly recognized Indian representative. During a whistle-stop train tour from Bombay to Lahore, Naoroji was welcomed by massive demonstrations that affirmed his broad and diverse support base. Decades before Mohandas K. Gandhi made extensive use of India's railway network for political purposes, Naoroji embarked on a train journey that confirmed an emerging mass appeal for nationalist activities.

The whistle-stop tour, along with the congratulatory letters and Indian newspaper editorials after his election, had larger implications. They helped confirm Naoroji's status as the first modern Indian political leader of a fundamentally *national* standing. The Parsi MP was, of course, identified with Bombay and its political milieu, but his name was associated with pan-Indian interests, causes, and aspirations rather than regional ones. This was perhaps best expressed by G. P. Pillai, a Malayali leader of the Congress and a prominent journalist in Madras. "If India were a Republic and the Republic had the right to elect its own President, the man who by the unanimous voice of his countrymen would be elected its uncrowned king is Mr. Dadabhai Naoroji," Pillai stated. "Others there are who have an Indian reputation but their provincial reputation is even greater than their Indian reputation. To Mr. Naoroji alone is accorded the proud privilege of belonging to all India. Though born in Bombay, Bombay cannot claim him as her son any more than Calcutta or Madras."[5]

Although an Indian leader, Naoroji was also the duly elected representative of a populous London constituency. By all accounts, he enthusiastically threw himself into parliamentary work concerning domestic British affairs. He was present for nearly every vote in the Commons and regularly spent twelve-hour days in Westminster, "all the time working and listening in the House to understand how to vote on every question." In 1893, Naoroji, himself a colonial subject, cast a vote in favor of Irish home rule. The following year, he was one of the key supporters behind a series of bills for improving the infrastructure of metropolitan London, including the completion of the iconic Tower Bridge over the Thames. Aside from these legislative activities in Parliament, Naoroji performed diverse other functions for his constituents, such as helping a Clerkenwell mother purchase her son's discharge from the Royal Navy and supporting costermongers (fruit and vegetable hawkers) facing eviction from a major local thoroughfare. And from across the British Isles, a broad spectrum of associations and unions flooded him with invitations to speak at and participate in meetings and rallies: Tilbury dockworkers, the Amalgamated Society of Railway Servants, suffragists in Bedford, and the Postal Telegraph Clerks' Association, to name a few.[6]

These activities did not distract Naoroji from his main goal: advancing an Indian parliamentary agenda. From the very beginning of his career in the Commons, he made the institution of simultaneous civil service examinations his primary legislative objective. This was not meant to be a sop to indigenous "competition wallahs." Rather, through invocation of his drain theory, Naoroji understood simultaneous examinations as the first step on the long road to self-government. It was, moreover, a first step that had a fighting chance of being achieved through Parliament. In his political corollary to the drain theory, Naoroji had established that the drain of wealth from India could be stanched if more Indians replaced Britons in the civil service. Simultaneous examinations—which would finally give Indians a real chance to qualify for positions in their own government—would begin the irreversible process of Indianizing the civil service. Thus, as he prepared to take his seat in Parliament, Naoroji harked back to the first phase in his political thought, reestablishing Indian poverty as his chief concern.

A Great Deal More than You Recognize

As member for India, Dadabhai Naoroji acquired a second set of constituents far removed from those in Clerkenwell: a vast network of Indian political actors that included Congress members, princely officials, and local community leaders. These individuals transmitted petitions, political intelligence, and statements of grievances to Naoroji, who then made use of this material on the floor of the Commons or in discussions with key Liberal ministers. Political actors in the subcontinent consequently influenced the shape and direction of Naoroji's emerging parliamentary agenda for India.

The first component of this agenda involved empowering Indians against colonial officials. With Naoroji in the Commons, Indians gained powerful new leverage against the British Indian bureaucracy. Thus, in early February 1893, M. Viraraghavachariar, writing from the Madras offices of the *Hindu*, informed Naoroji of the government's attempts to exclude Indian candidates for the position of Sanskrit professor at Madras Presidency College, as well its efforts to politically influence high court judges by appointing them members of the governor's executive council. Around the same time, ministers to the nizam of Hyderabad most likely sought Naoroji's assistance in exposing the British resident's reliance on a corrupt intermediary who was extorting large sums from the darbar. Naoroji brought up these matters in Parliament in the form of questions to the undersecretary of state for India, exerting high-level pressure upon the India Office for their resolution. In the matter of the Sanskrit professorship in Madras, at least, this pressure resulted in a favorable outcome: the appointment went to an Indian.[7]

Indians in the diaspora recognized Naoroji as their representative as well, and regularly sought his assistance. Members of the diaspora were some of the first to reach out to the Central Finsbury MP after his election. "I hope Mr. Dadabai [sic] Naoroji will not only represent the East Indians residing in India, but will also take an interest in those who have emigrated to this and other parts of the world," Veera Sawmy, an Indian in British Guiana, wrote in the columns of Aziz Ahmad's Glasgow-based paper, *Asia*, in September 1892. Sometime later that year, Naoroji received a memorial from the tiny and obscure Indian community of Madagascar, which loudly protested the British government's forfeiture of their interests upon the creation of a French protectorate on the island. Aside from bringing the memorial to the attention of the foreign secretary, Naoroji pursued the matter in Parliament, questioning the Foreign Office in 1894 on how it planned to respond to a spate of French attacks on Indian subjects.[8]

Like their co-nationals in Madagascar, Indians in South Africa quickly opened lines of communication with Naoroji. Here, Boers and British colonists alike were growing alarmed at the number of immigrants arriving from the subcontinent, which posed a threat to white political dominance. In the dusty mining town of Kimberley, Haji Ojer Ally, chairman of the newly constituted Coloured Agitation Committee, fired off letters protesting the Cape Colony's new Franchise and Ballot Act, championed by Cecil Rhodes to diminish the political power of Indian residents. Ally specifically sought Naoroji's help in convincing Lord Ripon, now colonial secretary, to advise Queen Victoria to withhold royal assent for the act—Indians' only hope for defeating Rhodes's measure. Further to the southeast in Durban, representatives of an Indian mercantile firm, Haji Mohamed Haji Dada & Co., apprised Naoroji of worsening conditions for Indians in the colony of Natal. "Now that you are in the House we confidently hope you will make it a special duty to protect your countrymen wherever they may be situated," they implored.[9]

Around two years later, another Indian in South Africa approached Naoroji: a self-described "inexperienced and young" Durban barrister by the name of Mohandas K. Gandhi. As Natal followed the lead of the Cape Colony and readied its own bill to disenfranchise Indians, Gandhi, thrust into a position of leadership vis-à-vis the European settler elite, turned to Naoroji for advice. "You will . . . oblige me very greatly if you will kindly direct and guide me and make necessary suggestions which shall be received as from a father to his child," he wrote in July 1894. Thus commenced around a decade of regular correspondence between the future Mahatma and Naoroji, who helped transmit Gandhi's South African dispatches to British ministers, Indian Congress members, and the press. Like Veera Sawmy in British Guiana and the Durban merchants of Haji Mohamed Haji Dada & Co., Gandhi understood Naoroji's political duties to extend to the entire Indian diaspora. He was confident that the MP would come to the assistance of Natal Indians, using his influence "that always has been and is being used on behalf of the Indians, no matter where situated."[10]

One MP, of course, could not shoulder the burden of Indian affairs both subcontinental and diasporic. In order to advance his work, Naoroji increasingly relied upon a circle of fellow members of Parliament, all of them Liberals or Irish, who took an interest in Indian political matters. His strongest pillar of support was a fellow Congress member, William Wedderburn. Having retired from the Indian civil service in 1887, Wedderburn threw himself into Congress work. He entered the Commons through a by-election in 1893. While not a gifted speaker—"Sir W.W. is regarded as a bore alike in public & in private," judged the ever-opinionated Henry Hyndman—Wedderburn's zeal for the Congress agenda, and for the organization's strategy of pursuing its work through Parliament, was matched only by Allan Octavian Hume and the honorable member for Central Finsbury. Michael Davitt's abbreviated tenure as MP for North-East Cork in early 1893—he was expelled from Parliament for bankruptcy—briefly raised Naoroji's hopes for cementing a solid Irish-Indian alliance (Naoroji thereafter unsuccessfully lobbied Davitt to accept the presidency of the 1894 Madras Congress). In the eventual Congress president for 1894, Alfred Webb, the Indian MP found an equally energetic Irish ally. A Quaker with a staunch belief in universal liberty, Webb was naturally drawn to the cause of Indian political reform. Upon re-signing his parliamentary seat in 1895, he confided to Naoroji that "losing opportunities of helping or at least showing sympathy with India" was the "bitterest pill I have to swallow."[11]

Within the burgeoning British temperance movement, Naoroji found two more loyal friends in Parliament. William Sprotson Caine, MP for East Bradford, was as enthusiastic about Indian political reform as he was condemnatory of drink. He attended the Congress's 1890 session in Cal-cutta and, from the backbenches of the Commons, channeled his invec-tive against the Indian opium trade with China, a cause in which he was supported by Naoroji. Samuel Smith, MP for Flintshire, had known Naoroji for more than three decades—since their days as Liverpool cotton traders in the late 1850s. Smith adopted many of Naoroji's views on In-dian poverty and, with Caine and the Indian MP at his side, presided over the Anglo-Indian Temperance Association. Together, these men, bound by the progressive alliances that Naoroji had long nurtured, began to for-mally coordinate their activities in the Commons. Wedderburn, Naoroji, and Caine founded an Indian Parliamentary Committee in July 1893, which soon grew in size to a whopping 154 MPs.[12]

Possessing the support and confidence of Indians dispersed around the globe, and the sympathies of several fellow parliamentarians, Naoroji now began formulating a distinctly Indian legislative agenda premised on the subcontinent's staggering poverty. The Indian MP began by distrib-uting copies of a booklet, *Poverty of India*, consisting of Naoroji's two 1876 papers of that name, to ministers in Gladstone's government. He attempted to access confidential reports and statements on Indian poverty—occasionally meeting with stony silence or the rebukes of in-credulous India Office officials. In speeches to the Commons, he chided Britons for "not giv[ing] a single thought to the sufferings of men who are being ground to the very dust" by India's "extreme poverty." On occasion, he spoke in bolder terms about the drain of wealth and the consequences of foreign rule. "Lord Macaulay has said that 'the heaviest of all yokes is the yoke of the stranger,'" Naoroji told the chamber on the evening of March 28, 1893, provoking an angry chorus of "Oh, oh!" from Conserva-tive benches. "So long as this House does not understand that the yoke as it at present exists practically in India is 'the heaviest of all yokes,' India has no future, India has no hope. (Loud cries of 'Oh, oh!') You may say 'Oh, oh!' but you have never been, fortunately—and I hope and pray you may never be—in the condition in which India is placed in your hands."[13]

In spite of such forthrightness about Indian poverty, the Central Finsbury MP, for the most part, adopted a policy of pronounced political moderation, employing far more caution than he ever did on the campaign trail. His rhetoric was sometimes cloyingly moderate—and, given his previous statements and policy positions, occasionally disingenuous. In his maiden address to Parliament, Naoroji affirmed that India was "governed on the lines of British freedom and justice." He lavished praise on Great Britain for endowing India with freedom of speech—in spite of being well aware of the Raj's history of onerous sedition and press censorship laws. In interviews with the British press, he downplayed Indian demands for representative government—in spite of, as early as 1868, identifying and clamoring for "that great end, a Parliament or Parliaments in India," and, much more recently, appealing to Gladstone to grant "Real Living Representation" to Indian subjects. If Naoroji hoped that such cautious language would take the steam out of his opponents, he was clearly mistaken. They had a long memory. While reporting on the relatively anodyne nature of a speech on British rule that Naoroji delivered in early 1893, the *Pioneer* of Allahabad, a mouthpiece of Anglo-Indian interests, reminded its readership that the speaker was still "the spokesman of Indian self-government."[14]

Such caution, and occasional obfuscation, continued as Naoroji brought the question of simultaneous civil service examinations before Parliament. Simultaneous examinations enjoyed a broad spectrum of support among British and Indian political figures. Its moderate and relatively unambitious nature, Naoroji hoped, would mask its more ambitious ends—namely, the irreversible process of Indianization of the services, an essential foundation for self-government. But some more astute political observers were able to call the MP's bluff. In an interview for the London-based *Pearson's Weekly*, Naoroji dismissed speculation that he had in mind anything more ambitious than civil service reform. "Home rule is scarcely the word; we don't want anything in the least like what the Irish want," he affirmed. His interviewer shot back: "Come, Mr. Naoroji, do you mean to say that the end and object of all political agitation in India is to get a handful of young men into the Civil Service!" Naoroji's reply must have confirmed the reporter's suspicions. "Ah no," he stated, "it means a great deal more than you recognize."[15]

On March 1, 1893, Naoroji tabled a bill in the House of Commons that called for the simultaneous holding in India and Great Britain of the first round of civil service examinations. The bill, however, was met with the steely opposition of Lord Kimberley, the secretary of state for India. It consequently failed to advance to its second reading, where it could have been debated by MPs. Undaunted by this failure, Naoroji began pursuing his next best option: introducing a resolution supporting simultaneous examinations. A resolution, of course, was non-binding, but it would initiate debate and thereby force William Gladstone's ministry to take a stance on the topic. It also provided some symmetry to Naoroji's career: in 1868, Naoroji had worked behind the scenes to support the first so-called member for India, Henry Fawcett, as he introduced a similar resolution before the Commons. Immediately after the failure of his bill, therefore, Naoroji began assiduously lobbying his fellow MPs on the subject of Indian civil service reform. He did so in spite of establishing—via a question put to the undersecretary of state for India—that the government was steadfastly opposed to the principle of simultaneous examinations.[16]

Naoroji chose to confront this opposition by catching government ministers unawares. Late in the night of June 2, 1893—well after most sensible parliamentarians had departed Westminster and retired to their beds—Herbert Paul, the Liberal MP for Edinburgh South and a member of the Indian Parliamentary Committee, introduced Naoroji's resolution on the floor of the Commons. After Paul's speech, which clearly bore Naoroji's stamp, the member for Central Finsbury rose to second the resolution. He framed civil service reform as something that would restore "the good name of the British people" among a skeptical Indian public. Avoiding direct reference to Indian poverty, which could attract the ire of disbelieving Conservative elements, he instead argued that the question at hand was one of justice and honor—reversing more than a century of misrule in India. Naoroji was careful to lay full blame for Indian misrule upon Anglo-Indian officials, who were guilty of "subterfuges and unworthy and un-English means." Members of the Commons, he concluded, had an opportunity to rectify the unfortunate situation and thereby strengthen the empire, ensuring that "their power might rest upon the strongest foundation of the contentment of the people . . . which would be unshakable for ever."[17]

Conservative MPs did not take the bait. George Chesney, a decorated veteran of the Indian Mutiny, a retired Anglo-Indian official, and now member for Oxford, led the charge against the resolution. Chesney had shot to fame in 1871 for writing *The Battle of Dorking*, an alarmist work of fiction about a German invasion of England—and an implicit warning that Britain was in danger of losing its military and imperial dominance. Paul and Naoroji's proposal to loosen the British stranglehold on the civil service, therefore, made Chesney see red. He saw no point "hiding the fact that India was held at present by the sword." On that account, it was unthinkable to "do away with the English Agency in the government of India." Chesney, furthermore, drew upon several classic racial arguments to dismiss the fitness of Indian candidates. There was "no similarity between the moral and intellectual conditions" in India and Britain, and he sternly warned that "it would be in the highest degree undesirable to flood India with Bengalee civil servants." In resorting to racial tropes, Chesney was ably helped by a fellow Conservative MP, George Curzon. Curzon, whose desire to become the Indian viceroy was common knowledge in Westminster, coolly stated that Europeans were more likely to have the requisite "high moral character" and "wide culture and experience" necessary to be a "ruling type of man."[18]

Chesney and Curzon's arguments must have deeply stung Naoroji, who had labored against such racist drivel for decades. Yet it was George Russell, undersecretary of state for India and a fellow Liberal MP, who attacked Naoroji's resolution with the most obnoxiously prejudiced arguments. Citing the "great, fundamental, racial difficulty" as the primary reason for the government's opposition to simultaneous examinations, Russell asserted that Indians were, "as a race, . . . less richly endowed with the gifts of government." The undersecretary of state was also skilled in the art of self-contradiction. India, he continued, was "not composed of one race but of many," and once more singled out Bengalis for particular contempt. The "fierce, turbulent races" of the north and west, Russell stated, "would resent, and very strongly resent, any attempt on the part of the Bengalese [sic] natives to exercise administrative control over them." It was best to keep the Englishman at the helm.[19]

After Russell, Chesney, and Curzon had delivered their blows against the resolution, Herbert Paul moved for a vote, no doubt anticipating that the late-night session would be capped off with an embarrassing defeat. After all, aside from Naoroji and William Wedderburn, no one else in the chamber had spoken in favor of the resolution. Naoroji, however, was far more sanguine. He had canvassed support from a large number of MPs, many of them members of the Indian Parliamentary Committee, and had ensured that—unlike so many members of the government and numerous Tories, who had long ago retired for the night—they stayed put in the chamber. These MPs might have remained silent during the debate, but they were present for the vote. Once the speaker had tallied the ayes and nays, 84 votes for the resolution and 76 against, the undersecretary of state for India realized to his utter horror that embarrassing defeat was his fate, not Paul's. The vote marked the first defeat for Gladstone's ministry since the 1892 general elections. And it had been brought about by the prime minister's fellow Liberals.[20]

Naoroji had not simply caught the government unawares—he had quite literally caught his opposition asleep. On June 5, members in the Commons peppered a red-faced Gladstone with questions on how the government would react to the successful resolution. The prime minister could only respond that he needed a few days to consider the matter. In the subcontinent, Anglo-Indian organs, jolted out of a similar state of somnolence about civil service reform, reacted with trepidation. With Naoroji gaining allies in the Commons, they fretted over the broader implications of increased parliamentary intervention in Indian affairs. "In these days," rued the *Pioneer*, "we may wake to find . . . the Opium Revenue cut off or the machinery of the administration revolutionised by a snap vote, secured by men who make no pretence to knowledge." Indian papers, meanwhile, celebrated a rare victory over the ruling sahibs. "Whatever the decision now, the final issue is clear enough; it is only a question of sooner or later" for the institution of simultaneous examinations, the *Indian Spectator* confidently predicted. "India cannot be too thankful to the House for their righteous resolution."[21]

A few months after Dadabhai Naoroji's victory in the House of Commons, tragedy struck his family. Ardeshir, his son, had spent the past decade establishing himself as a respected doctor in the princely state of Kutch, even earning a promotion and commendation from Khengarji, the ruling maharao. Watching at a distance from London, Naoroji beamed with pride about his son, who earlier had caused him so much distress with his lackadaisical school record in college and his obsession with guns. Moreover, in the absence of his father, Ardeshir was now taking an active role in the education of his siblings: he encouraged his younger sister, Maki, herself an aspiring physician, to join him in Kutch in order to receive some medical training. But one day in early October 1893, after he had completed his hospital duties in the town of Mandvi, Ardeshir suddenly collapsed and died of heart failure. He was barely thirty-five years old. Ardeshir left behind four daughters and three sons—and his young widow, Virbai, was pregnant with their eighth child. Naoroji learned of the news via a series of brief telegrams dashed off from Kutch and Bombay.[22]

He was utterly devastated. In the subsequent days and weeks, Naoroji completely withdrew from public life, quietly mourning within the confines of his London residence. An immediate return to Bombay, where he would at least be in the comforting embrace of family members, was simply out of the question. Meanwhile, both in the imperial capital and halfway around the world in India, friends rushed to assist the family. Behramji Malabari cabled the darbar of Kutch, securing monetary support for Ardeshir's children and a pledge to employ Virbai as a teacher within the royal household. R. M. H. Griffith, Naoroji's indefatigable secretary, took charge of the MP's correspondence and stood in for him at several appointments and social functions. With Griffith's assistance, the Naoroji household in Bombay learned of the great sympathy that Ardeshir's death had generated in faraway England: messages and resolutions of condolence poured in from political associations, churches, and countless private individuals. "It all shows how human we are here, not quite so bad as you Indians make us out sometimes to be," he wrote to Fram Dadina, widowed Virbai's brother. "We have many funny ways, but a good many of us are all right at bottom when you have rubbed the varnish off."[23]

Naoroji's grief was complicated by another factor: realization that he had to quickly get back to work. With every passing day and week away from Westminster, he risked sapping the momentum of his parliamentary agenda for Indian reform. Friends such as Allan Octavian Hume and Malabari had the unpleasant task of coaxing Naoroji to curtail his absence from public life and the political arena. In letters that interspersed messages of condolence with urgent news from India, they set out a heavy agenda of work to capitalize on the recent resolution in the House of Commons. "I know you have enough of faith and fortitude to bear up against this grievous loss," Malabari counseled. "Remember, all India is your son."[24]

A New Life Is Coming over the Country

A non-binding resolution, passed in the teeth of government opposition and voted upon when relatively few MPs were present, did not constitute any guarantee for the speedy institution of simultaneous examinations. Recognizing the weakness of their position, Dadabhai Naoroji and his Indian allies sought to force the government's hand by coordinating mass demonstrations of support across the subcontinent. In response to those classic arguments of his opponents—the unfitness of Indians to rule, the superior moral character of the European, and the "racial difficulty," as George Russell had put it, of Bengalis ruling over their more warlike cousins—Naoroji hoped to unleash a powerful, unified movement displaying popular enthusiasm for civil service reform.

Starting in the summer of 1893, early nationalists once again constructed sophisticated and wide-ranging networks for achieving their political objectives. Their efforts received a shot in the arm shortly after the passing of the civil service resolution, when Naoroji signaled his willingness to serve as the president of the Congress at its December 1893 Lahore session. Congress leaders set to work to turn Naoroji's

homecoming—his first time on Indian soil since entering Parliament—
into another demonstration of support for simultaneous examinations.
These political activities unfolded on a scale hitherto unseen in India, in
terms of both popular reach and geographic breadth. Agitation for civil
service reform, which swept across the country between mid-1893 and
late 1894, constituted a significant achievement for the early nationalist
movement: it demonstrated that the Congress was not simply a debating
chamber for a handful of elites.

Naoroji and Behramji Malabari once more acted as central nodes. Early
in May, a month before Herbert Paul introduced the resolution in the
Commons, Malabari had already dispatched a "private circular" on civil
service reform to members of the Indian press, urging them to "discuss
the subject heartily." By early July, he reported to Naoroji that "the press
has taken up the question earnestly." In the National Liberal Club's writing
room in London, meanwhile, Naoroji furiously drafted letter after letter
addressed to Congress branches across the country, urging demonstrations, meetings, and petitions in favor of simultaneous examinations.
"This is a supreme moment," he wrote in one letter dispatched to Surendranath Banerjea in Calcutta. "Write to every part of India, rouse it up . . .
All the moral forces and exertions of the past 40 years from 1853 when
the first political associations were formed in India have now come to fru-
ition." Naoroji wanted nothing short of "petitions innumerable" to "pour
into the Commons."[25]

Replies came in waves through the remainder of summer. From Madras, M. Viraraghavachariar discussed plans to hold public meetings "all
over the Presidency," subsequently claiming that signatures for petitions
were being collected "in every town & village." From Barisal in eastern
Bengal, the secretary of the local Congress standing committee informed
Naoroji of the imminent dispatch of several petitions to Parliament. And
from Agra, Ahmedabad, Allahabad, Lucknow, Meerut, Poona, and elsewhere came more petitions, reports of meetings, and messages of support. Even villagers from Vengurla, a Konkan coastal hamlet situated a
few miles north of the Portuguese Goan frontier, canvassed neighboring
towns for signatures and informed Naoroji of their progress. Seeking support for the resolution, Naoroji did not limit his correspondence to po-

litical elites in major cities. He was, as these replies demonstrate, in touch with a broad range of Indians dispersed around the country.[26]

As the Central Finsbury MP started arranging his travel plans for the Lahore Congress, his Conservative and Anglo-Indian opponents attempted to pick away at the movement for simultaneous examinations. In early August 1893, the *Pioneer* somehow came into possession of one of Naoroji's earlier letters to the Madras Congress committee, where he had exhorted members to commence agitation via public meetings and petitions. Publishing the full letter on its front page, the *Pioneer* cited the correspondence as proof that the recent popular demonstrations in India were nothing more than shams stage-managed by "Graduates and Lawyers." The *Times* of London gleefully republished the Allahabad paper's "exposure," claiming that "the whole agitation is artificial and is merely the work of the Congress wirepullers obeying Mr. Naoroji's detailed instructions."[27]

A month later in the Commons, George Chesney complemented the actions of the *Times* and the *Pioneer* by launching a lengthy ad hominem attack against Naoroji. He ridiculed his fellow MP for having "taken up the position as a sort of general Representative of India." Many others in Parliament, Chesney continued, had "a much larger and much more recent experience of India and Indian affairs than the hon. gentleman who represents Finsbury." Chesney acknowledged in the course of his speech that he figured prominently in this august group of individuals. Naoroji's problem was that he was a "stranger." "I would remind him that as regards the people of India he belongs to an alien race," Chesney remarked. Parsis were "aliens separated from the people of India by religion, by race, by caste, by tradition, and by history," and if British rule were ever to collapse, "they would assuredly be driven out of India" on the heels of the English.[28]

By dismissing Naoroji as an alien, the member for Oxford played an unwitting role in shaping the Indian MP's itinerary and reception upon his return to native shores. In order to rebut these attacks and highlight public support for simultaneous examinations, Naoroji decided to turn his upcoming journey to Lahore into a whistle-stop tour of western and northern India. Halting at various cities and towns on the route northward, and visiting locations of importance to Hindus, Muslims, and Sikhs, Naoroji hoped to demonstrate not only his popularity among all Indians, but also the representative nature of the Congress movement and the agitation for civil service reform.

He was, for example, insistent on active Muslim participation in the Lahore Congress. Naoroji had been deeply dismayed by opposition to the Congress offered by prominent Muslim leaders—including two close friends, Kazi Shahabudin, his revenue minister during the Baroda diwanship, and Sayyid Ahmad Khan, the social reformer and educator. By the fall of 1893, the MP recognized, Congress outreach to Muslims had become all the more critical. Hindu revivalist forces, unfurling the banner of cow protection, instigated an orgy of communal violence in northern India, as well as deadly riots in Bombay. This had further polarized Muslims from the Congress. Naoroji therefore issued strict instructions via Malabari to Lahori Congress members: "Impress upon them to have as many Mahamadans with them as possible in all their doings." He was careful to include Aligarh—home to Sayyid Ahmad Khan's Mohammedan Anglo-Oriental College—on his railway itinerary, reach out to the Aga Khan, and organize a mass meeting with the qazi of Bombay.[29]

In spite of such public overtures toward Muslim leaders, it would be wrong to see Naoroji's brief tour through northern and western India as nothing but a choreographed event. Congress organizers—or "wire pullers," as the Times would have it—did indeed plan a few receptions in Bombay, Lahore, and elsewhere. However, neither they nor Naoroji was prepared for the overwhelming public response that ensued. Naoroji's return to India was marked by mass demonstrations of a scale routinely described in the press as "unparalleled," "unprecedented," and "historical." This was in spite of Congress leaders' earnest attempts to temper the celebrations out of respect for Ardeshir Naoroji's recent passing. Even the Times was forced to concede that the demonstrations were "striking." The MP's brief halts at Ahmedabad, Delhi, Amritsar, Allahabad, and elsewhere drew thousands of spectators, while in Bombay and Lahore he literally brought these cities to a halt. These demonstrations did much more than disprove Chesney's allegations against Naoroji: they indicated how early nationalism and the Congress movement were exciting a degree of mass participation across the country.[30]

The MP's reception in Bombay provided for a dramatic beginning. According to one account, half a million people lined Bombay's streets to mark his arrival on Indian soil on the afternoon of December 3, 1893—an exceptionally significant number considering that the city's population hovered around a million. Standing and salaaming to the crowds from within a carriage, Naoroji commenced a four-mile procession from Apollo Bunder through the lanes of Fort, Bhuleshwar, and Girgaum to his home in Khetwadi, where he was reunited with his family members. Bystanders heaped flowers into his carriage, while more petals streamed down from windows, balconies, and rooftops lined with spectators. So great were these offerings that one reporter quipped that Naoroji was "nearly asphyxiated with the flowers." As the procession entered Hornby Road, Parsi priests from Dadyseth Agiary offered benedictions to the MP in the sacred languages of Avestan and Pahlavi. Naoroji was next greeted by "the performance of some ceremony peculiar to the Madrassees," parties of laborers and millworkers, and the cheers of passengers on trams that had been haplessly stranded amid the crowds. In Bhuleshwar, Brahmin priests emerged from a temple to offer their blessings. It took around two hours for the procession to reach its destination, where Naoroji was hurried into his dwelling amid a surge of more well-wishers. Sometime before reaching home, he received a telegraphed message from Madras, announcing that ten thousand people had gathered in the capital of the southern presidency to welcome his return, give "emphatic denial to the gross misrepresentations of Colonel Chesney," and request that the MP visit their city.[31]

By featuring participants of diverse ethnic, religious, and socioeconomic backgrounds, Bombay set the tone for future demonstrations honoring Naoroji. Similar ovations followed in Poona and the cities of Gujarat. After a three-mile procession through Poona's streets—a "miraculous welcome" attended by residents "without any distinction of class or caste"—Naoroji was greeted by Bal Gangadhar Tilak at the Hirabaug town hall. "I think he would be best described by calling him the great teacher of the new religion—the new political religion of India," Tilak said of Naoroji before an audience that included Gopal Krishna Gokhale, a rising leader in the Congress, and the city's municipal commissioners.

Naoroji passed some days at home in Bombay before boarding the Ahmedabad Mail at Grant Road Station and commencing his journey northward. At Surat, crowds gathered at one o'clock in the morning to witness Naoroji's brief halt, while in Baroda he was greeted by the diwan and the city's nagarsheth or head Jain merchant. Arriving at Ahmedabad the next morning, Naoroji surveyed a crowd of nearly ten thousand people that had gathered opposite the station. As the *Times of India* recorded, "The mills stopped work for two hours, and thousands of mill-hands were present." Naoroji paid his respects to Ranchhodlal Chhotalal, founder of the city's first cotton mill, and praised the success of Ahmedabad's indigenous industrial economy.[32]

After Ahmedabad, Naoroji left the limits of Bombay Presidency and his traditional political base. But the demonstrations did not abate. Beawar in Rajputana staged illuminations as Naoroji's train pulled into the town station at one o'clock in the morning. Ajmer awoke to the strains of an "excellent band" at two o'clock. Delhi's reception, in the words of a correspondent for the Lahore *Tribune,* marked "a new era in the history of upper India." In spite of a civil service officer's discouragement of any celebrations, members of the city's municipal committee, a delegation from Awadh, and between five thousand and eight thousand residents packed the station to welcome Naoroji. From here, Naoroji was put at the head of a procession of four hundred carriages that moved down Delhi's grand central artery, Chandni Chowk. More demonstrations followed in Ambala, Ludhiana, Phagwara, and Jalandhar before Naoroji took a longer halt in Amritsar. The holy city of the Sikhs responded with the biggest demonstrations the MP had experienced since Bombay. Around fifty thousand people lined its bazaars and streets, according to one estimate telegraphed to the *Tribune.* Naoroji was conducted to the Golden Temple, where Sikh granthis led a special service, invested the MP with a "sacred cloth," and fastened golden and pink scarves to his Parsi headgear. After taking a sip of holy water from the pool, Naoroji was escorted to the window of the temple's *darshani* gate, where "cheers and acclamations[—]wah! wah! jai! jai!—burst forth from the vast assemblage of 20,000 men and women."[33]

Naoroji's train finally pulled into Lahore Junction at midday on December 26. Denizens of the Punjabi capital marked the end of Naoroji's journey with another demonstration that powerfully reaffirmed the MP's cross-communal popularity. A correspondent for the *Manchester Guardian* reported that the railway station's entrances were completely blocked by crowds extending half a mile into the distance. "Nothing approaching this demonstration has ever before been witnessed in the Punjaub," he observed. From the station—where the Congress president was met with loud cries of "Dadabhai Naoroji ki jai!" and "Long live electors of Central Finsbury"—Naoroji was taken on a four-hour procession. This procession, which "rolled on like a turbulent river" through Anarkali Bazaar and the walled city, led Naoroji past mosques, temples, and gurudwaras, whose entrances, courtyards, and balconies were packed with the followers of Lahore's three main faiths. Quite often, the demonstrations took on an explicitly religious form: individuals stopped Naoroji's carriage to perform *aarti*, give *ashirvad*, and sing *bhajans*. A famous sweet maker, Surjan Singh, upturned a giant plate of sticky *bedana* over spectators. In an open square next to Lahore's waterworks, the poet Syed Nazir Hussain Nazim read out verses in Urdu that he had composed for the occasion, using the MP's name to draw "an augury that henceforth *naoroz* (*new era*) would dawn on India." As the poet finished his recitation, delegations streamed in to present addresses to the MP: groups of students, civic leaders, and a deputation of Lahori Muslims asking Naoroji to bring "the special grievances of the Mahomedans" to the attention of the Commons.[34]

Naoroji's journey through Punjab had taken him through its biggest cities and into some of its most sacred sites. But on the morning of December 27, when he delivered his presidential address before the Congress, he returned to the domain of high politics. In his address, the MP responded to ovations he had received across India, and also assessed India's political progress. This was a speech of great significance, and not simply because it marked the conclusion of a long journey from the halls of Westminster back to the Congress pandal. Rather, the Congress address was significant because it perfectly encapsulated the second phase of Naoroji's career. It was the best expression of the early nationalist strategy for achieving Indian reform in Great Britain and, specifically, through Parliament. And it marked the high point of Naoroji's confidence in British institutions and the British electorate.

As he approached the Congress pandal, Naoroji knew that he had to speak to two audiences—one in India and the other in faraway Westminster. At first he attempted to speak to both: he spelled out necessary political reforms while carefully noting that these demands did not undermine Indians' fundamental loyalty to the crown. The MP thanked members of the Punjab Congress committee for inviting him—"not a Punjabi, not a Muhammadan, nor a Sikh"—to preside. He rebuked the forces of communalism, praising the efforts of various Hindu and Muslim associations to forswear a repetition of the cow-protection-related violence from earlier in the year. "The highest wish of my heart," Naoroji noted, "is that all the people of India should regard and treat each other as fellow-countrymen." Common nationality must trump all other identities. "Whether I am a Hindu, a Muhammadan, a Parsi, a Christian, or of any other creed, I am above all an Indian," he declared. "Our country is India, our nationality is Indian."[35]

By choosing him as president, Naoroji continued, Punjabis had also affirmed their support for simultaneous examinations, "the only method in which justice can be done to all the people of India." Naoroji proceeded to speak of the gravity of Indian poverty and the great difficulties of bringing this to the attention of British legislators and voters. In this arduous task, he stated, Indians could thankfully rely on the assistance of various progressive allies. Singling out the Irish for their steadfast support, Naoroji read out a message from Michael Davitt, who informed Congress delegates that "every one of Ireland's Home Rule Members in Parliament is at your back." In spite of difficulties and setbacks, the MP urged Congress members to maintain faith. "Our faith in the instinctive love of justice and fair play of the people of the United Kingdom is not misplaced," he professed.[36]

Although in the shadow of the Badshahi Masjid, and with nearly a thousand Congress delegates before him, Naoroji began to direct his speech more and more toward his parliamentary audience in London. The presidential address soon took on the form of a final, earnest appeal to the Gladstone ministry to sanction simultaneous examinations. Civil service reform, he argued, fit in with the "moderate and reasonable" agenda of the Congress and would immensely benefit both India and the empire at large. Here, the MP characterized simultaneous examinations as being fundamentally in the interest of Britain and Britons. "I regard the enormous European Services as a great political and imperial weakness," Naoroji continued, noting that the drain of wealth was breeding disaffection. Instead of perpetuating a cycle of poverty and discord, Naoroji held up an alternative imperial vision. With a reformed civil service and a reduced drain of wealth, India would prosper, allowing the empire to be held together through mutually beneficial economic ties rather than military force. A prosperous India that traded on equal terms with Britain, Naoroji believed, would mean that "the United Kingdom would not for a long time hear anything about her 'unemployed.'" Partnered with an economically strong India, Great Britain could also "defy half-a-dozen Russias." This message of economic and political security for the United Kingdom was what Naoroji sought to convey to his fellow MPs. He concluded with the hope of seeing "the British holding out the hand of true fellow-citizenship and of justice to the vast mass of humanity of this great and ancient land of India with benefits and blessings to the human race."[37]

As he stepped away from the pandal and toward the cheering crowds that had assembled on this cold Punjabi morning, Naoroji's thoughts were in London. He had stated his case to MPs, outlining how simultaneous examinations would strengthen India, the empire, and, most fundamentally, Great Britain. Naoroji now eagerly awaited a response from the Liberal ministry.

Departing Lahore, Dadabhai Naoroji passed another three weeks traveling around India. He embarked eastward to Kanpur, Agra, Aligarh, and Allahabad—where his procession included a herd of elephants. With time running short, the MP abandoned plans to journey further onward to Calcutta and Madras, instead returning to Bombay before boarding a Europe-bound steamer on January 20, 1894.

Naoroji's nearly two months in the subcontinent elicited a wide variety of responses and reactions. The Indian media put forth several interpretations of the ovations that were staged from the southern coast through the plains of Punjab. There were, of course, direct references to George Chesney and his ilk, with several newspapers noting how Naoroji's Parsi ethnicity had not precluded him from winning enthusiastic support from a broad spectrum of Indians. In Calcutta, the *Amrita Bazar Patrika* insisted that Naoroji was not simply "a Member of Parliament but *our own* member." The *Gujarati*, meanwhile, argued that "he is as much a Hindu and a Mahomedan as he is a Parsi and all the races are equally proud of the great Parsi patriot who has risen superior to all racial prejudices." Bal Gangadhar Tilak's English broadsheet, the *Mahratta*, agreed: "The fact can no longer be denied by the most prejudiced Anglo-Indian, and even a Chesney . . . will find it difficult in future to forget that Mr. Dadabhai is the real representative of the whole of India."[38]

A few publications, both in India and in Britain, argued that the public demonstrations signified popular support for simultaneous examinations. Here it was Naoroji, who was desirous of pressing this interpretation upon fellow MPs and the British public at large, who offered the most enthusiastic commentary. "The whole foundation of the British rule rests mainly on the confidence in its honor," the MP scribbled in a press statement drafted aboard his Europe-bound steamer, "and of this honor the people regard the Resolution for simultaneous examinations as signal proof." This was a difficult claim to make. Back in London, a journalist, C. S. Bremner, interviewed Naoroji and frankly expressed her doubts. "I can't say that the concession appears to me a sufficient explanation for an outburst of enthusiasm from a great nation," she offered, "though it is very modest of you to attribute it to that source." Naoroji was not flattered. While "to the outsider," he maintained, it appeared "a small cause to produce an effect so great; yet it is the real explanation."[39]

In spite of Naoroji's steadfast claims, the true significance of the visit lay elsewhere. It was not merely a riposte to Anglo-Indian prejudice, nor was it just a show of support for simultaneous examinations. As newspapers across India noticed, the whistle-stop tour and Lahore Congress had generated palpable nationalist sentiment. There was now excited talk about "Young India," heralded by the erstwhile leader of Young Bombay. Early nationalism was engendering unified demands for political reform. It was an especially welcome development given the communal violence that had scarred several Indian cities only a few months beforehand, and a possible salve for Muslim alienation from the Congress. As the *Sahachar*, a Bengali weekly in Calcutta, remarked, "This time the Hindu, the Musalman, the Sikh, the Bengali, the Hindustani, the Maharatti, the Parsi, the Panjabi and the Madrasi have spoken with one voice." The *Tribune* of Lahore, meanwhile, waxed eloquently about the symbolism of Naoroji's reception in the capital of Punjab. "It seemed like a dream: all Lahore turning out to greet not a Governor, not a Prince Royal, not a Maharaja with brocaded troops and regiments on elephants—but a Parsi gentleman . . . who had devoted himself to the service of his country," the paper noted. "Seeing the sight and understanding its true import, no one need despair of the future of India."[40]

At the same time, there had been an undeniable popular dimension to the demonstrations greeting the member for India. Papers noted that the "rich and the poor, the educated and uneducated" had welcomed Naoroji. Among the crowds that Naoroji attracted on his railway journey northward, the Western-educated elite could only have made up a fraction. The MP had been greeted by millworkers, laborers, and other ordinary Indians, who had then conveyed him to locations associated with authority and legitimacy, such as the broad imperial avenue of Chandni Chowk and the Golden Temple. Surveying the full extent of Naoroji's reception in India, the *Native Opinion* pointed to its obvious significance. "Can we not take this," it asked, "as the surest indication . . . that a new life is coming over the country, that a new awakening has obtained a sure footing, not only in a microscopic minority but in the masses too, and that it is rapidly filtering down and down still?"[41]

Look upon This Picture and upon That!

Dadabhai Naoroji's brief stay in India in 1893–1894 thus stirred something perceptibly new in the country: amplified political interest and participation, an expanded base of support for the Congress, and widening interest in political reform. It bred a moment of increased confidence and optimism in India's political future. By the time of his return voyage to London, after eighteen months in office, the member for India believed that he had laid the groundwork for sustained political reform. Indian political actors, both in the subcontinent and in the diaspora, had recognized his position of power in London and pressed their claims against British authorities. They, too, seemed to acknowledge the importance of Parliament in resolving their disputes.

In order to build on this groundwork, Naoroji now looked forward to working with the Gladstone ministry on executing civil service reform. He was confident that the Liberal government would eventually come around on the issue. "Of course the Indian Government is against carrying the resolution into effect," he conceded to a *Daily News* correspondent upon returning to London, "but it must be carried into effect," as the ruling sahibs could not ignore the will of Parliament. India's enthusiastic response to the resolution added further moral weight. "All things have now become possible," Naoroji remarked optimistically to another reporter.[42]

But the MP's optimism was not to last. If the whistle-stop tour and Lahore Congress had been triumphs for Naoroji—an affirmation of faith in a British parliamentary strategy for Indian reform—then his return to the Commons in early 1894 came like a crash. The strategy of pursuing Indian reform in Britain, after all, came with one major risk. Indians could petition Parliament or speak forcefully and eloquently about the need for political change, but there was no guarantee that MPs would actually listen to them. And members of the Liberal ministry had clearly chosen not to heed Naoroji's presidential address in Lahore. They instead relied on a very different source: Anglo-Indian civil servants. Unbeknownst to the member for Central Finsbury, the secretary of state for India, panicked by Herbert Paul's successful resolution, had in the summer of 1893 begun polling Indian officials on the viability of simultaneous examinations. These officials responded with vigorous condemnation. "There is no disguising what this agitation for simultaneous examinations means," sneered one officer, warning of a threat to British domination in India. Moreover, Lord Lansdowne, the viceroy, made cynical use of the recent communal violence over cow protection to unequivocally reject the proposal. He argued that with more Indians in positions of power, "we cannot undertake to be responsible for the public safety." And so Gladstone's government, armed with "expert" opinion, remained stonily silent on the issue. Month after month, it refused to entertain queries from Naoroji or other like-minded MPs. "If the Simultaneous Exam. question has to hang fire like this, you will have to make a fresh fight about it," Behramji Malabari suggested to Naoroji in April 1894.[43]

However, Indian civil service reform was not simply hanging fire—it was steadily retreating into the distant background. Indian affairs were crowded out by the failure of the second Irish home rule bill, Gladstone's resignation in early 1894, and Lord Rosebery's ascent to the position of prime minister. Correspondingly, Naoroji's letters to fellow Congress members began taking on a markedly desperate tone. In July 1894, he pleaded with Surendranath Banerjea for more active demonstration of support in India for simultaneous examinations. "This is the supreme moment of India's fortunes," he declared. "If we fail, our doom of slavery is fixed for generations." Naoroji was not simply asking Banerjea for further petitions and meetings. He wanted sustained agitation. "What is *absolutely necessary*," he instructed, "is that the agitation should be *unceasing*."[44]

Desperation gave way to bitterness, and bitterness emboldened Naoroji. As the headiness of the Lahore Congress slipped into memory, Naoroji began forcefully propounding the drain theory from the floor of the Commons, throwing to the wind the caution and moderation he had displayed during earlier debates. Reviving his positions of the late 1870s and early 1880s, he once more pronounced British policy in India to be "evil." During another late-night session in Westminster in mid-August 1894, only around thirteen months after the vote on simultaneous examinations, Naoroji launched a lengthy tirade against the impoverishing effects of British administration. "If there was any condemnation of the existing system" in India, Naoroji held, "it was in the result that the country was poorer than any country in the world." Repeating his arguments from "Poverty in India" about how the European-dominated civil service resulted in an economic and moral drain, he charged that "the evil of the foreign rule involved the triple loss of wealth, wisdom, and work. No wonder at India's material and moral poverty!"[45]

The Central Finsbury MP then embarked upon a risky strategy: he pinned the blame of India's gross poverty upon several contemporary MPs and government officials, a few of whom were perhaps in the chamber that night. Lord Salisbury was among the first. Naoroji latched onto a statement from 1881 in which the Tory leader had proclaimed that "India must be bled"—that its resources had to be drained for greater imperial purposes. While sardonically praising Salisbury for laying bare the central premise of British policy in the subcontinent, Naoroji unequivocally warned that "this bleeding of India must cease." The member for India also cast his eye toward Government House in Calcutta, training

Debate on Indian cotton duties in the House of Commons in 1895. Naoroji, at center, tells his fellow British MPs, "You are an alien people." *Graphic*, March 2, 1895, p. 236.

Reproduced from the Center for Research Libraries, Chicago.

his focus on the viceroy, Lord Lansdowne. Naoroji reminded the viceroy that his grandfather had, through his sponsorship of the East India Company Charter Act of 1833, attempted to "break our chains" and promote the true welfare of Indians. Nevertheless, Lansdowne "now rivetted back those chains upon us" by coming out in opposition to simultaneous examinations. "Look upon this picture and upon that!" Naoroji exclaimed. "And the Indians were now just the same British slaves."[46]

However, the full extent of Naoroji's disillusionment became evident only when he turned to the honorable member for Midlothian, William Gladstone. Though no longer prime minister, the eighty-four-year-old statesman was still a formidable presence in the Commons. Naoroji commended Gladstone's efforts to grant Irish home rule, quoting extensively from his speeches on the unwisdom of holding Ireland in bondage through military power and political oppression. But "this applied to India with a force ten times greater" than Ireland, Naoroji reminded him. "While giving emancipation to 3,000,000 of Irishmen," was Gladstone preparing to end his six-decade-long political career with the perpetuation of unjust policies that would "only further enslave the 300,000,000 of India?" He put a similar question to Lord Rosebery: "Would he begin his promising career as Prime Minister by enslaving 300,000,000 of British subjects?"[47]

Naoroji increasingly dwelt on the idea of slavery, occasionally offering vivid comparisons with other subject peoples. Replying to the Queen's Speech on February 12, 1895, he proclaimed, "In a way a great mass of the Indians were worse off than the slaves of the Southern States [of America]. The slaves being property were taken care of by their masters. Indians may die off by millions by want and it is nobody's concern." By early 1895, however, it was unclear if anyone in the Commons—aside from the few core members of the Indian Parliamentary Committee, such as William Caine and William Wedderburn—was seriously paying attention to Naoroji. Shortly after the Queen's Speech, the *Illustrated London News* offered a pathetic description of the MP. "Mr. Naoroji clings with affecting tenacity to the belief that the House of Commons can be induced to listen to speeches about India," the paper scoffed. "So he delivered to empty benches a plaintive wail about the financial condition of the Indian Empire." *Punch* also mocked the member for India. "Read a paper of

prodigious length; beat the tom-tom for nearly an hour," the comic magazine summarized Naoroji's parliamentary performance. "In churches, an
incumbent sometimes reads himself in. NAOROJI reads his congregation
out. Mayn't be quite so black as the MARKISS [Salisbury] painted him, but
he's quite as long-winded as could have been expected."[48]

The most humiliating blows came in July 1895, during the general elections. Naoroji lost his seat in Central Finsbury, one of dozens of Liberal
MPs swept out of power during a Unionist Conservative torrent that put
Lord Salisbury back into office as prime minister. Even worse, the Tories
now had their own member for India in Parliament: Mancherji Bhownaggree, who had been returned from Bethnal Green in the East End. For
reasons both personal and political, Naoroji was devastated by this news.
Bhownaggree, a fellow Parsi and once a close friend, had campaigned for
him in 1892 and celebrated his victory. However, Bhownaggree quickly
found the Central Finsbury MP far too extreme in his politics, and he re-
aligned his political views with the Conservative Party. Dismissing "the
Congress fad of Radicalism," he began to consider his own electoral prospects. A number of influential Conservatives nurtured his ambitions:
they recognized that a Tory Indian MP would both undercut Naoroji's influence and repudiate any remaining stains from the black man incident
of 1888. One such Conservative supporter was Lord Harris, the governor
of Bombay Presidency and a rather Janus-faced politician. Harris had
warmly cheered Naoroji in public while pouring invective behind his
back ("I am much disgusted at Dadabhai Nowroji getting in to the House,"
he privately grumbled to the outgoing secretary of state for India, Lord
Cross, in July 1892. "Why Englishmen should elect natives I can't for the
life of me see; they can't govern themselves, why should they govern us?
This man is of the priestly class I believe, & that class as a rule, I don't say
he does, wash themselves night & morning in cows urine!"). George Birdwood, one of Naoroji's oldest British friends, also played a major role in
orchestrating Bhownaggree's candidacy. In the summer of 1895, defeat
came with a strong whiff of betrayal.[49]

The rout of "Dadabhai Narrow-majority," Conservative papers quipped,
was a foregone conclusion; Congress leaders in India, meanwhile, reeled
from the election of a man they mocked as "Mancherji Bow-and-agree."
The ex–Central Finsbury MP, for his part, wasted no time in reaching out

to long-standing allies, hoping to find a new way back into the halls of power at Westminster. "A reactionary Indian is in the House," he wrote to Michael Davitt in January 1896. "May I ask you to help me obtain an Irish Seat." However, the Irish Parliamentary Party was still in the midst of a leadership crisis and Davitt himself was fast losing his faith in parliamentary methods. Naoroji's longtime Irish supporter could offer him no help.[50]

Out of the Commons, coming to terms with the strong Tory ministry now in charge of Indian policy, and with his parliamentary strategy for Indian reform lying in tatters, Dadabhai Naoroji surveyed his options. Thus began the final stage in his political career.

CHAPTER 7

Swaraj

"WE ARE HAVING AWFUL TIMES HERE. GOD ALONE CAN HELP INDIA."[1]
These words, uttered by Behramji Malabari, conveyed with devastating succinctness the mood in India at the turn of the twentieth century. And they were echoed by many of Dadabhai Naoroji's nationalist colleagues. As the new Conservative government in London tightened the screws of Anglo-Indian autocracy, Congress leaders feared that they had reached a dead end to their movement. "I am getting more and more disheartened as regards the political prospects of the country," W. C. Bonnerjee confessed. Natural disasters soon dwarfed political ones. Following weak monsoons in 1895 and 1896, famine of a scale and deadliness not seen since the 1860s and 1870s gripped large swaths of the subcontinent. In the Bombay Presidency, a ferocious outbreak of the plague, and the government's high-handed response to the epidemic, added to the general misery. "Everything is out of joint at this wretched time," complained Gopal Krishna Gokhale, who compared official antiplague measures in Poona to absolutist terror worthy of the Russian czar. Once Indian indignation manifested itself in violence—on June 22, 1897, two Maharashtrian revolutionaries assassinated Walter Charles Rand, the special plague commissioner in Poona, and his military escort—the mood became far grimmer. Were these assassinations a harbinger of the future?[2]

Worse was in store. In late 1899, as European capitals prepared for glittering fin de siècle celebrations, famine—"the most wide-spread famine ever known in India," according to Romesh Chunder Dutt—returned with even more brutal force, ravaging districts uncomfortably close to Bombay. Nearly eight decades beforehand, famine had likely prompted Naoroji's parents to abandon Gujarat. Now, from London, Naoroji observed as his family's native Navsari and Dharampore, along with neighboring Gujarati districts, once more anticipated a season of mass starvation. It provided a somewhat gruesome symmetry to his life and career. And it pushed Naoroji and his closest political colleagues to speculate how these disasters—generating a wave of popular anger across India toward colonial authorities—might augur a violent end to the Raj. "How long do you think the present system in India will last now?" Henry Hyndman asked Naoroji in January 1900. "From what I can hear, there is a growing feeling among the dominant class here that we are on the verge of a *serious crisis*." Allan Octavian Hume spoke with greater certainty about impending catastrophe. "I fear that the time for constitutional agitation has passed," he noted. Hume saw only one possible trajectory for India: "oceans of blood."³

For a time, so did Dadabhai Naoroji. The last phase of Naoroji's political career, which unfolded between 1895 and 1906, was marked by profound bitterness and worry. Frustrated by four decades of attempts to bring about Indian reform through constitutional means, he warned colonial authorities that Indian disaffection would soon manifest itself in a violent uprising, a second Mutiny. He made such predictions as early as August 1895, only days after losing his reelection campaign in Central Finsbury. "The violation of the pledges made to India time after time has been scandalous," Naoroji told a London correspondent during an interview. "I prophesy that this constant violation of pledges, this persistent opposition to Indian interests, and the deterioration and impoverishment of the country by an evil administration, must lead, sooner or later, to a rebellion."⁴

But Naoroji was not the type of person to wallow in gloom and despair. He used the steady stream of calamitous news reports from India in order to issue a stern message to Britons: now is the time to act. He warned of imminent rebellion in the unflinching hope that London would finally deliver those reforms that would prevent it. Ultimately, Naoroji realized that this was not enough. Beginning in 1903, he began to openly proclaim the need for Indian self-government. At first, keenly aware of the might of the most powerful empire in human history, he spoke of "Self-Government under British Paramountcy," hoping for autonomy like that enjoyed by Canada or Australia. Finally, however, he made a bolder and simpler demand. Addressing the 1906 session of the Indian National Congress, which was racked by division between moderate and radical factions, Naoroji called for swaraj—self-government without any necessary qualifications. Only swaraj, he declared, could release India from the devastating cycles of famine and pestilence. Only swaraj could save the country from the curse of ever-worsening poverty—poverty that otherwise promised a future of rank violence and destruction.

The last phase of Dadabhai Naoroji's career was marked by sustained agitation. He spoke in the bold, unfettered language of constant protest. "India is bleeding to death," Naoroji bluntly informed an audience of genteel congregationists in northwest London. "You have brought India to this condition by the constant drain upon the wealth of that country." He adopted a far more punishing schedule of daily work, refusing to let health problems and advanced age restrict his movements. In spite of warnings from friends and doctors, Naoroji continued until his eightieth year to deliver several speeches and lectures in the course of a single day, an especially arduous task in an era before loudspeakers and microphones. As he reevaluated old friendships—"the Liberal Government is as bad as the Conservative," he confided to an Irish correspondent—Naoroji took care to incorporate new allies, both anti-imperialists in faraway America and a rising generation of Indian leaders. These allies included men and women with far more radical and revolutionary politics. Above all, Naoroji refused to slow down, and he refused to give up.[5]

Empress of Famine, Queen of Black Death

What did it mean to agitate? "Agitation is the civilised, peaceful weapon of moral force, and infinitely preferable to brute physical force when possible," Dadabhai Naoroji remarked.[6] It meant constant protest, mass meetings, petitioning, propaganda, and demonstrations. And it entailed direct confrontation with colonial officials.

Through dire predictions of an imminent rebellion in India, Naoroji signaled to the ruling sahibs that the days of conciliatory loyalism were well and truly over. This caused significant consternation in Whitehall and Westminster. One of Naoroji's last achievements as an MP had been to help secure a royal commission—the Welby Commission, which began its work after the 1895 general election—to scrutinize the finances of the Indian government and military. Royal commissions were normally staid, academic investigations. But Naoroji, who served as both a member and a witness, turned the Welby Commission into a launching pad for furious attacks against the government, using language that, in India, would have been considered borderline seditious or treasonous. "The British people stand charged with the blood of the perishing millions and the starvation of scores of millions," he declared in its proceedings. While testifying before the commission, Naoroji entered into a heated exchange with an Anglo-Indian member, James Peile, about the future form of the Raj's administration. "I want to ask you, in general, what it is that you want," Peile demanded. "Do you wish to sweep away the whole English civil service?" "Yes," shot back Naoroji, although he conceded that the highest offices in India, such as the viceroy and provincial governors, could remain, at the moment, in British hands. Peile was incredulous: "And by degrees you would evict them all?" "We may go on gradually higher up," Naoroji replied.[7]

During the late 1890s, Naoroji agitated most forcefully about the famine and plague epidemic sweeping through western India. This provoked an often fiery confrontation with the new Conservative secretary of state for India, Lord George Hamilton. Hamilton, a veteran MP of aristocratic Anglo-Irish stock, was a formidable opponent—and someone who diametrically opposed most of Naoroji's political positions. He poured cold water on the idea of a drain of wealth. He celebrated and nurtured the autocratic nature of the Raj, regarding Queen Victoria's Proclamation of 1858, which promised a modicum of equality to her Indian subjects, as "one of the great mistakes that ever was made." On several occasions, Hamilton even declared Britain's premier imperial possession to be a "savage country." Naoroji quickly realized that only one strategy would work with the new secretary of state: deliberate provocation.[8]

He began by joining hands with Henry Hyndman for what was termed, appropriately enough, a "serious agitation" about the famine and plague. Together—and with the combined forces of the Congress and the Social Democratic Federation behind them—the two old friends sought to embarrass the Conservative ministry while shocking the British public about the gravity of these twin disasters. They might have played a role in distributing gruesome pictures and illustrations of famine victims to British dailies, which left India Office officials red-faced as they read their morning papers. In February 1897, Hyndman barged into a famine relief meeting in Mansion House, the residence of the lord mayor of London. Before an audience that included George Hamilton and the leading lights of the British elite, Hyndman denounced the British Indian government for diverting famine relief funds toward frontier military adventures. Even after police forcibly evicted him from Mansion House, Hyndman hankered for confrontation. He pronounced Queen Victoria "the Empress of Famine and the Queen of Black Death."[9]

Following the theatrics at Mansion House, Naoroji and Hyndman organized a series of meetings and rallies across the United Kingdom in order to work up popular protest against the handling of the famine. They summoned some of Britain's leading leftist figures to their cause. A mass protest meeting in Westminster on February 10, 1897, for example, featured Ramsay MacDonald, the future British prime minister; Tom Mann, a veteran union leader; Robert Bontine Cunninghame Graham, founder of the Scottish Labour Party; and Edward Spencer Beesly, a confidant of Karl Marx. These leaders and others popularized the idea of an impending rebellion in India. Michael Davitt called British rule a "curse" and predicted that Indians "would take measures to relieve India from that rule." Hyndman linked rebellion in India with a looming social revolution at home, noting that "the same class who sweated the Indian people sweated the English workers." Naoroji, for his part, momentarily refrained from repeating his predictions about a second Mutiny. George Hamilton nevertheless took umbrage at his association with these radical figures. "Naoroji & Co. are getting more violent," he warned the viceroy, Lord Elgin, a day after the Westminster protest.[10]

In India, not all political leaders reacted positively to Naoroji's activities. They fretted about Hyndman's brash tactics and questioned the political creed of his Social Democratic Federation. Naoroji, for his part, staunchly defended socialism to his friends in the subcontinent. "It is an unexpected good fortune that the Indian cause has been taken up by a powerful and advancing organization to whom the future largely belongs," he noted. Defending Hyndman, however, proved to be far more difficult. As time wore on, the socialist firebrand became markedly impatient with the political moderation of other Congress leaders, intemperately lashing out at William Wedderburn and Romesh Chunder Dutt. He also adopted stridently militant positions on Indian affairs. Naoroji had always defined agitation as a peaceful method. His warnings about a future rebellion in India were never meant to be incitements to violence. But now Hyndman was openly making such incitements. Surveying the Boxer Rebellion in China, fueled by antipathy toward European imperialism, he told Naoroji that a similar uprising was now India's "only chance of being saved." The Indian leader recoiled from such pronouncements. "My desire and aim has been not to encourage rebellion but to prevent it," he told Hyndman. Naoroji subsequently chose to limit his public association with the Social Democratic Federation and its famine protest activities.[11]

There were, of course, many other avenues for carrying out sustained agitation. In order to further annoy and provoke recalcitrant Conservative leaders, Naoroji flooded their offices with letters. In these letters, he exposed the hypocrisy and racism that undergirded British policy in India. To Lord Lansdowne, the former Indian viceroy now serving as secretary of state for war, Naoroji hurled accusations of a policy of "race-distinction" in the British army, one that prevented the promotion of non-Europeans. Flustered officials at the War Office eventually declined to continue correspondence, leaving his charges unrefuted. Naoroji embodied the War Office's tacit acknowledgment of "race-distinction" in a widely distributed pamphlet.[12]

To his bête noire at the India Office, Lord George Hamilton, Naoroji protested against similar racial bars that kept Indians out of all arms of the bureaucracy. And he sought to unsettle India Office bureaucrats by once more raising the specter of rebellion. Violation of promises and pledges, Naoroji warned, provided for "the sowings of bitter seeds; and although their bitter fruit may not be reaped in our time, the bitter fruit must and will come in some form or other." He elaborated in another note. "What will naturally happen will be secret societies and assassinations," Naoroji confidently predicted. "Your European Civil Service and all Civilian Europeans are your greatest weakness. In the midst of the hundreds of millions, the European Civilian population will be swept away. You have had some experience of it," he noted in an almost wry tone, "in that unfortunate mutiny."[13]

Fortunately for Naoroji, Hamilton took the bait and responded. The secretary of state lashed out at his opponent. "You announce yourself as a sincere supporter of British rule; you vehemently denounce the conditions and consequences which are inseparable from the maintenance of that rule," he wrote. These conditions and consequences were, of course, maintenance of a British-dominated civil service and the transfer of Indian revenue to Great Britain. While acknowledging that "heavy annual remittances have to be made to this country [the United Kingdom] for services rendered and monies borrowed," Hamilton steadfastly disavowed the existence of a drain and loudly denied that India was becoming more impoverished. "I assert you are under a delusion," he continued, remarking that—in spite of "periodic visitations of pestilence and famine"—conditions in India had vastly improved under British rule. Naoroji used Hamilton's inconsistent statements to great effect. As he had done with the War Office correspondence, he published the letters in full. Hamilton's remarks, not surprisingly, generated indignant responses from India, still reeling from mass famine and plague.[14]

By 1898, the India Office responded to Naoroji's radicalized tenor by sending spies to some of his public meetings. At least two spies were dispatched to separate meetings of the London Indian Society, where Naoroji sought to politicize young Indians in the imperial capital for study and work. The spies recorded attendees' condemnation of various aspects of Indian policy, such as a repressive new sedition law passed in 1898, and noted Naoroji's continued pronouncements of looming disaster in the homeland. But they also took care to record who, aside from Indian students, took part in proceedings. A report of a late December 1898 gathering mentioned "a young African native with English friends" in the audience. In May 1901, a spy at another London Indian Society meeting remarked of attendees that "quite 2 / 3 of them were women." One of the speakers was "an Indian born in South Africa" ("evidently with some negro blood," he sneered).[15]

Whether they recognized it or not, the India Office sleuths had documented evidence of one final component in Dadabhai Naoroji's program of agitation. As he adopted a more radical tenor, Naoroji embraced numerous other emancipatory causes, pioneering links with anti-imperialist leaders and movements around the world. The geographical horizons of his political work became truly global. Much of this work, it is true, entailed continued engagement with the Indian diaspora. For example, Naoroji entertained requests and petitions from distressed coolies in Trinidad. In Australia, a collection of Indians originally from Punjab, Bombay, the West Indies, and Mauritius—along with a few Ethiopians—pleaded for help in fighting against the new commonwealth's whites-only policy, "knowing what a deep and earnest interest you take in the welfare and happiness of the various coloured races." From Durban and Johannesburg, Mohandas K. Gandhi sent Naoroji near-weekly dispatches about the new indignities that South African authorities hurled at the Indian community. Armed with these dispatches, Naoroji generated even more correspondence with British officials in Whitehall. Could Indians in Natal, he asked Joseph Chamberlain, secretary of state for the colonies, in October 1897, really believe that they were "British subjects" and "not slaves"?[16]

Increasingly, however, Naoroji was drawn to the causes of other downtrodden people, regardless of their links to India or whether they lived under the British flag. As the nineteenth century drew to a close, he participated in a vibrant current of worldwide anti-racist activity, much of it centered in London. Naoroji was particularly interested in the global African diaspora. While still in Parliament, he befriended Catherine Impey, the founder of *Anti-Caste,* a British journal that campaigned against all forms of racial prejudice and drew particular attention to lynchings in the American South. It was through Impey that Naoroji later met Ida B. Wells, an African American journalist and civil rights activist who, in 1909, helped establish the National Association for the Advancement of Colored People (NAACP). Moved by Wells's stirring testimony on the horrors of Jim Crow and an epidemic of lynch mob violence, which she delivered during speaking tours in Great Britain in 1893 and 1894, Naoroji joined a group of progressive MPs, journalists, and clergymen in founding an English Anti-Lynching Committee. This was noticed across the Atlantic. "His name on the list [of founders]," observed the *Christian Recorder*, an African American newspaper published in Philadelphia, "reminds us that lynching is a barbarity unknown to countries called heathen, a product of regions themselves Christian."[17]

Impey and Wells might have also introduced Naoroji to the growing number of black activists in the imperial capital. Among these individuals was Henry Sylvester Williams, a Trinidadian, who in 1900 organized the Pan-African Conference in London. This conference—which drew delegates from Africa, the West Indies, and the United States, including W. E. B. Du Bois—featured discussion on self-government for British African colonies. Du Bois authored a proclamation condemning imperialism and the exploitation of "the black world." While hardly any evidence on the conference survives, it is clear that Naoroji played some role in its organization. Williams occupied an office that was strategically placed next door to the British Committee of the Indian National Congress on Parliament Street in Westminster. And shortly before the conference convened, he sent a brief note to Naoroji thanking him for a donation. The Indian leader continued to take an interest in Williams's work long after the conference had concluded. During the British general election of 1906, Naoroji assisted Williams in searching for a parliamentary constituency. Although unsuccessful in this endeavor, he helped Williams and John Archer, another black activist, win elections to London municipal councils the same year.[18]

Naoroji's outreach to the global African diaspora was a pathbreaking example of colored solidarity, an audacious thrust against dominant racial attitudes and norms. It happened just a few years after one Indian leader, Swami Vivekananda, denounced color prejudice while on speaking tours in America, and around the same time that another leader, Gandhi, began taking a marked interest in the work of Booker T. Washington and his Tuskegee Institute in Alabama. And it signified that the tenets of Indian nationalism had universal reach and appeal. Perhaps Naoroji regarded his outreach to the Pan-African Conference, Williams, and Archer as the best of all possible ripostes to Lord Salisbury's "black man" jibe. Regardless, by pioneering ties between Indian and black leaders, he helped pave the way for more such cooperation in Britain, America, and elsewhere during the twentieth century.[19]

Naoroji's interest in the African diaspora was symptomatic of something else: his deepening curiosity about events unfolding in the United States. America had long fascinated the Indian leader. He had, after all, made pointed comparisons with the United States in his earlier studies of Indian poverty and the drain of wealth. From the late 1870s onward, he sustained correspondence with several Americans. Eager to further explore how greatly the American experience differed from that of his homeland, Naoroji peppered Washington bureaucrats with questions about railway construction, industrial expansion, and trade balances. Already a voracious reader of newspapers from around the globe—he exchanged French and German dailies with Henry Hyndman—Naoroji began leafing through titles such as the *New York Tribune* and *New York Sun* by the 1890s. This allowed him to gauge American attitudes about Indian affairs, and also to quickly pounce upon American commentators who made ill-informed remarks. When the Episcopal bishop of New York, Henry Codman Potter, argued that Indian famines were proof of the Raj's good governance—"Great Britain had stopped tribal warfare and slaughter and, in consequence, population increased"—this man of the cloth quickly received a lengthy sermon on the matter in Naoroji's hand.[20]

Amid similar reportage that betrayed a pronounced American ignorance about India, Naoroji identified one sympathetic voice, George Freeman, a contributor to the *Sun*. He began corresponding with Freeman in the summer of 1897. This was, most likely, the first-ever instance of cooperation between an American anti-imperialist and an Indian nationalist. Through a stream of letters, press clippings, and books mailed across the Atlantic, Naoroji helped catapult the career of a man who would, in time, become one of the earliest and staunchest American supporters of Indian revolutionaries.[21]

Freeman had anti-imperialism sewn into his very identity. An Irishman born as George Fitzgerald, he changed his name, sometime after sailing beyond the limits of direct British jurisdiction, in order to make a political point. In New York, he was active in the Irish republican organization Clan-na-Gael, which channeled the revolutionary energies of Irish Americans across the United States. Freeman, however, was not simply another Irish political contact for Naoroji—nor was he an exclusively American interlocutor. The two men exchanged notes about a broad range of global affairs. Since Freeman had lived in Canada, and since he had actively espoused the dominion's separation from the British Empire, Naoroji gained insight into anti-imperialist politics north of the American border. He queried Freeman about the causes of the Rebellion of 1837–1838 in Lower Canada, where politically and economically marginalized French Canadians revolted against British rule, and drew parallels with the current political situation in India. Freeman spoke of British misrule in the West Indies and railed against the Boer War in South Africa, which commenced in 1899.[22]

In their correspondence, Naoroji revealed advanced, practically Marxist political views that recognized a fundamental link between capitalism, imperialism, and race. Capitalist greed, he argued, was the primary cause for the miseries of colonized and oppressed peoples, whether they lived under the Union Jack, the Stars and Stripes, or the standards of other imperial powers. "I am afraid the race question will become in time a burning one," he noted in 1898. "The backward races in other parts of the world seem destined to have a bad time. The European greed will be too much for them." As ever, the specter of rebellion in India occupied his mind. It was the gravest warning that the current system would not hold. "There is no remedy for all our evils till the fundamental evil of greed is remedied—ether by a peaceful change of system or forced by a revolution—and a successful revolution in India means the annihilation of British India."[23]

George Freeman liked what he read. He duly requested copies of Naoroji's economic writings. Freeman then dispatched crates of these articles and pamphlets to universities, public libraries, and leading newspapers in the United States, remarking that they offered "entirely novel views of British Rule in India." Soon, leading anti-colonial voices across America were learning more about the former Indian MP. In Boston, Edward Atkinson, founder of the American Anti-Imperialist League, told Freeman that Naoroji's 1880 pamphlet "Condition of India" confirmed his opinions about the "doubtful benefit of English rule." Atkinson began directly corresponding with the Indian leader. Naoroji, for his part, eagerly encouraged Freeman's interest in subcontinental affairs. With his assistance, Freeman established contacts with Indian journalists and began receiving Indian newspapers: under the shadow of the Brooklyn Bridge, he leafed through pages of Calcutta's *Amrita Bazar Patrika*. This opened further doors. Freeman took up correspondence with M. Viraraghavachariar of the *Hindu*, while the *Madras Standard* began reproducing some of his articles from the *New York Sun*. He soon met with Bipin Chandra Pal, the radical Bengali leader who toured America in 1900.[24]

Around the same time that Freeman began poring through Naoroji's writings on the drain of wealth, American battleships opened fire on Spanish fortifications in Cuba, Puerto Rico, Guam, and the Philippines. The brief Spanish-American War of 1898, which forcefully demonstrated the arrival of an American empire, anguished both correspondents. And it set Freeman's mind to work about how best to agitate against the United States' acquisition of formerly Spanish colonies. Amid the miasma of yellow journalism and jingoistic sentiment, he predicted that America's new colonial subjects would soon suffer from the same withering poverty that British rule had inflicted on India—and that such impoverishment would, in time, stoke a violent rebellion similar to the one Naoroji foresaw in India's future. "The moneyed class is pushing the U.S. government into the grabbing of tropical territory with semi-civilised populations for American 'boys' of the political carpet-bagger class to be sent out to govern and exploit," he wrote. Naoroji's literature "contains a clear warning against it."[25]

Freeman recruited the Indian leader in an attempt to influence various American politicians. He facilitated the delivery of Naoroji's writings to members of the US Senate. Most significantly, he sought out the leading voice of American Progressives, William Jennings Bryan, who passionately argued against the United States' newfound imperial fervor. Through an unnamed contact in Nebraska, Freeman transmitted to Bryan several of Naoroji's papers along with a tract written by Henry Hyndman. Bryan, the unnamed contact noted from Omaha, was "astonished at what he learned" about British imperialism in India. Freeman's contact agreed that the Indian example could serve as a potent counteractive to jingo fever. "Now, if ever, the Indians should inundate this country with material and patriotic literature, before the ever watchful British devil gets possession of American public opinion and prejudices against the claims of India," he urged. Bryan, meanwhile, referenced Naoroji in a few speeches and articles, including a *New York Journal* piece declaring that Britain's plunder of India was the sternest warning against American imperialism. When Freeman finally met Bryan in New York in January 1900, the Progressive leader remarked about "the instruction he had derived from reading your [Naoroji's] writings."[26]

Naoroji's correspondence with George Freeman appears to have died away in 1901. Perhaps, as was the case with Hyndman, the Parsi leader took objection to his increasingly radical and revolutionary tenor. In 1903, Freeman established the *Gaelic American*, a newspaper that encouraged Indian rebellion, celebrated the rising incidence of revolutionary terrorism in the subcontinent, and, in a sign of definite rupture between the two men, occasionally savaged Naoroji's relative political moderation. With time, the plucky Irish American journalist became "regarded by Indians in New York as the real leader of the anti-British movement." He consorted with the Parsi revolutionary Bhikhaiji Cama, helped smuggle proscribed literature into India, and assisted Taraknath Das, a Bengali revolutionary then studying at a Vermont college, to publish a short-lived radical paper, the *Free Hindusthan*, in 1908. Freeman seems to have been peripherally involved in the Ghadr (Revolution) Party, the band of Indian radicals primarily based on the American West Coast, and he was directly involved in the so-called Hindu-German Conspiracy, where Ghadr operatives sought German arms and assistance during the First World War.[27]

All of this far postdates our story. What is significant is that without Naoroji, Freeman likely would have not gained the insights and contacts that later made his revolutionary avatar possible. Naoroji harnessed the energies of American anti-imperialists like Freeman long before other Indians—such as Lala Lajpat Rai, Har Dayal, or Gandhi—made productive use of the same strategy. Of equal significance, Freeman enabled a unique episode in the Indian leader's long career: the application of his economic thought in the domain of US foreign and colonial policy.

Dadabhai Naoroji's ideas had indeed spread well beyond the perimeter of the British Empire.

Self-Government under British Paramountcy

Agitation entailed a nearly round-the-clock schedule of protest, speaking, travel, meetings, and writing, one that would have utterly exhausted most other septuagenarians. But Dadabhai Naoroji refused to slow down. He also refused to fully abandon the strategies that had marked the two earlier phases of his political career. In spite of the humiliations that he had faced in Parliament, Naoroji labored to return to the Commons in order to champion Indian reform. In the late 1890s, he canvassed constituencies around Great Britain, narrowing his focus to Halifax in Yorkshire and South Hackney in London's suburban fringes. Henry Hyndman pledged the Social Democratic vote if Naoroji was able to secure a Liberal Party nomination. However, when a general election was finally announced in September 1900, shortly after his seventy-fifth birthday, Naoroji suffered a severe bout of bronchitis. His doctor sternly warned him of a certain attack of pneumonia, likely to be fatal at his advanced age, if he undertook the rigors of a campaign. And so Naoroji sat out the so-called khaki election, where Boer War jingoism ensured that the Conservatives retained their commanding presence in Parliament. Naoroji responded to the Liberals' trouncing by preparing for the next general election.[28]

The following year, Naoroji published his best-known work: a nearly seven-hundred-page tome entitled *Poverty and Un-British Rule in India*. This was largely a compendium of the papers he had authored during the first phase of his career, an assertion of the drain theory's heightened relevance as mass famine continued its ravages in the subcontinent. In the introduction, Naoroji augured "a disastrous explosion of the British Empire." But, through the deliberate use of the term "un-British," he retained a sliver of hope of an official change of course. "True British rule will vastly benefit both Britain and India," he maintained. It was a faint echo of the rosy optimism of an earlier era.[29]

Poverty and Un-British Rule provoked strong interest across the subcontinent and around the world. It helped further expand the global reach and application of his ideas. Some months after its publication, for example, an Armenian in Nicosia requested a copy from Naoroji. "Here in Cyprus, we have been discussing the question 'whether the net effect of British rule has been to impoverish Cyprus,'" he remarked. "We have had no famines so far, but we are fast approaching hopeless indebtedness. We are studying the matter by analogy." Nearer by in Scotland, Joseph Booth, an unconventional missionary who had begun preaching political gospel in Nyasaland in addition to the Bible, saw the utility of *Poverty and Un-British Rule* for denouncing British colonialism in Africa. He and an "African friend" hawked the book along the streets of Glasgow and Edinburgh.[30]

During the first two years of the twentieth century, Naoroji was at an impasse. He clearly did not relish being the prophet of imminent doom for British India. After all, he was far more interested in practical political solutions and implementable programs of reform. Events around the world further worked up the Indian leader. In South Africa, the British concluded the Boer War in 1902 by promising the restoration of self-government to the erstwhile Boer republics. That same year, Naoroji probably assailed his American contacts for information on the Cooper Act, whereby the US Congress gave a modicum of representative government to Filipinos after they waged a bitter and unsuccessful war against their new colonial masters. These concessions, granted so quickly to former adversaries, made the continuance of authoritarian British rule in India appear all the more egregious. Yet, like Hyndman, Naoroji worried that many of his Congress colleagues were behaving in a far too moderate and timid manner, seemingly unable to build momentum for anything like what the Boers or Filipinos were being promised.

It was time to make a bold demand. Conscious of his own advancing years, Naoroji knew that it was also time to impress such a demand on the next generation of Congress leaders.

He set to work on these tasks in 1903, in his seventy-seventh year. That July, Romesh Chunder Dutt approached Naoroji for support in clamoring for lower land tax rates for Indian peasants, a cause that Naoroji had heartily supported in the 1870s. Dutt was instead upbraided by his senior nationalist colleague, who utilized unusually forceful language. Land tax agitation was simply the "wrong course," Naoroji retorted; he had already

trodden and abandoned it years ago. What good would it accomplish
when, in fact, the whole colonial system needed to be swept away? "Your
agitation about land tax is the very thing the Anglo Indians welcome,"
Naoroji stated. "It draws a red herring across the *real evil* at the bottom,"
the drain of wealth caused by colonialism. He pleaded with Dutt not to
waste his time on piecemeal reform. "The Fundamental *cause*, the cause
of the whole mischief is the 'Foreign domination' and as long as that continues, there is no hope." Naoroji urged Dutt to join him in rousing India's masses for a greater aim, "Self-Government under British Paramountcy." It might take another fifty years to achieve this object, but
any further delay in articulating this demand would only exacerbate the
cycles of famine and pestilence. "At my age it will not be my lot to take
any long part in this great battle," Naoroji concluded, "and I am therefore
the more anxious to see that younger hands and hearts set themselves to
work."[31]

What did it mean to have self-government under "British Paramountcy"? Similar to what he had stated before the Welby Commission,
Naoroji conceded that Britons could retain the highest Indian government positions for the moment. He drew comparisons to self-governing
British colonies such as Canada, South Africa, and Australia—a parallel
that, at the height of Pax Britannica, was probably India's best hope. But
in his correspondence with Dutt, he also suggested a future association
between Britain and India that was essentially economic in nature. Instead of any fuzzy notions of imperial citizenship, Naoroji envisioned
the bonds of empire whittled down into a mutually beneficial trading relationship. Many Britons, he told Dutt, well understood the consequences of centuries of colonial plunder. "If the people of India once understood their condition and their strength the British will have either to
leave precipitately, or be destroyed in India," he noted. Or, Naoroji hoped,
"if they see the danger of the disaster in good time and apply the remedy,
to save the Empire by putting an end to the Drain," Britons could find
"their true benefit in trade with a prosperous and vast people." "British
Paramountcy" was a necessary rider for the moment, but, in the long run,
it would not amount to much.[32]

Self-government, rather than fear of a second Mutiny, now became
Naoroji's rallying cry. And he sought out a rising Congress leader far

younger than Dutt, Gopal Krishna Gokhale, to take up the cause. From 1903 onward, Naoroji wasted few opportunities in order to impress upon the Poona nationalist that self-government should be "the '*Mission*' and *Aim* of the Congress." He urged him to bring up the demand in addresses to Indian youth—they, after all, were far more receptive to the idea than many older, established Congressmen. Before Gokhale traveled to Banaras to preside at the 1905 Congress, Naoroji even attempted to force his endorsement of self-government via a publicly distributed letter. "Self-government is the only remedy for India's woes and wrongs," he declared to the incoming president. "For this purpose we must strengthen this Congress, our great body, representative of all India, to go on making every possible effort to accomplish this end." Gokhale tiptoed around the idea of self-government in his presidential address. Banaras Congress officials buried the letter at the end of the session's report.[33]

Naoroji therefore had mixed success with his nationalist colleagues. But he fared far better in raising the profile of Indian self-government before another Congress: the International Socialist Congress, forum of the Second International. With Henry Hyndman's assistance, Naoroji participated in the Amsterdam Socialist Congress held in August 1904. He was a rare non-European representative invited to join a gathering of the world's leading leftist voices. On August 17, he was called to address an audience that included figures such as Rosa Luxemburg, Karl Kautsky, and Jean Jaurès. As Naoroji approached the podium, these individuals, and the rest of the delegates, rose to their feet and observed a moment of silence for the millions of Indians cut down by famine. Naoroji then issued an "appeal to the workmen of the whole world" for "help and sympathy" in India's political struggle. Socialism, he confirmed, was part of the remedy. "Imperialism of brute force is barbarism," Naoroji stated. "The Imperialism of civilization is the Imperialism of equal rights, equal duties, and equal freedoms." He concluded with a call for self-government, although some delegates (including Hyndman) were ruffled by his insistent qualification of "British Paramountcy."[34]

As exponents of world socialism displayed their solidarity with India, events were moving fast in the subcontinent. The viceroy, Lord Curzon, seemingly eager to cement his unpopularity in India, moved ahead with official plans to partition the sprawling province of Bengal, justified on

Participants in the Amsterdam Socialist Congress, 1904. In the first row are Henry Hyndman (third from left) and Naoroji (third from right). Rosa Luxemburg (sixth from left) and Karl Kautsky (fifth from right) stand in the second row.
Reproduced from the International Institute of Social History, Amsterdam.

the grounds of administrative expediency. A wave of resentment built up among Bengalis once the government's real motives became clear: to fashion a border that would, in the words of one Anglo-Indian official, "split up and thereby weaken a solid body of opponents to our rule." This resentment crystallized into furious political activity across Bengal. Naoroji welcomed the demonstrations and mass meetings that marked the early, moderate phase of anti-partition agitation. "I am thankful that I have lived to see the birthday of the freedom of the Indian people," he remarked in one address to the London Indian Society. He also threw his support behind a widening call to boycott British-made goods and instead patronize only swadeshi (domestic) products.[35]

Bengal's partition, however, would unleash transformations that were of far greater consequence than Naoroji's decision to make self-government, rather than imminent rebellion, the central theme of his political activities. Curzon's division of the province was, first and foremost, a fillip to a rising generation of radical and revolutionary Indian nationalists. These men (and, occasionally, women) did not share Naoroji's persistent optimism about the goodwill of the British people, nor did they believe that Britons would readily concede self-government. As agitation in Bengal matured into the swadeshi movement, the radicals—willing to speak enthusiastically about *both* rebellion and self-government—began to loudly criticize Naoroji's methods and political views as being too moderate.

This was a major development, and one that unfolded at breakneck speed. Throughout his political career, Naoroji had represented the vanguard of Indian nationalist thought. Many of his pronouncements and actions had deeply unsettled moderate leaders. To such men, Naoroji *was* the radical. Dinsha Wacha scolded him for participating in London Indian Society meetings where young Indian radicals employed "intemperate" and "violent" language. Within the British Committee of the Indian National Congress, W. C. Bonnerjee reacted with horror at Naoroji's radicalized denunciations of British pillage and plunder. And by associating with "a motley gathering of Continental agitators" at the Amsterdam Socialist Congress, Naoroji alienated more friends and allies in Britain and India. The emergence of political leaders who appeared more radical than Naoroji, therefore, was a relatively new development. During the late 1890s, men such as Bal Gangadhar Tilak of Maharashtra, Aurobindo Ghosh of Bengal, and Lala Lajpat Rai of Punjab established their more extremist credentials, but—with the possible exception of Tilak—they posed no serious challenge to Naoroji. These men, furthermore, did not affiliate Naoroji with established moderates such as Gopal Krishna Gokhale or Pherozeshah Mehta.[36]

What is striking is that Naoroji personally knew many of these radicals, and remained on amicable terms with a few of them for the remainder of his political career—even as they began to speak against him. Some of the most prominent radical leaders had grown up around Naoroji during the 1890s and early 1900s. They had looked to him as a mentor or friend. Bipin Chandra Pal participated in one of the London Indian Society meetings that had been monitored by an India Office spy: the Bengali extremist, identified in the spy's report as a "Brahmo lecturer," sat just to the right of Naoroji upon the dais. Shyamji Krishnavarma, who edited the *Indian Sociologist* in London and excoriated moderates in the paper's columns, by his own admission had known Naoroji "for nearly thirty years." In 1905, Naoroji helped inaugurate India House in London—which later became a hotbed of student radicalism—alongside Krishnavarma and Lala Lajpat Rai. Finally, Bhikhaiji Cama, the Parsi revolutionary who based herself in France, looked after Naoroji's granddaughter Perin while she pursued higher education at the Sorbonne.[37]

Many of these leaders had grown radical from the very same experiences that so embittered Naoroji at the turn of the century: the reactionary policies of the Tory ministry, famine and plague, and Curzon's imperious viceroyalty. But, contrary to their effect on Naoroji, these experiences had extinguished any hope among radicals of achieving Indian political rights through Parliament, lobbying the British public, and other aspects of a nationalist strategy that concentrated its activities in the imperial capital at the expense of the colony. Yet Naoroji stubbornly clung to his faith in British institutions and the British people. A constitutional strategy for political reform, one that shunned extralegal tactics and abhorred any use of violence, necessitated that he keep this faith alive. For this reason, while he celebrated the fact that Bengalis had embarked upon a sustained agitation that could help the cause of self-government, Naoroji continued to place the burden of responsibility upon British shoulders—and hope that, this time, they would not disappoint.

Some radicals urged Naoroji to change his tactics and recognize that many in India were no longer willing to hold out hope for Britain to deliver on long-promised reforms. Prominent in this group was Bal Gangadhar Tilak, who had warmly welcomed Naoroji to Poona in December 1893 during his whistle-stop tour between Bombay and Lahore. In September 1906—as moderate Congress members equivocated over whether or not to support the boycott of foreign goods, patronization of swadeshi articles, and other new methods of protest that were sweeping through Bengal—Tilak penned a lengthy letter to Naoroji. He addressed the senior nationalist in tones of respect and deference, stating, "You are the *guru* of us all in political matters & I need not say that I highly value the privilege of receiving advice from you." But he adamantly maintained that a difference existed between them, and that "the present controversy is one of methods." Tilak pleaded for Naoroji to shift the focus of Congress activities from Great Britain to India. "All that the Congress has been hitherto doing is to pass resolutions every year & submit the same to Govt.," he argued. "This was supplemented by educating the public opinion in England. Can we not go a step further?" What Tilak had in mind, specifically, was "self-help" and "self-reliance" for the Indian people. "Svadeshi [sic], boycott, strikes, national education, are pointed out as instances or directions in which the Congress may do useful work," he continued, referring to the activities over the past year in Bengal. While he assured Naoroji that "no one has the least idea of taking to the revolutionary methods," Tilak ended his letter on a note of desperation. "We have prayed & petitioned so long," he stated. There was, in his mind, no logic in continuing to confine the nationalist movement to purely constitutional methods, ones that a new generation of radicals branded as sheer mendicancy.[38]

Other radicals, unlike Tilak, decided to directly attack Naoroji. From 1905 onward, his fiercest and most persistent critic was Shyamji Krishnavarma. Originally from Kutch, Krishnavarma had served as the diwan of Junagadh before relocating to the United Kingdom, where he became an admirer of Herbert Spencer and befriended Henry Hyndman. In 1904, he founded a monthly paper, the *Indian Sociologist,* which quickly evolved into the mouthpiece of Indian radicals and revolutionaries in Great Britain. In its columns, Krishnavarma praised Naoroji's economic analysis of Indian poverty, but argued that his political career had been "by no means so advantageous to the cause of his countrymen." Indian representation in the House of Commons, Krishnavarma believed, would achieve nothing; it could even "retard India's progress towards freedom and independence" by distracting from calls for representative government at home. With Naoroji's campaign fundraising experiences clearly in mind, he denounced "wasting the resources of India on a few Indians' admission into the British Parliament." Naoroji's steadfast faith in the British people and his continued declarations that Indians would eventually receive justice from British hands further repelled Krishnavarma. "If Mr. Dadabhai Naoroji thinks that the liberty and justice which the English so much love will be extended to India, he is sadly mistaken."[39]

But Krishnavarma saved his most damning criticisms for a later edition of the *Indian Sociologist,* published in November 1906. Here he surveyed

Naoroji's long career of five decades and asked what he had achieved. The East India Association, where Naoroji had enunciated many components of his drain theory during the late 1860s and early 1870s, had fallen into the hands of Anglo-Indians. The organization was "now altogether inimical to Indian interests." Naoroji's signal achievement in the House of Commons, the resolution in favor of simultaneous examinations, had resulted in no tangible outcome. Krishnavarma took issue with the very idea of simultaneous examinations, arguing that it was unwise to encourage Indian youths to join the civil services and thereby "become unjust agents of an oppressive foreign government." Indianization of the bureaucracy, Krishnavarma held, would not alter the fundamental power dynamics of an authoritarian British Indian government. "It causes us no pleasure to say unpalatable truths about a man who for many years had the reputation of laboring in his country's cause," he remarked. He then delivered his final blow. Having evaluated Naoroji's various activities, Krishnavarma pronounced, "we find that his political work has been a sad failure."[40]

Shyamji Krishnavarma's devastating verdict was prompted by yet more events unfolding in Bengal. The Congress's 1906 session was scheduled to meet in late December in Calcutta, the epicenter of the swadeshi movement, where the widening chasm between moderate and radical nationalists was daily apparent. Through the summer of 1906, members of the Calcutta Congress committee tackled the thorny issue of who should serve as president. Radicals pushed vigorously for Tilak, someone who was completely unacceptable to the moderate establishment. But the rising tide of swadeshi activism—given added fuel by the new secretary of state for India, John Morley, who refused to modify the partition of Bengal—added weight to their demands. The Congress movement appeared dangerously close to a rupture. From Calcutta, Naoroji began receiving frantic messages from moderate leaders. "Tilak's nomination will be strenuously opposed by a large section of our Congress friends and will infallibly lead to a split in our camp," Surendranath Banerjea warned. Banerjea, therefore, pleaded for Naoroji's assistance: would he agree to preside at the Calcutta session? Naoroji, it was hoped, would be equally acceptable to moderates and radicals. "Your Presidentship will be universally and loyally accepted by all and will avert a split," Banerjea professed. Bhupendranath Basu concurred. "Without the presence of a man of your personality, the whole Congress movement will be split beyond rehabilitation," he stated.[41]

In September 1906, shortly after his eighty-first birthday, Naoroji signaled that he was willing to travel to Calcutta and accept the presidency of the Indian National Congress.

Bande Mataram

Nineteen hundred and six was the most dramatic year in Dadabhai Naoroji's long life. He waged a final parliamentary campaign in North Lambeth, the London constituency that overlooked Westminster Palace from across the foggy Thames. North Lambeth had a progressive bent. Yet, as in Central Finsbury, internecine local politics cast a shadow over his prospects. In spite of securing the Liberal nomination from a bevy of local party and labor organizations, Naoroji soon found himself in an acrimonious three-cornered race—not including the Conservative rival. He was ultimately outmaneuvered. "Why should an old man of 80 want to get into the House of Commons?" was the common refrain among Liberal Party functionaries. In spite of warnings from friends, Naoroji decided to stand as an independent Liberal with some Labour and Social Democratic backing. He lost badly, securing only 733 of the approximately 5,000 votes cast, finishing third. Yet he refused to give up. Naoroji reached out to the Irish Parliamentary Party one last time, asking if they could give him the seat of one of its newly elected MPs. Bhikhaiji Cama even offered to go to Ireland in order to carry out negotiations. When this did not come to pass, Naoroji held out hope that John Clifford, a non-conformist leader, could help get him into the Commons through a by-election.[42]

Nineteen hundred and six saw the Liberals returned to power after ten solid years of Conservative rule. Naoroji responded to the welcome change of government by dispatching letters to the new prime minister, Henry Campbell-Bannerman. In these letters, he began outlining a specific plan for instituting Indian self-government. He drew up timetables for Indianizing the vast majority of the civil service. As for the handful of remaining British executives, Naoroji continued, they must be paired with "at least one Indian of popular choice to begin with." In London, three Indians needed to be appointed to the Council of India, the India Office's principal advisory body. Meanwhile, Naoroji relied on William Wedderburn and Gopal Krishna Gokhale to make a truly audacious suggestion to John Morley: that he be appointed as one such Indian member of the council. This elicited howls of disbelief in Whitehall. "The India Office as a body was dead set against Mr. Dadabhai," remarked Gokhale. Naoroji remained optimistic that something would work out. "He was so cheerfully confident that I felt ashamed of my own doubts in the matter," Gokhale confided to Naoroji's old colleague from Baroda, Hormusjee Ardeseer Wadya.[43]

Nineteen hundred and six was, for Naoroji and a vast spectrum of Indian political actors, ultimately dominated by the Calcutta Congress. The aged leader's acceptance of the presidential chair excited opinion across the subcontinent from both radicals and moderates. Surendranath Banerjea and Bhupendranath Basu were correct about Naoroji being acceptable to both parties. With the exception of Bipin Chandra Pal and Shyamji Krishnavarma, whose remarks on Dadabhai Naoroji's "sad failure" were part of a much longer tirade against his proposed presidency, radicals approved of Naoroji's selection. Bal Gangadhar Tilak withdrew his name from consideration as president and conveyed his support in a letter to Wedderburn. "Mr. Dadabhai is coming here to preside at the next session & *there is no one in the Congress who will venture to go against his wishes*," he stated.[44]

By the fall of 1906, therefore, Naoroji found himself in a peculiar situation in India. Moderate leaders continued to find him too radical. Radical leaders found him too moderate. Both factions, however, accepted his leadership of the Congress. Furthermore, in the months leading up to the Calcutta session, both factions attempted to appropriate Naoroji. Moderate organs believed that Naoroji would save the Congress from falling into extremist hands. The *Hindi Punch*, an illustrated satirical magazine modeled on the well-known London title, featured a cartoon where "Lady Congress," perched at the edge of a cliff, peered down into the murky depths of "extremist views," while "Mr. Punch" led her away on the path "to moderation." Tilak, meanwhile, wrote in his Marathi paper, *Kesari*, that "there is practically no difference between the views of Mr. Dadabhai and those entertained by the extreme party in the Congress." Naoroji's most recent pronouncements "bear evidence of a feeling of utter exasperation" with British intransigence. "His published opinions," Tilak concluded, "show that he is an advanced extremist himself."[45]

Such remarks, emanating from both the moderate and radical camps, placed an enormous weight of expectation upon Dadabhai Naoroji's frail shoulders. On November 29, 1906, Naoroji, now showing some signs of his eighty-one years, departed London. Narrowly missing a breakfast meeting with Mohandas K. Gandhi, who was in the imperial capital to lead a deputation of Transvaal Indians to the Colonial and India Offices, he boarded a morning train at Victoria Station and thus commenced his long journey eastward to India. During a brief halt at a Paris station later that evening, Naoroji met his granddaughter Perin. Perin, whether her grandfather knew it or not, was now complementing her studies at the Sorbonne with lessons in revolutionary thought from Bhikhaiji Cama—and instruction in bomb making from Cama's Polish revolutionary contacts. The new political winds were even influencing members of the Grand Old Man's very household.[46]

Naoroji arrived in Bombay on the afternoon of December 14. Once more, his arrival in the city was marked by mass demonstrations of support and a long procession through the city, winding its way from Apollo Bunder to Hornby Road and through Girgaum and Khetwadi. Once more, Naoroji embarked on a whistle-stop train tour through India, this time cutting through the Deccan en route to Calcutta.[47]

But something was also different, signifying the vast changes of the past few years. While in Bombay, Naoroji inaugurated a cooperative store for swadeshi goods at Bori Bunder. He received a message from Indian students in Japan, welcoming his return to the subcontinent with the cry "Bande mataram!" (Hail, mother). Those words, an invocation to the motherland popularized during the swadeshi movement, echoed across railway platforms thronged with well-wishers as Naoroji's train proceeded toward Bengal. And at the Nagpur railway station, a group of local residents thrust a memorial into Naoroji's hands. "We all have not come to see you here as Dadabhoy or a member of Parliament, or a gentleman living so long in England but as a protector of poor Indians, who are surrounded on all sides, by the cruel enemies or English rulers," the memorial began. The Nagpur residents, who had probably suffered through both the recent famine and plague, pleaded with Naoroji to out-line a bold, decisive agenda for the Congress at Calcutta. "Be not preju-diced by the interpretence [impertinence] of Hon. Gokhale or Mehta or Waccha," they counseled. They offered their own take on where Naoroji figured in the moderate-extremist spectrum, maintaining that "if there are any men, who are struggling for the welfare of India . . . they are you, Tilak, Lala Lajpatrai or Bipin Chundrapal & Shamji Krishnaji." And they hoped that if Naoroji effected the necessary changes to the Congress, he would thereafter be "worshipped as Sivaji"—Shivaji Maharaj, the Maratha king who had made his own bold declaration of swaraj centuries before-hand in his fight against the Mughals.[48]

It was with much anticipation, therefore, that Indians of different po-litical persuasions awaited Naoroji's presidential address. Would he sup-port the new methods of protest employed during the swadeshi move-ment, or would he plead for a return to petitions and memorials? Would he boost the moderates or the radicals, or would he try to forge some sort of consensus that could avert a split in the Congress? What would he say about how self-government could be achieved? Naoroji, no doubt, was also deeply worried and anxious about how best to carry out his heavy responsibilities. For five decades he had worked to advance Indian po-litical demands. He had been a principal architect of the Congress and the chief exponent of its strategy for achieving reform through Westmin-ster. Now, in the last few years of his life, he had to issue a call that would take into account both the radical challenge to this strategy and his own bitter experience of engaging with British institutions. He had to account for a movement in Bengal that was popular and broad-based but threat-ened to embrace both political extremism and violence. As he prepared his address, Naoroji weighed the various economic and political ideas he had developed during the three stages of his career. He composed a speech that, in many ways, reflected the evolution of his own thought, focusing on the drain, the need to Indianize the civil services, and the necessity of influencing Parliament and the British public. But he also built on these ideas in order to present a clear road map for the achievement of self-government.

As many as twenty thousand individuals, "crowded to suffocation," gathered to hear the presidential address on December 26, held in an open area on Russa Road in Tollygunge. It was quite likely the largest political gathering held in India to date—a markedly different affair from previous Congress sessions, which had only attracted hundreds or perhaps a few thousand. Participants heralded the Congress president's arrival at the pandal, precisely at two o'clock in the afternoon, with cries of "Bande mataram." In the audience assembled moderates such as Dinsha Wacha and Pherozeshah Mehta, radicals like Tilak, and Samuel Smith, Naoroji's friend since their days as Liverpool cotton traders fifty years ago, someone who had assiduously supported Indian reform when both men were MPs in the Commons. Gokhale strode onto the platform alongside the president. Naoroji spoke a few words, sat down, and handed his speech to Gokhale to read. While age had rendered it impossible for him to make a sustained address to an enormous crowd, Naoroji's gesture was strategic. It quite literally made Gokhale voice his own political credo, a task he had long attempted to do.[49]

Through Gokhale's more robust vocal chords, Naoroji began by drawing upon the first two phases of his career. His views on the drain had now advanced to the point where he demanded immediate "reparation" from Great Britain "for our past sufferings." Turning to parliamentary politics, Naoroji declared that India continued to enjoy strong support from allies such as the Irish and radical Liberals. Events of the past few years had even yielded India new friends, members of the recently founded Labour Party. In spite of his own disheartening experience in the Commons, Naoroji urged Congress members to support the election of more Indian MPs. "We must have many Indian Members in Parliament till we get self-government," he stated.[50]

Naoroji then began to draw upon his experiences from the last few years. Building upon his conversations with George Freeman and other anti-imperialists, he placed the Indian nationalist movement in the context of a broad range of emancipatory movements around the world. He noted the achievements of the Russian Revolution of 1905, where peasants had brought about the establishment of a representative parliament, the Duma. Russians, subject to the whims of "the greatest autocrat in the world," the czar, had proven that there were no prerequisites for representative government. Therefore, Naoroji believed, "it is futile to tell me that we must wait till all the people are ready" for a similar form of government in India. "We can never be fit till we actually undertake the work and the responsibility." Developments elsewhere strengthened the case for immediate and significant political rights. "China in the East and Persia in the West of Asia are awakening and Japan has already awakened," Naoroji noted. The Qing Empire in China was quickly reforming in a desperate attempt to fend off Sun Yat-sen and his fellow nationalists; the Constitutional Revolution in Persia had, just a few months beforehand, led to the creation of a representative Majles; and Japan had done the unthinkable—the defeat of a European power—during the Russo-Japanese War, while steadily pursuing reform at home. During these "present times of spreading emancipation," Naoroji asked, were Indians to remain "under the barbarous system of despotism, unworthy of British instincts, principles and civilization?"[51]

In light of these developments, Naoroji declared that India must have "'Self-Government' or *Swaraj* like that of the United Kingdom or the Colonies." His wording was significant. Naoroji deployed the vernacular term that Tilak had been popularizing for the past few years, which in turn harked back to the declarations made by Shivaji. He offered no qualification of "British Paramountcy" for self-government, and his reference to "the United Kingdom or the Colonies" was quite probably deliberately vague. It left open the possibility that India could evolve into a self-governing territory like Australia or Canada, which remained in the empire, or a truly autonomous nation like Britain. Critically, in previous statements—such as the message he had sent to Gokhale and the Banaras Congress of 1905—Naoroji had only referred to "self-government like that of the colonies."[52]

Naoroji then proceeded to do something highly unusual for a Congress presidential address, which normally took the form of a review of developments over the past year. Having raised the demand for swaraj from the Congress pandal, thereby binding the organization to this objective, he laid out a concrete agenda for the future transfer of administrative responsibilities from British to Indian hands. There were four key components of this agenda. First, not surprisingly, was the civil service. The time had come for the investiture of "all administration in every department in the hands of the people of India." "Not only has the time fully arrived," he added, "but [it] had arrived long past." Simultaneous examinations were to be immediately instituted, but only for a short period, after which all civil service examinations were to be held in India. By going a step beyond simultaneous examinations, a cause he had championed for nearly four decades, Naoroji took his political corollary of the drain theory to its logical conclusion. The full Indianization of the bureaucracy would eliminate what Naoroji believed to be the most significant part of the drain. The second component of his agenda was the military. This was another source of the drain: instead of defending the country, whole divisions of the army were deployed abroad and utilized "entirely for British imperial purposes." As long as the army continued to perform this function, therefore, British taxpayers, not Indian ones, needed to begin picking up the bill.[53]

Representative institutions constituted the third component. Here Naoroji returned to a point he had made earlier: it was a fallacy to claim that Indians were "not ready" to enjoy such institutions. After all, he pointed out, this argument had been deployed against much of the middle and working classes in Britain until recently, and it was still being employed to deny the franchise to British women. Naoroji did not elaborate on the scope of Indian enfranchisement but warned against limiting the vote to the English-educated elite. The spread of vernacular education and literature, he pointed out, had made a large mass of the Indian populace fluent in contemporary political matters. And this led to the final component of Naoroji's agenda for self-government. "Education must be most vigorously disseminated among the people—free and compulsory primary education, and free higher education of every kind," he declared. Education, he believed, "will bring the accomplishment of self-government far more speedily than many imagine." This was a deeply personal issue for Naoroji. "It was free education that I had at the expense of the people," he noted, "that made me and others of my fellow-students and subsequent fellow-workers to give their best to the service of the people for the promotion of their welfare." In his last major political speech, Naoroji thus vindicated the experiments of the Bombay Native Education Society during the 1830s, which had once made education accessible to a young boy from a poor Parsi family.[54]

So far, Naoroji's presidential address had encouraged many of the radicals in the audience. In spite of cumbersome quotations from British statesmen and detailed references to British historical precedents, he had spoken of steps to be taken in India, not Westminster. He had demanded that the British government immediately begin transferring authority to Indians, not to effect piecemeal change but in order to achieve self-government. Naoroji next turned to the question of methods. His initial statements once more buoyed radical hopes. He endorsed swadeshi enterprise. "'Swadeshi' is a forced necessity for India in its unnatural economic muddle," Naoroji claimed.[55]

But that was as far as he was willing to go. Naoroji avoided taking a public position on the boycott of foreign goods, national education, strikes and other elements of the agenda of "self-reliance" and "self-help" that Tilak had outlined in his earlier letter. Instead, he clung to his established position of constitutional agitation. He called for more "petitions, demonstrations and meetings, all quite peacefully but enthusiastically conducted." With regard to influencing Parliament, Naoroji believed that "the fact that we have more or less failed hitherto, is not because we have petitioned too much but that we have petitioned too little." And so he called for a "Petition of Rights" to be drawn up in India and dispatched to the king and Parliament. Speakers should be sent "to all the nooks and corners of India" in order to "inform the people in their own languages of our British rights and how to exercise and enjoy them." Another delegation would travel to Great Britain in order undertake that much-attempted task, lobbying the British public.[56]

At this point in his speech, Naoroji must have anticipated the swell of disappointment among radical Congress members. So he chose to recount his own doubts and frustrations, especially those from the last phase of his career, when he began speaking of imminent rebellion in India. "I have been for some time past repeatedly asked whether I really have, after more than half a century of my own personal experience, such confidence in the honour and good faith of British statesmen and [the] Government," he related. "Since my early efforts," Naoroji continued, "I must say that I have felt so many disappointments as would be sufficient to break any heart and lead one to despair and even, I am afraid, to rebel." These disappointments had "not been of the ordinary kind" but, rather, "far worse and keener." Citing the simultaneous examinations resolution in the House of Commons as an example, Naoroji noted that the government had been unwilling to countenance any defeat. "I fought and won on several occasions," Naoroji claimed, "but the executive did not let us have the fruit of those victories—disappointments quite enough, as I have said, to break one's heart."[57]

"But I have not despaired," Naoroji told his audience. His disappointments, failures, and frustrations had taught him the value of perseverance, and he urged members of the Congress to not let similar failures push them to extremes. "You cannot stop at any stage, disappointments notwithstanding, or you lose all you have gained and find it far more difficult afterward even to begin again. As we proceed, we may adopt such means as may be suitable at every stage, but persevere we must to *the end*." And so, in conclusion, Naoroji urged the Congress to reject the temptations of violent methods and proceed along constitutional lines. "Agitate, agitate over the whole length and breadth of India in every nook and corner—peacefully of course—if we really mean to get justice from John Bull."[58]

Extremists of Today, Moderates of Tomorrow

By the conclusion of the Calcutta session, the Congress had passed resolutions endorsing swadeshi, supporting the boycott of foreign goods, and condemning the partition of Bengal. It passed a further resolution on self-government, though it watered down Naoroji's language and referred only to the system of government prevailing in the "British Colonies." Moderate and radical leaders did not come to blows, as many had feared, although their differences were clearly apparent in oftentimes raucous committee proceedings. Bipin Chandra Pal's paper, *Bande Mataram*, attacked Pherozeshah Mehta for his "high handedness" during debates on various resolutions."[59]

Yet there was consensus that the Calcutta session had pushed the Congress into a new stage of its evolution. This opinion was propounded well beyond the confines of the Congress pandal. Aside from filling the columns of Indian and British newspapers, Naoroji's speech garnered international attention. In Ireland, nationalists latched onto Naoroji's declaration of self-government. "Mr. Redmond and Mr. Naoroji have clasped hands across continents, and both have behind them peoples well united and determined," the Dublin correspondent of the *New York Times* commented, referring to John Redmond, who now occupied Charles Stuart Parnell's place as the leader of the Irish Parliamentary Party. In Washington, D.C., W. E. B. Du Bois, who six years beforehand had attended the Pan-African Congress in London, printed excerpts of Naoroji's address in his magazine, *Horizon*. "The speech of Naoroji before the National Congress of India was worthy of men who want to be free," Du Bois remarked. "The dark world awakens to life and articulate speech. Courage, Comrades!"[60]

Not surprisingly, Naoroji's address was closely followed by British Indian officials. The ruling sahibs of Calcutta cast a weary eye toward the aged nationalist. The viceroy, Lord Minto, found his speech "very long and unpractical." "He seemed to attempt to foreshadow an administration which he knows to be impossible," Minto informed John Morley, the secretary of state for India. Minto was also stung by the Congress president's refusal to pay him a visit at Government House. "Naoroji much to my surprise went off home without attempting to see me," he complained in another letter to Morley. "I fully expected he would ask for an interview which I would gladly have given him, and I suspect his not doing so was out of regard to 'extremist' susceptibilities."[61]

Aside from Minto's grumblings, Morley relied on the testimony of Samuel Smith. On the evening of December 26, Smith put down his thoughts about his old friend's address. "It was a remarkable sight," he wrote to Morley. "The huge tent was crowded with at least 12,000 people. The most perfect quietness and order prevailed." Naoroji, whose words conveyed "a deep feeling of disappointment at recent events," made "a thoroughgoing demand for full Indian self-government: very logical, very well expressed, and founded upon our promises and precedents." While Smith offered his own reservations about the feasibility of self-government in India, he could "feel the force of the appeal. No one with a sense of humanity could but feel the great wave of emotion which is carrying India towards an unknown future. It was an epoch-making occasion." Indians, he concluded, were fast losing their patience with Great Britain, and Naoroji's demands had accentuated the "universal feeling that national self-consciousness was at last awakened." The India Office could no longer stymie political progress. "Action of some kind," Smith warned Morley, "will be expected before long." These were among the last words that Smith ever wrote. He died in Calcutta two days later, casting a pall of gloom over the Congress proceedings and bringing to a dramatic end a political career that had long concerned Indian rights.[62]

It was left to the Indian press to muse over whether the presidential address had helped the radicals or the moderates. Opinion was bitterly divided among papers in both camps. In some cases, even a single paper provided starkly different takes. "The Congress has been saved," proclaimed the *Jame Jamshed* of Bombay, a moderate organ. "To Mr. Dadabhai belongs the credit of having rescued it from utter and irreparable wreck this year." But in another column the *Jame* recoiled at the contents of his speech. The paper was "sorely disappointed" that Naoroji did not deliver "prudent and sober advice to the extremists." It pronounced him guilty of having "flattered the Bengalis," a high crime among non-Bengali moderates who viewed the swadeshi movement with pronounced skepticism. "He said not a word against the mischievous boycott agitation in Bengal, nor did he ask the Bengalis to wisely accept the partition as a 'settled fact,'" the *Jame* averred. While offering different perspectives on his speech, most other moderate papers agreed with the *Jame* that Naoroji had headed off a split in the Congress. The Calcutta session had "secured a permanent stability for the movement," commented the *Behar Herald* of Patna. "Neither the Moderates nor the Extremists have cause for complaint." Calcutta's *Amrita Bazar Patrika*, which was straddling the lines of moderation and radicalism at the time, celebrated the consolidation of a "strong, united Congress."[63]

A number of radical organs condemned Naoroji's speech, worrying that the Calcutta Congress represented an undesired compromise with the moderate old guard—one that would snuff out promising sparks of rebellion. "Never was the speech of a President of the Congress so insipid, meaningless and timid as that delivered by Mr. Dadabhai this year," charged the *Vihari*, a Marathi weekly. Instead of preaching "mendicancy," the paper wished that Naoroji had spoken of the "armed resistance" of the Boers or even tactics that the English had employed in the past against their rulers, "such as rising in rebellion against them or banishing or beheading them." Meanwhile, in Calcutta, Bipin Chandra Pal's *Bande Mataram* labeled Naoroji's faith in constitutional methods as "cheap patriotism." Italy could never have wrested its freedom through mere petitions and demonstrations; Japan, furthermore, had shown in its recent conflict with Russia that "moral force" alone was not enough. Shyamji Krishnavarma republished Pal's words in the *Indian Sociologist* and offered his own stinging remarks. In studied contrast to the *Vihari, Bande Mataram,* and *Indian Sociologist* was *Kal,* a Poona broadsheet. This paper claimed that because of sedition laws, Naoroji had embedded a "secretly intended meaning" in his words. "Mr. Dadabhai is an extremist himself," *Kal* noted, and by mentioning how his disappointments had almost pushed him to rebel, he had signaled to other Indians that self-government could be achieved by "having recourse to violent remedies." Consequently, "the extremist party has achieved a signal victory this year in the Congress."[64]

In its very last declaration, *Kal* might have been closer to the mark. While many radicals dwelled gloomily upon Naoroji's refusal to endorse violent methods, Bal Gangadhar Tilak appeared pleased by the presidential address. According to him, Naoroji, through his clear declaration of swaraj, had unmistakably shifted momentum within the Congress movement from the moderates to his camp. "Very few amongst the moderates ever dreamt that he would go so far as he has done, but as the new position has been most clearly defined by their own idol, they have to make the best of the situation," Tilak noted in the columns of *Kesari.* Naoroji had successfully prodded Gopal Krishna Gokhale to adopt swaraj. Another radical Congress member had noticed that Pherozeshah Mehta left the Congress "perfectly discomfited." With Gokhale and Mehta in mind, Tilak declared that "the Congress and *swarajya* are now so indissolubly connected together that however much the moderates may dislike the combination, they will have to put up with it." Naoroji's presidency had, indeed, been a victory for the radicals.[65]

A few days after the Congress had dispersed, Tilak delivered a landmark speech at Calcutta's venerable College Square. "The Extremists of today will be the Moderates of tomorrow," he pronounced before a gathering of students, "just as the Moderates of today were Extremists yesterday." He had the recent Congress president in mind. Tilak broached the topic of methods, fixating upon Naoroji's remarks about his disappointments and the temptation to rebel. The younger generation, Tilak maintained, "were entitled to draw their own conclusion from his disappointments."

By relying only upon "petitions and prayers," they would find it "impossible to gain any concessions."[66]

But Tilak, unlike Pal or Krishnavarma, did not hold up violent methods as the necessary alternative. Instead, he drew upon Naoroji's economic thought to justify another way forward. "Your industries are ruined utterly, ruined by foreign rule; your wealth is going out of the country and you are reduced to the lowest level which no human being can occupy," he reminded his audience, borrowing Naoroji's familiar language on the drain of wealth. "The venerable leader who presided over the recent Congress was the first to tell us that the drain from the country was ruining it, and if the drain was to continue, there was some great disaster awaiting us." Invoking Naoroji's drain theory, Tilak urged supporters to widen the boycott of foreign goods and propagate swadeshi. Boycott was now India's best response to the drain. It was a form of non-violent agitation, which Naoroji had so assiduously preached during the last phase of his career, but with different methods. "We are not armed, and there is no necessity for arms either," he urged. "We have a stronger weapon, a political weapon, in boycott."[67]

Naoroji, it is true, had remained conspicuously silent about the boycott in his speech. This did not matter to Tilak. "Mr. Dadabhai, in openly declaring his adherence to swadeshi as best adapted to the unnatural economic conditions prevailing in this country, has tacitly given his support to boycott," he claimed.[68] Regardless of whether this was true, there was something significant about Tilak's words. In pressing the radical cause onward, something that would precipitate the splintering of the Congress in less than twelve months, the seniormost radical leader had looked to Naoroji for legitimacy. In their interpretations of his presidential address, many moderates had assailed Naoroji for being too extreme, and many radicals had pilloried him for being too timid. But for Tilak, who would dominate the next phase of the nationalist movement, Dadabhai Naoroji was an essential part of the way forward.

Conclusion

"I AM IN THE BEST OF HEALTH," Dadabhai Naoroji had noted on his eighty-first birthday, just a few months before setting sail to India for the Calcutta Congress. Yet the strain of that journey and the heavy responsibilities he undertook at Calcutta ultimately took their toll. "How weak and frail he looked," commented the British missionary and educationist Charles Freer (C. F.) Andrews, one of the thousands who crowded before the pandal to listen to Naoroji's presidential address. In late January 1907, after spending a few weeks with family in Bombay, Naoroji decided to sail back to London in the improbable hope that he could resume his political activities. Almost immediately after returning to the imperial capital, he suffered a series of grievous health setbacks: respiratory ailments, fevers, general weakness. Travel and work had "more or less exhausted the vitality of all my organs," he wrote in an unusually candid manner to his family in India, "and each one is having its revenge." Unlike in the past, there were no quick recoveries. Friends and relatives began pleading with Naoroji to retire from public life. "This last India visit of yours has completely shattered your health," Homi Dadina, Naoroji's son-in-law, surmised from Bombay. "We are informed on all hands that your medical adviser is also of the same opinion, and though he has pressed you very much to retire for good, you decline to do so." Knowing that his father-in-law was averse to any idea of retirement or rest, Dadina struck upon a different strategy for enticing him back home: "The public think that your advice and counsel would be more beneficial to them here in this crisis through which the country generally is passing."[1]

By August, a month shy of turning eighty-two, Naoroji's stubborn refusal to slow down finally gave way. He decided "to go to India for good," resolving to spend his remaining days with his family in Bombay. George Birdwood, Naoroji's longtime friend, now retired from the India Office, agreed with the decision. "And it is in India you should die," Birdwood remarked. "That will give the necessary dramatic unity to your life." Later in the month, rumors reached Bombay that Naoroji had taken a turn for the worse and was on the verge of death. "Shops, libraries, and places of business were closed or about to be closed, and the people were preparing for universal mourning for a national calamity," reported the *Hindi Punch*. "From all parts of the country, from temples, mosques[,] churches and every household prayers will go up to Heaven to the Giver of all Good for the speedy recovery of the great and beloved patriot," the *Madras Standard* proclaimed.[2]

Naoroji pulled through. He returned to Indian shores in early November 1907, arriving at Prince's Dock in Bombay after strict orders had been given against any public demonstrations of welcome. The least excitement, family and friends worried, might prove fatal. In spite of predictions that he had only days or months to live, Naoroji, as usual, defied the odds and persevered, surviving for nearly another decade. But that decade was an unusually quiet one for a man used to being at the very center of nationalist politics. Along with his aged wife, Gulbai, he domiciled himself in a turreted seaside bungalow in Versova. Now a chaotic neighborhood within modern Mumbai's vertiginous concrete landscape, Versova was, a century ago, a tiny and isolated fishing village north of Bombay proper, a place where the postal address indicated its obscurity: "Via Andheri, BB&CI [Bombay, Baroda, and Central India] Railway." Here, along a palm-fringed beach with a commanding view of the Arabian Sea, Naoroji largely cut himself off from public affairs. Instead of having a packed daily schedule of appointments, he entertained only select visitors: a number of established and rising leaders of the Congress, delegations of *stri sabhas* or women's social reform and educational organizations, and the occasional Anglo-Indian official. Until his ninetieth year, he maintained his habit of writing correspondence in his own hand, although the flood of incoming letters from political leaders began to abate. Ordinary Indians, nevertheless, continued to write for political advice and support. Others trekked to Versova just to catch a fleeting glimpse of the frail patriot. A Maharashtrian woman, for example, published a vivid account about how she watched from afar as the nonagenarian "Hindusthānche pitāmah"—a Marathi rendering of Naoroji's moniker, "the Grand Old Man of India"—was carried in a cane chair to a waiting motor vehicle, which took him on a daily drive along the beach to get fresh air.[3]

Family affairs, not nationalist ones, now finally became the primary focus of his life. Of the many roles that Dadabhai Naoroji pioneered in the nationalist movement, one was, unfortunately, that of the absent husband and father. We know hardly anything about Gulbai: among the thousands of letters that Naoroji wrote and received, there are only a handful of passing references to his wife. Their marriage did not seem to be a happy one. Rustom P. Masani, Naoroji's first biographer, painted a deeply unflattering portrait of her. By all accounts, Naoroji remained a faithful husband to Gulbai—but, aside from a brief period in the mid-1860s, after his former business partner Mancherji Hormusji Cama had fabricated the story of Naoroji's intention to convert to Christianity and marry an Englishwoman, he saw no need to bring along his wife during his long stints of residence in London. This was highly unusual treatment, to say the least, for a man who otherwise championed female education, women's suffrage, and the relative equality of the sexes. Gulbai passed away in May 1909 in Versova, bringing to an end a marriage that, in spite of lasting for seventy-five years, remains for the historian largely a blank slate.[4]

By all accounts, Naoroji had a close and loving relationship with his two surviving children, daughters Maki and Shirin, and his grandchildren, of which there were at least ten. They carried on a regular stream of correspondence between Bombay and London; the youngest grandchildren appended doodles and brief messages in Gujarati. While Gulbai remained ensconced in Bombay, Naoroji encouraged his children and grandchildren to occasionally join him in London and pursue educational opportunities across Europe. Maki, who chose to follow in the footsteps of her deceased brother, Ardeshir, and become a doctor, received medical training in Edinburgh and London (she became Naoroji's chief caretaker during his retirement in Versova). In 1906, Meher, Ardeshir's eldest daughter, might have become the first Indian woman to receive a medical degree from the University of Edinburgh. She completed her studies as one sister, Perin, enrolled at the Sorbonne and another sister, Gosi, prepared to go to Oxford. During weekends and holidays, they descended on Naoroji's home in south London, where their grandfather carved time out of his busy schedule to take them to concerts or plays.[5]

But there had been occasions when distance and Naoroji's political responsibilities created clear rifts in the family. In April 1895, for example, Behramji Malabari wrote a frank letter to Naoroji about domestic unhappiness in Bombay. Virbai, Ardeshir's widow, complained to Malabari that "the elders were not careful about the needs of the youngers & that their first duty was towards the family"—a comment that, Malabari judged, was directed toward her absent father-in-law. The joint family setup in Bombay, where Naoroji's wife and daughters shared their Khetwadi house with the family of Mancherji Merwanji Dadina, resulted in frequent flare-ups. Maki, in particular, complained of Dadina's fierce temper and harsh treatment. Her correspondence "about the unhappiness of herself and her mother," Naoroji confessed to Malabari, "has made me miserable." Some years later, Maki pleaded with her father to return to Bombay for her wedding to Dadina's son Homi. Although he was clearly torn about the matter, Naoroji sternly—and a little heartlessly—reminded Maki about his greater nationalist obligations in London. "Surely you will not compare the presence at your wedding to my throwing away my duty and my whole life-work," he told her. "No dear, give up the idea of my presence." In retirement in Versova, Naoroji had time to reflect on whether such decisions had been, in hindsight, the correct ones to make.[6]

Retirement from political activity was one of the most difficult challenges that Naoroji faced during his long life. For an individual who had labored for five decades to construct much of the nationalist movement, sudden detachment and disengagement required steely willpower. During the Surat Congress in December 1907, a single Maratha *chappal* (slipper), flung from the crowd at Pherozeshah Mehta and Surendranath Banerjea,

brought to an end the vaunted unity of the Congress that some newspapers had so confidently announced a year beforehand. Moderate and radical differences finally reached their violent breaking point. The Congress session dissolved into chaos and physical brawls, and the radical
faction, with Bal Gangadhar Tilak at its head, formally seceded from the
organization. Naoroji maintained absolute silence, refusing to comment
on the split.

Occasionally, however, he caused panic among friends and relatives by
threatening to reengage with political matters. In 1912, after King George
V and Queen Mary became the first reigning British monarchs to visit
their Indian empire, Naoroji urged Indians to welcome the royal couple
by demanding self-government. He reiterated this demand in lengthy letters that he composed to Lord Crewe, the secretary of state for India, and
Lord Hardinge, the viceroy. Hormusjee Ardeseer Wadya, Naoroji's right-
hand man from his Baroda days, intervened and asked him to desist. "If
serious attention were paid it might lead you into a controversy which
we all desire you now to avoid," Wadya pleaded. Three years later, in September 1915, Naoroji enraged Dinsha Wacha and Pherozeshah Mehta by
agreeing to become president of the Home Rule League—a new, more politically strident organization set up by Annie Besant—and endorsing a
campaign for the immediate establishment of home rule for India. Besant,
head of the Theosophical Society in Adyar and a political firebrand, was
hardly a popular figure among Bombay moderates, who balked at the agitation for immediate home rule. "You don't know how far mischief has
already been caused by your acceptance of the Presidentship of the Home
Rule League," Wacha scolded Naoroji. "We have been so much embarrassed that you can't realise it."[7]

Finally, in November 1915, Naoroji learned of efforts to reintegrate Tilak
and other radicals into the Congress, as well as the push to reach a consensus between the Congress and the Muslim League, an infant party that
challenged the Congress's cross-communal aspirations. There is a chance
that he might have been invited to some deliberations that eventually led
to the Lucknow Pact, the grand compromise between these parties. By
now, however, even Naoroji had realized the limitations that came with
advanced age. "I shall not be able to accept any office," he regretfully

ANNIE BESANT AND DADABHAI NAOROJI.

Annie Besant, her supporters, and an aged Naoroji in 1915. This photograph was probably taken when Naoroji agreed to be president of Besant's Home Rule League.

Theosophist, November 1915. From the author's collection.

informed William Wedderburn before the Congress's December 1915 session. He was, after all, ninety.[8]

Dadabhai Naoroji made his last public appearance on January 28, 1916, when Bombay University conferred upon him an honorary doctorate of law in recognition of his political service. After a formal ceremony held under the neo-Gothic spires of the university's Convocation Hall, Naoroji was placed in the back of a motorcar and treated to one final procession through Bombay's streets. Schools and markets closed for the day, while Congress and Muslim League volunteers cleared a path through the crowds for the motorcar to proceed. This procession was markedly different from the overtly political celebrations that had occurred in 1893 and 1906, on the eve of his Congress presidencies. Naoroji halted outside at least three girls' schools, thereby harking back to the earliest endeavor in his career: female education. When he had first taken up the cause of female education seven decades beforehand, during the heady era of reform that was Young Bombay, he had few students and no female instructors. Now, around three hundred pupils of the Young Ladies' High School in Fort, joined by their all-female teaching staff, welcomed him with songs. The school's female principal presented Naoroji with a bouquet of flowers. At the Chanda Ramji Girls' High School in Bhuleshwar, members of the Gujarati Hindu Stri Mandal, a women's association, draped garlands over his frail shoulders. As the *Bombay Chronicle* noted, these ovations, made by the current torchbearers of female education in the city, "must have given peculiar satisfaction to him."[9]

On Saturday, June 30, 1917, Dadabhai Naoroji passed away peacefully at the Cumballa Hill home of his grandson-in-law. Once news of his death was made public, a crowd of around fifteen thousand individuals congregated along Gowalia Tank Road, then on Bombay's sleepy northern edge. Here were Indian men and women of various faiths and backgrounds, "leaders of the different communities—men of wealth and intellect—intermingling with the poor and the illiterate." Bal Gangadhar Tilak arrived to pay his respects, as did an aged Dinsha Wacha and two rising stars in the Congress, Muhammad Ali Jinnah and Sarojini Naidu. Benjamin Horniman, who, as editor of the *Bombay Chronicle,* became one of the most fearless British critics of his fellow countrymen's colonial exploits, was also present. "To have witnessed the silent but eloquent tributes of the thousands who attended his funeral was to realize the lasting hold that the departed patriot had secured in the hearts of his countrymen," he observed. This cross section of Indian society, its political leadership, and a handful of sympathetic Britons gathered behind white-robed Parsi pallbearers who carried the Grand Old Man of India toward the Towers of Silence at Malabar Hill, where he was laid to rest according to Zoroastrian rites.[10]

Below the gates to the Towers of Silence, Narayan Chandavarkar, a moderate Congressman who had frequently clashed with Naoroji and his more radical brand of politics, delivered an impromptu eulogy. "The premier son of India, the man who typified in himself the best traits not merely of Indian character, but of character universally personified, is laid low," he remarked. "And yet he is not dead. The sun, that rose just ninety-three years ago over India, is set, but, I say, it is set to rise again in the form of regenerated India."[11]

In the century that has passed since Narayan Chandavarkar uttered those words, the name of Dadabhai Naoroji has pronouncedly dimmed in public consciousness, overshadowed by the legacies of those nationalist leaders who finally delivered on the promise of swaraj for India. The struggle for freedom evolved in dramatic ways in the years immediately after Naoroji's death. It acquired new methods, millions of new recruits, and a dizzying assortment of new political and social objectives. Who among the Congress leaders gathered outside the Towers of Silence in 1917 could have anticipated the events of the next four years? The Rowlatt Acts, which considerably enhanced the coercive powers of the colonial administration, proved that, in spite of promises of Indian political reform that were finally emanating from Westminster, the Raj would cling to its worst authoritarian impulses. General Reginald Dyer, by brutally killing hundreds of peaceful protesters in Amritsar in April 1919, inflicted a fatal blow to any lingering faith in British justice and fair play. And Mohandas K. Gandhi, by launching the non-cooperation movement in 1920, charted a new course in anti-colonial resistance. He hammered the final nail into the coffin of a nationalist politics defined by strictly constitutional agitation, petitioning, and forbearance.

In this context, many of Naoroji's political conceptions and methods appeared hopelessly out of date. What was the use of clamoring for civil service reform when the new watchword was non-cooperation? How could any number of Indian MPs play a constructive role in distant Westminster? The Grand Old Man and his politics retreated into relatively distant memory.

In spite of this, Naoroji's legacy remains far-reaching and pervasive, albeit in a quiet and unobtrusive way. His bedrock political and economic ideas and his towering example as an anti-imperialist pioneer are the twin components of his legacy. It is a legacy that extends far beyond the subcontinent. In the United Kingdom, a new generation of non-white political leaders has reexamined his landmark election to Parliament, hailing the Central Finsbury MP as a pioneer of the British Asian community. They have embraced him as a black man in ways that would have utterly befuddled Lord Salisbury. Meanwhile, as British society fitfully confronts its imperialist past, Naoroji remains as relevant as ever. His documentation of Indian poverty still serves as a powerful counteractive to chronic outbreaks of imperial nostalgia.[12]

Across the world during the twentieth century, Naoroji's economic writings provided ammunition to anti-colonial liberation movements. His drain theory found echoes in the thought of diverse leaders such as Kwame Nkrumah, who led Ghana to independence in 1957; Sukarno, the first president of Indonesia; and Eric Williams, a noted scholar and prime minister of Trinidad and Tobago. Williams's landmark 1944 book, *Capitalism and Slavery*, complemented Naoroji's work by sketching out a similar economic drain in the British West Indies, one where the blood of African slaves cemented the fortunes of Liverpool and London. Sukarno, for his part, maintained that Naoroji, alongside men such as Bal Gangadhar Tilak, Mohandas K. Gandhi, and Jawaharlal Nehru, was one of the Indian leaders who most inspired Indonesian nationalists in their struggle against Dutch colonialism.[13]

Naturally, it is in India where Naoroji's legacy has been the most pervasive. It is simply impossible to imagine how the nationalist movement would have developed without him. More than any other early nationalist figure, Naoroji established its key institutions, mentored its leaders, chalked out its initial goals and strategies, and elucidated foundational economic grievances. While nurturing the Indian polity, he gave it strong international roots, enmeshing Indian nationalism within a much broader anti-imperialist stream. In moments of despair, such as during the long night of Conservative rule in the late 1890s and early 1900s, he preached faith and perseverance. He simply refused to give up, no matter the odds.

Of equal importance, Dadabhai Naoroji demonstrated to subject peoples that they could stand up to their colonial masters. They could speak truth to power. Shredding racist arguments, disproving official economic statistics, and condemning colonial policies from the very floor of the House of Commons—these were not just courageous acts. They were subversive ones as well. True, Naoroji regularly declared his loyalty to British rule and his faith in the British people. More often than not, however, he used such declarations as a shield from behind which he could launch even more devastating assaults against the Raj. Naoroji shook up the smug confidence that buttressed the British Empire. He utterly demolished the idea that imperialism was beneficial to the colonized, laying bare its real consequences while putting colonial officials on the defensive. With every angry denunciation that he elicited from an Anglo-Indian organ or an official in Calcutta or Whitehall, and with every ordinary Briton whom he won over to the cause of Indian reform, Naoroji exposed fractures in the edifice of empire, fractures that future nationalists would exploit and widen.

In the years after his death, many nationalists branded Naoroji as an unabashed moderate, savaging those very same declarations of faith in British goodwill and dismissing his methods as sheer mendicancy. By the year 1930, one of his grandsons, Jal, even had to defend his deceased grandfather in the columns of the *Times of India* against the absurd charge that he was a loyalist of empire. "In his own house conversation regarding the British Empire in India was generally punctuated by such phrases as bleeding white, poverty, organised loot, Swaraj, un-British rule, false promises, and so on," wrote Jal, a Tata executive who was also a close friend of Jawaharlal Nehru. "Dadabhai Naoroji had an absolute conviction that India had no future within the British Empire unless there was a complete change of outlook on the part of the Britisher."[14] Defenses such as these had little effect in changing the opinions of critics of early nationalism.

Still, even while accounting for only his concrete political achievements, it is markedly difficult to agree with Shyamji Krishnavarma's damning verdict that the Grand Old Man's career was a "sad failure." Subsequent leaders recognized the momentousness of his declaration of swaraj. "No speech delivered by a president of the National Congress ever had more far-reaching effects than that of Dadabhai in 1906," remarked C. F. Andrews, who became one of Gandhi's closest friends. By the time that Andrews penned those words in 1938, he recognized that Naoroji's address had actually contributed to the split of the Congress and the diminishing influence of the moderates. The tone of Naoroji's demand also had far-reaching implications. "It was not only that Lokmanya Tilak's phrase had been adopted, and that 'self-government' was now put forward as a right," Andrews continued, "but it was also for the first time, in such a place, that the form and nature of India's demand was expressed by an Indian word, *Swaraj*, the meaning of which could be easily understood throughout the length and breadth of India by the simplest villager as well as by the educated class."[15]

This was something that had also been recognized by, of all people, Bipin Chandra Pal, who had been one of Naoroji's fiercest detractors within the radical camp. Before the Calcutta Congress, Pal had ridiculed Naoroji's declared goal of "Self Government under British Paramountcy." "Either British paramountcy would mean nothing," he argued, "or self-government would mean nothing." He similarly mocked Naoroji's idea of self-government as it existed in white-settler colonies like Australia or Canada. But Pal, it seems, was eventually won over by the Grand Old Man. He was deeply encouraged by Naoroji's insistence that self-government could be "as in the United Kingdom," opening up the possibility of complete national autonomy for India. "This is really the same idea that had been proclaimed by us," he told fellow radicals. It was the use of the term "swaraj," once more, that truly moved Pal. This had emotion and power that could appeal to the nation. Speaking in Madras in mid-1907, Pal recalled a few passing words that Naoroji made to delegates at the very end of the Calcutta Congress. "He declared that as the result of the labour of the last 50 years, this generation had been able to discover this great national ideal of Swaraj," Pal stated. "He said, the generation that is passing away gives you, youngmen [*sic*], this idea. It devolves on you to work it out in practice." And so Pal came to see Naoroji's Calcutta speech as an inspiring call to action.[16]

What about methods? By the time of the 1906 Calcutta Congress, it is true, petitioning and related methods were largely discredited. But Naoroji's strategy of achieving reform through Whitehall and Westminster remained an essential component of the nationalist movement through independence. Even Gandhi and Nehru traveled to London to confer with imperial officials, while cultivating support among British progressives and the working class. The Mahatma famously mingled with laborers of the East End and mill hands in Lancashire, children and grandchildren of workers whom Naoroji had wooed from the 1880s onward. Both Tilak and Lala Lajpat Rai sought support from members of the Labour Party.

By 1919, Tilak himself was in London engaging with the British Committee of the Indian National Congress, a body whose work he had disparaged only a decade earlier.[17]

Other Indian leaders engaged with British politics to various degrees. In 1922, Shapurji Saklatvala followed in the footsteps of Naoroji and Mancherji Bhownaggree by becoming the third Indian—and the third Parsi—elected to the House of Commons. Like Naoroji, Saklatvala ran from a progressive and working-class constituency, Battersea, and plunged himself into British political affairs. He joined the Communist Party of Great Britain, became a well-known figure in the British labor movement, and served as the British representative for the All-India Trade Union Congress. V. K. Krishna Menon, who became Nehruvian India's premier diplomat, also blazed a trail in Britain very similar to that of Naoroji. Under the banner of the India League, a London-based organization that he led from the early 1930s onward, Menon lobbied the British public through speeches to working-class audiences, women's groups, and church congregations. The league forged an alliance of sympathetic MPs who pressed Parliament for purna swaraj (complete independence) for India. In 1934, Menon, running on the Labour ticket, was elected as a councilor in the London borough of St. Pancras, next door to Finsbury.[18]

The next generation of Congress leaders clearly understood their debts to Naoroji. Languishing in a British jail in 1934, Jawaharlal Nehru reflected on his exposure of Indian poverty, which, the future prime minister claimed, "served a revolutionary purpose and gave a political and economic foundation to our nationalism." Sarojini Naidu, who first met Naoroji while a student in London, believed that he "kindled the torch of freedom in India." "This child of an exiled community stood up and said that India must be free," she noted at a memorial meeting in 1936. "It required marvellous courage for any man to say that openly when even to whisper a thing like that was considered sedition."[19]

Gandhi remained one of Naoroji's staunchest admirers and one of the most prolific commentators on his legacy—even as he started to dispose of Naoroji's methods and faith in British justice. In both South Africa and India, the Mahatma marked Naoroji's birthdays with speeches or editorial messages in his newspapers. Naoroji, he pronounced in one such speech, was a rishi. "I myself and many others like me have learnt the lessons of regularity, single-minded patriotism, simplicity, austerity and ceaseless work from this venerable man." He began his famous treatise, *Hind Swaraj*, with a stern defense of the Grand Old Man against the criticisms of Indian revolutionaries. In the summer of 1909, Naoroji's granddaughter Gosi met Gandhi in London. "He simply worships you," she wrote to her grandfather. For Gandhi, still in the thick of his satyagraha in South Africa, even Naoroji's failures had been inspirational. He held up Naoroji as a model of perseverance. "If we would but remember that Mr. Dadabhai has been struggling for the last forty years or more," he wrote to fellow South African Indians in his paper, *Indian Opinion*, "we would find in the thought a great deal to console us that, after all, our struggle has only just commenced, and that we have not been without silver linings to the clouds which have hung over us." Henry Polak, Gandhi's faithful deputy in South Africa, expressed a similar sentiment while on a visit to Bombay in 1909. "It has been largely the recollection of your sustained self-sacrifice on behalf of India, covering a period of over half-a-century, that has been our inspiration in the Transvaal during the last three bitter years," he told Naoroji.[20]

Upon completing his work in South Africa and returning to Indian soil in January 1915, one of the very first tasks that Gandhi undertook was a visit to Naoroji. Gandhi continued to think of the veteran leader as he pioneered the next stage of the nationalist movement. He acknowledged his debts to Naoroji's economic writings for teaching him about the horrific dimensions of Indian poverty. And in 1924, a year before the centenary of Naoroji's birth, the Mahatma put forth an innovative proposal. He urged Indians to honor the Grand Old Man by spinning khadi, a rough cloth worn by the poorest of the poor, on a *charkha* or spinning wheel. The charkha had become a preeminent symbol of Gandhian nationalism—a weapon of the poor against economic injustice, a tool for national uplift. Gandhi believed, however, that it was also a fitting tribute to Naoroji—and something that Naoroji would have appreciated if he had been alive to witness the changed political atmosphere in India. "All activities which encourage its use amount to an imitation of Dadabhai's virtues," he noted. This was not simply an attempt to appropriate part of the Grand Old Man's legacy. Rather, the Mahatma recognized something important about Naoroji's political thought: that it was

marked by constant evolution. Unlike so many of his nationalist colleagues, Naoroji radicalized as he aged. Well into his late seventies and
early eighties, he continued to embrace new ideas instead of retreating into
the safety of his own core convictions. He continued to embrace change.[21]

By identifying the charkha with Naoroji, therefore, the Mahatma raised
a tempting question: if the Grand Old Man had lived and remained politically active for several more years, would he have adopted Gandhi's
methods? Would there have been a fourth phase in his political career?

Gandhi clearly thought so. After all, by the launch of the non-
cooperation movement in late 1920, several of Naoroji's grandchildren
had pledged themselves to the principles of satyagraha. This included
Perin Naoroji, who had earlier dabbled in revolutionary activities under
the tutelage of Bhikhaiji Cama and Vinayak Damodar Savarkar, only to
realize the futility of violent methods. As avowed Gandhians, Naoroji's
grandchildren believed themselves to be following in the footsteps of
their grandfather.

It was a link that Rustom P. Masani, Naoroji's first biographer and a
moderate critic of the Mahatma, eventually came to see. In December 1931,
Masani and Gandhi found themselves to be fellow passengers aboard the
SS *Pilsna*, leaving the Italian port of Brindisi for Bombay. The Round Table
Conference in London—where Prime Minister Ramsay MacDonald, who
had known Naoroji, presided over negotiations for a future constitutional
arrangement for India—had recently failed. India steeled itself for a new
round of civil disobedience—one during which Perin Naoroji would face
an especially long and brutal stint in jail. Somewhere in the Arabian Sea,
Masani struck up a conversation with the Mahatma. "Don't you think,"
Masani asked, "Dadabhai's policy, which the present generation ridicules
as a mendicant policy, was the right one, considering the circumstances
prevailing?" "Yes," Gandhi replied. He then quickly added, "And I believe
that if he were alive today he would follow the same policy that I have
been pursuing for the last few years."[22]

At the intersection of Dr. Dadabhai Naoroji Road and Mahatma Gandhi
Road in south Mumbai is a small statue of the Grand Old Man. He is seated
on a modest plinth, hemmed in by pavement booksellers and shaded by

a massive banyan tree. Among the thousands of people who pass by the statue each day—professionals, laborers, students, and recently arrived migrants to India's City of Dreams—few stop to notice. Few have time to do so. An endless stream of honking cars, overcrowded buses, and the occasional horse or cow lumber by, providing a vivid tableau of modern Indian life but further relegating the Grand Old Man to the background. To the left and right of the statue are the headquarters of banks and multinational corporations that have powered India's economic growth in the post-liberalization era, a development that has helped lift hundreds of millions out of desperate poverty. Some of these multinationals have begun acquiring prestigious British brands, raising panic in the former heart of empire about a very different drain of wealth. In front of the statue is the Bombay High Court, a setting for some of the most dramatic moments of the nationalist movement and now a symbol of the modern Indian state. The Bombay Stock Exchange and Rajabai Tower of Mumbai University loom farther afield. As the Grand Old Man stares directly south from the pedestal, he establishes a line of sight with Elphinstone College, his alma mater.[23]

It is a perfect monument to Dadabhai Naoroji—unobtrusive and hardly noticed, yet at the center of it all.

TIMELINE

1820S

SEPTEMBER 4, 1825 Dadabhai Naoroji born in Khadak in Bombay's Native Town.

1829 (?) father Naoroji Palanji passed away.

1830S

EARLY 1830S enrolled as a student in the central English school of the Bombay Native Education Society.

1836 (?) married to Gulbai Shroff, aged seven.

1839 underwent the Zoroastrian navar ceremony (first initiation ceremony for the Zoroastrian priesthood) at Wadia Atash Behram, Bombay.

1840S

MAY 1, 1840 enrolled at Elphinstone College.

1845 completed studies at Elphinstone College.

1845 (?) Erskine Perry, chief justice of the Bombay supreme court, proposed sending Naoroji to England to be trained as a barrister. The idea was shot down by orthodox Parsis who feared Perry wanted to convert Naoroji to Christianity.

NOVEMBER 1, 1845 appointed as assistant master at Elphinstone College.

1848 led efforts to found the Students' Literary and Scientific Society.

1848 OR 1849 appointed as assistant professor at Elphinstone College.

1849 published first monthly edition of the Gujarati-language *Dnyan Prasarak*.

OCTOBER 1849 Students' Literary and Scientific Society opened six girls' schools in Bombay. Naoroji supervised a school in Baharkot, just outside of Fort.

1850s

JANUARY 20, 1851 appointed to the Bombay Board of Education.

AUGUST 3, 1851 joined Navrozji Fardunji in founding the Rahnumae Mazdayasnan Sabha, a vehicle for Zoroastrian religious reform in the Parsi community.

NOVEMBER 15, 1851 published the first edition of *Rast Goftar*.

AUGUST 26, 1852 delivered his maiden political speech at the meeting that inaugurated the Bombay Association.

OCTOBER 1852 appointed as acting professor of mathematics and natural philosophy at Elphinstone College after Joseph Patton, the previous professor, departed Bombay due to severe illness.

1854 appointed as full professor of mathematics and natural philosophy at Elphinstone College, becoming the first-ever Indian to hold this rank at a British-administered institution of higher education.

JUNE 27, 1855 departed Bombay aboard the steamer *Madras,* beginning his voyage to Great Britain to help establish Cama & Co., the first Indian commercial firm in the United Kingdom.

AUGUST 22, 1855 arrived in Southampton. Once Cama & Co. was established, Naoroji became its representative in Liverpool, primarily dealing in the cotton trade.

MARCH 1856 appointed as professor of Gujarati at University College in London.

1858 resigned from Cama & Co. and returned to Bombay.

1859 Ardeshir, a son, born in Bombay.

JANUARY 9, 1859 departed Bombay for Great Britain.

POST-JANUARY 1859 took up the case of Rustamji Hirjibhai Wadia, the first Indian candidate for the Indian civil service, who was barred from taking the civil service examination due to a last-minute reduction of the age limit.

POST-JANUARY 1859 established Dadabhai Naoroji & Co. in London.

1860s

MARCH 13, 1861 delivered "The Manners and Customs of the Parsees" to the Liverpool Philomathic Society.

MARCH 18, 1861 delivered "The Parsee Religion" to the Liverpool Literary and Philosophical Society.

SEPTEMBER 22, 1861 the Zoroastrian Fund, the modern-day Zoroastrian Trust Funds of Europe, established in London. This was the first-ever

Asian religious organization established in the United Kingdom. Naoroji was elected as a trustee.

SEPTEMBER 9, 1863 arrived back home in Bombay from London after Mancherji Hormusji Cama spread a rumor that he was about to convert to Christianity and marry an Englishwoman.

1864 OR 1865 Shirin, a daughter, born.

APRIL 29, 1865 departed Bombay for Great Britain, taking along with him his mother, Manekbai; wife, Gulbai; son, Ardeshir; and baby daughter, Shirin.

MARCH 27, 1866 delivered "The European and Asiatic Races" to the London Ethnological Society.

JUNE 1866 Dadabhai Naoroji & Co. went bankrupt.

DECEMBER 1, 1866 established the East India Association in London.

MAY 2, 1867 delivered "England's Duties to India" at the first meeting of the East India Association in London.

JULY 5, 1867 delivered a paper on Mysore state to the East India Association in London.

FEBRUARY 5, 1868 submitted a petition to the secretary of state for India on female education.

MAY 2, 1868 submitted a petition to the secretary of state for India on the admission of educated Indians into the Indian civil service.

OCTOBER 10, 1868 Maki, his second daughter, born in Bombay.

1870S

JULY 27, 1870 delivered "Wants and Means of India" to the Society of Arts in London.

FEBRUARY 15, 1871 delivered "On the Commerce of India" to the Society of Arts in London.

MONSOON 1871 toured south Gujarat, Kathiawar, and Kutch to investigate local poverty.

1872 first considered standing for a seat in the House of Commons.

JULY 1873 Malharrao, gaikwad of Baroda, sent a dispatch on the darbar seating controversy, written by Naoroji, to the secretary of state for India. In return for his services, the gaikwad gave Naoroji Rs. 50,000 in the form of a trust for the education of his children.

JULY 11 AND 15, 1873 delivered testimony in London before the Select Parliamentary Committee on East India Finance. The committee chairman and the secretary of state for India refused to publish a statement authored by Naoroji in its final report. Naoroji eventually delivered this statement to the Bombay branch of the East India Association in 1876 under the title of "Poverty of India."

AUGUST 6, 1873 defended his acceptance of Rs. 50,000 from the gaikwad at a meeting of the East India Association in London.

EARLY NOVEMBER 1873 departed Great Britain for India.

EARLY DECEMBER 1873 arrived at Baroda in order to begin his diwanship.

DECEMBER 23, 1873 Malharrao sent a note to Robert Phayre, the British resident, stating that Naoroji had begun his duties as diwan.

DECEMBER 27, 1873 signed a proclamation asking subjects to report any cases of oppression or bribery by government servants in Baroda.

EARLY JULY 1874 offered to resign as diwan after the gaikwad ordered him to revive the older, more corrupt judicial system. The gaikwad ultimately relented.

JULY 31, 1874 listed his demands to the gaikwad for reforms in Baroda state, including the abolition of nazarana, the resignation of particular darbaris, and his direct involvement in any future government appointments.

AUGUST 9, 1874 tendered his resignation as diwan due to the gaikwad's administrative interference. Naoroji withdrew his resignation after Malharrao relented.

AUGUST 11, 1874 Robert Phayre sent a message to Malharrao advising him not to appoint Naoroji as diwan.

AUGUST 14, 1874 Malharrao informed Phayre that Naoroji had been diwan since December 1873. Malharrao asked once more for military honors to be extended to Naoroji.

NOVEMBER 2, 1874 Malharrao asked British authorities to remove Phayre as resident.

NOVEMBER 9, 1874 Phayre nearly poisoned in Baroda.

DECEMBER 21, 1874 Naoroji and his ministers tendered their resignations from office.

1875 mother, Manekbai, passed away.

JANUARY 11, 1875 Naoroji and his colleagues departed Baroda.

LATE JANUARY 1875 Malharrao deposed as the gaikwad of Baroda by British authorities.

JULY 1875 elected as a member of the Bombay Municipal Corporation and town council.

FEBRUARY 28, 1876 delivered "Poverty of India, Part I" to the Bombay branch of the East India Association.

APRIL 27, 1876 delivered "Poverty of India, Part II" to the Bombay branch of the East India Association.

AFTER SEPTEMBER 1876 departed Bombay for London.

1880s

MAY 24, 1880–JANUARY 4, 1881 corresponded with the secretary of state for India on the economic productivity of Punjab. The correspondence was eventually published as "Condition of India."

APRIL 1881 returned to Bombay from Great Britain, intending to stay in India for good, after closing down Dadabhai Naoroji & Co. in London.

SEPTEMBER 16, 1882 submitted a statement to the Hunter Commission on Indian Education, analyzing the British Indian government's dismal underfunding of education.

JANUARY 1883 started *Voice of India* in Bombay with Behramji Malabari.

LATE 1883 TO JUNE 1884 suffered a serious health setback, necessitating convalescence in the Gujarati seaside town of Tithal.

NOVEMBER 29, 1884 delivered a speech in Bombay to mark the retirement of the viceroy, Lord Ripon. Naoroji invoked, for the first time in public, the idea of self-government for India.

JANUARY 1885 met with Allan Octavian Hume and other Bombay political leaders in order to discuss setting up the Indian National Congress.

JANUARY 31, 1885 Bombay Presidency Association inaugurated with Naoroji as one of its vice presidents.

SEPTEMBER 1885 appointed to the Bombay legislative council by the governor, Lord Reay.

DECEMBER 28–30, 1885 first session of the Indian National Congress held in Bombay.

LATE MARCH 1886 departed Bombay for London with the ambition of standing for Parliament.

APRIL 12, 1886 arrived in London and began meeting with prominent Liberal Party officials for campaign support.

JUNE 18, 1886 unanimously endorsed as the Liberal parliamentary candidate for Holborn by the Holborn Liberal Association.

JUNE 24, 1886 held his first public meeting as the official Liberal candidate for Holborn.

JULY 5, 1886 polling day in Holborn. Naoroji, who polled 1,950 votes, was defeated by the Conservative incumbent, Francis Duncan, who polled 3,651 votes.

NOVEMBER 11, 1886 departed London for Bombay.

DECEMBER 27–30, 1886 served as president of the Congress's second session, held in Calcutta. He delivered his presidential address on December 27.

LATE FEBRUARY 1888 friends encouraged Naoroji to investigate standing for Parliament from Central Finsbury.

MAY 25, 1888 in a letter to the *Freeman's Journal* of Dublin, Michael Davitt encouraged Charles Stuart Parnell to choose Naoroji for an open parliamentary seat in Sligo, Ireland.

AUGUST 15, 1888 selected as the official Liberal candidate for Central Finsbury, although the proceedings of the Central Finsbury Liberal and Radical Association's meeting were eventually challenged. Richard Eve soon emerged as a rival Liberal candidate.

SEPTEMBER 5, 1888 met Francis Schnadhorst, secretary of the National Liberal Federation, who advised Naoroji not to retire from the Central Finsbury race or give in to calls for arbitration.

NOVEMBER 29, 1888 Prime Minister Lord Salisbury, in Edinburgh, called Naoroji a "black man."

JANUARY 21, 1889 complimentary banquet given to Naoroji at the National Liberal Club in response to Lord Salisbury's "black man" remark.

JULY 27, 1889 British Committee of the Indian National Congress established in London.

1890s

LATE JUNE 1890 Richard Eve retired from the Central Finsbury race.

JULY 16, 1890 spoke at an international women's conference in London organized by the Women's Franchise League.

JANUARY 1891 Frederick A. Ford launched a challenge to Naoroji for the Liberal candidacy in Central Finsbury.

JUNE 11, 1892 Liberal MP Richard Causton visited Naoroji and asked for "some overture for peace" to resolve the dispute in Central Finsbury.

MID-JUNE 1892 Frederick A. Ford terminated his candidacy, leaving Naoroji as the recognized Liberal candidate in Central Finsbury.

JULY 6, 1892 polling day in Central Finsbury. Naoroji won, polling 2,959 votes to Conservative rival Frederick Thomas Penton's 2,956 votes. In a subsequent recount, Naoroji's margin of victory widened to five votes.

AUGUST 9, 1892 delivered his maiden address to the House of Commons.

MARCH 1, 1893 tabled a bill in the House of Commons for simultaneous civil service examinations. The bill failed to muster sufficient support for debate.

JUNE 2, 1893 resolution for simultaneous civil service examinations passed in the House of Commons.

JULY 27, 1893 helped to found the Indian Parliamentary Committee, a group of MPs sympathetic toward Indian concerns.

OCTOBER 7, 1893 son, Ardeshir, passed away in Kutch.

NOVEMBER 17, 1893 departed London for Bombay, returning to India to preside at the Lahore Congress.

DECEMBER 3, 1893 arrived in Bombay and greeted by as many as 500,000 people during a procession through the city.

DECEMBER 25, 1893 arrived in Lahore after a whistle-stop train tour through western and northern India.

DECEMBER 27–30, 1893 served as president of the Lahore Congress. He delivered his presidential address on December 27.

JANUARY 20, 1894 departed Bombay for London.

EARLY FEBRUARY 1894 arrived in London.

JULY 5, 1894 Mohandas K. Gandhi wrote his first letter to Naoroji, asking for guidance in South African political matters.

JULY 16, 1895 polling day in Central Finsbury. Naoroji, who polled 2,873 votes, was defeated by the Conservative Unionist candidate, William Frederick Barton Massey-Mainwaring, who polled 3,588 votes. Mancherji Bhownaggree, standing as a Conservative, won election to Parliament from Bethnal Green.

FEBRUARY 10, 1897 held a mass meeting in Westminster with Henry Hyndman addressing the Indian famine.

MARCH 25, 1897 testified before the Welby Commission.

1900S

SEPTEMBER–OCTOBER 1900 general election held in Great Britain. Naoroji was unable to contest a parliamentary seat due to illness.

AUGUST 29, 1901 selected as the official Liberal candidate for North Lambeth by the North Lambeth Liberal and Radical Club and National Democratic League.

OCTOBER 1901 published *Poverty and Un-British Rule in India*, a compilation of his economic writings from the past thirty years.

JULY 3–6, 1903 outlined the objective of "Self-Government under British Paramountcy" in correspondence with Romesh Chunder Dutt.

AUGUST 14–18, 1904 attended the International Socialist Congress in Amsterdam along with Hyndman.

JANUARY 15, 1906 polling day in North Lambeth. Naoroji, running as an independent Liberal candidate, was defeated, earning only 733 votes.

JULY 12, 1906 asked by Surendranath Banerjea to preside at the upcoming Calcutta Congress. Banerjea apprised Naoroji of a likely split between moderate and radical factions unless Naoroji accepted the presidency.

NOVEMBER 8, 1906 accompanied Gandhi to a meeting with Lord Elgin, secretary for the colonies, at the Colonial Office.

NOVEMBER 13, 1906 unanimously invited by the Congress reception committee to preside at the upcoming Calcutta Congress.

NOVEMBER 22, 1906 accompanied Gandhi to a meeting with John Morley, secretary of state for India, at the India Office.

NOVEMBER 29, 1906 departed London for Bombay.

DECEMBER 14, 1906 arrived in Bombay and greeted with a procession through the city.

DECEMBER 26–29, 1906 served as president of the Calcutta Congress. He delivered his presidential address on December 26, calling for swaraj.

JANUARY 19, 1907 departed Bombay for London, hoping to continue his political work in the imperial capital.

FEBRUARY 8, 1907 arrived in London.

EARLY OCTOBER 1907 after months of ill health, resolved to return to India "for good" and departed London.

NOVEMBER 7, 1907 arrived in Bombay and began his retirement in Versova.

MAY 15, 1909 wife, Gulbai, passed away.

1910S

JANUARY 12, 1915 Gandhi, who had recently arrived in India after completing his South African career, visited Naoroji before attending a welcoming reception at the Petit family house in Bombay.

JANUARY 28, 1916 given an honorary doctorate of law by Bombay University. After the convocation ceremony, Naoroji was taken on one final public procession through Bombay.

JUNE 30, 1917 passed away at Palitana House, Cumballa Hill, Bombay.

KEY INDIVIDUALS

BANERJEA, SURENDRANATH (1848–1925) Prominent moderate Congress leader from Calcutta. Along with Romesh Chunder Dutt, he qualified for the Indian civil service in 1869, but he was later dismissed on very spurious grounds, likely due to racism. He was the editor of the *Bengalee* and a leader of the Indian Association in Calcutta, from which he started the National Conference, a precursor to the Congress. Banerjea took an early and confrontational role in the swadeshi movement but worried about its increasingly radical tenor. He was instrumental in convincing Dadabhai Naoroji to accept the presidency of the Indian National Congress's 1906 Calcutta session.

BELL, EVANS (1825–1887) British proponent of Indian princely state interests. He arrived in India in 1842 as a military officer and was stationed in Nagpur. Here he fought on behalf of the deposed Bhosle family after the governor-general of India, Lord Dalhousie, annexed Nagpur state. He was ultimately charged with insubordination. Bell wrote a number of works arguing in favor of princely state autonomy and helped form the India Reform Society in London. In 1866, he became one of the first members of Naoroji's East India Association.

BHAGVATSINHJI, THAKUR OF GONDAL (1865–1944) Ruling prince of Gondal state in Kathiawar, reigning from 1870 until his death. He was recognized as one of the most progressive Indian princes. Bhagvatsinhji was also one of Naoroji's most steadfast financial supporters during the Central Finsbury campaign.

BHOWNAGGREE, MANCHERJI (1851–1933) Conservative MP for Bethnal Green between 1895 and 1906 and the second-ever Indian (and Parsi) elected to the British Parliament. Bhownaggree served as the Bombay-based agent for the ruling thakur of Bhavnagar before relocating to London, where he assisted Naoroji in his Central Finsbury campaign. He subsequently found Naoroji too politically radical for his tastes and—with assistance from George Birdwood and Lord Harris, the governor of Bombay—launched his successful campaign in Bethnal Green, aiming to become a Conservative "member for India." As an MP, Bhownaggree was reviled by Indian nationalists as an Anglo-Indian stooge, although he did provide critical assistance to Mohandas K. Gandhi in South African affairs.

BIRDWOOD, GEORGE (1832–1917) India Office official, scholar of Indian art and history, and a staunch Conservative. In spite of his very different political leanings, Birdwood was one of Naoroji's oldest and most trusted friends; their friendship dated from 1858 and lasted until 1917, when they died days apart. Birdwood resided in Bombay between 1854 and 1868, where he became a professor at Grant Medical College. Unlike many other Anglo-Indians, he actively sought out friendships and associations with Indians, becoming an extremely popular figure in the city. After returning to Britain and securing a position in the India Office, he continued to mentor and assist Indians who were in the United Kingdom for work or study. Birdwood played an active role in Mancherji Bhownaggree's decision to contest a parliamentary seat as a Conservative in 1895, something that might have temporarily frayed his friendship with Naoroji.

BONNERJEE, WOMESH CHUNDER (W. C.) (1844–1906) First president of the Congress (at its 1885 session in Bombay). Originally from Calcutta, Bonnerjee lived primarily in London after he qualified as a barrister. He was a moderate leader who helped steer the British Committee of the Indian National Congress. Bonnerjee unsuccessfully stood as a Liberal candidate for Parliament in the 1892 general elections.

BUTLER, JOSEPHINE (1828–1906) Prominent British women's rights activist. In the 1860s, she began campaigning for women's suffrage and also began a prodigious career as a writer, authoring books and tracts on various women's rights issues. Butler took an active interest in Indian political affairs in connection with her work to repeal the Indian Contagious Diseases Acts. She recruited Naoroji as a strong supporter of her repeal efforts; in return, Butler supported Naoroji's parliamentary ambitions.

CAMA, BHIKHAIJI (1861–1935) Radical nationalist who spent much of her life in exile in Paris. Cama became close to Naoroji and his family while residing in London in 1905 and 1906, where she also came into contact with Henry Hyndman and Shyamji Krishnavarma. In Paris, she looked after Naoroji's granddaughter Perin, a student at the Sorbonne, and introduced her to other revolutionaries in the city. In 1907, Cama attended the International Socialist Congress in Stuttgart and held up a flag that, she announced, stood for an independent India.

CAMA, KHARSHEDJI NASARVANJI (1815?–1885) Wealthy Parsi shetia (commercial elite) who served as Naoroji's colleague and financial benefactor in numerous Young Bombay endeavors. He provided financial support for the Dnyan Prasarak Mandli, the Rahnumae Mazdayasnan Sabha, and the girls' schools operated by the Students' Literary and Scientific Society. He cofounded *Rast Goftar* with Naoroji in 1851.

CHESNEY, GEORGE (1830–1895) Indian army officer and advocate of increased British military spending (he authored *The Battle of Dorking* in 1871, a sensational account of a German invasion of Great Britain). He retired from India in 1891 and was elected as the Conservative MP for Oxford in 1892. Chesney became one of Naoroji's most vocal opponents in the House of Commons, calling into question Naoroji's ability to act as an Indian representative.

CRAWFURD, JOHN (1783–1868) British diplomat in Java and Siam, later appointed to fill Stamford Raffles's post in Singapore in 1823. Toward the end of his life, Crawfurd served as president of the London Ethnological Society. Naoroji's 1866 paper "The European and Asiatic Races" was a response to Crawfurd's racist rants about the inferiority of Asians in comparison to Europeans.

DAVITT, MICHAEL (1846–1906) Outspoken Irish nationalist leader, founder of the Irish Land League, and MP. Davitt and Naoroji were close friends, although many Indian nationalists in the 1880s and 1890s found Davitt far too radical and resented Naoroji's association with him. Keenly interested in Indian affairs, Davitt suggested offering an Irish seat in Parliament to Naoroji in 1883 and 1888. Naoroji asked him for help in finding an Irish parliamentary seat in 1892 and 1896, and encouraged him to accept the presidency of the Congress in 1894.

DICKINSON, JOHN (1815–1876) Vocal critic of British Indian policy. He founded the India Reform Society in 1853, which organized public meetings and published a number of tracts that were strongly critical of policies pursued by Lord Dalhousie, the governor-general. Like Evans Bell, Dickinson took a marked interest in princely state affairs. Dickinson was an early member of Naoroji's East India Association. Along with Navrozji Fardunji, he helped draft a petition to the House of Commons in 1874 on Indian parliamentary representation.

DIGBY, WILLIAM (1849–1904) Social campaigner and journalist. Digby edited the *Madras Times* before returning to Great Britain in 1879. He stood unsuccessfully as a Liberal candidate for Parliament in 1885 and 1892. Digby was one of Naoroji's most important supporters during the Holborn and Central Finsbury campaigns, acting as an intermediary between Naoroji and Francis Schnadhorst in the latter campaign. He was secretary of the British Committee of the Indian National Congress and editor of its newspaper, *India*, between 1890 and 1892. In 1901, he published *"Prosperous" British India*, a scathing account of Indian poverty and famines.

DUTT, ROMESH CHUNDER (1848–1909) One of the earliest Indian members of the civil service, retiring as divisional commissioner of Burdwan in 1897. He was president of the 1899 Lucknow Congress. Dutt authored the two-volume *Economic History of India* during his residence in London, where he participated in the activities of the British Committee of the Indian National Congress. In 1900, he contemplated standing for Parliament. Dutt's correspondence with Naoroji in July 1903 prompted Naoroji to enunciate the demand for "Self-Government under British Paramountcy."

EVE, RICHARD (1831–1900) Solicitor and unsuccessful Liberal candidate for Parliament. Eve polled second to Naoroji in the disputed vote of the Central Finsbury Liberal and Radical Association of August 15, 1888. He eventually challenged Naoroji and waged a campaign against him, but retired from the race in June 1890.

FAWCETT, HENRY (1833–1884) Professor of political economy at Cambridge University and a Liberal MP. Due to a shooting accident in 1858, he was left permanently blind, but refused to let his handicap impair his education and work. Fawcett was deeply influenced by John Stuart Mill and quickly joined the most progressive ranks of Liberal MPs. From the late 1860s until his death, Fawcett was known as the "member for India" in Parliament for his advocacy of Indian interests.

FORD, FREDERICK A. (1849?–1910) Represented Central Finsbury in the London County Council from 1889 until 1892. He was the husband of the well-known Victorian feminist Florence Fenwick Miller. Ford polled third in the August 15, 1888, vote at the Central Finsbury Liberal and Radical Association. He entered the Central Finsbury race in early 1891 as a rival Liberal candidate to Naoroji, posing a much more serious threat than Richard Eve. Ford dropped out of the race, most likely due to Liberal Party pressure, in June 1892, just weeks ahead of the general election.

FREEMAN, GEORGE (GEORGE FITZGERALD) (BORN C. 1836) Irish American journalist and Indian revolutionary supporter. Very little is known about his life. He lived in London before immigrating to Canada, where he became an outspoken advocate of Canada's separation from the British Empire. After moving to New York, he joined the Clan-na-Gael, an Irish republican organization, and contributed to the *New York Sun*. He corresponded with Naoroji between 1897 and 1901, establishing what was most likely the first-ever instance of cooperation between an American anti-imperialist and an Indian nationalist. Freeman thereafter drifted into radical circles, associating with the Ghadr Party and assisting in the so-called Hindu-German Conspiracy during the First World War.

GANDHI, MOHANDAS K. (1869–1948) Gandhi lived in London between 1888 and 1891, where he studied for the bar. Here he met Naoroji for the first time in 1888. He began a lengthy correspondence with Naoroji in 1894 after he relocated to South Africa. Naoroji helped publicize and distribute Gandhi's reports, which detailed discriminatory activity against Indians in South Africa, and lobbied British colonial officials on Gandhi's behalf. He also assisted with Gandhi's 1906 deputation to London.

GHOSH, LALMOHAN (1849–1909) Member of the Indian Association of Calcutta. In 1885, he became the first Indian to stand for election to the British Parliament, waging an unsuccessful campaign as a Liberal in Deptford. He made a second unsuccessful attempt in 1886. Ghosh was president of the 1903 Madras session of the Congress.

GLADSTONE, WILLIAM EWART (1809–1898) Leader of the Liberal Party in the late Victorian era, serving as prime minister four times. Gladstone was known as the "Grand Old Man," a moniker that inspired Indians to dub Naoroji as the "Grand Old Man of India" by the early 1890s. He rallied to Naoroji's defense after Lord Salisbury's "black man" remark in 1888. Naoroji's election to the Commons coincided with Gladstone's fourth and last ministry, lasting from 1892 until his resignation from office in early 1894.

GOKHALE, GOPAL KRISHNA (1866–1915) One of the most prominent leaders of the moderate faction of the Congress in the early twentieth century. Mentored by Mahadev Govind Ranade, Gokhale joined the Congress in 1889 and served as its president at its 1905 Banaras session. He was a professor at Fergusson College in Poona. Gokhale worked closely with Naoroji during the

Welby Commission, traveling to London along with Dinsha Wacha in order to deliver evidence. From 1904 onward, Naoroji cultivated Gokhale as a supporter of Indian self-government.

GRIFFITH, ROBERT MORGAN HOLT (R. M. H.) (1840–1906) Campaign secretary for Naoroji during his first campaign in Central Finsbury and secretary during his term in Parliament. Griffith distinguished himself as one of Naoroji's most loyal and steadfast supporters, helping him navigate local political divisions in Clerkenwell. He was also the proprietor of the *Weekly News and Clerkenwell Chronicle*.

HAMILTON, LORD GEORGE (1845–1927) Appointed as secretary of state for India in 1895 by the Conservative ministry of Lord Salisbury. He became the longest-serving secretary of state for India, leaving office only in 1903. Hamilton was widely disliked by Naoroji and other Indian nationalists, who blamed him for relative indifference to the plague epidemic and famines of the late 1890s.

HUME, ALLAN OCTAVIAN (1829–1912) Considered the "father of the Indian National Congress." Hume arrived in India in 1849 and joined the civil service, being first stationed in Etawah. He resigned from the civil service in 1882 and thereafter served as an advisor to Lord Ripon during his viceroyalty. Hume worked with Naoroji and other Bombay political leaders to begin preliminary organization of the Congress in January 1885. In the summer of 1885, he visited the United Kingdom in order to drum up support for the proposed Congress amongst Liberal politicians. Naoroji relied on Hume's extensive contacts after arriving in London in 1886 with the intention of standing for Parliament.

HYNDMAN, HENRY (1842–1921) Socialist leader and founder of the first socialist political party in Great Britain (the Democratic Federation, established in 1881, which in 1884 became the Social Democratic Federation). Hyndman most likely first met Naoroji in 1878 after reading the latter's "Poverty of India." He subsequently adopted Naoroji's views on the drain of wealth. In 1897, he embarked on a speaking tour with Naoroji in order to highlight the catastrophic famine in India. In 1904, he attended the International Socialist Congress in Amsterdam with Naoroji. By the late 1890s, Hyndman, brash and outspoken, had become critical of Naoroji's and the Congress's political moderation, instead speaking of the need for open rebellion against British rule.

JAMBHEKAR, BAL GANGADHAR SHASTRI (1812–1846) Assistant professor at Elphinstone College and one of Naoroji's college instructors.

Jambhekar was responsible for selecting Naoroji for admission into Elphinstone College. Originally from the south Konkan coast, he was brought to Bombay in 1826 and educated at the Bombay Native Education Society's central English school. Recognized as a brilliant polymath, Jambhekar taught subjects ranging from Shakespeare to integral calculus.

KAZI SHAHABUDIN (1832–1900) Diwan of Kutch until 1874. In the early 1870s, he resided in London, where he became involved in the East India Association. During Naoroji's diwanship in Baroda, he served as head of the revenue department. Kazi was diwan of Baroda from 1883 until 1886. He was appointed to the Bombay legislative council in 1886 and later became a critic of the Congress.

KRISHNAVARMA, SHYAMJI (1857–1930) Radical nationalist influenced by Herbert Spencer and Henry Hyndman. He was the founder of the Indian Home Rule Society and India House in London, as well as editor of the *Indian Sociologist* (published in London and, later, Paris). Krishnavarma became Naoroji's most virulent critic in the radical camp by 1905.

MALABARI, BEHRAMJI (1854–1912) Social reformer, poet, and journalist known as the "right-hand man of Dadabhai Naoroji." Malabari took over the *Indian Spectator* in 1880, which became one of the most respected Indian periodicals under his watch. In 1883, he and Naoroji founded *Voice of India*, a newspaper meant to counter the Anglo-Indian dominance of Indian news coverage in Great Britain. Although he joined the Congress for only a brief period—he strongly disagreed with its refusal to take up social reform matters—Malabari took an active part in nationalist political activity. He played an indispensable role in Naoroji's parliamentary campaigns, cobbling together financial and logistical support across India (including significant financial support from princes), coordinating support from Indian newspapers, and seeking assistance from Liberal Party functionaries. A tireless campaigner on behalf of Indian women's rights, he championed the controversial Age of Consent Bill of 1891, which earned him the ire of Bal Gangadhar Tilak.

MALHARRAO, GAIKWAD OF BARODA (1831–1882) Ruler of Baroda state from 1870 until 1875. He appointed Naoroji as his diwan in 1873, a move that accentuated bad relations between the Baroda darbar and the British resident, Robert Phayre. Malharrao retained corrupt darbaris in spite of Naoroji's attempts to appoint his own ministers and institute administrative reform. Ultimately, in December 1874, he allowed Naoroji to follow through on persistent threats of resignation. In early 1875, Malharrao was removed from the throne by British authorities and subsequently convicted of involvement in an attempted poisoning of Phayre. He died in exile in Madras.

MEHTA, PHEROZESHAH M. (1845–1915) One of the most dominant figures in Bombay politics during the late nineteenth and early twentieth centuries, known as the "uncrowned king of Bombay." Mehta was president of the Congress in 1890. He strenuously opposed Naoroji's decision to stay in the United Kingdom after the 1886 general elections. Mehta became one of the best-known leaders of the moderate faction of the Congress. He was reportedly deeply unhappy with Naoroji's presidential address at the Congress's 1906 Calcutta session, believing that it had aided the radical camp.

NAVROZJI FARDUNJI (1817–1885) Journalist, assistant professor at Elphinstone College, cofounder of the Bombay Association, and one of the earliest and most prominent social and religious reformers in the Parsi community. He was popularly known as the "Tribune of the People." Navrozji served as a mentor to Naoroji and other members of Young Bombay. He worked closely with Naoroji in promoting female education, establishing the Rahnumae Mazdayasnan Sabha, and running *Rast Goftar*. Navrozji was an active participant in the East India Association, both in Bombay and London. He was involved in Bombay municipal affairs in the 1870s and 1880s as a member of the town council.

PAL, BIPIN CHANDRA (1858–1932) Prominent radical leader of the Congress. He became acquainted with Naoroji while in London in the late 1890s but soon after established himself as one of his staunchest critics, finding Naoroji's politics far too moderate. He objected to Naoroji's formulation of "Self-Government under British Paramountcy," calling it too timid, and criticized Naoroji for ruling out violent methods for achieving self-government. Pal helped run *Bande Mataram* in Calcutta.

PENTON, FREDERICK THOMAS (1851–1929) Elected as the Conservative MP for Central Finsbury in 1886 in spite of the constituency's radical Liberal leanings. Naoroji defeated him by three votes, according to the initial count, during the 1892 general election. Penton initiated a lengthy recount and voter scrutiny that ultimately validated Naoroji's election, widening his margin of victory to five votes. He descended from a prominent Clerkenwell landholding family.

PHAYRE, ROBERT (1820–1897) British resident of Baroda during Naoroji's diwanship. Suspicious of Naoroji's political activities in London, Phayre skillfully took advantage of divisions in the Baroda darbar in order to thwart many of Naoroji's efforts at reform. He was removed from his post in late 1874 after he was nearly poisoned, an attempt later linked to Malharrao.

RANADE, MAHADEV GOVIND (1842–1901) Noted economic thinker, social reformer, and leader of the Congress. He graduated from Elphinstone College and Bombay University and served as a judge on the Bombay High Court. His judicial career prevented Ranade from accepting a ministerial position during Naoroji's diwanship in Baroda. Naoroji and Ranade both served in the Bombay legislative council in 1885–1886. He helped found the Poona Sarvajanik Sabha and remained an active member until Bal Gangadhar Tilak seized control of the organization in 1896. Thereafter, Ranade and Gopal Krishna Gokhale founded the Deccan Sabha.

RIPON, 1ST MARQUESS OF (GEORGE FREDERICK SAMUEL ROBINSON) (1827–1909) Indian viceroy from 1880 to 1884. He was popular among early Indian nationalists due to his comparatively progressive and reformist stance on Indian policy. During Frederick A. Ford's insurgent Liberal candidacy in Central Finsbury, he attempted to lobby National Liberal Federation officials on Naoroji's behalf. Ripon served as secretary of state for the colonies from 1892 until 1895.

SALISBURY, 3RD MARQUESS OF (ROBERT ARTHUR TALBOT GASCOYNE-CECIL) (1830–1903) Conservative leader and British prime minister. Salisbury was secretary of state for India from 1866 to 1867 and from 1874 to 1878; he was prime minister from 1885 to 1886, from 1886 to 1892, and from 1895 to 1902. In November 1888, he labeled Naoroji as a "black man" undeserving of election to Parliament, triggering widespread support for Naoroji and boosting his candidacy in Central Finsbury.

SCHNADHORST, FRANCIS (1840–1900) Secretary of the Liberal Central Association and the National Liberal Federation, which functioned as headquarters for the Liberal Party. He offered assistance to Naoroji in finding a constituency for the 1886 general elections and, in 1888, pledged to support Naoroji against Richard Eve's insurgent Liberal candidacy in Central Finsbury. Relations between Naoroji and Schnadhorst frayed during Frederick A. Ford's insurgent candidacy, pushing Naoroji to publish a controversial pamphlet, "Mr. D. Naoroji and Mr. Schnadhorst," in early 1892.

SMITH, SAMUEL (1836–1906) Successful cotton merchant and Liberal MP. Smith first met Naoroji in the late 1850s while both men were engaged in the Liverpool cotton trade. He made several visits to India, steadily becoming a supporter of Indian political reform and championing Indian causes in the

House of Commons, where he was an MP from 1882 until 1885 and from 1886 until 1905. Smith took special interest in temperance matters, becoming president of the Anglo-Indian Temperance Union. He died in Calcutta a few days after witnessing Naoroji's presidential address at the 1906 Congress session.

TILAK, BAL GANGADHAR (1856–1920) Radical Indian nationalist and editor of the English-language *Mahratta* and Marathi-language *Kesari*. Tilak pioneered a brand of Hindu nationalism through the development of public celebrations of Ganpati and the birthday of Shivaji. He captured the Poona Sarvajanik Sabha from moderate leaders in 1896. Tilak was suspected of involvement in the 1897 assassinations of Walter Charles Rand, special plague commissioner in Poona, and Charles Egerton Ayerst, his military escort, and was subsequently imprisoned for sedition. He emerged as one of the leading radical nationalists in the early 1900s, popularizing the term "swaraj." Tilak pleaded with Naoroji to adopt tenets of the radical camp, such as the boycott of foreign goods and national education. Proposed by radicals to be president of the 1906 Calcutta Congress, he stood aside when Naoroji indicated his willingness to accept the position. At its 1907 session in Surat, Tilak led the radical faction out of the Congress. He was imprisoned between 1908 and 1914 and rejoined the Congress at the 1916 Lucknow session.

WACHA, DINSHA (1844–1936) General secretary of the Congress and a long-serving member of the Bombay Municipal Corporation. He served as president of the Congress in 1901. Along with Behramji Malabari, Wacha was one of Naoroji's closest confidants and one of his most regular correspondents. He served as an editor of the English columns of *Kaiser-i-Hind* and was active in the Bombay Millowners' Association. Within the Congress, Wacha was closely associated with moderate stalwarts such as Pherozeshah Mehta and Gopal Krishna Gokhale.

WADYA, HORMUSJEE ARDESEER (1849–1928) Moderate leader of the Congress and one of Naoroji's political protégés. Wadya most likely first met Naoroji when he was studying in University College in London during the late 1860s. During the Baroda diwanship, he was known as Naoroji's right-hand man and served as chief magistrate. He remained actively involved in princely state affairs in Gujarat.

WEDDERBURN, WILLIAM (1838–1918) One of the Congress's earliest guiding figures, along with Naoroji and Hume. Wedderburn joined the Bombay civil service in 1860. He helped Naoroji found the Bombay branch of the East India Association in 1869. After retiring from the civil service in 1887, he plunged into the work of the Congress, serving as president at its 1889 Bombay session. Wedderburn was elected to Parliament in 1893, serving alongside Naoroji in the Commons for two years. He served as a commissioner for the Welby Commission in the late 1890s, once more alongside Naoroji. In 1900, Wedderburn retired from the Commons, but he remained actively involved in the British Committee of the Indian National Congress for the rest of his life.

WOOD, W. MARTIN (1828–1907) one of Naoroji's closest friends and a long-time political ally. Wood edited the *Times of India* in the early 1870s. He joined Naoroji in lobbying the India Office on behalf of the interests of various princely states. Wood was a member of the British Committee of the Indian National Congress.

A NOTE ON SOURCES

During his lifetime, Dadabhai Naoroji amassed a simply voluminous trove of letters. The overwhelming majority of his correspondence can be found today within the Dadabhai Naoroji Papers at the National Archives of India in New Delhi. This is a rich and curiously underexplored collection. In spite of scholarly neglect, the Naoroji Papers constitute an indispensable resource for understanding aspects of nineteenth-century India and Victorian Britain.

The Naoroji Papers have a long and complicated history. Like many of his nationalist colleagues, Naoroji meticulously saved his incoming letters and kept tissue-thin press copies of his outgoing letters (he occasionally produced handwritten duplicates). We know that contemporaries in Bombay such as Navrozji Fardunji, Pherozeshah Mehta, Behramji Malabari, and Dinsha Wacha all followed the same habits and amassed sizable collections of personal papers as well. However, among this group of individuals, Naoroji's is the only collection that has survived more or less intact (some of Pherozeshah Mehta's papers can be found at the National Archives of India and the Nehru Memorial Museum and Library). Modern India has a relatively dismal record of archival preservation. Due to the carelessness of descendants or organizations tasked with preservation, and with the assistance of an adverse climate, numerous important collections have literally crumbled to dust. In this sense, it is extremely fortunate that the Naoroji Papers have survived—although there has been significant damage and loss. By tracing the history of the Naoroji Papers, we can better understand the processes of decay and neglect that make writing Indian biographies such a challenging endeavor.[1]

When he retired in 1907, Dadabhai Naoroji brought along all of his London correspondence to Versova, where it was kept alongside earlier correspondence already stored in Bombay. Much of this earlier correspondence, however, dating from Naoroji's youth through 1876, was by this time "found to be worm-eaten." It was destroyed after the family gave up their earlier residence in Khetwadi. After Naoroji died in 1917, his remaining papers were entrusted to the newly formed Dadabhai Naoroji Memorial Prize Fund, although they likely remained in the family's bungalow in Versova. Rustom P. Masani, Naoroji's first biographer and a trustee of the Prize Fund, was the first individual to comprehensively examine this collection. He noted that correspondence from 1876 onward was still intact, "but it had suffered from the ravages of time and transport." We must assume that Masani's consultations resulted in further damage and loss. While he did an enormous favor to researchers by putting lengthy extracts of correspondence into print, Masani might have inadvertently lost, destroyed, or misplaced numerous important letters, leaving major gaps in the surviving correspondence. His biography is now the only record of certain crucially important letters to and from Mohandas K. Gandhi, Henry Hyndman, Dinsha Wacha, and George Freeman.[2]

Masani did not attempt to estimate the extent of the Dadabhai Naoroji Papers. Four years after his biography was published, however, another individual, Jehangir P. Wadia, gave a vivid description of the collection's makeup and condition. Wadia had been employed by the Dadabhai Naoroji Memorial Prize Fund to compile a "bibliography" of the papers. He focused on Naoroji's outgoing letters, noting the existence of "about 35 press-copy books (each of 500 pages) containing copies of letters written by Dadabhai since 1886." This material was in a precarious state. "Sometimes pages crumbled into pieces while being turned," Wadia noted. "Some of the books partially eaten up by worms emitted a bad stink." Wadia estimated that he went through 15,000 letters that he deemed to be of historical importance, leaving aside a massive heap of other material. He typed out a nearly two-hundred-page index of items, documenting numerous letters that no longer exist: letters exchanged with Mahadev Govind Ranade from the early 1880s, correspondence from the Baroda diwanship, and letters pertaining to the Congress's first few years of existence. Unfortunately, that was the extent of Wadia's efforts. He was unsuccessful in convincing Prize Fund trustees to give him more time to organize and index the collection. The Naoroji Papers returned to a dusty storage space, where they continued to molder away in Bombay's tropical heat.[3]

In 1952, Rustom P. Masani approached R. P. Patwardhan, a retired educational official, with a seemingly innocuous proposal: would he edit and publish a series of selected correspondence from the Naoroji Papers? The task, Masani advised, might take "a couple of years." In reality, it would take much of the remainder of Patwardhan's life. Over the next few years, Patwardhan transported small packets of letters to his residence in Poona. He soon realized the enormous challenges of working with the Naoroji Papers. "The paper of some letters had become so brittle, through lapse of time, that the least touch broke it into little bits," he noted. "On some the writing had grown faint, and it was necessary to handle them very, very delicately so as to straighten them and then to put them in hard-board covers, before any attempt could be made to read them . . . All this produced at times a feeling of despondency, and I wondered whether I should not give up the job, as Sir Rust[o]m had told me others had done before me." By this time, one of Patwardhan's greatest challenges was deciphering the press copies of Naoroji's outgoing letters. In some letters, handwriting had become blurry or washed out. In others, the high acid content of the ink had begun eating through the paper, turning words into strings of holes.[4]

After around fifteen years of labor, Patwardhan prepared four typed manuscripts, which he divided into two separate volumes of edited correspondence. He estimated that he had consulted "about 40,000 papers."[5] In 1977, the last two of these manuscripts were published under the title of *Dadabhai Naoroji Correspondence, Vol. II.* Patwardhan died in 1980, before he could secure the publication of the two remaining manuscripts that constituted the first volume of the series. These manuscripts were assumed lost after Patwardhan's death, but S. R. Mehrotra, a prominent historian of the nationalist movement, located them in 1990. In 2016, Mehrotra and I published *Dadabhai Naoroji: Selected Private Papers* (Oxford University Press), which in part relied upon material from one of these manuscripts. I anticipate that there is scope for at least two further volumes of this series, which would consist of unpublished material from Patwardhan's manuscripts—including many letters that no longer exist—and additional material in the Naoroji Papers that I have collected. Patwardhan's unpublished manuscripts (cited as R. P. Patwardhan Manuscripts or RPPM in this book), meanwhile, have been deposited at the National Archives of India.

The Naoroji Papers made their final journey in 1968, when they were transferred to the National Archives of India from Poona. They arrived in an even more damaged state. Once staff compiled an index, they determined that the Naoroji Papers consisted of 25,000 items, plus a stack of items that remained uncataloged (I estimate that this uncataloged portion consists of 5,000 items).

Thus, perhaps 10,000 items went missing during Patwardhan's consultation. Worryingly, this comprised some of the most valuable items: Naoroji's outgoing letters. Currently, only around 3,700 letters authored by Naoroji exist. Given the size of Naoroji's extant outgoing correspondence, Mehrotra and I estimate that around 16,300 of Naoroji's own letters were lost between the late nineteenth century and today. Since the bulk of these letters were in the form of fragile press copies, it is no surprise that they long ago disintegrated. The National Archives of India has undertaken significant preservation work, but a substantial chunk of the extant outgoing correspondence is simply unreadable due to damage that occurred decades ago. All of this presents a colossal challenge to the historian. In order to reconstruct Dadabhai Naoroji's life from his papers, one has to primarily rely upon letters that he did not write.

The National Archives of India has divided the Naoroji Papers into five parts, each of which has its own index. The vast majority of correspondence can be found in Part I, while a smaller series of family correspondence can be found in Part II. Most of the correspondence in these two parts dates from 1886 until Naoroji's retirement in 1907. Part I contains several very lengthy series: letters from R. M. H. Griffith, Behramji Malabari, and Dinsha Wacha, as well as Naoroji's outgoing letters. Part III, "Miscellaneous Papers," consists of letters, flyers, and other publications, most of which relate to the organizations and clubs that Naoroji joined while in London. This collection also includes a series of items on Naoroji's parliamentary campaigns, a handful of images and maps, and—unexpectedly—floor plans for the Naoroji house in Khetwadi. Within Part IV, one can find more than two hundred press clippings that Naoroji saved. Some of these press clippings, especially from Indian periodicals, are quite valuable, considering that original runs of many newspapers and journals no longer exist. Part V is titled "Notes and Jottings." This is a motley collection of scribbled notes, accounts, balance sheets, and lists, most in Naoroji's hand. One surviving volume of Naoroji's diary, dating from 1886, can be found here, as well as a few biographical pamphlets.

This leaves us with the uncataloged items. For some reason, National Archives staff did not index a few thousand items. I have been able to leaf through some of this material, which, unlike the rest of the Naoroji Papers, consists of a significant amount of non-English material. There are numerous Gujarati letters and printed items, but also several documents in Hindi, Urdu, Persian, and French. And there are a number of unusual finds: wedding invitations, Gujarati songs and poems about Naoroji, cartoons, and at least one death certificate. I found two thick bundles of Gujarati letters that were too damaged to

A Note on Sources   295

consult: one appears to date from Naoroji's diwanship in Baroda, and the other appears to be correspondence with Parsi cricketers who toured Great Britain in 1886.

In the early 1980s, the National Archives of India and the Shastri Indo-Canadian Institute jointly microfilmed the Naoroji Papers. The National Archives and the University of Toronto's Robarts Library retain copies. Unfortunately, the quality of the microfilm is extremely poor, rendering large segments completely unreadable. Many letters are also missing. In the past few years, National Archives staff have begun digitizing segments of the Naoroji Papers.

Aside from the National Archives of India, a small but significant portion of the Naoroji Papers can be found at the Nehru Memorial Museum and Library in New Delhi. For some reason, these letters were never sent to R. P. Patwardhan for consultation. A number of Naoroji's outgoing letters can be found here, along with items penned by Allan Octavian Hume, Behramji Malabari, and ordinary British workers and electors.

Beyond the Naoroji Papers, there are numerous other collections in India that help shine light on the life of the Grand Old Man. Within the National Archives of India, the Gopal Krishna Gokhale Papers and the Romesh Chunder Dutt Papers contain important correspondence. The Maharashtra State Archives in Mumbai have some useful material: records pertaining to Naoroji's diwanship in Baroda, educational reports from the 1840s and 1850s, and the records of Elphinstone College. Farther up the road, the J. N. Petit Library holds the most extensive run of *Rast Goftar*, the Gujarati paper that Naoroji cofounded in 1851. Sadly, this does not include volumes for 1851 through 1854, when Naoroji exercised the most editorial control. In Ahmedabad, one can consult scans of Naoroji's letters to Gandhi at Sabarmati Ashram. As far as I can tell, the Baroda Record Room, which contains the records of the erstwhile princely state of Baroda, does not hold any records from Naoroji's diwanship.

In the United Kingdom, the British Library's India Office Records contains a wealth of material relevant to many aspects of Naoroji's life. One can find important correspondence within the William Digby Papers and the George Birdwood Papers, as well as several volumes of the East India Association's minute books. Letters in the Lord George Hamilton Papers offer scathing opinions on the Congress and its primary leaders. Since Naoroji was in frequent communication with various colonial and India Office bureaucrats, the Judicial and Public records contain a number of relevant files. Finally, material on Naoroji's relations with princely states, including the Baroda diwanship, can be found in Residency and Foreign Department records. I consulted the British Library's newspaper collection while it was still housed in Colindale. The collection, now partly digitized, includes local papers from Finsbury, such as the *Weekly News and Chronicle* and the *Finsbury and Holborn Gazette,* as well as Liberal-leading broadsheets such as the *Star.*

Apart from the British Library, it is worthwhile to make the trip to the Islington Local History Centre, located within the perimeter of the old parliamentary constituency of Central Finsbury. Here one can view the picture book of Bombay that the city's leading citizens sent after the 1892 elections, a token of thanks "to the Electors of Central Finsbury for their generous and high minded action in electing Mr. Dadabhai Naoroji as their Member of Parliament."

ABBREVIATIONS

BL	British Library
DNP	Dadabhai Naoroji Papers
IOR	India Office Records
MSA	Maharashtra State Archives
NAI	National Archives of India
NMML	Nehru Memorial Museum and Library
NNR	Native Newspaper Reports
RPPM	R. P. Patwardhan Manuscripts
WDP	William Digby Papers

NOTES

Introduction

1. As Michael H. Fisher has pointed out, David Ochterlony Dyce Sombre was technically the first Indian elected to Parliament, winning election from Sudbury as a Whig Radical in 1841. He was subsequently disqualified on grounds of bribery. Dyce Sombre was born in Sardhana in India to parents of mixed European and Indian ancestry. He was raised by Begum Sombre (Begum Samru), the wealthy ruler of Sardhana state. In spite of these Indian connections, Dyce Sombre insisted that he was European, and certainly did not display any intentions to represent Indian interests in Parliament. See Michael H. Fisher, *The Inordinately Strange Life of Dyce Sombre: Victorian Anglo-Indian MP and a "Chancery Lunatic"* (New York: Columbia University Press, 2010). "London Correspondence," *Freeman's Journal*, July 7, 1892; "Colour Disabilities," *Imvo Zabantsundu (Native Opinion)*, July 28, 1892.

2. This picture book is currently held by the Islington Local History Centre in London. S. R. Mehrotra, *A History of the Indian National Congress* (New Delhi: Vikas Publications, 1995), 26; *Mahratta*, July 10, 1892, in NNR, Bombay, July 16, 1892, MSA; "Mr. Dadabhai Naoroji's Election," *Tribune*, July 20, 1892, 4. There is hardly any information with which to reconstruct Naoroji's relationship with Muhammad Ali Jinnah. I have only come across one insignificant reference to Jinnah in Naoroji's papers. Jinnah claimed to have served as Naoroji's secretary at the 1906 Calcutta Congress, but this was hardly a mark of distinction, as Naoroji relied on numerous secretaries. Stanley A. Wolpert, *Jinnah of Pakistan* (New York: Oxford University Press, 1984), 11, 26; Ramachandra Guha, *Gandhi before India* (New Delhi: Allen Lane, 2013), 76.

3. "People of Chikmagalur to Electors of Central Finsbury," 25 July 1892, NAI, DNP, C-132; "Rural Election to the Congress," *India*, March 1, 1893, 70; British Guiana East Indian Institute to Dadabhai Naoroji, October 6, 1892, NAI, DNP, B-220.

4. *The First Indian Member of the Imperial Parliament, Being a Collection of the Main Incidents Relating to the Election of Mr. Dadabhai Naoroji to Parliament* (Madras:

Addison, 1892), 111; Charles W. Barker to Naoroji, July 19, 1892, NAI, DNP, B-47 (6).

5. "The Grand Old Man of India," in *Collected Works of Mahatma Gandhi* (New Delhi: Publications Division, Ministry of Information and Broadcasting, 1960), 4:268; "Resolutions at Gujarat Political Conference—I," in *Collected Works of Mahatma Gandhi* (New Delhi: Publications Division, Ministry of Information and Broadcasting, 1963), 14:67.

6. "Second Indian National Congress," in *Essays, Speeches, Addresses and Writings (on Indian Politics) of the Hon'ble Dadabhai Naoroji*, ed. Chunilal Lallubhai Parekh (Bombay: Caxton Printing Works, 1887), 341.

7. "Mr. Dadabhai Naoroji at Walthamstow: 'India Must Be Bled,'" in Dadabhai Naoroji, *Poverty and Un-British Rule in India* (London: Swan Sonnenschein, 1901), 646.

8. There is no direct evidence that Naoroji and Karl Marx ever met each other— although, as I discuss in Chapter 2, both men knew the socialist politician Henry Hyndman, and Hyndman might have discussed Naoroji's drain theory with Marx. I have found no evidence of contact between Naoroji and J. A. Hobson, whose *Imperialism: A Study* was published just a year after Naoroji's best-known work, *Poverty and Un-British Rule in India*. Dadabhai Naoroji, "The Condition of India," in *Poverty and Un-British Rule in India* (London: Swan Sonnenschein, 1901), 216.

9. Rustom P. Masani, *Dadabhai Naoroji: The Grand Old Man of India* (London: G. Allen & Unwin, 1939). There have been two other biographies of note. See Omar Ralph, *Naoroji, the First Asian MP: A Biography of Dadabhai Naoroji, India's Patriot and Britain's MP* (St. John's, Antigua: Hansib, 1997); and Munni Rawal, *Dadabhai Naoroji, a Prophet of Indian Nationalism, 1855–1900* (New Delhi: Anmol Publications, 1989). A handful of volumes of his writings and correspondence also exist. For the most recent volumes, see *Dadabhai Naoroji Correspondence*, ed. R. P. Patwardhan, vol. 2, part 1 (New Delhi: Allied, 1977); *Dadabhai Naoroji Correspondence*, ed. R. P. Patwardhan, vol. 2, part 2 (New Delhi: Allied, 1977); and *Dadabhai Naoroji: Selected Private Papers*, ed. S. R. Mehrotra and Dinyar Patel (New Delhi: Oxford University Press, 2016).

10. For economic work, see especially chapter 8 in Bipan Chandra, *The Rise and Growth of Economic Nationalism in India: Economic Policies of Indian National Leadership, 1880–1905* (New Delhi: People's Publishing House, 1966); chapter 7 in Manu Goswami, *Producing India: From Colonial Economy to National Space* (Chicago: University of Chicago Press, 2004); B. N. Ganguli, *Dadabhai Naoroji and the Drain Theory* (New York: Asia Publishing House, 1965); and Savak Jehangir Katrak, "Imperialism Viewed from Below: A Study of the Political and Economic Ideas of Dadabhai Naoroji," Ph.D. diss., Harvard University, 1971. For work on Naoroji as a parliamentary candidate, see Antoinette M. Burton, "Tongues Untied: Lord Salisbury's 'Black Man' and the Boundaries of Imperial Democracy," *Comparative Studies in Society and History* 42, no. 3 (July 2000): 632–661; Julie Codell, "Decentring and Doubling Imperial Cosmopolitan Discourse in the British Press: Dadabhai Naoroji and M. M. Bhownaggree," *Media History* 15, no. 4 (2009):

371–384; David Charles Mellor, "The Parliamentary Life of Dadabhai Naoroji, the Great 'Parsi Patriot' between 1885–1895: With Special Reference to the Voice of India and Indian Spectator," *Journal of the K. R. Cama Oriental Institute*, no. 52 (1985): 1–113; and Sumita Mukherjee, "'Narrow-Majority' and 'Bow-and-Agree': Public Attitudes towards the Elections of the First Asian MPs in Britain, Dadabhai Naoroji and Mancherjee Merwanjee Bhownagree, 1885–1906," *Journal of the Oxford University Historical Society* 2 (2004): 1–20. For works on British anti-colonialism, see Mira Matikkala, *Empire and Imperial Ambition: Liberty, Englishness and Anti-Imperialism in Late-Victorian Britain* (London: I. B. Tauris, 2011); and Nicholas Owen, *The British Left and India: Metropolitan Anti-Imperialism, 1885–1947* (Oxford: Oxford University Press, 2007). For an excellent work on Indians in Britain, see Rozina Visram, *Asians in Britain: 400 Years of History* (London: Pluto Press, 2002). For work on the Parsis, see especially John R. Hinnells, *Zoroastrians in Britain* (Oxford: Clarendon Press, 1996); Eckehard Kulke, *The Parsees in India: A Minority as Agent of Social Change* (Munich: Weltforum Verlag, 1974); and Jesse S. Palsetia, *The Parsis of India: Preservation of Identity in Bombay City* (Leiden: Brill, 2001). For work on the Indian liberal tradition, see C. A. Bayly, *Recovering Liberties: Indian Thought in the Age of Liberalism and Empire* (Cambridge: Cambridge University Press, 2012). For work on early Indian nationalism, see John R. McLane, *Indian Nationalism and the Early Congress* (Princeton, NJ: Princeton University Press, 1977); S. R. Mehrotra, *The Emergence of the Indian National Congress* (Delhi: Vikas Publications, 1971); Mehrotra, *A History of the Indian National Congress*; and Anil Seal, *The Emergence of Indian Nationalism: Competition and Collaboration in the Later Nineteenth Century* (London: Cambridge University Press, 1968). Mehrotra's books provide the most comprehensive, thoroughly researched accounts of early Indian nationalism. Sukanya Banerjee has also addressed Naoroji in her work on imperial citizenship. See chapter 1 in *Becoming Imperial Citizens: Indians in the Late-Victorian Empire* (Durham, NC: Duke University Press, 2010).

11. Due in part to current interest in intellectual history, a number of biographical works have recently appeared on South Asian figures ranging from Ashoka to Narasimha Rao. For an earlier essay on the "meagre harvest" that is South Asian biography, see Ramachandra Guha, "A Bare Cupboard," *Times Literary Supplement*, August 30, 2002, 12. Not surprisingly, two Marxist thinkers, M. N. Roy and R. Palme Dutt, led the way in fomenting dismissive attitudes toward early Indian nationalism. See M. N. Roy, *India in Transition* (Geneva, 1922); and R. Palme Dutt, *India To-Day* (London, 1940). I relied extensively on S. R. Mehrotra, who spent years combing through Naoroji's papers, for information on the relatively few scholars who have engaged with this collection.

1. Young Dadabhai, Young Bombay

1. "Chetavnī," *Pārsī Mitr*, June 30, 1855, 238, 239; B. B. Patell, ed., *Pārsī Prakāsh* (Bombay: Duftur Ashkara Press, 1888), 1:676–677.
2. Dadabhai Naoroji to Norman Fraser, August 5, 1904, RPPM.

3. By the mid-1860s, missionaries and the government provided the bulk of annual expenditure on girls' schools outside of Bombay. In Bengal, Indians provided only Rs. 132 during 1865–1866, while the presidency government expended Rs. 29,000. A further Rs. 41,000 came from other sources, including missionaries. In the North-West Provinces, the government expended Rs. 35,000 during 1865–1866, while missionaries appeared to provide around half of the Rs. 23,000 from other sources. In Madras, the government spent Rs. 5,500 during 1866–1867, while missionary donations accounted for nearly all of the Rs. 36,000 arriving from other sources. Meanwhile, in Bombay, the presidency government expended only Rs. 341 for 1866–1867. In contrast, Indians during the same year provided Rs. 40,000. Missionary contributions were negligible. Naoroji to Stafford Northcote, February 5, 1868, NAI, DNP, N-1 (17).

4. Naoroji to Fraser, August 5, 1904, RPPM.

5. Rustam Barjorji Paymaster, *A Farman of Emperor Jehangir Given to Dr. Dadabhai Naoroji's Ancestors Three Centuries Ago and a Short History of His Dordi Family of Navsari; with Poems on Dadabhai Naoroji by Rustam Barjorji Paymaster; Specially Published for the Dadabhai Naoroji Centenary* (Bombay: Fort Printing Press, 1925), 9–10, 5–6, 16–17.

6. *Gazetteer of the Bombay Presidency, Volume IX, Part II. Gujarat Population: Musalmans and Parsis* (Bombay: Government Central Press, 1899), 192; Rustom P. Masani, *Dadabhai Naoroji: The Grand Old Man of India* (London: G. Allen & Unwin, 1939), 20; Marianna Postans, *Western India in 1838* (London: Saunders and Otley, 1839), 1:280.

7. Jim Masselos, "Migration and Urban Identity: Bombay's Famine Refugees in the Nineteenth Century," in *Bombay: Mosaic of Modern Culture*, ed. Sujata Patel and Alice Thorner (Bombay: Oxford University Press, 1996), 29.

8. Ibid., 30.

9. The statistic of 8.7 people per house is for Dongri, one of the overlapping localities that encompassed Khadak. Amar Farooqui, *Opium City: The Making of Early Victorian Bombay* (Gurgaon: Three Essays Collective, 2006), 73, 58; Dinsha Wacha, *Shells from the Sands of Bombay; Being My Recollections and Reminiscences, 1860–1875* (Bombay: K. T. Anklesaria, 1920), 468, 477; Govind Narayan Madgaonkar, *Govind Narayan's Mumbai: An Urban Biography from 1863*, ed. Murali Ranganathan (Delhi: Anthem Press, 2012), 52.

10. Naoroji's navar ceremony took place in 1839 at the Wadia Atash Behram in Chandanwadi (present-day Princess Street), Bombay. Naoroji to Fraser, August 5, 1904, RPPM; Chhaganlal D. Mehta, "Hindno dādo," *Māsik Mitr,* July 1911, 42; Rustam Barjorji Paymaster, ed., *Pārsī Prakāsh* (Bombay: Frasho-Gard Printing Press, 1923), 4:191.

11. Wacha, *Shells from the Sands of Bombay*, 362.

12. "Introduction," in Ramchandra Vithal Parulekar, ed., *Survey of Indigenous Education in the Province of Bombay (1820–1830)* (Bombay: Asia Publishing House, 1951), 1:xxi; "Extract Minute by the Hon. Mountstuart Elphinstone, Governor of Bombay, Dated December 13, 1823," *Appendix to the Report from the Select Committee of the House of Commons on the Affairs of the East-India Company, 16th August 1832, and Minutes of Evidence* (London: J. L. Cox and Son, 1833), 367.

13. Naoroji to Fraser, August 5, 1904, RPPM.

14. Ibid.

15. *Dadabhai Naoroji Correspondence*, ed. R. P. Patwardhan, vol. 2, part 1 (New Delhi: Allied, 1977), xiv; Naoroji to Fraser, August 5, 1904, RPPM.

16. Naoroji to Fraser, August 5, 1904, RPPM.

17. Postans, *Western India in 1838*, 1:56–57.

18. Naoroji to Fraser, August 5, 1904, RPPM.

19. "Extract from the Fourth Report (1827) of the Bombay Native Education Society," in Ramchandra Vithal Parulekar and C. L. Bakshi, eds., *Selections from Educational Records (Bombay): Part II, 1815–1840* (Bombay: Asia Publishing House, 1955), 105–107; "Extract from the Bombay Secretariat Records: G.D. Volume 485 of 1839," in Ramchandra Vithal Parulekar and C. L. Bakshi, eds., *Selections from Educational Records (Bombay): Part III, 1826–1840* (Bombay: Asia Pub. House, 1957), 252; "Bombay Board of Education Report Excerpts," 1842–1844, NAI, DNP, uncataloged item.

20. After 1839, Elphinstone College continued to exist de facto, but only as the upper division of a newly created Elphinstone Institution, which included a junior school. See chapter 3 in Naheed Ahmad, "A History of Elphinstone College, 1827–1890: A Case Study in the Early Formation of an English-Educated Intelligentsia in Bombay," Ph.D. diss., Wolfson College, Oxford, 1982.

21. Ibid., 218; Robert E. Speer, *George Bowen of Bombay: Missionary, Scholar, Mystic, Saint* (New York: Missionary Review of the World, 1938), 170.

22. Wacha, *Shells from the Sands of Bombay*, 529.

23. "Address to Professor Bell," *Bombay Times and Journal of Commerce*, May 16, 1846, 317; Khurshedji Rustomji (K. R.) Cama to Naoroji, October 25, 1901, NAI, DNP, C-21 (1).

24. Masani, *Dadabhai Naoroji*, 31; *Memoirs and Writings of Āchārya Bāl Gangādhar Shāstri Jāmbhekar, 1812–1846: Pioneer of the Renaissance in Western India and Father of Modern Mahārāshtra*, ed. G. G. Jambhekar (Poona: G. G. Jambhekar, 1950), 1:iv, viii; "The Elphinstone Memorial: Report of Proceedings of a Public Meeting of the Students and Ex-Students of the Elphinstone College and Institution on the 11th January 1860 in Honor of the Late Hon'ble Mountstuart Elphinstone," Asiatic Society of Mumbai; Aroon Tikekar, "Naoroji Furdoonji and the 'Young Bombay Party': Reflections on the Early Debate on Reform in Western India," in *Mārga: Ways of Liberation, Empowerment, and Social Change in Maharashtra*, ed. Masao Naitō et al. (Delhi: Manohar, 2008), 198.

25. Patell, *Pārsī Prakāsh*, 1888, 1:481.

26. *Report of the Board of Education for the Years 1840, 1841* (Bombay: American Mission Press, 1842), 4; *Report of the Board of Education for the Year 1844* (Bombay: Government Press, 1845), 5–6.

27. *Report of the Board of Education for the Year 1843* (Bombay: Government Press, 1844), 5, 6; Masani, *Dadabhai Naoroji*, 36. The letter of recommendation, which survives as a transcription made by Naoroji, is in an extremely damaged state, and only the letters "Jo" are readable in the transcribed signature. Based on the letter's content, however, there is little reason to doubt that it was authored by Harkness. April 30, 1846, NAI, DNP, uncataloged item.

28. Naoroji to Fraser, August 5, 1904, RPPM; Masani, *Dadabhai Naoroji*, 37–39.

29. Bhawanishankar Shridhar Pundit, ed., *Rāosaheb Keshav Shivrām Bhāwlkar yānche ātmavrutta* (Nagpur: Vidharbha Samshodan Mandal, 1961). The next highest-ranking instructor after Naoroji, Bomanji Pestonji, earned only Rs. 55 even though he had one year of seniority over Naoroji. Naoroji's old classmate Ardeshir Framji Moos had a salary of Rs. 40. MSA, Elphinstone College Records, vol. 9; *Report of the Board of Education from January 1, 1850 to April 30, 1851* (Bombay: Bombay Education Society's Press, 1851), 31.

30. "Annual Report of the Elphinstone Institution, Bombay, for the Year 1852," in *Report of the Board of Education, Bombay, from May 1, 1852, to April 30, 1853* (Bombay: Bombay Education Society's Press, 1853), 84; Dadabhai Naoroji, "Advantages to Be Derived from the Study of Mathematics," *Jame Jamshed*, December 28, 1906 (republication), NAI, DNP, Part III, G-3.

31. *Report of the Board of Education, Bombay, from May 1, 1854 to April 30, 1855* (Bombay: Bombay Education Society's Press, 1855), 54–55.

32. "Extract from the Fourth Report (1827) of the Bombay Native Education Society," in Parulekar and Bakshi, *Selections from Educational Records (Bombay): Part II*, 57; *Report of the Board of Education, Bombay, from May 1, 1854 to April 30, 1855*, 26.

33. Naoroji to Erskine Perry, May 5, 1852, NAI, DNP, N-1; Ahmad, "A History of Elphinstone College," 131–132.

34. "Chuckerbuttyism in Bombay," *Times of India*, September 20, 1851, 618.

35. Jim Masselos, *Towards Nationalism: Group Affiliations and the Politics of Public Associations in Nineteenth Century Western India* (Bombay: Popular Prakashan, 1974), 28. For a study that posits conflict between a new intelligentsia and the shetia elite, see Christine E. Dobbin, *Urban Leadership in Western India: Politics and Communities in Bombay City, 1840–1885* (London: Oxford University Press, 1972), especially chapters 2 and 3.

36. K. R. Cama to Naoroji, October 25, 1901, NAI, DNP, C-21 (1); *A Brief Account of the Framjee Cowasjee Testimonial and the Principal Correspondence Relating to the Framjee Cowasjee Institute* (Bombay: Union Press, 1871), 10; Patell, *Pārsī Prakāsh*, 1888, 1:624–625. In this book, I have been unable to address Naoroji's lifelong involvement in the affairs of the Iranian Zoroastrians. Naoroji worked with Manekji Limji Hataria, the Parsi emissary to the Iranian Zoroastrians during the second half of the nineteenth century, and corresponded with Ardeshir Reporter, one of Manekji's successors. While in Great Britain, Naoroji twice met with the shah of Persia in order to lobby for reforms such as the abolition of the *jiziya* tax against non-Muslims. I hope to address this aspect of Naoroji's career in a future article.

37. *Fourth Report of the Students' Literary and Scientific Society, and of Its Vernacular Branch Societies* (Bombay: Duftur Ashkara Press, 1853), 6; "Students' Literary and Scientific Society," *Bombay Times and Journal of Commerce*, July 28, 1849, 509.

38. *Proceedings of the Students' Literary and Scientific Society, Bombay, for the Years 1854–55 and 1855–56* (Bombay: Bombay Gazette Press, 1856), 5.

39. "The Late Mr. C. N. Cama," *Times of India*, February 9, 1885, 6; Patell, *Pārsī Prakāsh*, 1888, 1:512.

40. Daniel J. Sheffield, "In the Path of the Prophet: Medieval and Early Modern Narratives of the Life of Zarathustra in Islamic Iran and Western India," Ph.D. diss., Harvard University, 2012, 173–174.

41. Kaikhosro N. Kabraji, *Ehvāle "Rāst Goftār" yāne "Rāst Goftār tathā Satya Prakāsh"* [History of the "Rast Goftar" and "Rast Goftar and Satya Prakash"] (Bombay: Duftur Ashkara Press, 1901), 48, 51, 52.

42. *Rāhānumāe mājdīsnā eheve nāmnī sabhānī pehelī, bījī tathā trījī bethaknī ūpaj nīpajno eheval* [Proceedings of the first, second, and third meetings of the Rahnumae Mazdayasnan Sabha] (Bombay: Duftur Ashkara Press, 1851), 8–9, 5.

43. *Rāhānumāe mājdīsnā*, 3, 9; Ratan Marshall, *Gujarātī patrakāritvno itihās* (Surat: Sahitya Sangam, 2005), 111; Masani, *Dadabhai Naoroji*, 61; Masselos, *Towards Nationalism*, 45.

44. *Rāhānumāe mājdiasnā eheve nāmnī sabhānī navmī bethaknī ūpaj nīpajno eheval* [Proceedings of the ninth meeting of the Rahnumae Mazdayasnan Sabha] (Bombay: Mumbai Samachar, 1852), 37–38, 1; Patell, *Pārsī Prakāsh*, 1888, 1:586; R. P. Karkaria, "Revival of the Native Press of Western India: The Rast Goftar," *Calcutta Review*, October 1898, 238.

45. J. P. Naik, ed., *A Review of Education in Bombay State, 1855–1955* (Poona: Director, Government Printing, Publications and Stationery, Bombay State, 1958), 2; "Second Annual Report (1817) of the Bombay Education Society," in Parulekar and Bakshi, *Selections from Educational Records (Bombay): Part II*, 7; Dobbin, *Urban Leadership in Western India*, 57.

46. "The 'Bengal Hurkaru' on Parsee Affairs," *Bombay Times and Journal of Commerce*, May 31, 1848, 414.

47. Sanjay Seth, *Subject Lessons: The Western Education of Colonial India* (Durham, NC: Duke University Press, 2007), 137; J. V. Naik, "Bhau Mahajan and His Prabhakar, Dhumketu and Dnyan Darshan: A Study of Maharashtrian Response to British Rule," *Indian Historical Review* 13–14, nos. 1–2 (July 1986): 147; *Report of the Board of Education from January 1, 1850 to April 30, 1851*, 267; Masani, *Dadabhai Naoroji*, 44.

48. Naoroji's statement was composed for the Indian Education or Hunter Commission of 1882. Masani, *Dadabhai Naoroji*, 85; "A Note Submitted to the Education Commission of 1882 by Dadabhai Naoroji," in *Evidence Taken by the Bombay Provincial Committee, and Memorials Addressed to the Education Commission (Bombay, Vol. II)* (Calcutta: Superintendent of Government Printing, India, 1884), 104; Mary Carpenter, "On Female Education in India," *Journal of the National Indian Association*, November 1871, 230; Naoroji to Fraser, August 5, 1904, RPPM.

49. Patell, *Pārsī Prakāsh*, 1888, 1:506–507; *Proceedings of the Students' Literary and Scientific Society*, 9; Masani, *Dadabhai Naoroji*, 45.

50. Students' Literary and Scientific Society, Bombay. *Report of the Session of 1871–72* (Bombay: Union Press, 1873), 21; *Fourth Report of the Students' Literary and Scientific Society*, 7, 9, 10.

51. *A Brief Account of the Framjee Cowasjee Testimonial,* 11; Patell, *Pārsī Prakāsh,* 1888,
    1:507; "Religious & Social Reform," *Indu Prakash,* March 23, 1885, in Sorabji
    Bamanji Munshi to Naoroji, March 1, 1902, NAI, DNP, M-210 (25); *Proceedings
    of the Students' Literary and Scientific Society, Bombay, for the Years 1854–55 and
    1855–56* (Bombay: Bombay Gazette Press, 1856), 10–11; "The Late Mr. C. N.
    Cama," 6.

52. *Proceedings of the Students' Literary and Scientific Society,* 13–14, 40–41; Naik, *A Re-
    view of Education in Bombay State,* 388; Vaman Pandurang Khanolkar and Ram-
    chandra Vithal Parulekar, eds., *Indigenous Elementary Education in the Bombay
    Presidency in 1855 and Thereabouts (Being a Departmental Survey of Indigenous Educa-
    tion)* (Bombay: Indian Institute of Education, 1965), 106–107.

53. Perry to Naoroji, April 11, 1851, NAI, DNP, P-106 (8); Perry to Naoroji, May 6,
    1854, NAI, DNP, P-106; *Proceedings of the Students' Literary and Scientific Society,* 33.

54. "Inauguration of 'the Bombay Association,'" *Bombay Times and Journal of Com-
    merce,* September 1, 1852, 467.

55. "The Humble Petition of the Members of the Bombay Association, and Other
    Native Inhabitants of the Presidency of Bombay," in *First Report from the Select
    Committee on Indian Territories; Together with the Minutes of Evidence, and Appendix*
    (London: House of Commons, 1853), 480.

56. MSA, General/Education/No. 717; Masani, *Dadabhai Naoroji,* 71.

57. B. B. Patell, ed., *Pārsī Prakāsh* (Bombay: Sanj Vartaman Press, 1910), 2:64; Mary
    Carpenter, *Six Months in India* (London: Longmans, Green, 1868), 1:251; "Parsee
    Munificence," *Manchester Guardian,* March 2, 1864, 3; "Admission of Educated
    Natives into the Indian Civil Service (East India Association)," in *Essays, Speeches,
    Addresses and Writings (on Indian Politics) of the Hon'ble Dadabhai Naoroji,* ed.
    Chunilal Lallubhai Parekh (Bombay: Caxton Printing Works, 1887), 88. Plans
    for the university fellowship and loan company were dashed by the severe
    commercial crisis in Bombay following the conclusion of the American Civil
    War. "The Indian Association," *Journal of the National Indian Association,* January
    1871, 3.

58. Historiographically, Indian leadership in education in Bombay is important.
    Historians of social and educational matters in Bombay have tended to overrely
    on periodicals and reports authored by Britons—not surprising, considering
    the destruction and loss of so much vernacular material from the nineteenth
    century—but such sources, replete with patronizing and moralizing language
    on how Indians did not appreciate the value of education, or how Indians
    needed to be coaxed into supporting schools and colleges, must be used with
    care. Read uncritically, they facilitate scholarship that privileges the role of im-
    perial ideologies and assigns far too much influence to British officials and in-
    structors. Closer inspection and interrogation of available sources reveals a
    definite gap between rhetoric and reality in the sphere of British Indian educa-
    tional policy. The legacy of Indian educational leadership and philanthropy in
    Bombay—and, particularly, Naoroji's role in facilitating reform movements
    based on education, and his establishment of girls' schools that were indepen-
    dent of government assistance—shows us how Indians compensated for this

gap. It shows us how our historical narratives of Indian education, many based on sources filled with biases and inaccuracies, need a measure of revision. Naoroji to Northcote, February 5, 1868, NAI, DNP, N-1 (17); "Financial Administration of India," in *Essays, Speeches, Addresses and Writings (on Indian Politics) of the Hon'ble Dadabhai Naoroji*, ed. Chunilal Lallubhai Parekh (Bombay: Caxton Printing Works, 1887), 138.

59. Naoroji to Fraser, August 5, 1904, RPPM; "A Note Submitted to the Education Commission of 1882 by Dadabhai Naoroji," 88, 89.

2. Of Poverty and Princes

1. "Varshādnī moshamnī Mumbaīthī Edannī shafar," *Rāst Goftār*, July 29, 1855, 239; "Edanthī Mālthā sudhīnī shafar," *Rāst Goftār*, October 7, 1855, 317, 318.

2. "Māltāthī Inglandnī shafar," *Rāst Goftār*, October 14, 1855, 325; "Pārīshnu egjībīshan," *Rāst Goftār*, December 16, 1855, 399–400; "Pārīshnu egjībīshan," *Rāst Goftār*, December 23, 1855, 407–408; "Pārīshnu ekjībīshan," *Rāst Goftār*, December 30, 1855, 418–419. These articles were published anonymously but were clearly written by Dadabhai Naoroji. A contemporary English daily, furthermore, identified Naoroji as the author. See *Bombay Times and Journal of Commerce*, October 20, 1855, 2. My thanks to Murali Ranganathan for help in tracking down these difficult-to-procure articles.

3. "Financial Administration of India," in *Essays, Speeches, Addresses and Writings (on Indian Politics) of the Hon'ble Dadabhai Naoroji*, ed. Chunilal Lallubhai Parekh (Bombay: Caxton Printing Works, 1887), 140; Dadabhai Naoroji to Behramji Malabari, October 22, 1884, NAI, DNP, N-1 (188).

4. Naoroji to Lord George Hamilton, February 26, 1901, NAI, DNP, E-72 (98); J. V. Naik, "Forerunners of Dadabhai Naoroji's Drain Theory," *Economic and Political Weekly*, November 24, 2001, 275.

5. "Poverty of India, Part II," in *Essays, Speeches, Addresses and Writings (on Indian Politics) of the Hon'ble Dadabhai Naoroji*, ed. Chunilal Lallubhai Parekh (Bombay: Caxton Printing Works, 1887), 218–219.

6. Stanley Wolpert labeled Naoroji's views on the drain of wealth as "tempting oversimplifications," something that a more serious student of economics like Ranade would never formulate. Bipan Chandra evaluated Naoroji's arguments with deep skepticism, charging that his fixation on the Indian civil service was "narrow-mindedness to the length of inanity." Stanley Wolpert, *Tilak and Gokhale: Revolution and Reform in the Making of Modern India* (Berkeley: University of California Press, 1962), 107; Bipan Chandra, *The Rise and Growth of Economic Nationalism in India: Economic Policies of Indian National Leadership, 1880–1905* (New Delhi: People's Publishing House, 1966), 651–652; Anil Seal, *The Emergence of Indian Nationalism: Competition and Collaboration in the Later Nineteenth Century* (London: Cambridge University Press, 1968).

7. For more on bigamy within the Parsi community, and Parsi efforts to outlaw it, see Mitra Sharafi, *Law and Identity in Colonial South Asia: Parsi Legal Culture, 1772–1947* (New York: Cambridge University Press, 2014), 170–173.

8. Rustom P. Masani, *Dadabhai Naoroji: The Grand Old Man of India* (London: G. Allen & Unwin, 1939), 86–87, 93–95; Naoroji to Ardeshir Naoroji, February 21, 1879, NAI, DNP, Part II, 13 (1879).

9. "Condition of India," in *Essays, Speeches, Addresses and Writings (on Indian Politics) of the Hon'ble Dadabhai Naoroji*, ed. Chunilal Lallubhai Parekh (Bombay: Caxton Printing Works, 1887), 487.

10. Sven Beckert, *Empire of Cotton: A Global History* (New York: Alfred A. Knopf, 2014), 329; Masani, *Dadabhai Naoroji*, 92–95.

11. Dinyar Patel, "Viewpoint: How British Let One Million Indians Die in Famine," BBC News, June 11, 2016, http://www.bbc.com/news/world-asia-india-36339524; Dadabhai Naoroji, "Irrigation Works in India," *Journal of the East India Association* 3 (1869): 3.

12. For an excellent overview of contemporary British theories on the causes of Indian famines, see chapters 1 and 9 in Mike Davis, *Late Victorian Holocausts: El Niño Famines and the Making of the Third World* (London: Verso, 2001).

13. "On the Commerce of India," in *Essays, Speeches, Addresses and Writings (on Indian Politics) of the Hon'ble Dadabhai Naoroji*, ed. Chunilal Lallubhai Parekh (Bombay: Caxton Printing Works, 1887), 112, 114.

14. "The East India Association," *London Review*, September 21, 1867, 325.

15. "England's Duties to India," in *Essays, Speeches, Addresses and Writings (on Indian Politics) of the Hon'ble Dadabhai Naoroji*, ed. Chunilal Lallubhai Parekh (Bombay: Caxton Printing Works, 1887), 29, 27.

16. "The Wants and Means of India," in *Essays, Speeches, Addresses and Writings (on Indian Politics) of the Hon'ble Dadabhai Naoroji*, ed. Chunilal Lallubhai Parekh (Bombay: Caxton Printing Works, 1887), 97.

17. Ibid., 102–103; "The First Indian National Congress," in *Essays, Speeches, Addresses and Writings (on Indian Politics) of the Hon'ble Dadabhai Naoroji*, ed. Chunilal Lallubhai Parekh (Bombay: Caxton Printing Works, 1887), 327.

18. "The Wants and Means of India," 100, 103; "Poverty of India, Part I," in *Essays, Speeches, Addresses and Writings (on Indian Politics) of the Hon'ble Dadabhai Naoroji*, ed. Chunilal Lallubhai Parekh (Bombay: Caxton Printing Works, 1887), 184–190; Davis, *Late Victorian Holocausts*, 40.

19. C. A. Bayly refers to this strategy as the "turning of the defence witnesses." Bipan Chandra also details this technique, although he does not mention Naoroji's use of it. C. A. Bayly, *Recovering Liberties: Indian Thought in the Age of Liberalism and Empire* (Cambridge, New York: Cambridge University Press, 2012), 196; Chandra, *The Rise and Growth of Economic Nationalism in India*, 15.

20. "Poverty of India, Part I," 197–198, 200, 204, 205, 207.

21. Ibid., 162.

22. Ibid., 174, 183.

23. In the course of his research on Indian agriculture, Naoroji most likely contacted and corresponded with a range of knowledgeable individuals across the subcontinent. Kazi Shahabudin, a friend and the former diwan of Kutch, supplied his calculations on costs of living for agricultural laborers in the Bombay Presidency. While calculating Bengali rice production for "Poverty of India,"

Naoroji relied upon the observations of a Parsi manager at a Port Canning rice mill. "Condition of India," 427, 433, 432, 415, 437.

24. "Poverty of India, Part II," 277. For Naoroji's rebuttal of Danvers's views, see "Condition of India," 441–464. Naoroji particularly sought to disprove Danvers's argument that railways generated wealth for India.

25. Navrozji Fardunji, "To the Editor of the 'Bombay Gazette,'" *Times of India*, December 28, 1876, 3; Hyde Clark, "Enterprise in the East Indies," *Journal of the Society of Arts*, September 16, 1870, 848; William Sowerby, "The Condition of India Question," *Times of India*, August 1, 1876, 2.

26. "The Indian Civil Service," in *Essays, Speeches, Addresses and Writings (on Indian Politics) of the Hon'ble Dadabhai Naoroji*, ed. Chunilal Lallubhai Parekh (Bombay: Caxton Printing Works, 1887), 500.

27. *Minute of Proceedings of the Bombay Association* (Bombay: Bombay Gazette Press, 1852), 18–19; J. Cosmo Melvill to Naoroji, March 29, 1859, NAI, DNP, I-13 (2).

28. Masani, *Dadabhai Naoroji*, 98.

29. "England's Duties to India," 29, 30.

30. Ibid., 50, 38, 29; "Expenses of the Abyssinian War," in *Essays, Speeches, Addresses and Writings (on Indian Politics) of the Hon'ble Dadabhai Naoroji*, ed. Chunilal Lallubhai Parekh (Bombay: Caxton Printing Works, 1887), 53; "Financial Administration of India," 146–149.

31. "On the Commerce of India," 123, 134; "Financial Administration of India," 138.

32. "The Wants and Means of India," 105, 106, 103.

33. "Admission of Educated Natives into the Indian Civil Service (East India Association)," in *Essays, Speeches, Addresses and Writings (on Indian Politics) of the Hon'ble Dadabhai Naoroji*, ed. Chunilal Lallubhai Parekh (Bombay: Caxton Printing Works, 1887), 75; "Admission of Educated Natives into the Indian Civil Service (Memorandum)," in *Essays, Speeches, Addresses and Writings (on Indian Politics) of the Hon'ble Dadabhai Naoroji*, ed. Chunilal Lallubhai Parekh (Bombay: Caxton Printing Works, 1887), 496; "On the Commerce of India," 132.

34. "Financial Administration of India," 141, 143, 144.

35. "Condition of India," 477; "England's Duties to India," 26, 30–31.

36. "Summary: Bombay," *Pioneer*, June 26, 1871, 4; "Mī. Navrojjī Fardunjī," *Rāst Goftār*, February 16, 1873, 108; Dadabhai Naoroji, "Poverty of India," in *Poverty and Un-British Rule in India* (London: Swan Sonnenschein, 1901), 1.

37. "Poverty of India, Part I," 160, 196, 210, 212. Curiously, Naoroji briefly returned to the idea of a "legitimate drain" in 1881. "Condition of India," 446–447.

38. Naoroji's earliest correspondence with US officials is likely lost. The earliest surviving correspondence I have found in the Naoroji Papers dates from January 24, 1882. "Poverty of India, Part I," 210, 208.

39. Ibid., 212, 213.

40. Kim Wagner, "'Treading upon Fires': The 'Mutiny'-Motif and Colonial Anxieties in British India," *Past and Present*, no. 218 (February 2013): 159–197; "England's Duties to India," 35; "Condition of India," 469, 477.

41. "Poverty of India, Part II," 275; "The First Indian National Congress," 325.

42. "The Indian Civil Service," 500.

43. Ibid., 502, 501; "Retirement of Lord Ripon," in *Speeches and Writings of Dadabhai Naoroji*, ed. G. A. Natesan, 2nd ed. (Madras: G. A. Natesan & Co., 1917), 168–169.

44. Ian Copland, *The British Raj and the Indian Princes: Paramountcy in Western India, 1857–1930* (Bombay: Orient Longman, 1982), 1; Barbara N. Ramusack, *The Indian Princes and Their States* (Cambridge: Cambridge University Press, 2008), 174.

45. J. V. Naik, "An Early Appraisal of the British Colonial Policy," *Journal of the University of Bombay, Arts Number* 44–45, no. 80–81 (1976): 253, 256; S. R. Mehrotra, *The Emergence of the Indian National Congress* (Delhi: Vikas Publications, 1971), 85.

46. *The State and Government of India under Its Native Rulers*, India Reform, no. IX (London: Twentieth Century Press, 1899), 14–15, 17–18, 19–20, 24–27, 28, 36, 49.

47. Sorabji Jehangir, *Representative Men of India* (London: W. H. Allen & Co., 1889), 139–141; Evans Bell, *The Mysore Reversion: "An Exceptional Case"* (London: Trübner & Co., 1865), iv.

48. "Mysore," in *Essays, Speeches, Addresses and Writings (on Indian Politics) of the Hon'ble Dadabhai Naoroji*, ed. Chunilal Lallubhai Parekh (Bombay: Caxton Printing Works, 1887), 65, 61.

49. "Kutch: Relations of the Rao with His Bhyad," October 2, 1868, BL, IOR, L/PS/6/560, Coll. 12.

50. "Admission of Educated Natives into the Indian Civil Service (Memorandum)," 493; "Poverty of India, Part I," 194.

51. Naoroji to Ishvarlal Ochumanty, September 5, 1871, NMML, DNP, II, #493; "Annual Meeting of the East India Association," *Journal of the East India Association* 6 (1872): 226; "Important Letter from the Maharaja Holkar," *Journal of the East India Association* 6 (1872): 223; Naoroji to Haji Ahmad Isaji, February 23, 1872, NMML, DNP, II, #497; "Bombay Branch of the East India Association," *Journal of the East India Association* 6 (1872): 245; list of members of the East India Association in Junagadh, 1872, NAI, DNP, uncataloged item.

52. "Memorial of Gaekwar Regarding His Position in Relation to Governor of Bombay," 1873, MSA, Political/Baroda/No. 1856; "Annual Meeting of the East India Association," *Journal of the East India Association* 7, no. 2 (1873): 122–123.

53. "Annual Meeting of the East India Association," 123.

54. Bartle Frere to Naoroji, November 7, 1873, in Dadabhai Naoroji, *Baroda Administration in 1874: A Statement in Reply to Remarks in the Baroda Blue Book of 1875, Concerning Dadabhai Naoroji and His Colleagues* (London: Vincent Brooks, Day and Son, n.d.); Naoroji to Erskine Perry, November 2, 1873, NAI, DNP, N-1 (2471); Masani, *Dadabhai Naoroji*, 141, 146.

55. Masani, *Dadabhai Naoroji*, 146, 148.

56. "The Baroda Administration in 1874," in *Essays, Speeches, Addresses and Writings (on Indian Politics) of the Hon'ble Dadabhai Naoroji*, ed. Chunilal Lallubhai Parekh (Bombay: Caxton Printing Works, 1887), 395, 404; "Editorial," *Times of India*, December 14, 1874, 2; "Revenue Reforms of the State of Baroda," 1874, MSA, Political/Baroda/No. 1848; Lewis Pelly to the Secretary to the Government of India, Foreign Department, December 19, 1874, MSA, Political/Baroda/No. 1848.

57. "The Baroda Administration in 1874," 394.

58. Ian Copland, "The Baroda Crisis of 1873–77: A Study in Governmental Rivalry," *Modern Asian Studies* 2, no. 2 (1968): 97–98, 101; Masani, *Dadabhai Naoroji*, 148.

59. Ian Copland describes Robert Phayre as "honest, averagely intelligent, zealous in the execution of his duties, and somewhat tactless when dealing with 'inferiors.' At the same time he possessed qualities of drive, audacity and initiative which set him apart from the mass of his professional colleagues." This appears to be a far too sympathetic assessment of the man. Further exploration of archival materials in India and United Kingdom, and consideration of Naoroji's own records, has led me to judge Phayre as a much more complex—and occasionally devious—character. "The Baroda Crisis of 1873–77: A Study in Governmental Rivalry," 102; W. L. Merewether to Seymour Fitzgerald, August 25, 1870, "Col. Phayre's Official Quarrel as Pol. Supdt. Upper Scinde Frontier, with Col. Sir W. Merewether Commissioner in Sind, 1870," 1870, BL, IOR, R/2/536/312, File II; S. Gopal, *British Policy in India, 1858–1905* (Cambridge: Cambridge University Press, 1965), 106; Naoroji to Perry, November 2, 1873, NAI, DNP, N-1 (2471); Robert Phayre to C. Gonne, April 29, 1873, "Confidential Letters. Administration Report for 1872–73," 1873, BL, IOR, R/2/481/55, Item 377, No. 1; Phayre to Gonne, May 7, 1874, "Historical Sketch of Our Relations with the Baroda Government from 1820 to 1874," 1874, BL, IOR, R/2/481/55, Item 377, No. 2; "The Baroda Administration in 1874," 406.

60. Secretary to the Government of Bombay to the Secretary to the Government of India, March 5, 1874, *East India (Baroda). Report of the Commission Appointed to Inquire into the Administration of the Baroda State* (London: Her Majesty's Stationery Office, 1875), 64; "Baroda Administration Report for 1873/74," 1874, BL, IOR, R/2/481/55, Item 377.

61. "Baroda Administration Report for 1873/74," 1874, BL, IOR, R/2/481/55, Item 377; Masani, *Dadabhai Naoroji*, 157, 161.

62. Dinshah Ardeshir Taleyarkhan, *The Revolution at Baroda, 1874–75* (Bombay: Hormusjee Sorabjee & Co., 1875), 17–18; "Attempt to Poison Coll. Phayre the Resident," 1874, MSA, Political/Baroda/Vol. XVIII, No. 28; *East India (Baroda, No. 5). Correspondence Connected with the Deposition of Mulhar Rao* (London: Her Majesty's Stationery Office, 1875), 7.

63. Naoroji to Suchet Singh, August 25, 1887, NAI, DNP, N-1 (759); Tulaji Raje Bhosle to Naoroji, September 21, 1897, NAI, DNP, B-128; Maharana Shri Buldevji Naraindevji to Naoroji, July 14, 1892, NAI, DNP, uncataloged item.

64. "The Hon. Dadabhai Naoroji at the Town Hall," in *Essays, Speeches, Addresses and Writings (on Indian Politics) of the Hon'ble Dadabhai Naoroji*, ed. Chunilal Lallubhai Parekh (Bombay: Caxton Printing Works, 1887), 313–314; "Sir M. E. Grant Duff's Views about India," in *Essays, Speeches, Addresses and Writings (on Indian Politics) of the Hon'ble Dadabhai Naoroji*, ed. Chunilal Lallubhai Parekh (Bombay: Caxton Printing Works, 1887), 566, 573, 577–578, 572; Hormusjee Ardeseer Wadya to Naoroji, November 3, 1894, NAI, DNP, W-12 (9).

65. Henry Hyndman to Naoroji, September 12, 1901, NAI, DNP, H-221 (98); Hyndman to Naoroji, September 30, 1878, NAI, DNP, H-221 (1); Hyndman to Naoroji,

April 25, 1880, NAI, DNP, H-221 (3); "A Parsi Candidate for Parliament," *Pioneer*, June 7, 1886, 4.

66. Marcus Morris, "From Anti-Colonialism to Anti-Imperialism: The Evolution of H. M. Hyndman's Critique of Empire, c. 1875–1905," *Historical Research* 87, no. 236 (May 2014): 293–314; Karl Marx to Nicolai F. Danielson, February 19, 1881, in *K. Marx and F. Engels on Colonialism* (Moscow: Foreign Languages Publishing House, n.d.), 337. My thanks to Prabhat Patnaik for this reference. See his article "Marx and Naoroji," *Telegraph*, December 20, 2017. For more on Marx and Naoroji, see B. N. Ganguli, *Dadabhai Naoroji and the Drain Theory* (New York: Asia Publishing House, 1965), 42–46; and Manu Goswami, *Producing India: From Colonial Economy to National Space* (Chicago: University of Chicago Press, 2004), 227.

67. Naoroji to Mahadev Govind Ranade, April 23, 1884, NAI, DNP, N-1 (161); R. R. Dadina to Naoroji, April 12, 1884, NAI, DNP, D-10 (6).

68. Masani, *Dadabhai Naoroji*, 184–85; Naoroji to Ardeshir Naoroji, March 14, 1879, NAI, DNP, Part II, 19 (1879).

69. Masani, *Dadabhai Naoroji*, 185; Naoroji to Mancherji Merwanji Dadina, June 18, 1880, NAI, DNP, Part II, 24 (1880).

70. Naoroji to Ardeshir Naoroji, June 13, 1879, NAI, DNP, Part II, 52 (1879).

71. Naoroji to Ardeshir Naoroji, February 21, 1879, NAI, DNP, Part II, 13 (1879); "Bombay Branch of the East India Association," 244, 245.

3. Turning toward Westminster

1. Rustom P. Masani, *Dadabhai Naoroji: The Grand Old Man of India* (London: G. Allen & Unwin, 1939), 193; Jonathan Schneer, *London 1900: The Imperial Metropolis* (New Haven: Yale University Press, 1999), 196; Sukanya Banerjee, *Becoming Imperial Citizens: Indians in the Late-Victorian Empire* (Durham, NC: Duke University Press, 2010), 5.

2. "The Agitation of Indian Questions," *Times of India*, January 20, 1885, 4. See generally chapter 5 in S. R. Mehrotra, *The Emergence of the Indian National Congress* (Delhi: Vikas Publications, 1971).

3. M. Viraraghavachariar to Dadabhai Naoroji, February 29, 1888, NAI, DNP, C-113; *Dadabhai Naoroji Correspondence*, ed. R. P. Patwardhan, vol. 2, part 1 (New Delhi: Allied, 1977), 30; Naoroji to William Wedderburn, August 20, 1886, NAI, DNP, N-1 (633). For a more sympathetic account of the Britons who manned the Indian civil service, see David Gilmour, *The Ruling Caste: Imperial Lives in the Victorian Raj* (New York: Farrar, Straus and Giroux, 2005).

4. For more on Hume's meetings with prominent Liberals, see Mehrotra, *The Emergence of the Indian National Congress*, 402–403.

5. Ibid., 324. For work exploring the history of Irish-Indian political links, see Howard Brasted, "Indian Nationalist Development and the Influence of Irish Home Rule, 1870–1886," *Modern Asian Studies* 14, no. 1 (1980): 37–63; Mary Cumpston, "Some Early Indian Nationalists and Their Allies in the British Parliament, 1851–1906," *English Historical Review* 76 (April 1961): 279–297; Carla King,

"Michael Davitt, Irish Nationalism and the British Empire in the Late Nineteenth Century," in *Victoria's Ireland? Irishness and Britishness, 1837–1901*, ed. Peter Gray (Dublin: Four Courts Press, 2004), 116–130; Jennifer Regan-Lefebvre, *Cosmopolitan Nationalism in the Victorian Empire: Ireland, India and the Politics of Alfred Webb* (Houndmills: Palgrave Macmillan, 2009); and Michael Silvestri, *Ireland and India: Nationalism, Empire and Memory* (Basingstoke: Palgrave Macmillan, 2009).

6. This excepts, of course, David Ochterlony Dyce Sombre, who was technically the first Indian to stand for election in spite of identifying himself as a European. Michael H. Fisher, *The Inordinately Strange Life of Dyce Sombre: Victorian Anglo-Indian MP and a "Chancery Lunatic"* (New York: Columbia University Press, 2010).

7. Lynn Zastoupil, *Rammohun Roy and the Making of Victorian Britain* (New York: Palgrave Macmillan, 2010), 127.

8. Ibid., 127–128, 151–152.

9. Ibid., 162; Richard Philip Tucker, *Ranade and the Roots of Indian Nationalism* (Chicago: University of Chicago Press, 1972), 75; Manockjee Cursetjee, *A Few Passing Ideas for the Benefit of India and Indians* (Bombay: Bombay Education Society's Press, 1853), 3–4.

10. "England's Duties to India," in *Essays, Speeches, Addresses and Writings (on Indian Politics) of the Hon'ble Dadabhai Naoroji*, ed. Chunilal Lallubhai Parekh (Bombay: Caxton Printing Works, 1887), 31.

11. "Representative Government for India," *Journal of the East India Association* 1 (1867): 85, 82, 86, 84, 90, 91.

12. Minute book entry, March 11, 1874, BL, IOR, East India Association Papers, MSS Eur F 147/27.

13. Ibid. The arguments about technology and transportation are remarkably similar to those made around the same time in favor of parliamentary representation for Canada. See Ged Martin, "Empire Federalism and Imperial Parliamentary Union, 1820–1870," *Historical Journal* 16, no. 1 (1973): 79.

14. Minute book entries, October 21, 1874, and March 11, 1874, BL, IOR, East India Association Papers, MSS Eur F 147/27. Tucker claims that Ranade might have secured two hundred thousand signatures for this petition, which appears to be an error. *Ranade and the Roots of Indian Nationalism*, 75–76.

15. In 1867, for example, Fawcett caused significant embarrassment to the Conservative ministry by asking repeatedly why the "toiling peasant" in India was being required to pay for a lavish ball held in London for the sultan of Muscat. Leslie Stephen, *Life of Henry Fawcett*, 3rd ed. (New York: G. P. Putnam's Sons, 1886), 343–344.

16. Ibid., 385; Naoroji to Behramji Malabari, October 25, 1888, NAI, DNP, N-1 (1255).

17. Mehrotra, *The Emergence of the Indian National Congress*, 580–581; "India's Interest in the General Election (1885)," in *Essays, Speeches, Addresses and Writings (on Indian Politics) of the Hon'ble Dadabhai Naoroji*, ed. Chunilal Lallubhai Parekh (Bombay: Caxton Printing Works, 1887), 292–293.

18. Naoroji to W. Martin Wood, October 2, 1884, NAI, DNP, N-1 (180).

19. *Sic.* Naoroji to Gopalji Surbhai Desai, January 25, 1885, RPPM; Malabari to Naoroji, April 8, 1885, NAI, DNP, M-32 (54); Nasarvanji J. Moolla to Naoroji, February 27, 1885, RPPM.
20. Naoroji to Wedderburn, April 16, 1886, NAI, DNP, N-1 (533).
21. Naoroji to Wedderburn, June 25, 1886, NAI, DNP, N-1 (600); Henry Pelling, *Social Geography of British Elections, 1885–1910* (London: Macmillan, 1967), 35.
22. Naoroji to Wedderburn, June 25, 1886, NAI, DNP, N-1 (600)
23. Allan Octavian Hume to Naoroji, March 22, 1886, NAI, DNP, H-199.
24. Naoroji diary, April 17, 1886, NAI, DNP, Part V, 3–21; Naoroji to Wedderburn, May 7, 1886, NAI, DNP, N-1 (541); Naoroji diary, May 6, 1886, NAI, DNP, Part V, 3–21.
25. Naoroji turned down Hyndman's offer to dedicate a new edition of *The Bankruptcy of India* to him. George Birdwood to Naoroji, May 18, 1886, NAI, DNP, B-140 (1); Naoroji diary, May 17 and April 29, 1886, NAI, DNP, Part V, 3–21; Naoroji to Wedderburn, May 7, 1886, NAI, DNP, N-1 (541).
26. Naoroji diary, April 17 and May 6, 1886, NAI, DNP, Part V, 3–21.
27. Naoroji most likely knew Frank Hugh O'Donnell as well, but I have found no communication between the two men. Mary Cumpston claims that they were introduced in Paris but does not list her source. Cumpston, "Some Early Indian Nationalists and Their Allies in the British Parliament, 1851–1906," 282; Michael Davitt, *The Fall of Feudalism in Ireland; or, the Story of the Land League Revolution* (London: Harper & Brothers, 1904), 447; Henry Richard Fox Bourne to Naoroji, June 2, 1886, NAI, DNP, B-238; Naoroji diary, April 28, 1886, NAI, DNP, Part V, 3–21; Henry Hyde Champion to Naoroji, June 15, 1886, NAI, DNP, C-99.
28. Naoroji to Wedderburn, May 24, 1886, NAI, DNP, N-1 (554); Naoroji to Wedderburn, May 28, 1886, NAI, DNP, N-1 (561); Francis Wyllie to Naoroji, May 20, 1886, NAI, DNP, L-55; Naoroji diary, April 16 and May 3, 1886, NAI, DNP, Part V, 3–21.
29. Naoroji to Wedderburn, June 6, 1886, NAI, DNP, N-1 (569).
30. Naoroji, confident that Irish home rule was imminent, dismissed Chesson's idea of standing for an Irish seat. Naoroji diary, May 17, 1886, NAI, DNP, Part V, 3–21; Naoroji to Wedderburn, May 7, 1886, NAI, DNP, N-1 (541); Naoroji to Wedderburn, June 10, 1886, NAI, DNP, N-1 (585); Naoroji to Charles A. V. Conybeare, June 15, 1886, NAI, DNP, C-238; Naoroji to Wedderburn, June 17, 1886, NAI, DNP, N-1 (587).
31. Naoroji to Wedderburn, June 17, 1886, NAI, DNP, N-1 (587); Champion to Naoroji, June 15, 1886, NAI, DNP, C-99; "The Hon. Dadabhai Naoroji's Great Speech," in *Essays, Speeches, Addresses and Writings (on Indian Politics) of the Hon'ble Dadabhai Naoroji*, ed. Chunilal Lallubhai Parekh (Bombay: Caxton Printing Works, 1887), 302.
32. Harry T. Eve, circular, June 15, 1886, NAI, DNP, H-140; "The Hon. Dadabhai Naoroji's Great Speech," 303.
33. "The Hon. Dadabhai Naoroji's Great Speech," 304.
34. Ibid., 307, 308, 305; Naoroji to Wedderburn, June 25, 1886, NAI, DNP, N-1 (600); "The Hon. Dadabhai Naoroji at the Town Hall," in *Essays, Speeches, Addresses and Writings (on Indian Politics) of the Hon'ble Dadabhai Naoroji*, ed. Chunilal Lallubhai

Parekh (Bombay: Caxton Printing Works, 1887), 315; "The Hon. Dadabhai Naoroji at the Store-Street Hall," in *Essays, Speeches, Addresses and Writings (on Indian Politics) of the Hon'ble Dadabhai Naoroji,* ed. Chunilal Lallubhai Parekh (Bombay: Caxton Printing Works, 1887), 311.

35. Malabari to Naoroji, June 29, 1886, NAI, DNP, M-32 (98).

36. "Editorial Notes," *Indian Spectator,* July 4, 1886, 525–526; "The Indian Parliamentary Candidates," *Times of India,* June 30, 1886, 5; "India and England," *Pall Mall Gazette,* July 2, 1886; "The General Election: Holborn," *Daily News,* July 3, 1886; "India and the English Elections," *Huddersfield Daily Chronicle,* July 1, 1886, 4; "India and the English Elections," *Devon and Exeter Gazette,* July 1, 1886, 3.

37. "The General Election: Holborn," *Daily News,* July 2, 1886; Hyndman to Naoroji, June 25, 1886, NAI, DNP, H-221 (137); Naoroji diary, July 2 and July 3, 1886, NAI, DNP, Part V, 3–21.

38. Holborn had 9,802 registered voters for the 1886 election. "The General Election," *Times,* July 6, 1886, 6; Naoroji to Malabari, July 23, 1886, RPPM.

39. Naoroji to Sarah H. Gostling, July 8, 1886, RPPM; Hyndman to Naoroji, July 4, 1886, NAI, DNP, H-221 (10).

40. Naoroji to family, April 29, 1887, NAI, DNP, Part II, 9 (1887); Naoroji to Wedderburn, August 20, 1886, NAI, DNP, N-1 (633).

41. Wedderburn to Naoroji, September 13, 1886, NAI, DNP, W-48 (7); Malabari to Naoroji, August 3, 1886, NAI, DNP, M-32 (102).

42. Malabari to Naoroji, August 3, 1886, NAI, DNP, M-32 (102); Malabari to Naoroji, March 7, 1887, NAI, DNP, M-32 (130).

43. *Dadabhai Naoroji Correspondence,* ed. Patwardhan, vol. 2, part 1, 45; Hume to Lord Ripon, January 13, 1889, BL, Lord Ripon Papers, Add MSS 43616.

44. Naoroji to Wedderburn, August 20, 1886, NAI, DNP, N-1 (633); "United Kingdom Home Rule League," *Freeman's Journal,* August 12, 1886; *Dadabhai Naoroji Correspondence,* ed. Patwardhan, vol. 2, part 1, 43.

45. "The Imprisonment of Mr. John Dillon, M.P.," *Weekly News and Chronicle,* June 30, 1888, 2; Naoroji to Arthur J. Balfour, June 29, 1888, NAI, DNP, N-1 (1056); "Mr. Naoroji on Home Rule," *Weekly News and Chronicle,* September 22, 1888, 2; "The Conybeare Demonstration," *Reynolds's Newspaper,* June 30, 1889.

46. "India and Ireland," *Freeman's Journal,* May 28, 1888.

47. There is a chance that Naoroji had to retire from the Dublin delegation in order to travel to a conference in Switzerland. Naoroji to Charles Stuart Parnell, June 6, 1888, NAI, DNP, N-1 (1035); Birdwood to Naoroji, May 31, 1888, NAI, DNP, B-140 (8); Malabari to Naoroji, June 19, 1888, NAI, DNP, M-32 (173); Malabari to Naoroji, July 10, 1888, NAI, DNP, M-32 (176); letter to Naoroji dated June 26, 1888, quoted in Anil Seal, *The Emergence of Indian Nationalism: Competition and Collaboration in the Later Nineteenth Century* (London: Cambridge University Press, 1968), 284; Naoroji to Malabari, July 13, 1888, RPPM.

48. Champion told Naoroji that "with the working class element you will be very popular when they find out who you are." Champion to Naoroji, June 21, 1886, NAI, DNP, C-99 (1).

49. "The Clerkenwell-Green Meeting," *Weekly News and Chronicle*, November 17, 1888, 5; "Midnight Meeting of the Unemployed on Christmas Eve," *Reynolds's Newspaper*, December 23, 1888.

50. "The Honorable D. Naoroji on Poverty," *Weekly News and Chronicle*, October 20, 1888, 4; "The Split in Clerkenwell," *Finsbury and Holborn Guardian*, June 14, 1890, 5; Naoroji to Sidney Webb, October 18, 1888, NAI, DNP, N-1 (1234); "The Honorable D. Naoroji on Landlordism," *Weekly News and Chronicle*, November 3, 1888, 2; "The Honorable D. Naoroji on Landlordism and Ground Rents," *Weekly News and Chronicle*, November 3, 1888, 5.

51. "The Rights of Labour," pamphlet, 1890, NAI, DNP, Part III, G-25, 4, 5.

52. John Burns to Naoroji, September 6, 1888, NMML, DNP, I, #137. The earliest correspondence between Keir Hardie and Naoroji appears to date from 1905, although they were most likely already acquainted with one another.

53. "The Honorable D. Naoroji on Poverty," 4.

54. "Mr. Dadabhai Naoroji and Central Finsbury," *India*, August 26, 1892, 214. See chapter 1 in Antoinette M. Burton, *Burdens of History: British Feminists, Indian Women, and Imperial Culture, 1865–1915* (Chapel Hill: University of North Carolina Press, 1994).

55. For more on contagious diseases acts in India and across the British Empire, see chapter 2 in Philippa Levine, *Prostitution, Race, and Politics: Policing Venereal Disease in the British Empire* (New York: Routledge, 2003).

56. Josephine Butler and James Stuart to Naoroji, December 3, 1887, NAI, DNP, B-284 (3); Naoroji to Malabari, June 15, 1888, NAI, DNP, N-1 (1044); *Fédération Britannique, Continentale et Générale: Cinquième Congrès International Tenu du 10 au 13 Septembre 1889 à Genève* (Geneva: Secrétariat Général de la Fédération, 1890), 4, 91.

57. Alice Grenfell to Naoroji, July 15, 1892, NAI, DNP, W-141 (1); Helen New to Naoroji, January 22, 1895, NAI, DNP, I-37 (3); Julie Carlier, "A Forgotten Instance of Women's International Organising: The Transnational Feminist Networks of the Women's Progressive Society (1890) and the International Women's Union (1893–1898)," in *Gender History in a Transnational Perspective*, ed. Oliver Janz and Daniel Schönpflug (New York: Berghahn Books, 2014), 80, 81, 88; Women's Franchise League, "International Conference on the Position of Women in All Countries," conference program, July 1890, NAI, DNP, W-135 (10).

58. Butler to Naoroji, January 12, 1888, NMML, DNP, I, #141.

59. Butler to Naoroji, December 19, 1886, NAI, DNP, B-284 (1); Butler to Naoroji, January 14, 1888, NAI, DNP, B-284 (4).

60. Burton, *Burdens of History*, 2.

61. Butler to Naoroji, June 25, 1892, NAI, DNP, B-284 (13).

62. "The Royal Grants," *Times*, July 22, 1889, 6; "Lord Salisbury in Edinburgh," *Times*, December 1, 1888, 8.

63. For a detailed discussion of the domestic implications of the black man incident, see Antoinette M. Burton, "Tongues Untied: Lord Salisbury's 'Black Man' and the Boundaries of Imperial Democracy," *Comparative Studies in Society and History* 42, no. 3 (July 2000): 632–661. *Lord Salisbury's "Blackman"* (Lucknow: G. P. Varma and

Brothers Press, 1889), 4, 10–11, 26, 12; "Essence of Parliament," *Punch*, December 15, 1888, 287; "In Their Christmas Hampers," *Punch*, December 29, 1888, 303; Malabari to Naoroji, December 28, 1888, NAI, DNP, M-32 (200).

64. "London Correspondence," *Freeman's Journal*, December 11, 1888.

4. An Indian Emissary in the Heart of Empire

1. R. Ruff to Dadabhai Naoroji, telegram, January 2, 1891, NAI, DNP, uncataloged item.

2. Antoinette M. Burton, *At the Heart of Empire: Indians and the Colonial Encounter in Late-Victorian Britain* (Berkeley: University of California Press, 1998), 157; Amalendu Guha, "The Comprador Role of Parsi Seths, 1750–1850," *Economic and Political Weekly* 5, no. 48 (November 28, 1970): 1933–1936.

3. Gráinne Goodwin, "A Trustworthy Interpreter between Rulers and Ruled: Behramji Malabari, Colonial and Cultural Interpreter in Nineteenth-Century British India," *Social History* 38, no. 1 (2013): 1–25.

4. *Eighth Report of Her Majesty's Civil Service Commissioners* (London: George E. Eyre & William Spottiswoode, 1863), xviii.

5. *The Manners and Customs of the Parsees* (London: Pearson & Son, 1862); *The Parsee Religion* (London: Pearson & Son, 1862); F. Max Müller, "The Modern Parsis," in *Chips from a German Workshop* (New York: Charles Scribner's Sons, 1891), 1:167. For more on Naoroji's scholarly activities with regards to Zoroastrianism, see my article "Our Own Religion in Ancient Persia: Dadabhai Naoroji and Orientalist Scholarship on Zoroastrianism," *Global Intellectual History* 2, no. 3 (2017): 311–328.

6. S. R. Mehrotra, *The Emergence of the Indian National Congress* (Delhi: Vikas Publications, 1971), 224.

7. "List of Members and Report for 1867–8," *Journal of the East India Association* 2 (1868): 3–9.

8. "Annual Meeting, July 4, 1877," *Journal of the East India Association* 10 (1877): 270; Mehrotra, *The Emergence of the Indian National Congress*, 225, 295.

9. S. E. Garrington to Naoroji, November 21, 1892, NMML, DNP, #12.

10. Joseph G. Alexander to Naoroji, October 31, 1892, NMML, DNP, #2; James Hole to Naoroji, December 24, 1892, NMML, DNP, #10; T. Campbell to Naoroji, May 10, 1894, NAI, DNP, C-39 (1); Charles H. Hill and J. Hunt Stanford to Naoroji, October 7, 1893, NAI, DNP, H-113; Tom B. Chant to Naoroji, May 30, 1895, NAI, DNP, C-105 (1); Naoroji to Mrs. Pogosky, November 4, 1889, NAI, DNP, N-1 (1530).

11. Frederick W. Emett to Naoroji, January 23, 1894, NAI, DNP, E-48; W. J. Frost to Naoroji, October 11, 1894, NAI, DNP, F-89; W. J. Frost, "What Indian Boys Play At," *Chums*, May 15, 1895, 604.

12. Raymond Blathwayt to Naoroji, December 30, 1897, NAI, DNP, B-153; "Hap-Hazard Vegetarianism: A Talk with Mr. Dadabhai Naoroji," *Vegetarian*, January 29, 1898, 73.

13. "Hap-Hazard Vegetarianism," 73.

14. Rev. Thomas Thomson, "Crawfurd, John, F.R.S.," in *A Biographical Dictionary of Eminent Scotsmen* (London: Blackie and Son, 1870), 592–593.

15. John Crawfurd, "On the Physical and Mental Characteristics of the European and the Asiatic Races of Man," in *Transactions of the Ethnological Society of London (1861)* (London: John Murray, 1867), 5:59, 60, 64, 71, 76–77.

16. "The European and Asiatic Races," in *Essays, Speeches, Addresses and Writings (on Indian Politics) of the Hon'ble Dadabhai Naoroji*, ed. Chunilal Lallubhai Parekh (Bombay: Caxton Printing Works, 1887), 1, 3, 2, 5.

17. Ibid., 1–5.

18. Ibid., 14, 11.

19. Ibid., 16–17.

20. "Reviews," *Medical Times and Gazette*, May 11, 1867, 506.

21. "Admission of Educated Natives into the Indian Civil Service (East India Association)," in *Essays, Speeches, Addresses and Writings (on Indian Politics) of the Hon'ble Dadabhai Naoroji*, ed. Chunilal Lallubhai Parekh (Bombay: Caxton Printing Works, 1887), 81; "A Note Submitted to the Education Commission of 1882 by Dadabhai Naoroji," in *Evidence Taken by the Bombay Provincial Committee, and Memorials Addressed to the Education Commission (Bombay, Vol II)* (Calcutta: Superintendent of Government Printing, India, 1884), 96.

22. Naoroji to Behramji Malabari, October 12, 1888, NAI, DNP, N-1 (1225).

23. R. & J. Beck Ltd. to Naoroji, January 31, 1898, NAI, DNP, B-72 (5); William Hutchinson & Co. to Naoroji, October 28, 1901, NAI, DNP, H-213 (8); F. W. Ellis to Naoroji, April 24, 1901, NAI, DNP, E-42; A. Jacobs to Naoroji, April 2, 1907, NAI, DNP, J-4.

24. K. S. Bonnerjee to Naoroji, January 22, 1893, NAI, DNP, B-178; Rustom P. Masani, *Dadabhai Naoroji: The Grand Old Man of India* (London: G. Allen & Unwin, 1939), 76–77; Naoroji diary, April 28, 1886, NAI, DNP, Part V, 3–21; Lord Harris to Lord Lansdowne, December 8, 1893, BL, Lord Harris Papers, MSS Eur E256/7.

25. Masani, *Dadabhai Naoroji*, 145–46; Bhikhaiji Cama to Naoroji, January 27, 1906, NAI, DNP, C-13 (1); Mancherji Bhownaggree to Naoroji, June 5, 1892, RPPM; Naoroji to Messrs. Jeremiah Lyon & Co., June 2, 1891, RPPM; Aziz Ahmad to Naoroji, March 22, 1897, NAI, DNP, A-91 (37).

26. W. C. Bonnerjee to William Wedderburn, October 17, 1904, NAI, DNP, B-180 (37); Bhownaggree to Naoroji, Christmas greeting card, December 1891, NAI, DNP, B-130 (3); "Commercial Conversations. XXXVI.—With Mr. Dadabhai Naoroji, M.P.," *Commerce*, March 7, 1894, 361, in NAI, DNP, Part IV, 80.

27. In 2013, English Heritage unsuccessfully attempted to place a "blue plaque" historical marker at 72 Anerley Park. M. J. C. Mukerji, "Dadabhai Naoroji: A Character Sketch," *Hindustan Review*, September 1910, in NAI, DNP, Part IV, 207; "A Day of My Life—No. 26—Mr. Dadabhai Naoroji, Indian Patriot and Statesman," *Household Words*, June 27, 1903, 519, in NAI, DNP, Part IV, 148; R. M. H. Griffith to Naoroji, NAI, DNP, G-116 (257).

28. Griffith to Naoroji, July 3, 1889, NAI, DNP, G-116 (8). I am grateful to Sandra Golding, Griffith's great-great-granddaughter, for providing me with biographical information from her research of her family's history.

29. Griffith to Naoroji, telegram, May 13, 1890, NAI, DNP, G-116 (155); Griffith to Naoroji, telegram, September 25, 1890, NAI, DNP, G-116 (212); Griffith to Naoroji, April 13, 1891, NAI, DNP, G-116 (315).

30. Griffith to Naoroji, April 26, 1890, NAI, DNP, G-116 (154); Griffith to Naoroji, November 15, 1891, NAI, DNP, G-116 (430); Griffith to Naoroji, July 31, 1893, NAI, DNP, G-116 (780); Griffith to Naoroji, September 6, 1893, NAI, DNP, G-116 (1795); "Ninth Congress—Lahore—1893, Presidential Address," in *Speeches and Writings of Dadabhai Naoroji*, ed. G. A. Natesan, 2nd ed. (Madras: G. A. Natesan & Co., 1917), 23.

31. Naoroji to Malabari, May 11, 1888, NAI, DNP, N-1 (1010).

32. Naoroji to Malabari, August 16, 1888, NAI, DNP, N-1 (1116).

33. Vahid Jalil Fozdar, "Constructing the 'Brother': Freemasonry, Empire and Nationalism in India, 1840–1925," Ph.D. diss., University of California, Berkeley, 2001, 435–439; Alfred F. Goode to Naoroji, November 13, 1894, NAI, DNP, C-293 (2); Goode to Naoroji, November 30, 1894, NAI, DNP, G-13 (1); T. Cumner [?],October 11, 1900, NAI, DNP, C-295; Democratic Club, flyer, n.d., NAI, DNP, D-76 (1); Edward R. Pease to Naoroji, July 7, 1906, NAI, DNP, F-1 (4); F. A. Creed to Naoroji, November 8, 1894, NAI, DNP, F-86; Griffith to Naoroji, September 1, 1893, NAI, DNP, G-116 (803); Naoroji to Griffith, March 16, 1892, NAI, DNP, N-1 (2252); Griffith to Naoroji, May 10, 1895, RPPM.

34. Annie Chapman to Naoroji, December 8, 1899, NAI, DNP, C-107 (1); John Chapman to Naoroji, July 25, 1892, NAI, DNP, F-34 (26); Thomas Adams to Naoroji, July 27, 1904, NAI, DNP, A-13 (2); Buenos Ayres [*sic*] Electric Tramways Company to Naoroji, March 2, 1900, NAI, DNP, B-249.

35. London Socialist Sunday School Union, n.d. [1903], NAI, DNP, L-111; First of May Celebration Committee, April 29, 1907, NAI, DNP, F-39.

36. Naoroji to Wedderburn, July 16, 1886, NAI, DNP, N-1 (617); Naoroji to Malabari, August 25, 1887, NAI, DNP, N-1 (760); "Mr. Dadabhai Naoroji's—A Contradiction," n.d., in NAI, DNP, Part III, G-20; *Dadabhai Naoroji Correspondence*, ed. R. P. Patwardhan, vol. 2, part 1 (New Delhi: Allied, 1977), xxxiii.

37. Naoroji to Malabari, November 11, 1887, NAI, DNP, N-1 (849); Malabari to Naoroji, September 25, 1887, NAI, DNP, M-32 (155); Malabari to Naoroji, August 3, 1886, NAI, DNP, M-32 (102); Gopal Krishna Gokhale to Naoroji, May 3, 1897, NAI, DNP, G-64 (4); Gokhale to Naoroji, September 29, 1899, NAI, DNP, G-64 (13).

38. "Vegetarian Dishes," London Vegetarian Society, recipes, n.d., NAI, DNP, Part III, A-206 (1); Naoroji to P. J. Smith, January 15, 1898, NMML, DNP, II, #635; R. K. Tarachand to Naoroji, May 17, 1906, NAI, DNP, T-11 (11).

39. Masani, *Dadabhai Naoroji*, 71, 87.

40. Naoroji to family, June 11, 1888, NAI, DNP, Part II, 29 (1888). The precise address of Batliboi House was 16 Trebovir Road. "Sedition. Failure of Miss Perin A. D. Naoroji, a Friend of the Anti-British Extremist in Paris, to Obtain an Appointment in the Bikaner State. Precautionary Measures to Prevent Her Employment in Rajputana," June 1911, NAI, Foreign Department proceedings, 48, deposit.

41. "Indians in England," *Indian Magazine*, February 1887, 57; Rozina Visram, *Asians in Britain: 400 Years of History* (London: Pluto Press, 2002), 92; Malabari to Naoroji, June 6, 1890, NAI, DNP, M-32 (214).

42. Ahmad, "Testimonials and Criticisms," n.d., NAI, DNP, A-91 (39); Ahmad to Naoroji, November 20, 1891, NAI, DNP, A-91 (51); E. Horscroft to Naoroji, April 21, 1898, NAI, DNP, H-187.

43. Mynie Bell to Naoroji, December 3, 1887, NAI, DNP, B-85 (18); Naoroji diary, April 19, 1886, NAI, DNP, Part V, 3–21; Naoroji to Wedderburn, August 6, 1886, RPPM.

44. Romesh Chunder Dutt to Naoroji, September 7, 1900, NAI, DNP, D-161 (11); Dutt to Naoroji, September 21, 1900, NAI, DNP, D-161 (12); Dutt to Naoroji, September 25, 1900, NAI, DNP, D-161 (13); Dutt to Naoroji, May 2, 1903, NAI, DNP, D-161 (35); W. E. Williams to Naoroji, August 15, 1887, NMML, DNP, #12; Naoroji to Malabari, January 27, 1888, RPPM; Nandalal Ghosh to Naoroji, n.d., NAI, DNP, G-41 (1); Ahmad to Naoroji, September 5, 1891, NAI, DNP, A-91 (10); Ahmad to Naoroji, October 2, 1891, NAI, DNP, A-91 (44).

45. "Syllabus of Meetings," Edinburgh Indian Association, flyer, 1901 [?], NAI, DNP, E-15; W. W. Hunter to Naoroji, May 26, 1888, NAI, DNP, H-207 (9); Pandit Uma Sankar Misra and Manmohan Ghose to Naoroji, May 29, 1888, NAI, DNP, N-49 (1).

46. John R. Hinnells, *Zoroastrians in Britain* (Oxford: Clarendon Press, 1996), 107; Nasarvanji M. Cooper to Naoroji, March 12, 1906, NAI, DNP, C-249 (3). While technically incorrect, as it refers to the day before the new year, the word "pateti" was regularly deployed to describe new year's day of the Parsi Shenshai calendar.

47. Shapoorji A. Kapadia to Naoroji, April 23, 1906, NAI, DNP, P-45; Rustom H. Appoo to Naoroji, n.d., NAI, DNP, E-17; Appoo to Naoroji, May 14, 1906, NAI, DNP, E-17 (1); Appoo to Naoroji, May 31, 1906, NAI, DNP, E-17 (3); "Parsee Editor's Tragic Death," *Daily Telegraph and Deccan Herald*, August 19, 1911, 5.

48. "Parsee Editor and Ex-M.P.," *Daily Telegraph and Deccan Herald*, August 14, 1911, 5. Thanks to Alexandra Buhler for this reference. K. D. Cooper to Naoroji, December 8, 1901, NAI, DNP, C-248; Shankar Abaji Bhisey to Naoroji, July 16, 1909, NAI, DNP, B-126 (60).

49. S. Chelliah to Naoroji, February 14, 1902, NAI, DNP, C-125; Arthur Howell to Naoroji, July 1894, NAI, DNP, H-185; B. Collie to Naoroji, August 4, 1893, NAI, DNP, C-217; Bhisey to Naoroji, June 13, 1901, NAI, DNP, B-126 (7).

50. Chelliah to Naoroji, February 14, 1902, NAI, DNP, C-125.

51. Isidore Harris, "An Indian Reformer on Indian Affairs: Mr. Dadabhai Naoroji Interviewed," *Great Thoughts*, August 31, 1895, in NAI, DNP, Part III, G-17.

52. Masani, *Dadabhai Naoroji*, 7; Jivanlal Desai to Naoroji, October 6, 1883, NAI, DNP, D-87.

53. Hormusjee Ardeseer Wadya to Naoroji, March 17, 1896, NAI, DNP, W-12 (13); Naoroji to Dutt, January 31, 1871, NAI, Romesh Chunder Dutt Papers, serial no. 1; Dinsha Davar to Naoroji, August 27, 1897, NAI, DNP, D-42 (1).

54. Dutt to Naoroji, May 8, 1898, NAI, DNP, D-161 (2); S. Ghosh to Naoroji, June 9, 1902, NAI, DNP, G-42.

55. Many of these loans were probably never repaid. Four years after loaning money to Kelkar, Naoroji was still sending him reminders, written in "strong terms," about repayment. N. B. Wagle to Naoroji, October 16, 1902, NAI, DNP, W-14 (17); S. P. Kelkar to Naoroji, November 22, 1900, NAI, DNP, K-18; Kelkar to Naoroji, August 20, 1901, NAI, DNP, K-18 (8); Ahmad and Naoroji, bill, October 1, 1891, NAI, DNP, A-91 (14); G. K. Gadgil to Naoroji, May 19, 1905, NAI,

DNP, G-2 (5); Gokhale to Naoroji, July 12, 1897, NAI, DNP, G-64 (6); Ghose to Naoroji, May 23, 1894, NAI, DNP, G-39a (1); S. Chapman to Naoroji, July 7, 1894, NAI, DNP, C-112; George Edalji to Naoroji, January 1, 1903, NAI, DNP, E-10 (1).

56. Bhownaggree to Naoroji, June 5, 1892, RPPM; "Action against an Indian Prince," *Times of India*, July 28, 1891, 7; "Action against the Thakur of Gondal," *Times of India*, August 16, 1892, 6; Naoroji to Malabari, August 12, 1891, NAI, DNP, N-1 (1949); Dadabhoy Cursetjee Furdoonjee to Naoroji, November 2, 1901, NAI, DNP, F-94 (1); Furdoonjee to Naoroji, April 5, 1902, NAI, DNP, F-94 (2).

57. Malabari to Naoroji, April 30, 1886, NAI, DNP, M-32 (89); Naoroji to Shapurji D. Bhabha, January 30, 1890, NAI, DNP, N-1 (1339); J. B. Dubash to Naoroji, April 22, 1898, NAI, DNP, D-148 (1).

58. C. D. Furdoonjee to Naoroji, June 6, 1890, NAI, DNP, F-93.

59. "Report on a Meeting of the London Indian Society," January 2, 1899, BL, IOR, L/PJ/6/499, File 66.

60. Bhisey to Naoroji, June 13, 1901, NAI, DNP, B-126 (7); Bhisey to Naoroji, April 11, 1906, NAI, DNP, B-126 (43).

61. Joseph Baptista to Naoroji, June 26, 1899, NAI, DNP, B-42 (4); Baptista to Naoroji, March 8, 1901, NAI, DNP, B-42 (10).

5. The Central Finsbury Campaign

1. "Second Indian National Congress," in *Essays, Speeches, Addresses and Writings (on Indian Politics) of the Hon'ble Dadabhai Naoroji*, ed. Chunilal Lallubhai Parekh (Bombay: Caxton Printing Works, 1887), 332.

2. The last reference that I have found is from Dadabhai Naoroji's letter to John Slagg of February 8, 1885: "Never can a foreign rule be anything but a curse to any country, excepting only so far as it approaches a Native Rule." NAI, DNP, N-1 (244).

3. "The First Indian National Congress," in *Essays, Speeches, Addresses and Writings (on Indian Politics) of the Hon'ble Dadabhai Naoroji*, ed. Chunilal Lallubhai Parekh (Bombay: Caxton Printing Works, 1887), 323; S. R. Mehrotra, "Dadabhai Naoroji and the Demand for Swaraj," unpublished ms., n.d., 8.

4. Rustom P. Masani, *Dadabhai Naoroji: The Grand Old Man of India* (London: G. Allen & Unwin, 1939), 97; Naoroji to Allan Octavian Hume, November 11, 1887, NAI, DNP, N-1 (849); M. Viraraghavachariar to Naoroji, February 29, 1888, NAI, DNP, C-113.

5. Henry Lee to Naoroji, August 6, 1887, NMML, DNP, III, #747; J. George Brooke to Naoroji, January 9, 1888, NAI, DNP, B-228; Archibald Duff to Naoroji, February 17, 1888, NMML, DNP, #293.

6. F. L. Crelly to Naoroji, June 5, 1888, NMML, DNP, I, #129; G. E. Wade to Naoroji, November 24, 1887, NAI, DNP, III, #747.

7. Sumita Mukherjee, "'Narrow-Majority' and 'Bow-and-Agree': Public Attitudes towards the Elections of the First Asian MPs in Britain, Dadabhai Naoroji and Mancherjee Merwanjee Bhownagree, 1885–1906," *Journal of the Oxford University*

Historical Society 2 (2004): 7–8; Jonathan Schneer, London 1900: The Imperial Metropolis (New Haven: Yale University Press, 1999), 257–259. In a remarkably similar instance, we notice strong working-class support for John Archer, a black political activist from Battersea in the early twentieth century. These supporters loudly protested when the British media made an issue of Archer's race. In 1909, Archer became the mayor of Battersea, the first black individual to hold this position in a London borough. See Barry Kosmin, "Political Identity in Battersea," in Living in South London: Perspectives on Battersea, 1871–1981, ed. Sandra Wallman (Aldershot: Gower, 1982), 17–51.

8. James Blackshaw to Naoroji, May 30, 1898, NAI, DNP, B-148.

9. John Page Hopps, "Hottentots, Criminals and Black Men," Daily News, December 6, 1888; "Lord Salisbury and Mr. Naoroji," Reynolds's Newspaper, December 30, 1888.

10. The Hungarian leader referred to by Watson was most likely Louis Kossuth. "Mr. Naoroji in Newcastle," Times of India, March 11, 1889, 6; "Mr. Dadabhai Naoroji at Loughborough," Nottingham Evening Post, March 19, 1889, 4.

11. "Mr. Dadabhai Naoroji's Trouble: Lord Salisbury's Explanation," Times of India, January 8, 1889, 6; The Indian National Congress Cartoons from the Hindi Punch (from 1886 to 1901) (Bombay: Bombay Samachar Press, 1901); "Lord Rosebery in Edinburgh," Times, February 20, 1889, 9; "Lord Salisbury's 'Black Man': Banquet to Mr. Naoroji," Freeman's Journal, January 22, 1889.

12. Caroline Bressey, "Victorian 'Anti-Racism' and Feminism in Britain," Women: A Cultural Review 21, no. 3 (2010): 279–291; Hopps, "Hottentots, Criminals and Black Men."

13. Robert Spence Watson to Naoroji, December 29, 1888, NAI, DNP, D-77.

14. Naoroji to William Digby, August 16, 1888, RPPM; J. R. Bennett to Naoroji, September 18, 1888, NAI, DNP, H-136. The attempt to free Fenian revolutionaries was known as the "Clerkenwell Outrage," which killed several innocent people. See Andrew Whitehead, "Red London: Radicals and Socialists in Late-Victorian Clerkenwell," Socialist History 18 (2000): 4, 5–6, 3, 1, 9.

15. "Correspondence: The Split in Central Finsbury," Weekly News and Chronicle, September 22, 1888, 3.

16. Naoroji to Hume, April 5, 1888, RPPM; "Mr. Naoroji and His Candidature for Central Finsbury," Weekly News and Chronicle, September 15, 1888, 2; "Gossip," Weekly News and Chronicle, September 1, 1888, 4; "Central Finsbury: No Candidate Yet Properly Selected," Star, August 18, 1888, 2; Naoroji to family, n.d., RPPM.

17. "Central Finsbury: Some More Facts about and Protests against Mr. Naoroji's Selection," Star, August 20, 1888, 2; "Central Finsbury: No Candidate Yet Properly Selected," 2.

18. "Correspondence: The Split in Central Finsbury," 3; W. Martin Wood, "Central Finsbury," Star, August 23, 1888, 4; "East Finsbury," Star, September 11, 1888, 2; "The Central Finsbury Liberal and Radical Association: Selection of a Candidate. Stormy Proceedings," Weekly News and Chronicle, September 8, 1888, 2. We know very little about Richard Eve, who was a native of Kidderminster and a

solicitor by training. A profile in a Liberal Party organ described Eve as "one of the best known men in London, one of the truest and best Liberals the party has in it, one of the most unselfish and most ardent politicians ... If any man deserves a safe seat for the work he has done for Liberalism, it is Richard Eve." Eve had tried and failed to get into Parliament four times before his attempt at Central Finsbury. *The New House of Commons, with Biographical Notices of Its Members and of Nominated Candidates. 1885* (London: George Edward Wright, 1885), 80; "Mr. Richard Eve," *Liberal and Radical,* October 13, 1888, 227.

19. "What We Think," *Star,* August 17, 1888, 1; "What We Think," *Star,* August 18, 1888, 1; "Occasional Notes," *Pall Mall Gazette,* August 23, 1888, 4. The *Weekly News and Chronicle* quoted a general committee member as saying "Mr. Eve has 500 shares in the *Star.*" Notably, in its response to the *Pall Mall Gazette,* the *Star* denied that it was representing the interests of an individual, but at the same time completely avoided the issue of Eve's influence over the paper. "The Central Finsbury Liberal and Radical Association: Selection of a Candidate. Stormy Proceedings," *Weekly News and Chronicle,* September 8, 1888, 2; "What We Think," *Star,* August 24, 1888, 1.

20. "What We Think," August 18, 1888, 1.

21. "Correspondence: Selection of a Liberal Candidate for Central Finsbury," *Weekly News and Chronicle,* August 25, 1888, 3; "Central Finsbury: No Candidate Yet Properly Selected," 2; "The Candidature of Mr. Naoroji," *Weekly News and Chronicle,* September 29, 1888, 5.

22. John Burns to Naoroji, September 6, 1888, NMML, DNP, I, #137; "The Candidature of Mr. Naoroji," 5. Schnadhorst also met with Naoroji on September 5, counseling him "in very strong terms" not to quit the Finsbury race. If he quit, he would lose the confidence of supportive power brokers there, and thus would "not have any chance with any other Constituency." Francis Schnadhorst to Digby, August 18, 1888, BL, IOR, WDP, MSS Eur D 767/1/121; Schnadhorst to Naoroji, August 18, 1888, BL, IOR, WDP, MSS Eur D 767/1/122; Naoroji to Digby, May 25, 1891, BL, IOR, WDP, MSS Eur D 767/1/93–94.

23. Richard Eve decided to instead accept the Liberal candidacy for St. Georges in the East, a constituency in the Docklands. R. M. H. Griffith to Schnadhorst, July 1, 1890, NAI, DNP, G-116 (175); "Notes by 'Invisible,'" *Finsbury and Holborn Guardian,* January 11, 1890, 5; Griffith to Schnadhorst, July 1, 1890, NAI, DNP, G-116 (175); Central Finsbury Liberal and Radical Council, handbill, August 6, 1891, NAI, DNP, C-79 (2).

24. "The Central Finsbury Liberals," *Finsbury and Holborn Guardian,* January 10, 1891.

25. Ford was the husband of the well-known Victorian feminist Florence Fenwick Miller. According to Fenwick Miller's biographer, Ford had been active in Clerkenwell politics since at least 1884, when he was asked to stand for Parliament from Central Finsbury. He subsequently declined the offer, but left open the possibility that he would run in the future. He was elected to the London County Council in 1889. Rosemary T. Van Arsdel, *Florence Fenwick Miller: Victorian Feminist, Journalist, and Educator* (Aldershot: Ashgate, 2001), 214–215. Naoroji to Behramji Malabari, n.d. [most likely January 1891], RPPM.

26. Naoroji to Malabari, n.d. [most likely January 1891], RPPM.

27. Joseph Walton and Alfred Harper, "Central Finsbury Liberal & Radical Association: Report of the Special Committee on Ward Elections, 1891," March 20, 1891, in BL, IOR, WDP, MSS Eur D 767/6; "A New Candidate for Central Finsbury: A Chat with Mr. F. A. Ford," *Finsbury and Holborn Guardian*, May 23, 1891; "Notes by 'Invisible,'" *Finsbury and Holborn Guardian*, February 21, 1891, 5.

28. Naoroji to Digby, June 11, 1891, BL, IOR, WDP, MSS Eur D 767/1/90–92; Naoroji to Digby, April 23, 1891, BL, IOR, WDP, MSS Eur D 767/1/15–16.

29. Naoroji to Digby, May 4, 1891, BL, IOR, WDP, MSS Eur D 767/1/24–25; Naoroji to Michael Davitt, February 16, 1892, RPPM; Davitt to Naoroji, February 18, 1892, RPPM.

30. Digby to Naoroji, August 18, 1891, RPPM; Naoroji to Rustomji Dhanjibhai (R. D.) Mehta, March 3, 1887, RPPM; Malabari to Naoroji, August 29, 1887, NAI, DNP, M-32 (149); Naoroji, personal note, January 28, 1892, RPPM.

31. Dayaram Gidumal Shahani, *The Life and Life-Work of Behramji M. Malabari* (Bombay: Bombay Education Society's Press, 1888), xcv. Naoroji had stated his views on the Congress and social reform in his presidential address to the 1886 Calcutta Congress. Malabari responded: "But what do Mr. Dadabhai's remarks on the social question imply? Is it wise to draw a sharp line between social and political progress? It is certainly not consistent; for certain political leaders were telling us only last year that the two questions were only branches of one large question." "Editorial Notes," *Indian Spectator*, January 2, 1887, 5–6.

32. "Mr. Dadabhai Naoroji," *Indian Spectator*, March 17, 1889, 215. Legal scholars have noted that the manor of East Greenwich was referenced in many royal charters of American colonies, including those made for the Virginia Company, Hudson's Bay Company, and settlers in New England and the Carolinas. B. H. McPherson, "Revisiting the Manor of East Greenwich," *American Journal of Legal History* 42, no. 1 (January 1998): 35.

33. Naoroji also claimed to have relied upon Charles II's charter "in my paper on the Ilbert Bill." "Mr. Dadabhai Naoroji," 215; Naoroji to Malabari, April 12, 1889 [?], RPPM. An anti-Naoroji power broker, Mr. Shaw, appears to have challenged Naoroji's claim to be on a voting register list in Central Finsbury, prompting a hearing at the Central Finsbury Revision Court. At the hearing, Naoroji's subjecthood was recognized. "Mr. Naoroji's Vote," *Northampton Mercury*, September 26, 1890, 2.

34. "East Finsbury," 2; "Our London Letter (London, September 14, 1888)," *Indian Spectator*, October 7, 1888, 810.

35. Naoroji to Malabari, January 25, 1889, RPPM; Naoroji to Malabari, December 18, 1891, NAI, DNP, N-1 (3190).

36. Malabari, circular, January 27, 1892, NMML, DNP, II, #519; Malabari, circular, December 9, 1891, NMML, DNP, II, #521.

37. "Candidature of Mr. Dadabhai Naoroji," *Kaiser-i-Hind*, January 31, 1892, 3; "Comments," *Tribune*, February 21, 1892, 3; Malabari to Naoroji, February 13, 1892, NAI, DNP, M-32 (281); Griffith to Naoroji, March 7, 1892, NAI, DNP, G-116 (465).

38. Lord Ripon to Malabari, September 23, 1891, BL, Lord Ripon Papers, Add MSS 43616; Malabari, circular, December 9, 1891, NMML, DNP, II, #521; Naoroji to Malabari, March 11, 1892, RPPM; Naoroji to Malabari, February 10, 1892, RPPM.
39. Malabari to Naoroji, n.d., NAI, DNP, M-32 (270); Masani, *Dadabhai Naoroji*, 321. According to Hume, "Bengal gave no more than Rs 11,000" to Ghosh. Hume seemed so concerned about the difficulties of raising funds for Naoroji that, in the course of a lengthy conversation, Malabari "dropped the matter" entirely with him. Malabari to Naoroji, October 12, 1886, NAI, DNP, M-32 (109); Malabari to Naoroji, September 25, 1887, NAI, DNP, M-32 (155).
40. Malabari to Naoroji, November 16, 1888, NAI, DNP, M-32 (197); Malabari to Naoroji, August 29, 1887, NAI, DNP, M-32 (149); Malabari to Naoroji, August 15, 1887, NAI, DNP, M-32 (147). Tata's donation to a separate Congress fund was, in any case, relatively trifling, totaling Rs. 500. Malabari to Naoroji, March 7, 1887, NAI, DNP, M-32 (130); Jamsetji Tata to Naoroji, November 27, 1889, NAI, DNP, T-20 (1); Naoroji to Malabari, September 30, 1887, RPPM; Malabari to Naoroji, August 29, 1887, NAI, DNP, M-32 (149).
41. Malabari mentioned arranging meetings for Naoroji's "big affair"—his planned parliamentary run—with Sheikh Bavdinbhai, vizier of Junagadh, Manibhai Jasbhai, diwan of Kutch, and "the Rao," most likely Khengarji III of Kutch. A few days later, Malabari mentioned the ruling jam sahib of Jamnagar. Malabari also encouraged Naoroji to pay a visit to Kathiawar. Malabari to Naoroji, April 2, 1885, NAI, DNP, M-32 (51); Malabari to Naoroji, April 15, 1885, NAI, DNP, M-32 (56).
42. Masani, *Dadabhai Naoroji*, 321, 325; Malabari to Naoroji, February 23, 1888, RPPM; Malabari to Naoroji, November 29, 1890, NAI, DNP, M-32 (222); Malabari to Naoroji, January 3, 1891, NAI, DNP, M-32 (226a); Naoroji to Bhagvatsinhji, August 10, 1891, RPPM.
43. Naoroji to Malabari, March 4, 1892, NAI, DNP, N-1 (2232); Malabari to Naoroji, March 26, 1892, RPPM; Naoroji to Bhagvatsinhji, February 14, 1892, NAI, DNP, N-1 (2212).
44. Naoroji to Bhagvatsinhji, March 17, 1892, NAI, DNP, N-1 (2254).
45. "The General Election," *Standard*, June 23, 1892, 3.
46. Ripon to Naoroji, March 17, 1892, RPPM; J. E. Searle to Naoroji, April 30, 1892, RPPM.
47. Naoroji to Ripon, March 18, 1892, NAI, DNP, N-1 (2256a); Naoroji to Digby, April 29, 1892, BL, IOR, WDP, MSS Eur D 767/1/152–3; Griffith to Arnold Morley, May 6, 1892, NAI, DNP, G-116 (480).
48. Naoroji to Digby, June 11, 1892, BL, IOR, WDP, MSS Eur D 767/1/95–96; H. E. Fox-Bourne to Naoroji, April 14, 1892, RPPM; *The First Indian Member of the Imperial Parliament, Being a Collection of the Main Incidents Relating to the Election of Mr. Dadabhai Naoroji to Parliament* (Madras: Addison & Co., 1892), 31.
49. Naoroji to Digby, June 12, 1892, BL, IOR, WDP, MSS Eur D 767/1/97–98.
50. By the mid-1890s Ford had most likely divorced Florence Fenwick Miller, and thereafter slipped into obscurity. Van Arsdel, *Florence Fenwick Miller*, 215; "A Great Demonstration," *Holborn and Finsbury Guardian*, June 18, 1892, 2; Griffith to

Naoroji, June 17, 1892, NAI, DNP, G-116 (499); Griffith to Naoroji, June 17, 1892, NAI, DNP, G-116 (498).

51. Henry Mundy to Naoroji, June 27, 1892, NAI, DNP, C-82.

52. It appears that Pankhurst was to address a meeting at a local school; however, she had to cancel due to sickness. Health also prevented Nightingale from doing anything. "I am entirely a prisoner to my rooms from illness," she responded to Naoroji. Emmeline Pankhurst to Naoroji, June 23, 1892, NAI, DNP, P-20; Florence Nightingale to Naoroji, June 24, 1892, NAI, DNP, N-107 (1); "Editorial Notes," *Woman's Herald,* January 9, 1892, 8; W. Bethell to Naoroji, July 12, 1892, NAI, DNP, C-82 (17); Griffith to Naoroji, June 17, 1892, NAI, DNP, G-116 (499); Malabari to Naoroji, July 7, 1892, NAI, DNP, M-32 (295); Masani, *Dadabhai Naoroji,* 276, 278–279.

53. Masani, *Dadabhai Naoroji,* 278–279; Frederick Penton, "To the Electors of Central Finsbury (Clerkenwell)," handbill, University of Bristol Library, Special Collections, Arts and Social Sciences, Restricted Material 668; "Central Finsbury Parliamentary Election, 1892," *Finsbury and Holborn Guardian,* July 2, 1892, 4.

54. Edward Breen to Naoroji, June 30, 1892, NAI, DNP, B-204; George Bateman to Naoroji, July 7, 1892, NAI, DNP, B-61.

55. Masani, *Dadabhai Naoroji,* 282, 323; Political Sub-Committee Minutes, July 2, 1892, National Liberal Club Papers, National Liberal Club; Malabari to Naoroji, July 7, 1892, NAI, DNP, M-32 (295).

6. Member for India

1. There are, however, scattered references to Naoroji being referred to as the "Grand Old Man" before 1892. See, for example, *Essays, Speeches, Addresses and Writings (on Indian Politics) of the Hon'ble Dadabhai Naoroji,* ed. Chunilal Lallubhai Parekh (Bombay: Caxton Printing Works, 1887), 8. G. P. Pillai, *Indian Congressmen* (Madras: Price Current Press, 1899), 1.

2. "Dadabhai Naoroji, M.P.," *Kaiser-i-Hind,* July 10, 1892, 1; Thomas Davies to Dadabhai Naoroji, July 7, 1892, NAI, DNP, D-50.

3. *The First Indian Member of the Imperial Parliament, Being a Collection of the Main Incidents Relating to the Election of Mr. Dadabhai Naoroji to Parliament* (Madras: Addison & Co., 1892), 111, 112, 114.

4. "Central Finsbury Elections," December 13, 1892, National Archives of the United Kingdom, HO 45/9862/B13373.

5. Pillai, *Indian Congressmen,* 1.

6. Naoroji, election pamphlet, July 5, 1895, NAI, DNP, F-34 (37); Rustom P. Masani, *Dadabhai Naoroji: The Grand Old Man of India* (London: G. Allen & Unwin, 1939), 325; R. V. Barrow et al., February 18, 1895, NAI, DNP, H-178 (1); Christianna Cameron to Naoroji, July 23, 1893, NAI, DNP, C-31; Herbert G. Brooks to Naoroji, July 16, 1892, NAI, DNP, F-34 (22); Amalgamated Society of Railway Servants to Naoroji, October 14, 1894, NAI, DNP, A-38 (1); Elizabeth Clarke Wolstenholme Elmy to Naoroji, March 6, 1894, NAI, DNP, E-44; Charles H. Garland to Naoroji, February 16, 1895, NAI, DNP, P-186 (3).

7. M. Viraraghavachariar to Naoroji, February 9, 1893, NAI, DNP, C-113 (1); "The Professorship of Sanscrit at Madras College," March 3, 1893, *Parliamentary Debates*, vol. 9, Fourth Series (London, 1893), cols. 958–959; "The British Resident at Hyderabad," March 30, 1893, *Parliamentary Debates*, vol. 10, Fourth Series (London, 1893), cols. 1494–1495.

8. Aziz Ahmad to Naoroji, newspaper clipping from *Asia*, n.d. [late September 1892], NAI, DNP, A-91 (31); editor, *Madagascar News*, circular, October 21, 1892, NAI, DNP, M-6; Edward Gibbs to Naoroji, December 7, 1892, NAI, DNP, G-45; Mola Kadibhoy Alibhoy to Naoroji, September 24, 1894, NAI, DNP, uncataloged item; "Alleged Outrage on British Indians in Madagascar," *Parliamentary Debates*, vol. 28, Fourth Series (London, 1894), col. 447.

9. Haji Ojer Ally to Naoroji, October 24, 1892, NAI, DNP, A-35; Haji Mohamed Haji Dada & Co. to Naoroji, October 28, 1892, NAI, DNP, H-3 (1).

10. Sadly, this is not among the twelve of Gandhi's letters that survive in the Naoroji Papers. It has presumably been lost. Masani, *Dadabhai Naoroji*, 468–469; Ramachandra Guha, *Gandhi before India* (New Delhi: Allen Lane, 2013), 76.

11. Henry Hyndman to Naoroji, June 9, 1900, NAI, DNP, H-221 (79); Naoroji to Michael Davitt, October 2, 1894, Trinity College, Dublin, Michael Davitt Papers, 9347/514; Jennifer Regan-Lefebvre, *Cosmopolitan Nationalism in the Victorian Empire: Ireland, India and the Politics of Alfred Webb* (Houndmills: Palgrave Macmillan, 2009), 150–151; Alfred Webb to Naoroji, August 27, 1895, NAI, DNP, W-41 (1).

12. Masani, *Dadabhai Naoroji*, 81, 362–363; S. R. Mehrotra, *A History of the Indian National Congress* (New Delhi: Vikas Publications, 1995), 99; "Formation of an Indian Party in Parliament," *India*, August 1, 1893, 241.

13. R. M. H. Griffith to Naoroji, October 21, 1892, NAI, DNP, G-116 (553); Naoroji to Lord Reay, March 16, 1894, NAI, DNP, N-1 (2509); "East India (Civil and Military Services)—Resolution," March 28, 1893, *Parliamentary Debates*, 1893, vol. 10, cols. 1387, 1388, 1386, 1384–1385.

14. "Address in Answer to Her Majesty's Most Gracious Speech," August 9, 1892, *Parliamentary Debates*, vol. 7, Fourth Series (London, 1892), cols. 260–261; "Natives of India and the Civil Service," *Amrita Bazar Patrika*, July 30, 1893, 1; *The Duties of Local Indian Associations in Connection with the London Association* (London: W. Clowes & Sons, 1868), 6; Tejas Parasher, "Self-Rule and the State in Indian Political Thought, 1880–1950," Ph.D. diss., University of Chicago, 2019, 52; "Mr. Dadabhai Naoroji, M.P., on India," *Pioneer*, January 5, 1893, 3.

15. Masani, *Dadabhai Naoroji*, 335–336.

16. "Civil Services (East India) Bill," March 1, 1893, *Parliamentary Debates*, 1893, vol. 9, col. 764; *Amrita Bazar Patrika*, June 11, 1893, 2; "Indian Civil Service Examinations," April 13, 1893, *Parliamentary Debates*, vol. 11, Fourth Series (London, 1893), col. 202.

17. "Civil Service of India (Examination)—Resolution," June 2, 1893, *Parliamentary Debates*, vol. 13, Fourth Series (London, 1893), cols. 116, 113.

18. Ibid., cols. 124, 120, 123, 139, 138.

19. Ibid., cols. 127, 129, 127–128.

20. "The Indian National Movement," *Bombay Gazette*, January 16, 1894, in *India and Mr. Dadabhai Naoroji: An Account of the Demonstrations Held in His Honour as M.P.*

for Central Finsbury, during His Visit to India (Bombay: Commercial Press, 1898), 111–112.

21. "Indian Civil Service Examinations," *Pioneer,* June 6, 1893, 1; "Indian Civil Service Examinations," *Pioneer,* June 7, 1893, 1; *Pioneer,* June 8, 1893, 1; *Indian Spectator,* June 11, 1893, in NNR, Bombay, June 17, 1893, BL, IOR, L/R/5/148.

22. Ardeshir Naoroji to Naoroji, January 22, 1890, NAI, DNP, Part II, 9 (1890); Masani, *Dadabhai Naoroji,* 338; Behramji Malabari to Naoroji, October 14, 1893, NAI, DNP, M-32 (360). Ardeshir and Virbai's children were Meher (b. 1881), Gosi (b. 1884), Jal (b. 1886), Nurgis (b. 1887), Perin (b. 1888), Sarosh (b. 1891), Kershasp (b. 1893), and Khurshed (b. 1894).

23. Malabari to Naoroji, October 14, 1893, NAI, DNP, M-32 (360); Griffith to Fram M. Dadina, October 13, 1893, NAI, DNP, G-16 (831).

24. Malabari to Naoroji, October 14, 1893, NAI, DNP, M-32 (360).

25. Malabari to Naoroji, May 6, 1893, NAI, DNP, M-32 (337); Malabari to Naoroji, July 7, 1893, RPPM; Masani, *Dadabhai Naoroji,* 335.

26. Viraraghavachariar to Naoroji, June 28, 1893, NAI, DNP, C-113 (3); Viraraghavachariar to Naoroji, September 20, 1894, NAI, DNP, C-113 (4); Aswini Kumar Datta to Naoroji, July 9, 1893, NAI, DNP, D-39; Madan Mohan Malaviya to Naoroji, August 23, 1893, RPPM; Jivanlal Desai to Naoroji, July 26, 1893, NAI, DNP, D-87 (2); Gopal Krishna Gokhale to Naoroji, November 9, 1894, NAI, DNP, G-64; Raghunath S. Ingle to Naoroji, September 18, 1894, RPPM.

27. *Pioneer,* August 8, 1893, 1; "An Indian 'Agitation,'" *Times,* August 9, 1893, 3.

28. "East India Revenue Accounts," September 20, 1893, *Parliamentary Debates,* vol. 17, Fourth Series (London, 1893), col. 1773.

29. Masani, *Dadabhai Naoroji,* 256; Malabari to Naoroji, August 18, 1893, NAI, DNP, M-32 (352); Naoroji to Malabari, December 6, 1893, NAI, DNP, B-97; John R. McLane, *Indian Nationalism and the Early Congress* (Princeton: Princeton University Press, 1977), 272–273; *India and Mr. Dadabhai Naoroji,* 184, 214, 424.

30. *India and Mr. Dadabhai Naoroji,* 447, 204, xiii.

31. Ibid., 425, 533, 25–26c, 55.

32. *Sudharak,* December 18, 1893, in NNR, Bombay, December 23, 1893, BL, IOR, L/R/5/148; *India and Mr. Dadabhai Naoroji,* 91, 215, 141, 142.

33. *India and Mr. Dadabhai Naoroji,* 215, 216, 172, 173, 174–175.

34. "'The Member for India': Enthusiastic Reception at Lahore," *Manchester Guardian,* December 27, 1893, 5; "Arrival of Mr. Dadabhai Naoroji at Lahore," *Tribune,* December 27, 1893, 2–4.

35. "Ninth Congress—Lahore—1893, Presidential Address," in *Speeches and Writings of Dadabhai Naoroji,* ed. G. A. Natesan, 2nd ed. (Madras: G. A. Natesan & Co., 1917), 21, 55–56, 59.

36. Ibid., 28–29, 31.

37. Ibid., 27, 48, 41, 42, 64.

38. *Amrita Bazar Patrika,* December 10, 1893, 2; *India and Mr. Dadabhai Naoroji,* 354, 499.

39. Naoroji, draft press statement, included in Frederick W. Emett to Naoroji, January 23, 1894, NAI, DNP, E-48; *India and Mr. Dadabhai Naoroji,* 532–33.

40. *Sahachar,* January 3, 1894, in NNR, Bengal, January 13, 1894, BL, IOR, L/R/5/20; "Arrival of Mr. Dadabhai Naoroji at Lahore," 2.
41. *India and Mr. Dadabhai Naoroji,* 405, 406.
42. Ibid., 538, 533.
43. "Proposal to Hold Simultaneous Examinations in India and England for the Indian Civil Service," November 1893, NAI, Home Department, Public, 56–70; Malabari to Naoroji, April 21, 1894, NAI, DNP, M-32 (377).
44. Naoroji to Surendranath Banerjea, July 26, 1894, RPPM.
45. "Resolution," August 14, 1894, *Parliamentary Debates,* 1894, vol. 28, cols. 1055, 1059, 1061.
46. Ibid., cols. 1058, 1056.
47. Ibid., cols. 1063, 1065.
48. "Address in Answer to Her Most Gracious Majesty's Speech," February 12, 1895, *Parliamentary Debates,* vol. 30, Fourth Series (London, 1895), col. 570; "The House of Commons," *Illustrated London News,* February 16, 1895, 195; "Essence of Parliament: Extracted from the Diary of Tory, M.P.," *Punch,* February 23, 1895, 95.
49. Mancherji Bhownaggree to George Birdwood, March 9, 1894, BL, IOR, George Birdwood Papers, MSS Eur F 216/65; Lord Harris to Lord Cross, July 18, 1892, BL, IOR, Lord Harris Papers, MSS Eur E 256/1.
50. Naoroji to Davitt, January 15, 1896, Trinity College, Dublin, Michael Davitt Papers, 9348/529.

7. Swaraj

1. Behramji Malabari to Dadabhai Naoroji, March 18, 1900, NAI, DNP, M-32 (432).
2. W. C. Bonnerjee to Naoroji, April 4, 1901, NAI, DNP, B-180 (9); Gopal Krishna Gokhale to Naoroji, October 8, 1897, NAI, DNP, G-64 (12); Gokhale to Naoroji, August 6, 1897, NAI, DNP, G-64 (7).
3. Romesh Chunder Dutt, *Indian Famines: Their Causes and Prevention* (London: P. S. King & Son, 1901), 2; William Digby, *"Prosperous" British India: A Revelation from Official Records* (London: T. Fisher Unwin, 1901), 128–129; "Famine near Navsari," *Times of India,* March 20, 1900, 4; Henry Hyndman to Naoroji, January 22, 1900, NAI, DNP, H-221 (67); Allan Octavian Hume to Naoroji, n.d. [enclosed in letter from William Wedderburn dated November 8, 1903], NAI, DNP, W-48 (171).
4. Isidore Harris, "An Indian Reformer on Indian Affairs," *Great Thoughts,* August 31, 1895 (republished as pamphlet), NAI, DNP, Part III, G-17.
5. "Mr. Dadabhai Naoroji at Walthamstow: 'India Must Be Bled,'" in Dadabhai Naoroji, *Poverty and Un-British Rule in India* (London: Swan Sonnenschein, 1901), 645; Rustom P. Masani, *Dadabhai Naoroji: The Grand Old Man of India* (London: G. Allen & Unwin, 1939), 444.
6. "Twenty-Second Congress—Calcutta—1906: Presidential Address," in *Speeches and Writings of Dadabhai Naoroji,* ed. G. A. Natesan, 2nd ed. (Madras: G. A. Natesan & Co., 1917), 89.
7. "Royal Commission on the Administration of Expenditure in India," in Dadabhai Naoroji, *Poverty and Un-British Rule in India* (London: Swan Sonnenschein,

1901), 386; *Indian Expenditure Commission* (London: Her Majesty's Stationery Office, 1900), 3:167.

8. Lord George Hamilton to Lord Curzon, May 17, 1900, BL, IOR, Lord George Hamilton Papers, MSS Eur F 123/82; "Lord George Hamilton and 'India,'" *India*, August 18, 1899, 86.

9. Hyndman to Naoroji, October 23, 1896, NAI, DNP, H-221 (7); Hamilton to Lord Elgin, February 5, 1897, BL, IOR, Lord George Hamilton Papers, MSS Eur F 123/79; Tsuzuki Chushichi, *H. M. Hyndman and British Socialism* (London: Oxford University Press, 1961), 126–127.

10. "The Indian Famine—S.D.F. Indignation Meeting," *Justice*, February 20, 1897, 4; Hamilton to Elgin, February 12, 1897, BL, IOR, Lord George Hamilton Papers, MSS Eur F 123/79.

11. Masani, *Dadabhai Naoroji*, 398, 400; Hyndman to Naoroji, March 19, 1898, NAI, DNP, H-221 (54); Hyndman to Naoroji, July 21, 1900, NAI, DNP, H-221 (86).

12. "Copies of Correspondence between the War Office and Mr. Dadabhai Naoroji," pamphlet, in "Correspondence with Mr Dadabhai Naoroji Regarding the Eligibility of Natives of India for Appointments Made by the S of S in England to [1] the Educational Department [2] the Police Department [3] the Public Works Department from Cooper's Hill," BL, IOR, L/PJ/6/555, File 2168.

13. Naoroji to Hamilton, October 12, 1900, in "Correspondence with Mr Dadabhai Naoroji"; Naoroji to Hamilton, February 26, 1901 [included in Naoroji to Lord Morley and Lord Minto, June 25, 1908], NAI, DNP, E-72 (98).

14. "Correspondence between Mr. Dadabhai Naoroji and Lord G. Hamilton," *India*, May 24, 1901, 249, 250; M. Viraraghavachariar to Hamilton, June 20, 1901, in "Comments on Correspondence between the S. of S. and Mr Dadabhai Naoroji," BL, IOR, L/PJ/6/572, File 1174.

15. "Report on a Meeting of the London Indian Society," January 2, 1899, BL, IOR, L/PJ/6/499, File 66; H. J. Tozer, "Meeting of London Indian Society (24 May 1901)," May 25, 1901, in "Resolutions Passed at a Meeting of the London Indian Society," BL, IOR, L/PJ/6/570, File 970.

16. Hume to Naoroji, April 7, 1896, NAI, DNP, H-199 (5); "Trinidad: Coolie Wages," BL, IOR, CO 295/376; Coloured Progressive Association to Naoroji, November 11, 1902, NAI, DNP, C-225; "Dadabhai Naoroji on the Condition of Indians in South Africa," BL, IOR, L/PJ/6/726, File 1798; Naoroji to Joseph Chamberlain, October 11, 1897, Sabarmati Ashram Archives, S.N. 2568.

17. Catherine Impey to Naoroji, June 29, 1893, NAI, DNP, I-9; Caroline Bressey, "A Strange and Bitter Crop: Ida B. Wells' Anti-Lynching Tours, Britain 1893 and 1894," Centre for Capital Punishment Studies, London, 2003; Charles Alexander, "Boston on Lynching," *Christian Recorder*, September 13, 1894.

18. As Jonathan Schneer points out, there were clearly many links between Indian and black activists in London. Naoroji might have known another prominent black activist, Celestine Edwards. Both Edwards and Williams adopted language that was remarkably similar to Naoroji's. Jonathan Schneer, *London 1900: The Imperial Metropolis* (New Haven: Yale University Press, 1999), 210, 216, 224;

Henry Sylvester Williams to Naoroji, July 18, 1900, NAI, DNP, P-15; Rozina Visram, *Asians in Britain: 400 Years of History* (London: Pluto Press, 2002), 137–138.

19. Nico Slate, *Colored Cosmopolitanism: The Shared Struggle for Freedom in the United States and India* (Cambridge, MA: Harvard University Press, 2012).

20. O. P. Austin to Naoroji, n.d. [likely 1901], NAI, DNP, A-84 (3); Naoroji to Austin, January 28, 1901, NAI, DNP, A-84; Hyndman to Naoroji, December 29, 1897, NAI, DNP, H-221 (52); Hyndman to Naoroji, September 17, 1899, NAI, DNP, H-221 (63); Masani, *Dadabhai Naoroji*, 394, 445–446.

21. George Freeman to Naoroji, July 25, 1897, NAI, DNP, F-87. Jabez T. Sunderland, an American Unitarian minister who later corresponded with Mohandas K. Gandhi and Rabindranath Tagore, visited India in 1895–1896 and met with several Indian nationalist leaders. I have been unable to confirm whether Sunderland adopted his stridently anti-imperialist views at this early date. There appears to have been no correspondence between him and Naoroji.

22. James Campbell Ker, *Political Trouble in India (1907–1917)* (Calcutta: Superintendent of Government Printing, India, 1917), 221; Freeman to Naoroji, January 21, 1898, NAI, DNP, F-87 (1); Masani, *Dadabhai Naoroji*, 443; Freeman to Naoroji, February 28, 1899, NAI, DNP, F-87 (24); Freeman to Naoroji, January 30, 1900, NAI, DNP, F-87 (52); Freeman to Naoroji, January 21, 1898, NAI, DNP, F-87 (1).

23. Masani, *Dadabhai Naoroji*, 406, 443–444. As far as I can tell, none of Naoroji's outgoing letters to Freeman have survived. Masani's book therefore provides the only record.

24. Freeman to Naoroji, February 7, 1899, NAI, DNP, F-87 (21); Freeman to Naoroji, June 22, 1899, NAI, DNP, F-87 (36); Edward Atkinson to Naoroji, July 26, 1899, Massachusetts Historical Society, Edward Atkinson Papers, vol. 66; Freeman to Naoroji, April 11, 1899, NAI, DNP, F-87 (30); Freeman to Naoroji, March 17, 1899, NAI, DNP, F-87 (28); Freeman to Naoroji, March 2, 1900, NAI, DNP, F-87 (54).

25. Freeman to Naoroji, December 15, 1898, NAI, DNP, F-87 (16).

26. Freeman to Naoroji, January 17, 1898, NAI, DNP, F-87 (19); Freeman to Naoroji, January 1, 1899, NAI, DNP, F-87 (17); William Jennings Bryan, "England's Policy Is Our Warning," *New York Journal*, January 22, 1899, 29; Freeman to Naoroji, January 30, 1900, NAI, DNP, F-87 (52).

27. Ker, *Political Trouble in India (1907–1917)*, 221–222, 120; Michael Silvestri, *Ireland and India: Nationalism, Empire and Memory* (Basingstoke: Palgrave Macmillan, 2009), 27.

28. Hyndman to Naoroji, January 25, 1899, NAI, DNP, H-221 (59); Naoroji to Hyndman, October 11, 1899, NAI, DNP, N-1 (2668); Hyndman to Naoroji, October 12, 1899, NAI, DNP, H-221 (64); Naoroji to Renwick Seager, September 23, 1900, RPPM.

29. Dadabhai Naoroji, *Poverty and Un-British Rule in India* (London: Swan Sonnenschein, 1901), xii–xiii.

30. M. Sevasly to Naoroji, July 23, 1902, NAI, DNP, S-88a; Joseph Booth to Naoroji, August 20, 1906, NAI, DNP, B-181 (9); Harry Langworthy, *"Africa for the African":*

The Life of Joseph Booth (Blantyre: Christian Literature Association in Malawi, 1996).

31. Naoroji to Romesh Chunder Dutt, July 5, 1903, NAI, Romesh Chunder Dutt Papers, S.N. 4; Naoroji to Dutt, 3 July 1903, NAI, Romesh Chunder Dutt Papers, S.N. 3, S.N. 5.

32. Naoroji to Dutt, July 5, 1903, NAI, Romesh Chunder Dutt Papers, S.N. 4

33. Naoroji to Gokhale, September 16, 1904, NAI, Gopal Krishna Gokhale Papers, File 370, No. 9; Naoroji to Gokhale, October 29, 1905, NAI, Gopal Krishna Gokhale Papers, File 370, No. 12; Naoroji to Gokhale, November 26, 1905, in *Report of the Twenty-First Indian National Congress Held at Benares* (Banaras, 1906), Appendix C, iii.

34. Hyndman to Naoroji, June 24, 1904, NAI, DNP, H-221 (108); Masani, *Dadabhai Naoroji*, 431, 432; Daniel De Leon, *Flashlights of the Amsterdam International Socialist Congress, 1904* (New York: New York Labor News Company, n.d.), ix; Hyndman to Naoroji, June 29, 1904, NAI, DNP, H-221 (110).

35. Quoted in Sumit Sarkar, *The Swadeshi Movement in Bengal, 1903–1908* (New Delhi: People's Publishing House, 1973), 18; Masani, *Dadabhai Naoroji*, 449.

36. *Dadabhai Naoroji Correspondence*, ed. R. P. Patwardhan, vol. 2, part 2 (New Delhi: Allied, 1977), 597–598; Bonnerjee to Wedderburn, October 17, 1904, NAI, DNP, B-180 (37); "Mr. Dadabhai's Latest," *Times of India*, September 6, 1904, 4.

37. "Report on a Meeting of the London Indian Society," January 2, 1899, BL, IOR, L/PJ/6/499, File 66; "The Indian National Congress and Its President: A Professional Politician Once More to the Front," *Indian Sociologist*, November 1906, 41; Harald Fischer-Tiné, *Shyamji Krishnavarma: Sanskrit, Sociology and Anti-Imperialism* (New Delhi: Routledge, 2014), 62; Bhikhaiji Cama to Naoroji, November 2, 1906, NAI, DNP, Part II, 67 (1906).

38. Bal Gangadhar Tilak to Naoroji, September 21, 1906, NAI, DNP, T-73 (1).

39. "Mr. Dadabhai Naoroji and Indian Politics," *Indian Sociologist*, November 1906, 44; "Indians' Admission into British Parliament Retards India's Progress," *Indian Sociologist*, January 1906, 1; "The President-Elect of the Indian National Congress: The Fable of the Monkey and the Two Cats," *Indian Sociologist*, December 1906, 45–46.

40. "The Indian National Congress and Its President," 41. Many radicals found Krishnavarma's views on Naoroji too extreme. Some suggested ulterior motives. Lala Lajpat Rai remarked that "Mr. Shyamji is jealous of Naoroji and wants to pull him down in the estimation of Indians." Fischer-Tiné, *Shyamji Krishnavarma*, 129.

41. Surendranath Banerjea to Naoroji, September 13, 1906, NAI, DNP, B-33 (5); Bhupendranath Basu to Naoroji, September 13, 1906, NAI, DNP, B-59 (2).

42. Masani, *Dadabhai Naoroji*, 481–491; A. Birrell to Wedderburn, March 19, 1905, NAI, DNP, B-144 (1); "Monday's Polling," *Daily Mail*, January 16, 1906; Cama to Naoroji, January 27, 1906, NAI, DNP, C-13 (1); Cama to Naoroji, January 30, 1906, NAI, DNP, C-13 (2); Gokhale to Hormusjee Ardeseer Wadya, November 1, 1906, NAI, DNP, G-64 (20).

43. Naoroji to Henry Campbell-Bannerman, n.d. [1906], NAI, DNP, C-38 (1); Naoroji to Campbell-Bannerman, April 3, 1906, NAI, DNP, C-38; Gokhale to Wadya, November 1, 1906, NAI, DNP, G-64 (20).

44. Tilak to Wedderburn, September 21, 1906, NAI, DNP, T-73 (2).

45. "On Giddy Heights," in Barjorjee Nowrosjee, ed., *Cartoons from the Hindi Punch (for 1906)* (Bombay: Bombay Samachar Press, 1906); *Kesari*, December 18, 1906, in NNR, Bombay, December 22, 1906, BL, IOR, L/R/5/161.

46. Mohandas K. Gandhi to Naoroji, November 26, 1906, NAI, DNP, G-10 (5); Cama to Naoroji, November 22, 1906, NAI, DNP, C-13 (7); Nawaz Mody, "Perin Captain: From Dadabhai to Mahatma Gandhi," in *Women in India's Freedom Struggle* (Mumbai: Allied Publishers, 2000), 207.

47. "Mr. Dadabhai Naoroji: Arrangements for Reception," *Times of India*, December 10, 1906, 7.

48. *Sic.* The swadeshi store is today's Bombay Store. "Bombay Swadeshi Stores: Opened by Mr. D. Naoroji," *Times of India*, December 18, 1906, 5; "Indian Students" to Naoroji, December 1, 1906, NAI, DNP, I-23; "Mr. Dadabhai Naoroji: Departure for Calcutta," *Times of India*, December 24, 1906, 8; "Your Indians" to Naoroji, December 23, 1906, NAI, DNP, I-13a.

49. *Report of the Twenty-Second Indian National Congress Held at Calcutta* (Calcutta, 1907), 1, 16.

50. "Twenty-Second Congress—Calcutta—1906: Presidential Address," 71–72, 76, 85.

51. Ibid., 78, 79.

52. Ibid., 73; *Report of the Twenty-First Indian National Congress Held at Benares*, Appendix C, i. According to Dhanajay Keer, Tilak first used the term "swaraj" in 1897. Dhanajay Keer, *Lokmanya Tilak: Father of Our Freedom Struggle* (Bombay: India Printing Works, 1959), 119.

53. "Twenty-Second Congress—Calcutta—1906: Presidential Address," 74, 77, 80.

54. Ibid., 77–78.

55. Ibid., 91.

56. Ibid., 89, 86–87.

57. Ibid., 81, 82.

58. Ibid., 83, 90.

59. "The 22nd National Congress: Third Day's Proceedings," *Amrita Bazar Patrika*, December 29, 1906, 4–5; "Stormy Scenes in Subjects Committee: Threatened Split in Congress Camp," *Tribune*, December 30, 1906, 4.

60. "Notes from Dublin," *New York Times*, January 20, 1907, 8; "India," *Horizon*, February 1907, 8, 9.

61. Lord Minto to John Morley, January 2 and January 16, 1907, BL, IOR, Letters from Minto to Morley, MSS Eur D 573/11/f13.

62. Samuel Smith to Morley, December 26, 1906, BL, IOR, John Morley Papers, MSS Eur D 573/50.

63. *Jame Jamshed*, January 1, 1907, in NNR, Bombay, January 5, 1907, BL, IOR, L/R/5/162; *Jame Jamshed*, December 27, 1906, in NNR, Bombay, December 29, 1906, BL, IOR, L/R/5/161; *Behar Herald*, January 5, 1907, in NNR, Bengal, January 12, 1907, BL, IOR,

L/R/5/33; *Amrita Bazar Patrika*, January 1, 1907, in NNR, Bengal, January 12, 1907, BL, IOR.

64. *Vihari*, December 31, 1906, in NNR, Bombay, January 5, 1907, BL, IOR, L/R/5/162; *Punjabee*, January 5, 1907, in NNR, Punjab, January 5, 1907, BL, IOR, L/R/5/189; "The Presidential Address Dissected," *Indian Sociologist*, April 1907, 13–15; *Kal*, January 4, 1907, in NNR, Bombay, January 5, 1907, BL, IOR, L/R/5/162.

65. *Kesari*, January 8, 1907, in NNR, Bombay, January 12, 1907, BL, IOR, L/R/5/162; "Sir Pherozeshah Mehta Discomfited," *Indian Sociologist*, April 1907, 15; *Kesari*, January 8, 1907, in NNR, Bombay, January 12, 1907, BL, IOR, L/R/5/162.

66. *Bal Gangadhar Tilak: His Writings and Speeches*, ed. Aurobindo Ghosh (Madras: Ganesh & Co., 1919), 55, 64; *Mahratta*, January 13, 1907, in NNR, Bombay, January 19, 1907, BL, IOR, L/R/5/162.

67. *Bal Gangadhar Tilak*, 63, 64.

68. *Kesari*, January 1, 1907, in NNR, Bombay, January 5, 1907, BL, IOR, L/R/5/162.

Conclusion

1. Rustom P. Masani, *Dadabhai Naoroji: The Grand Old Man of India* (London: G. Allen & Unwin, 1939), 506, 508; C. F. Andrews, "Dadabhai Naoroji: His Life and Times," *Modern Review*, March 1940, 275; Dadabhai Naoroji to family, May 23, 1907, RPPM.

2. George Birdwood to Naoroji, August 26, 1907, NAI, DNP, B-140 (66); *Hindi Punch*, August 18, 1907, 19; "The Vigil!," *Hindi Punch*, August 18, 1907, 17.

3. "Pitāmah" technically means paternal grandfather. "Mr. Dadabhai Naoroji: Quiet Landing," *Times of India*, November 8, 1907, 7; Masani, *Dadabhai Naoroji*, 186; Yamunabai Bhat, "Varsovyāchī safar," *Gruhlakshmī*, December 1918, 10. Thanks to Murali Ranganathan for showing me this article in *Gruhlakshmī*, a Marathi women's journal.

4. Masani, *Dadabhai Naoroji*, 85; "A Cruel Bereavement," *Tribune*, May 18, 1909, 1.

5. Email correspondence with Roger Jeffery, director, Edinburgh India Institute, University of Edinburgh, November 8, 2014. Meher A. D. Naoroji received an MB ChB degree from the University of Edinburgh. A photograph of the female medical graduates of 1906 is available here: http://libraryblogs.is.ed.ac .uk/edinburghuniversityarchives/2013/11/12/1906-female-medical-graduates.

6. Behramji Malabari to Naoroji, April 25, 1895, NAI, DNP, M-32 (393); Naoroji to Malabari, February 26, 1892, RPPM; Mancherji Merwanji Dadina to Naoroji, October 28, 1892, RPPM; Naoroji to Maki Naoroji, November 5, 1896, NMML, DNP, II, #523.

7. Naoroji, draft statement, n.d. [January 1912], NAI, DNP, uncataloged item; Hormusjee Ardeseer Wadya to Naoroji, November 5, 1912, NAI, DNP, W-12 (27); *Dadabhai Naoroji Correspondence*, ed. R. P. Patwardhan, vol. 2, part 2 (New Delhi: Allied, 1977), 908.

8. Naoroji to William Wedderburn, November 27, 1915, NAI, DNP, N-1 (3100).

9. "Dadabhai Naoroji: Honorary Degree of LL.D. Conferred," *Bombay Chronicle*, January 29, 1916, 7, 10.

10. The Cumballa Hill home, Palitana House, was owned by Maneck Captain, who married Gosi Naoroji. I have been unable to confirm whether the marriage had taken place by the time of Dadabhai Naoroji's death. Benjamin Horniman, "*A Friend of India*": *Selections from the Speeches and Writings of B. G. Horniman* (Bombay: Fort Printing Press, 1918), 261; "Mr. Dadabhai Naoroji: The Funeral," *Times of India*, July 2, 1917, 8.

11. *Sic*. Naoroji was not ninety-three at the time of his death; he was a few months shy of turning ninety-two. "Mr. Dadabhai Naoroji: The Funeral," 8.

12. In 2014, Kusoom Vadgama, a British Asian historian, even suggested that Dadabhai Naoroji, not Gandhi, should be honored with a statue in London's Parliament Square. In the same year, the British government inaugurated the Dadabhai Naoroji Award, meant to recognize individuals who have furthered Indo-British cultural, economic, and educational relations. The award was discontinued in 2017. Dominic Kennedy, "Gandhi Statue 'Would Be an Affront to Women,'" *Times*, August 9, 2014; Prasun Sonwalkar, "UK Quietly Drops Dadabhai Naoroji Awards," *Hindustan Times*, November 4, 2017; Shashi Tharoor, *An Era of Darkness: The British Empire in India* (Delhi: Aleph, 2016).

13. Thanks to Nico Slate for bringing to my attention Kwame Nkrumah's ideas on the drain of wealth in colonial Africa. Kwame Nkrumah, *Class Struggle in Africa* (London: Panaf Books, 1970); Eric Williams, *Capitalism and Slavery* (Chapel Hill: University of North Carolina Press, 1944); V. Suryanarayan, *Together in Struggle: India and Indonesia, 1945–1949* (New Delhi: Prabhat Prakashan, 2018), 69.

14. Jal Naoroji, "What Dadabhai Naoroji Said," *Times of India*, July 11, 1930, 8.

15. C. F. Andrews and Girija Mukerji, *The Rise and Growth of the Congress in India* (London: George Allen & Unwin, 1938), 210, 211.

16. Bipin Chandra Pal, "The Gospel of Swaraj," in *Swadeshi and Swaraj (The Rise of New Patriotism)* (Calcutta: Yugagayatri Prakashak Ltd., 1954), 150, 157, 158.

17. S. R. Mehrotra, *A History of the Indian National Congress* (New Delhi: Vikas Publications, 1995), 99, 104–105.

18. For more on Saklatvala, see Mike Squires, *Saklatvala: A Political Biography* (London: Lawrence & Wishart, 1990). For more on Menon, see Rozina Visram, *Asians in Britain: 400 Years of History* (London: Pluto Press, 2002), 320–340.

19. Jawaharlal Nehru, *Toward Freedom* (New York: John Day Company, 1941), 270; "Though Dead, He Still Speaks to the People: Glowing Tributes to G.O.M. of India," *Bombay Chronicle*, September 5, 1936, 10.

20. "Birth Anniversary of Dadabhai Naoroji," in *Collected Works of Mahatma Gandhi* (New Delhi: Publications Division, Ministry of Information and Broadcasting, 1967), 25:102, 104; Mohandas K. Gandhi, *Hind Swaraj* (Madras: G. A. Natesan & Co., 1921), 2, 4; Gosi Naoroji to Naoroji, April 7, 1910, NAI, DNP, G-87 (1); "The Grand Old Man of India," in *Collected Works of Mahatma Gandhi* (New Delhi: Publications Division, Ministry of Information and Broadcasting, 1960), 4:50; Henry Polak to Naoroji, September 3, 1909, NAI, DNP, P-168 (2).

21. "Birth Anniversary of Dadabhai Naoroji," 103; "Mr. and Mrs. Ghandi [*sic*]: Entertained in Bombay," *Times of India*, January 13, 1915, 5; "Dadabhai Centenary," in

Collected Works of Mahatma Gandhi (New Delhi: Publications Division, Ministry of Information and Broadcasting, 1968), 28:11.

22. Masani, *Dadabhai Naoroji*, 11–12.
23. The current building that houses Elphinstone College was built in 1888. During Naoroji's time, Elphinstone College had been located close to the modern-day intersection of Mahapalika Marg and Dr. Dadabhai Naoroji Road.

A Note on Sources

1. The following paragraphs on the history of the Naoroji Papers are primarily drawn from my introductory essay to the volume I coedited with S. R. Mehrotra, *Dadabhai Naoroji: Selected Private Papers* (New Delhi: Oxford University Press, 2016). See also S. R. Mehrotra, "The Dadabhai Naoroji Papers," *Indian Archives* LIV, nos. 1–2 (2006): 1–18.
2. Rustom P. Masani, *Dadabhai Naoroji: The Grand Old Man of India* (London: G. Allen & Unwin, 1939), 11.
3. I have deposited Wadia's report, which was given to me by Mehrotra, at the Nehru Memorial Museum and Library.
4. *Dadabhai Naoroji Correspondence*, vol. 2, part 1, ed. R. P. Patwardhan (New Delhi: Allied, 1977), vii–viii.
5. Ibid., vol. 2, part 1, ix.

ACKNOWLEDGMENTS

This book grew out of eight years of work and study at Harvard University. While at Harvard, Sugata Bose, my advisor, helped me fundamentally transform my perspectives on South Asian history and expand my research interests beyond Parsi history, my original topic of research. Sven Beckert and Maya Jasanoff further developed the contours and scope of this book. They guided me toward understanding Dadabhai Naoroji's ideas and political trajectory in new ways, drawing in perspectives from global economic history and British history. Elsewhere at Harvard, I must thank Richard Delacy, Meena Hewitt, Tarun Khanna, Richard Lesage, and P. O. Skjærvo.

Like many young historians of South Asia, I have benefited from Ramachandra Guha's warm support, encouragement, and interest in my career and research. He took a very early interest in my biographical project on Naoroji, offered incisive commentary on earlier drafts, and provided me with invaluable help and advice as I turned those drafts into this book. This work draws significantly from his defense of the genre of biography within the historical profession. To the late S. R. Mehrotra I owe a profound debt of gratitude. He taught me the value of sustained and patient archival research (he remained a familiar figure in Indian libraries and archives well into his eighties). When I first contacted him by telephone in 2010, he informed me, "I have been waiting for your call." By this, he meant someone who was interested in researching and writing about Naoroji. For decades before our first telephone call, he had been carrying out this work almost single-handedly. Professor Mehrotra and I coedited a volume of Naoroji's correspondence that was published in 2016. It is a matter of personal regret that he did not live to see this book's publication.

I have been fortunate to receive research assistance and guidance from numerous other scholars from around the world. In particular, I must mention Gopalkrishna Gandhi, Sunil Khilnani, Prashant Kidambi, John McLeod, the late Edward C. Moulton, Enuga Reddy, Mitra Sharafi, and A. R. Venkatachalapathy. Peter Stansky, my undergraduate thesis advisor at Stanford, has continued to be an encouraging mentor in my years since college. In spite of his declining health, the late John Hinnells shared his research, read through my early scholarship, and engaged me in long conversations about Parsis and the Grand Old Man of India.

Several organizations have generously funded my research and writing. During my PhD program, I received an Institute of International Education (IIE) Fulbright-Nehru Fellowship and a Fulbright-Hays Doctoral Dissertation Research Abroad (DDRA) Fellowship for conducting archival research in India, the United Kingdom, and Ireland. Subsequent research, writing, and revisions were supported by a Provost Grant from the University of South Carolina, a National Endowment for the Humanities Fellowship, and a Fulbright-Nehru Academic and Professional Excellence Award. At the United States–India Education Foundation in New Delhi, I must particularly thank S. K. Bharathi, Priyanjana Ghosh, Neeraj Goswami, and Adam Grotsky for their assistance. I deeply appreciate the invaluable support provided to me by fellow members of the Zoroastrian community. I must thank the Vakhshoori Foundation and the Federation of Zoroastrian Associations of North America (FEZANA) for providing me with scholarships while I was enrolled in my PhD program. Within FEZANA I am particularly grateful to the trustees and benefactors of the Mehraban and Morvorid Kheradi Endowment as well as Dolly Dastoor, Roshan Rivetna, and Rohinton Rivetna.

At Harvard University Press, I have been very fortunate to have Sharmila Sen as an editor and Heather Hughes as an assistant editor. They have helped me trim the fat and sharpen the focus of this book. I must also thank Adriana Cloud for copyediting, Mary Ribesky for production editing, Stephanie Vyce for help with image and copyright matters, and the two anonymous readers who evaluated my manuscript.

Research for this book has taken me to numerous cities and countries around the world. In the Delhi area I must thank Yezad and the late Rati Kapadia, Niloufer and Noshir Shroff, Rukshana and Cyrus Shroff, and Shernaz Cama. The Kapadias and the Shroffs let me stay at their homes when I was just beginning my archival research. For over fifteen years, Shernaz Cama has been an invaluable guide for me in all matters pertaining to Parsi history. She encouraged me to apply for PhD programs and, since then, has always been ready to help and advise me in my research. She has also served as my official advisor during my Fulbright fellowships in India. The staff at the National Archives of India, where I worked for over two years, extended invaluable support to me as I went through the Dadabhai Naoroji Papers and related material. Several individuals went out of their way in their help, letting me be a part of the process of helping preserve and better organize the Naoroji Papers. I am particularly thankful to Sanjay Garg, the late Mushirul Hasan, Rajbala Jain, Jaya Ravindran, Rajmani Srivastava, and the staff of the Private Papers division. Mahesh Rangarajan's generous support and interest in my project made working at the Nehru Memorial Museum and Library particularly rewarding. His leadership at Teen Murti is keenly missed.

In Mumbai, S. A. Upadhyaya and the late Homi Patel provided very useful tutorials in nineteenth-century Parsi Gujarati. Jehangir Patel of *Parsiana* has been a wealth of information about Parsis and my go-to person for contacts within the community. Murali Ranganathan continues to be an encyclopedic guide for all matters concerning nineteenth-century Bombay. He has kindly read and commented on much of my work, including parts of this book. Elsewhere, I must thank the staff of the Asiatic Society of Mumbai, Maharashtra State Archives, and the J. N. Petit Institute; Manjiri Kamat of Mumbai University; Deepak Mehta of the Forbes Gujarati Sabha; Meher Mistry of Ramniranjan Jhunjhunwala College; Nawaz Mody of the K. R. Cama Oriental Institute; and Usha Thakkar of Mani Bhavan. Further afield in Navsari, Bharti Gandhi was a generous host at the Meherjirana Library. Arun Mehta and the staff of Vakils, as well as Arati Desai and Satish Sahney of the Nehru Centre, provided me with that rarest of all possible finds in Mumbai: a quiet, secluded place to read and write.

In Ahmedabad, Kinnari Bhatt and Dina Patel gave me generous help at the library of Sabarmati Ashram. Shirin and Makrand Mehta kindly shared with me their immense knowledge of Gujarati history. Aparna Sridhar expended a great amount of time and effort in helping me wade through difficult Parsi Gujarati material from the 1850s. Several members of the Ahmedabad Parsi community warmly extended their hospitality to me. In particular, I must thank Homai and the late Phiroz Khansaheb, the late Ratan Marshall, Meher and the late Rashid Medhora, Astad Pastakia, and Pearl and Cyrus Sabavala. Rumy Mistry of Vadodara helped me find out information about the Baroda Record Room.

At the British Library in London, I am thankful for the support and help provided by Ursula Sims-Williams and the staffs of Asian and African Studies reading room, Manuscripts reading room, and the old newspapers facility at Colindale. I appreciate the extremely professional help provided by staff at the National Archives at Kew in tracking down elusive material. Seth Alexander Thévoz facilitated access to the collections of the National Liberal Club. Staff and volunteers at the Islington Local History Centre let me rummage through their collections. John Drew of Cambridge enthusiastically shared his knowledge of Evans Bell and other Indian reformers who influenced Naoroji. At the Library of the University of Bristol, I must thank the staff at Special Collections for giving me access to the National Liberal Club pamphlets and assorted papers. In Dublin, I am grateful for the help provided by the staff at Trinity College Library. Carla King of St. Patrick's College shared with me her vast knowledge of Michael Davitt and his papers.

As an early career scholar, I have found the Department of History at the University of South Carolina to be an extraordinarily collegial and supportive place. I am particularly thankful for the mentorship that I have received from Christine Ames, Don Doyle, Kathryn Edwards, Woody Holton, Thomas Lekan, Lauren Sklaroff, and Patricia Sullivan. I also owe special thanks to the librarians and staff of the Thomas Cooper Library at the University of South Carolina.

Both during and after graduate school, I relied on a close group of colleagues and friends for writing and research support. I name only a few of these individuals here: Emilia Bachrach, David Boyk, Namita Dharia, Hardeep Dhillon, Daniel Elam, Isabel Huacuja Alonso, Sadaf Jaffer, Atiya Khan, Neelam Khoja, Madhav Khosla, Daniel Majchrowicz, Timsal Masud, Dinsha Mistree, Shruti Patel, Mircea Raianu, Santhosh Ramdoss, Rubina Salikuddin, Dan Sheffield, Sunit Singh, Vinay Sitapati, Mathu Subramanian, and Yuhan Vevaina.

Last, I must thank my family, both in the United States and India. Several family members—particularly my grandmothers, the late Mehru Parakh and the late Khorshed Patel—nurtured my interests in Indian and Parsi history. I must especially thank my parents, Phiroze and the late Aban Patel, for supporting my education and making all of this possible. My in-laws, Mahiar and the late Zinobia Madan, welcomed me into their house and made Mumbai a home-away-from-home for me. My wife, Parinaz Madan, has provided me with extraordinary support and encouragement. Parinaz has patiently put up with endless Naoroji trivia, my ramblings on late-nineteenth-century politics, excursions to obscure parts of Mumbai and London in search of early Indian nationalist landmarks, and even Naoroji-themed wedding invitations. She has been a sounding board for ideas, has assisted me with translating difficult Parsi Gujarati passages, and has proofread numerous drafts. Most significantly, she has shown me that that there are things in life far more important than dusty archives or particular events from one-hundred-and-twenty years ago. This book is for her, as an admittedly small token of my profound gratitude and love.

INDEX